UNIT IV READING FOR RESULTS

PREFACE

If business executives were asked to identify the single most important skill for success in the workplace today, they would more than likely answer the art of communicating. Communication is interaction; it is the transfer of thoughts and ideas from one mind to another and serves as the very foundation of all business activity. Communication is an art because it is not a single, isolated skill but rather a combination of interdependent skills–listening, speaking, reading, and writing.

Communicating for Results is today's response to a need in the marketplace for a straightforward, applied approach to teaching integrated communication skills. The approach of the authors is to present the purposes, strategies, and processes of listening, speaking, reading, and writing within business contexts, and then present application activities with real-world emphasis. The authors have also incorporated exercises that assess the student's knowledge of grammar, punctuation, and usage rules, which are provided in an appendix at the end of the text for student reference. Because *Communicating for Results* emphasizes integrated language arts instruction throughout, it is one of the most comprehensive communications texts available today.

FEATURES

Communicating for Results contains the following instructional tools:

- **Objectives.** Each unit begins with objectives that state the learning benchmarks and standards established for each unit.

- **Chapter Questions.** Each chapter begins with a series of questions designed to activate students' prior knowledge and serve as advance organizers for new learning to follow.

- **Marginal Definitions.** Terms that may be unfamiliar to students are defined in the margin to help students build their vocabulary and conceptual understanding while reading in context.

- **Case Scenarios.** Within each chapter, several Case Scenarios illustrate essential communication topics using business situations. Students are asked to analyze each case and share their perspectives and interpretations of the case.

- **Use Your Judgment.** Following each main topic within a chapter, Use Your Judgment exercises give students an opportunity to solve problems related to each topic.

- **In Brief.** At the end of each chapter, In Brief provides a concise synopsis of all major points covered within the chapter.

- **Words of Note.** At the end of each chapter, students are asked to define words that relate to the chapter topic. These words have not been defined in the margin, but will have been discussed within the text.

- **Check Your Recall.** Questions about the chapter concepts appear at the end of each chapter to provide students with an opportunity to actively review the material presented within each chapter.

- **Share Your Perspective.** Out-of-classroom activities are suggested to extend the learning activities in the chapter. These activities encourage students to do further research on chapter topics.

- **Focus on the Fine Points.** End-of-chapter grammar exercises ask students to locate and correct grammar, punctuation, and usage errors within business documents. These exercises require students to use their grammar skills to edit, proofread, and rewrite authentic documents.

- **Communicate for Results.** End-of-unit activities ask students to use all four communication skills to analyze problems that relate unit topics to the real world.

- **Listening, Speaking, Reading, and Writing Checklists.** At the end of Units II, III, IV, and V, students are asked to assess their communication skills by using a checklist that relates to each unit topic.

- **Abbreviated Grammar Reference.** An appendix at the end of the text helps students to understand grammar, punctuation, and usage rules as they relate to the grammar assessments in the text.

- **Glossary.** All key terms are listed and defined at the end of the text.

INSTRUCTIONAL RESOURCES

Workbook

The workbook for *Communicating for Results* reinforces concepts presented in the text. An introductory section explains how to use the workbook effectively with the text, and exercises are carefully integrated with the textbook to provide supplementary practice in listening, speaking, reading, and writing. The workbook also contains a section that deals with grammar and usage. These drills provide practice in dealing with many common problems in punctuation, capitalization, sentence structure, possessives, word usage, spelling, and grammar.

Instructor's Guide

The instructor's guide that accompanies *Communicating for Results* is a valuable teaching resource that provides general teaching suggestions, objectives, enrichment suggestions, and transparency masters. A test bank and answer keys for both the text and workbook are also provided.

Paradigm Reference Manual

The *Paradigm Reference Manual* is a comprehensive language reference guide created to give students efficient access to grammar and usage rules. The *Reference Manual* will provide students with the help they need as they plan, draft, write, and proofread their documents. This tool is also available online. The online version enables students to immediately access the information they need and view the reference pages on their computer screen while they are working with writing software.

Reference Manual Workbook

To give students additional practice with grammar and usage, the workbook that accompanies the *Paradigm Reference Manual* includes a variety of applications that give students ample practice in all areas of language usage. Using many job-related, problem-solving activities, the *Paradigm Reference Manual* and its accompanying workbook teach students to use the resources they will use on the job when planning, writing, and editing their documents.

A FINAL NOTE

Did you ever stop to think that language is acquired through listening, then speaking, then reading, and finally writing? Any weak link in that chain drastically affects the next skill. If hearing is impaired, speech is deficient. If reading is poor, writing is consequently weak. Communication, in one form or another, accounts for about 90 percent of our waking hours, and it is extremely important that we acquire and master each of these skills in order for the exchange of ideas to take place and be effective.

If we share or exchange ideas, we are each left with the possession of new ideas. This sharing leads to the development of further ideas, thereby enriching all participants, who may not have been able to develop these ideas individually. In sum, *Communicating for Results* is an enlightening textbook that focuses on teaching us how to communicate effectively.

UNIT 1

L earning how to communicate effectively involves recognizing the factors that influence the "success" of a message. This means that communication is more than the simple exchange of information; rather, it is the sum of many parts.

Communication is also a process. By understanding this process we can better analyze what is effective and what is not. In Unit I you will learn about the communication process and its variables, as well as factors and circumstances that have special implications for business. With this foundation you will move on to uncover the psychology of communication. This will give you an understanding of how point of view influences the process.

▼   **When you finish Unit I, you will**

- Understand the difference between, and the interaction of, verbal and nonverbal communication

- Recognize the basic barriers to effective communication

- Understand how international relationships and ethical issues create special concerns for effective communication in business

- Be able to determine your own and others' motivations, interests, beliefs, values, and needs when communicating

COMMUNICATION

IS

THE

SUM

OF

MANY

PARTS

UNDERSTANDING THE BASICS OF THE COMMUNICATION PROCESS

CHAPTER ONE

What is communication? What differences exist between verbal and nonverbal communication?

How does the communication process work?

How do business roles affect communication?

What factors interfere with good communication?

How do international relationships create special communication concerns?

If you charted your daily activity, you would find that you spend most of your time communicating. **Communication** is the process of conveying to others—and receiving from them—information, ideas, feelings, and beliefs. Because the process is vital to human interaction, communication skills affect your ability to understand others, to establish relationships, and to perform in most situations. The ability to communicate skillfully, therefore, directly affects your business success.

THE MEANS OF COMMUNICATION

You can improve your communication skills by being aware, day to day, of how you and others use the different means of communication to accomplish various purposes. The primary means we all use to convey and receive information are listening, speaking, reading, and writing. For example, you communicate whenever you

- Listen to your mechanic describe a problem with your car

- Speak with friends and relatives

- Read your favorite section of the newspaper

- Write a letter to a brother or sister

In the workplace, people must communicate to accomplish job-related tasks. How much time they spend using each means of communication will vary from person to person, from job to job, and from day to day:

As the examples on page 7 show, most workers use all four methods of communication—listening, speaking, reading, writing—to some degree every day. Each of these methods relies on words, so we consider each one a form of **verbal communication**. People, both in and out of the workplace, also send and receive messages through **nonverbal communication**. Let's take a closer look at these two types of communication.

Verbal Communication

Words are the "tools" of all verbal communication—speaking, writing, listening, and reading. How you use these tools will affect the success of your attempts to communicate. When you speak or write, you send or **transmit** messages to others; your purpose is to string words together in order to get a desired result. When you listen or read, you are on the receiving end; your purpose is to interpret the intended message and respond accordingly. To perform their jobs, workers must transmit and receive messages throughout the day. As you will see, we all face risks and responsibilities at both ends of a message.

Transmitting Communication: Speaking

Although you may seldom give formal speeches on the job, you probably will spend a good portion of your workday speaking with people. You may order supplies, call customers, discuss plans, ask and answer questions, handle telephone complaints, give instructions to subordinates, and participate in meetings. In many cases, you can plan ahead to improve these spoken communications. Planning involves defining to whom your message is to be sent and then to determine what you want your message to accomplish. Planning also involves identifying the information you want to include in your message. Brainstorming, outlining, and researching are methods you can use to help plan your communications.

Later in this text, you will learn techniques to help you improve your speaking effectiveness whether you are giving a presentation, making simple telephone calls, or participating in meetings.

C A S E   S C E N A R I O

Right from the Start

As a paralegal, Nate Warren found he needed to spend a great deal of time telephoning clients for information. He took careful notes but, nonetheless, he'd almost always forget to ask about something and would then need to call the client again. Of course, he usually got voice mail or a busy signal. The result? At the end of the day, Nate found himself rattled, frustrated, and buried in unfinished documents!

What problems might Nate's lack of planning cause for clients? What are the costs to his company? What planning could he begin to do to become more efficient and effective?

ANDY QUICKER:
"Because I'm in computer sales, most of my day involves listening to customers and reading technical manuals. When I first started in this business, an "old pro" told me, "Listening is half the sales rep's job. So stop talking and start listening." Once I started listening carefully, I really started selling systems!"

MARTHA MCHENRY:
"I do telemarketing, which means I talk on the telephone all day. That's how I sell our services. Because I work on commission, if I'm not selling, I'm not making any money! Talking and listening, that's what I do all day."

SHARON SCHURICT:
"You name it, I read it, consumer surveys; customer profiles; market studies; sales data; competitor profiles; budgets. As a marketing assistant, reading is the best way to stay on top of current trends. I also write summaries of what I read for distribution."

IT'S EASY TO WRING MORE OUT OF TELEPHONE CONVERSATIONS

by Mark McCormack

Most people agree that the telephone is the greatest business tool at our disposal. If you ask people why, though, they may not agree as easily.

To me, the greatest advantage of the telephone is its most obvious feature: The party on the other end of the line can't see you. If you can maintain your poise on the phone, it doesn't matter what circumstances you're in. You could be lounging in a bubble bath at home or surrounded by mayhem at the office; the party on the end of the line neither knows nor cares.

It's amazing how many people forget that.

They'll let an upsetting situation earlier in the day spill over into their telephone calls. They'll sound sullen or distracted or irritable. The problem is that the other party can quickly sense their foul mood and, with no other evidence to go on, might conclude that it is intentionally directed at him or her.

The biggest mistake people make on the phone is not letting their voice do the work. Before I reach for the phone, I pause briefly to collect my thoughts and decide what I want to convey solely through my voice. For example, if I'm talking to someone I haven't seen in a few weeks, I always remind myself to be enthusiastic: People tend to be more compliant and pleasant when they hear that I'm glad to be talking to them.

If I'm in a hurry, I'll start off by announcing that I only have a few minutes to talk. I find that tends to focus the other party; the person gets to the point quickly. It also makes me appear less rude when I have to end the call abruptly.

If you want to be more effective on the phone, look at your phone habits. Are you taking advantage of the fact that the other party can't see you? Or are you giving that advantage away from the things you say and the way you say them?

Distributed by King Features.

Transmitting Communication: Writing

The average business worker spends only a small portion of the workday writing, but that does not diminish the importance of the task. Written communications are a permanent record and often are subject to more scrutiny than other forms of communication. They represent you and your company. They are used to record and convey information of varying levels of importance and can have enormous impact on business functioning.

Even routine written messages are generally important, as the following situation illustrates.

A Matter of Time

Elise Shaw returned from lunch to find a message on her desk. Angela Herrara wanted to know when Elise's manager, Burt Winfield, would return from his trip so Ms. Herrara could arrange a meeting with him and the rest of the executive staff.

Elise checked Mr. Winfield's itinerary and saw that his flight was scheduled to land the next day at 9:56 a.m. She called Ms. Herrara's office and left a message that Mr. Winfield would return around 10:00 a.m. tomorrow.

Ms. Herrara scheduled a meeting of the executive staff for 10:30 the next morning. The next morning, everyone came to the meeting except Burt Winfield, who arrived 40 minutes late.

What did Elise neglect to think about? What should she have done differently?

Accurate written messages are vital in the business world. Perhaps the subject is technical, requiring lists of measurements and specifications. Perhaps a written record of a decision is needed for the files. A complex explanation may require step-by-step instructions. Or, a situation may call for a persuasive request. Business documents are written for a variety of purposes and require planning and skill in execution. For this reason they receive special attention in Part Five of this text.

Receiving Communication: Listening

Although listening dominates the typical workday, most business people have poor listening skills.

From Bad to Worse

First thing Monday morning Prestige Business Systems Sales Manager Alicia Yamato called a meeting of the local sales reps. At the meeting, she handed out copies of an article from Monday's *Daily Globe*. The headline read, "Prestige Shows Poor First-Quarter Profits—Will Services Be Cut?" Alicia said, "Now, before you panic, please listen. In spite of the headline, the article notes that customer support for our Venus software products will remain steady regardless of cuts in our customer-support personnel. Public Relations has already responded to the article, and the *Globe* will be running our reply tomorrow."

As soon as he saw the article, Jeff Lyman panicked. What were all his customers going to think when they heard the service on Venus products was to be cut? While Alicia talked, Jeff quickly began a list of reps whose customers might change to a competitive product line. When Alicia asked for questions, Jeff excused himself, went immediately to his phone, and called several reps outside the district. They were dismayed when Jeff told them about the bad publicity and the possible cuts in customer support for Venus products. By the end of the morning, Customer Service had been deluged with calls from across the country, all wanting to know why support for Venus was to be cut.

Why did Jeff miss the main point of Alicia's meeting? What effect did Jeff's not listening have? What should Jeff have done? Could Alicia have prevented Jeff's actions? How?

Jeff's participation in the situation described is, unfortunately, quite realistic. When he should have been listening carefully, he was doing other things.

People tend to believe that, while reading is a learned skill, listening is a natural skill, one that need not be taught. But this belief is incorrect. Hearing is automatic for most people, but hearing and listening are different. Listening can be taught, and often must be. Because listening is our primary means of gathering information, good listening skills are extremely important for successful communication. All business situations require **active listening,** which we will explore further in Chapter 3.

Some Typical Obstacles to Effective Listening

- Concentrating on your reply instead of listening to another's message

- Speaking too quickly after another has spoken without considering what you have heard

- Turning a discussion immediately to your own interests instead of allowing another speaker to determine the direction of the discussion

- Tuning out a discussion if it is dull or if it does not appear to address your interests or concerns

- Reacting emotionally to certain words instead of focusing on the speaker's main ideas

- Being easily distracted by any movement or sound in the area

Receiving Communication: Reading

In the previous situation, Jeff said, "I can hardly believe this headline!" Jeff read the headline and nothing else, missing the information in the rest of the article.

Reading business documents is part of every job. It is different from reading textbooks, novels, newspapers, and most other media because (1) the subjects are different, (2) your reasons for reading are different, (3) what business documents direct you to do is different, and (4) your relation to the writer is different. In Chapters 7 and 8 you will learn techniques that focus on business-related reading needs. These techniques will help you develop the skill of thinking as you read business documents.

Nonverbal Communication

Besides verbal communication, which relies on words, we also communicate nonverbally through gestures and other body movements. Nonverbal messages are those you send when you smile, sneer, raise an eyebrow, shrug your shoulders, nod in agreement or disagreement, cross your arms, or grit your teeth. Even more subtle actions such as body posture, keeping your coat on indoors, failing to offer a handshake, or arriving late for meetings communicates to others.

C A S E   S C E N A R I O

Routine Habit

The weekly budget meeting at Leading Edge Productions was a "routine" meeting every week: same day, time, place, and participants. Charlie Burrows made it a habit to arrive at every meeting ten minutes late.

On Friday, as Charlie walked in, Connie Turnbull, a coworker, noticed that Harold Rankowski, who'd been speaking to the group, sneered momentarily before turning back to the board and continuing with his presentation.

At lunch, Connie joined Charlie in the cafeteria. "That was some look you got from Harold this morning," she remarked. "You noticed that too, huh?" replied Charlie. "What's his problem?" "Well, you *were* late," Connie pointed out. Impatient, Charlie responded, "Connie, you know all those meetings start out with the same old thing: Harold gives a ten-minute play-by-play that we could read off the budget sheet in thirty seconds!"

"But, Charlie," Connie continued, "You wouldn't be late for a meeting with Jack, would you?" "Of course not!" exclaimed Charlie. "He's the president of the company. I'd never keep him waiting. It wouldn't be professional or political!" Connie raised her eyebrows. "But you think it's okay to keep your coworkers waiting?"

"Now wait, Connie that's not fair," Charlie objected. "You know I think the budget meetings are important."

What doesn't Charlie understand? What message is he sending by arriving late to budget meetings? What could happen as a result of his behavior?

The previous case scenario illustrates why it is important to pay attention to how we communicate nonverbally. Consider the following features of nonverbal messages:

context

the words and ideas that surround a word, term, or idea and can throw light on its meaning; the environment or setting in which something occurs or is communicated

1. **They are subject to interpretation.** There is no "literal" meaning to a given action; it must be considered in the ***context*** in which it occurs. For example, a wave of the hand can mean "goodbye" or it can mean "I'm over here"; tapping fingers can communicate "I like this tune on the radio" or "Let's move things along; I'm getting impatient."

2. **They can be unintentional.** Have you ever had a blush betray your emotions? This type of nonverbal message is not only unintentional, it is virtually uncontrollable as well. There are also circumstances in which, unless we undertake careful self-examination, we will send nonverbal messages without even realizing it. A distracted listener will have eyes that roam the room; he or she may not realize that the speaker interprets the wandering eyes as disinterest or ***disdain***.

disdain

a feeling of scorn or contempt

3. **They can compete with, even negate, verbal messages.** If you say one thing and do another, your verbal messages are likely to be ignored. For example, a supervisor who asks workers to be committed and put in overtime when it is needed, but who himself will not work evenings or weekends, probably will not win the loyalty of his crew. As the saying goes, "Actions speak louder than words."

As we have seen, our nonverbal messages can be just as important as our verbal messages. For this reason, effective communicators are sensitive to nonverbal signals. As they speak and listen, they control their actions, gestures, facial expressions, and body language; they also "read" the nonverbal signals sent by others.

1   **USE YOUR JUDGMENT**

An excellent way to understand nonverbal communication is to watch television without sound. Watch a talk show, for example, with the volume off. Identify specific ways people communicate meaning without words. List ten gestures, facial expressions, and other body language you observe, and describe the meaning that each communicates.

Identify a career that interests you. Then, list:

a. Three people to whom you would most often listen in this position
b. Three kinds of materials that you would typically read
c. Three people to whom you would most often speak (other than those in *a*)
d. Three kinds of documents you would write

Using any combination of *a*, *b*, *c*, and *d*, describe three communication situations you might encounter if you were employed in this career.

THE COMMUNICATION PROCESS STEP-BY-STEP

A *process* is a series of actions, steps, procedures, or operations intended to achieve a specific purpose. Every office has processes workers follow to enter orders, correct payroll errors, authorize payments, order supplies, and so on. Communication is also a process, one whose purpose is always to transmit or receive a message. As you already know, people transmit messages by speaking and writing, and they receive messages by listening and reading. Figure 1.1 identifies three steps in the **communication process**:

1. The sender forms a message.

2. The message is transmitted from sender to receiver.

3. The receiver translates the message.

Here, **sender** can mean speaker(s) or writer(s). **Message** can mean conversation or discussion, memo or letter, shrug or nod, or any other type of message. And **receiver** can mean listener(s) or reader(s).

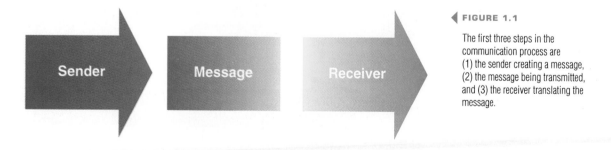

◀ FIGURE 1.1

The first three steps in the communication process are (1) the sender creating a message, (2) the message being transmitted, and (3) the receiver translating the message.

The communication process is complete only when the receiver provides **feedback**, that is, some indication that she or he has received the message:

1. The sender forms a message.

2. The message is transmitted from sender to receiver.

3. The receiver translates the message.

4. *The receiver provides feedback.*

Figure 1.2 shows all four steps in the communication process.

Keep in mind that a message in a memo, for instance, is not "received" if the receiver has it in hand but does not read it. Similarly, the message is not "received" if the receiver reads the memo but does not understand its content. Feedback, both verbal and nonverbal, keeps the communication process going because it either confirms that the message was received as intended or it cues the sender that the message failed.

Now let's take a closer look at the role of each element in the communication process.

The Sender

Whenever you speak, write, gesture, or even move within a communication context, you send a message. Your reasons for sending messages will vary. You might

FIGURE 1.2 ▶

Feedback completes the communication process by confirming that the intended message was received.

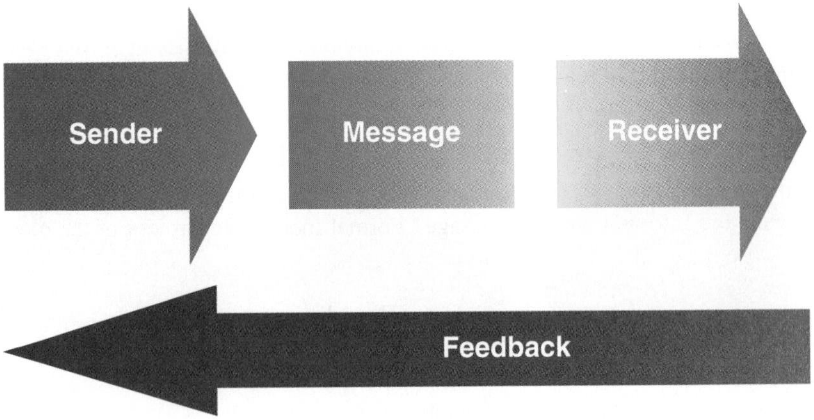

Sender → Message → Receiver

← Feedback

have an idea or a need that must be expressed in a written or spoken message. For example:

- You have an idea that will simplify the order-processing system. You talk with others to gather information to support your idea, and you draft a memo to your manager.

- You realize the monthly sales report is three days late. You call the Sales Department to ask the manager when you can expect to have last month's report.

- The office copier has broken down. The control panel indicates the problem must be serviced by a maintenance person. You telephone the manufacturer and request a service call.

In other situations, your motivation for sending messages might be to respond or react to other messages:

- You find a note on your desk that Mr. Mahabir called. You respond by returning his call.

- You read a memo requesting information. You respond by writing a memo providing that information.

- You read a newspaper report that one of your competitors is expanding its advertising campaign. You react by clipping the article and passing it on to your manager.

The Message

The **message** is the basic content of your communication. It is the information or idea you are transmitting. The **medium** is the form you use to deliver that content, and as you have already learned, it can be verbal or nonverbal.

If, for example, you want to inform Rae Fisher that you will take vacation on Monday, February 9, that information is your message. You will send that message verbally, of course, but which medium will you use? Telephone call? Face-to-face conversation? Informal written message? Formal memo? Regardless of the medium you choose, your message is the same.

If the message is simple and straightforward, perhaps a telephone call is best. If you will have a chance to deliver the message face-to-face, you may wait to do so. In other cases, you may prefer to send a written message. But "writing" covers a number of choices. Your message can be handwritten, typewritten, or word processed. In addition, it can be transmitted by hand delivery, the postal system, courier service, electronic mail, or fax machine. Factors influencing how you choose to transmit a message include the

- Importance of having a written record of the information

- Need for sending the information immediately

- **_Proximity_** of the receiver

- Number of people receiving the message

- Level of formality necessary

- Expectations of the receiver

proximity

closeness, nearness—the quality or state of being nearby or very close

The Receiver

Each step of the communication process is important, but the receiver's role is critical. A message must be received, or there is no communication. Therefore, for every message you send, there are two important goals:

1. The receiver will understand your message.

2. The receiver will respond to your message in the desired way.

To increase the likelihood that a message gets results, the sender needs to consider who the receiver is, which, of course, will vary depending on the situation. As the sender, you need to ask: Is the receiver

- One person? Several people? A large audience?

- A coworker? Your manager? A company executive? A customer? A supplier?

- Someone you know very well? An acquaintance? A stranger?

In addition, the sender needs to consider the receiver's needs, background, and likely attitude to the message.

Let's apply this piece of advice to the situation with Rae Fisher. Earlier your task was to decide on a medium you might use to inform Rae of your vacation on Monday, February 9. As the situation was described, your purpose was simply to inform Rae, and February 9 had no special significance. In other words, you assumed you were simply passing on a routine message.

But what if the circumstances are different? What if Rae had planned a February 9 meeting with key customers that you are scheduled to attend? Or what if your supervisor wants no vacation time taken until after February? In these cases, Rae's needs and attitudes are likely to be different, and in turn, she is likely to receive your message differently. By considering your receiver's possible reactions to your message, you can anticipate and avoid problems, getting the feedback you want. We will explore the area of individual needs and attitudes as they relate to communication in the next chapter.

Feedback

Feedback, the receiver's response to your message, tells you whether the receiver understood the message as you intended. Consider the following scenarios:

- You left a message with your travel agent, Lars Nielson, to book a flight. Lars returns your call and says, "I booked your round-trip ticket to Chicago and will send you a written confirmation immediately. In the meantime, get a pen and jot down these flight numbers . . ."

- You spent four hours last Friday on the phone, straightening out a customer complaint. Today you receive a short note from the customer, expressing appreciation for how you handled the problem.

- You submitted a requisition form for office supplies to the Purchasing Department. A memo from the department, with the form attached, explains that they cannot process your requisition form until you obtain your manager's authorization.

In each situation, the feedback—whether a phone call, note, or memo—communicates to you that your message was received clearly. In the third example, the feedback is especially important: It shows that though your message was received, it was not as you intended. The feedback enables you to correct your mistake.

This example also illustrates an important characteristic of the communication process. Feedback often plays two roles: It can serve both as feedback to one message and as a new message in itself. Thus, by giving feedback, the receiver of the first message often becomes the sender of the second message. To illustrate this, let's reconsider a small part of Charlie and Connie's conversation in which Connie was trying to teach Charlie about nonverbal communication:

"But, Charlie," Connie continued, "You wouldn't be late for a meeting with Jack, would you?" "Of course not!" exclaimed Charlie. "He's the president of the company. I'd never keep him waiting. It wouldn't be professional or political!" Connie raised her eyebrows. "But you think it's okay to keep your coworkers waiting?"

In this brief interchange, both characters play sender and receiver. Charlie's explanation of his prompt arrival for meetings with Jack serves both as feedback to Connie's question (message) and as a new message to Connie (it requires Connie's feedback). Connie's response also serves both as feedback to Charlie's message and as a new message in itself. This illustrates the realistic give-and-take of the communication process.

USE YOUR JUDGMENT

Identify two specific communication situations in which you were a sender and two in which you were a receiver. For each situation, identify the other person involved in the process. Then, using the sender/message/receiver/feedback diagram (Figure 1-2, page 14), describe briefly the message and the feedback.

BUSINESS ROLES AND COMMUNICATION

Business communications can be described as external and internal. **External communication** takes place with anyone outside of the organization—customers, stockholders, and job applicants, to name a few. **Internal communication** takes place within an organization and can be upward, downward, or lateral. Figure 1.3 illustrates these roles and levels of communication.

FIGURE 1.3 ▶

The roles and levels of communication

INTERNAL	EXTERNAL
CEO's Supervisors Managers	Customers Stockholders
upward	
Coworkers Peers *lateral* **YOU** *lateral* Associates Competitors	
downward	
Employees Subordinates	Vendors Suppliers

When you communicate with someone who is your superior, you are participating in **upward communication**. When the sender or receiver is a *peer*, the exchange is **lateral communication,** communication at the same level. Anytime you interact from a position of authority, it is called **downward communication**.

The relationship between the sender and receiver has implications for the message. In general, the level of formality and solicitation goes up when communications are external and/or upward. Internal communications that are lateral or downward tend to be more relaxed, depending ultimately on the "personality" of the organization.

peer

an equal; a person of equal standing with another based on age, grade, status, education, or work position

BARRIERS TO EFFECTIVE COMMUNICATION

Like other complex processes, the communication process has many potential obstacles, barriers that prevent clear, effective communication. The barriers may stem from nonverbal communication or verbal communication. They may exist at the sender's end of the process, at the receiver's end, or both.

Sending Barriers

Sending barriers occur when the sender says or does something that jeopardizes the flow of communication.

C A S E   S C E N A R I O

Computer Glitch

Arnita Howard sells computer systems. One client, Jerry Wilson, specifically tells her that he knows little about computers, but he needs something for his office. Arnita knows exactly the right computer for Jerry, one that is currently on sale at a real value. She immediately steers Jerry to the system she has in mind, saying, "I think you'll like this system, Jerry, it's very popular! It has a 60 megahertz 486 microprocessor, 8 megabytes of RAM, all you would ever need. It comes loaded with software, even has a math coprocessor. Of course, if you'd like, you could start with a 4 megabyte system that's fully expandable . . ."

"Wow, Arnita," Jerry replied. "Maybe I need to think about this some more." To himself, he thought, "I think I'll call Marco and ask him where he bought his computer."

Why didn't Arnita make the sale? What could she have done differently? How were Arnita and her company hurt? Was Jerry hurt as well? In what way?

Like Arnita, we often assume that others know the words we know so well. As a result, we unwittingly create communication barriers.

Using words imprecisely can also cause miscommunication:

- In her annual report, Joanne Koonitz repeatedly uses the word "profit" in such a way that readers cannot tell when she means *net profit* and when she means *gross profit*.

- When Bart Oramendi mentions in a letter the closing of "the warehouse," his customers assume he means the Washington Street warehouse, not the Portland Avenue warehouse.

The sender also interferes with a message by using poor grammar or distracting mannerisms, or by dressing inappropriately. In these situations, the sender's verbal message is lost or diminished by competing nonverbal messages.

Another sending barrier results from uncertainty. The sender who does not have a good grasp of his or her purpose for communicating is likely to relay a muddled and ineffective message.

Receiving Barriers

Receiving barriers can be just as harmful to the communication process as sending barriers. As you will see, most of these barriers can be dismantled with a little self-awareness.

net profit

profit remaining after the deduction of all necessary charges and outlay such as wages, taxes, and insurance

gross profit

overall profit before the deduction of charges and outlay such as wages, taxes, and insurance

FIGURE 1.4 ▶

Inappropriate dress and distracting mannerisms can alter the sender's intended message.

Sales from Bob's new marketing plan have not lived up to his expectations

A receiver can allow personal prejudices to influence whether a message is received. For instance, an older man who stubbornly believes all managers should be male and over forty is not likely to hear and believe a statement about the effectiveness of a new manager who happens to be a woman in her thirties.

Receivers who do not read or listen closely or actively enough can also disrupt the communication process. When information is not clear, many receivers do not accept responsibility for getting clarification from the sender.

Consider the situation with Arnita Howard and Jerry Wilson. Jerry wants to buy the computer system that best suits his needs, yet he tunes out Arnita because she uses *jargon* (*megabytes, coprocessor, fully expandable*) he does not understand. If, instead, he were to stop Arnita, remind her of his limited expertise, and ask her to clarify some of the terminology, Jerry might have found that Arnita's is the best system for him. Because he simply tunes her out, he loses the opportunity to learn about this system. He may end up buying an inferior or more costly system elsewhere.

jargon

the technical terminology or characteristic idiom of a special activity or group; obscure and often pretentious language marked by unnecessarily long words and descriptions

Although senders are responsible for sending clear messages, listeners should be ready to recognize potentially unclear messages and accept responsibility for getting clarification. Consider how barriers in the following situations could easily be avoided, but instead are allowed to interfere with the messages:

- In her annual report, Joanne Koonitz repeatedly used the word "profit" without clarifying whether she meant net or gross profit. Instead of asking Joanne to clarify the term, those who even noticed the problem assumed she meant "gross profit." Many readers ended up calling Joanne to express concern that the figures in the report were inconsistent.

- In his letter, Bart Oramendi mentioned the closing of "the warehouse" without specifying whether he was referring to the one on Washington Street or Portland Avenue. Rather than calling Bart for clarification, one customer lost a day's time by shipping to the closed warehouse.

Such misunderstandings cause daily problems ranging from minor events to serious, costly errors. Fortunately, both receiving and sending barriers can be minimized with conscious effort. Later chapters will address techniques to help ensure that you listen, read, write, and speak with care.

USE YOUR JUDGMENT 4

Describe recent situations where you observed (or created) a sending barrier to communication and a receiving barrier to communication.

INTERNATIONAL COMMUNICATION

Many of today's businesses operate globally. As Figure 1.5 shows, international trade is common for many American companies. More than ever before, American business people communicate internationally.

Depending on your company and your duties, you may find yourself communicating with foreign business people daily, hosting foreign visitors, or even traveling to foreign countries to represent your company. To handle these situations, you need to be aware of language barriers and cultural barriers to effective communication.

Language Barriers

As a speaker of English, you have an advantage in international communication because English is the language most often used in international communication. Therefore it is especially important for you to be sensitive to the business people who are willing to communicate in a language other than their own. You will likely meet some foreign business people whose English is less than fluent. Even fluent speakers may be unfamiliar with many of the phrases that pepper the average American's everyday speech. By being aware of the potential barriers and following some basic guidelines, you can increase the effectiveness of your communications with nonnative-English speakers.

FIGURE 1.5 ▶

International communication is becoming a bigger part of the American business scene.

Speaking and Writing Guidelines

In speaking and writing, the most effective way to communicate with people from other cultures is to speak or write their language. Although they may know English, your use of their language shows a respect for them and their culture. However, English-speaking people are less likely to use other languages simply because many people from other countries have learned English as a second language. Thus, it is likely you will communicate in English in your business relationships with people from other cultures.

Many international business people began studying English as children and know formal, standard English well. What these international business people lack is experience speaking in informal situations, situations in which they would learn slang and *idioms*. In speaking and writing, always choose words and phrases that represent formal, standard English instead of less formal regional dialect or idioms. Phrases like *up the creek*, *off the handle*, and *in the wings*, for example, have nothing to do with creeks, handles, and wings. Because they might confuse non- native speakers, such phrases should be avoided.

When speaking to business people for whom English is a second language, try to gauge their understanding. Look for nonverbal clues that show they are confused or have a question. Pause briefly between statements to allow listeners to translate for themselves. Speak slightly more slowly than you would to native English speakers, and *enunciate* clearly to allow listeners to hear and distinguish the different sounds we take for granted. Do not talk more loudly than usual; increased volume does not increase comprehension! Finally, understand that, depending on their culture, listeners may consider it inappropriate for them to interrupt to ask questions.

idiom

dialect; the language peculiar to a people or to a district, community, or class; an expression having a meaning that cannot be derived from the combined meaning of its individual words (for example: *Monday week* for *the week after next Monday*)

enunciate

to pronounce words very clearly

Listening and Reading Guidelines

Be patient and considerate when communicating with a nonnative speaker, and accept your share of the responsibility for communicating. If the speaker mispronounces a word, stumbles while trying to remember the right phrase, or uses the wrong term, do not tune that speaker out. Do not correct a speaker's English unless a particular error creates a significant problem related to your business relationship. If you must correct the speaker, be subtle and diplomatic.

When reading, try to look past errors in grammar or usage and focus instead on the writer's intent. When listening, provide positive nonverbal cues to show when you understand and, when necessary, ask questions that will help clarify the speaker's meaning. Always provide nonverbal cues to show you are listening attentively.

```
C   A   S   E       S   C   E   N   A   R   I   O
```

Mixed-Up Message

Monica Conroy, a production coordinator, wrote a letter to Anton Levesque, a client in Versailles, France. In her letter, she said:

> This morning I called three manufacturers to ask for bids on your equipment parts. One company was completely off the wall as far as our production schedule was concerned, and its costs were way out in left field. The other two companies were right on the money. When we make our final selection, I will make sure that the company we select follows our schedule and does not put our project on a back burner. As far as the shipping date is concerned, the ball is in my court. I'll keep you informed, of course.

Monica faxed the letter to Anton and gave a copy to her supervisor, Luis Gonzalez. Luis was immediately worried that Anton would have difficulty reading the letter. Later that day, Anton called him asking for clarification.

Why did Anton have difficulty reading Monica's letter? When he saw the letter, what else could Luis have done? If you were Monica, what steps would you take to help yourself avoid this situation in the future? How might Luis have avoided the incident in the first place? What can he do now to prevent a similar occurrence?

denotation

the direct, specific meaning of a word or term as found in the dictionary

connotation

something suggested by a word or term that is not part of its direct, specific meaning—connotation depends on the culture and past experience of the persons using or hearing a word or term

Whether you are listening or reading, be aware that nonnative-English speakers may choose English words that lead you to question their tone or implication. A person may, for example, use the word *ignorant* instead of *uninformed* without understanding that, while the words have a similar **denotation**, their **connotations** are quite different. Although nonnative-English speakers usually know the denotations of English words, you cannot assume they know the connotations of each word. Therefore, do not allow inexact word choice to damage your business relationship.

Cultural Barriers

Although language differences present potential barriers in communicating with international business people, communication barriers often go beyond language. Insensitivity to cultural differences can seriously impair communication between business associates.

C A S E   S C E N A R I O

A Question of Culture

When his Nebraska-based medical technology company opened its branch office in India, Jack Haggerty wrote a letter congratulating the manager of the new office, Gopal Murti. He ended his letter by saying, "In honor of our new partnership, I'm shipping you a box of prime Nebraska steaks. Enjoy!" He placed the letter and instructions for ordering and shipping the steaks on his assistant's desk before leaving on a ten-day business trip.

Priscilla Carlton, Jack's assistant, found the letter and the gift the next day. She was surprised. She knew that many people in India were Hindu; in Hinduism, the cow is sacred and cannot be eaten. If Mr. Murti were Hindu, he would most certainly be insulted by the gift. But Priscilla didn't know whether Mr. Murti was Hindu. She decided not to question the gift, after all Jack was the boss. So she sent the letter and ordered the steaks.

What might have happened as a result of Jack's and Priscilla's actions? What do you think of the way Priscilla handled this situation? What else might she have done, with what results? What advice would you give Jack?

Obviously, Jack did not mean to offend but to compliment Mr. Murti. Jack should have consulted someone with a basic knowledge of Indian customs to find out what type of gift is acceptable in that culture when a coworker is promoted or appointed to a new post. Then he might have learned of the inappropriateness of his selection.

Customs, attitudes, beliefs, and values vary from country to country. Most are deeply rooted, developed over centuries in most cases. Just as national customs differ, business customs, practices, and expectations also differ.

Cultural differences are more than merely interesting; they can affect your international business and personal relationships, as Jack Haggerty's ill-chosen gift pointed out. But just as you cannot quickly master a foreign language, you cannot quickly learn the customs, attitudes, opinions, and beliefs of many other peoples; in fact, the latter is even more difficult. However, you can be aware that such differences exist and learn them as needed to avoid barriers to communicating globally.

Cultural Contrasts

- In Latin America, rushing a business meeting is considered bad taste.

- Chinese business people exchange small gifts with guests.

- For the French, the corner office is not the most important, as it generally is in the United States.

- In the Middle East and in China, "personal space" (the distance between two people) when talking is just a few inches, far less than the few feet we generally prefer in the United States.

- In Turkey and many Asian countries, people are offended if visitors show the soles of their shoes, as they might, for example, when crossing their legs.

- Americans use a gesture to say "okay" formed by making a circle with thumb and forefinger and extending the three remaining fingers. In Japan, this means "money." In France, it means "zero." In many Arab countries, it is a curse. In some other countries, it is obscene.

- To an American, a thumbs-up gesture means things are going well. To an Australian, this is an obscene gesture.

- Many Latin American business people view a hug as Americans view a handshake. Furthermore, Americans tend to favor a "firm" handshake, but many Europeans and Middle Eastern people view this firmness as overly aggressive.

Among many people from other cultures, Americans have a reputation for acting superior and lacking understanding of other cultures. This "smugness" may stem from the prestige the English language enjoys and the widespread acceptance of everything American, from jeans to rock 'n' roll to fast food. Certainly Americans, like other nationals, should take pride in their country's accomplishments, but these accomplishments do not make American customs and attitudes superior.

Thus, to be effective when communicating with international business people, you need to learn their customs. To interact blindly is to risk offense, embarrassment, and loss of business.

Guidelines for Intercultural Communication

The following broad guidelines will help you to develop some common sense in relating with people from different parts of the world:

- Be patient with and considerate of people who have taken the trouble to learn your language and understand your culture.

- Understand that full language and cultural knowledge is possible only for people who live within a culture.

- Rid yourself of prejudices. Generalizations such as "People A are sneaky, People B cannot be trusted, People C are dirty, People D are dumb" are simplistic and destructive. If you have heard only negative comments about certain other cultures, embrace any situation as an opportunity to learn the other side.

- Avoid judging people's customs and beliefs and comparing them with yours. All people are rightfully proud of their heritage and culture.

- Avoid clumping cultures simply because they are in the same part of the world. For example, some Americans tend to view Chinese, Japanese, Korean, Taiwanese, and other Southeast Asian cultures as "Oriental" or "Asian," but these cultures differ in many ways.

USE YOUR JUDGMENT 5

Read the following situation. List the ways in which Gloria's language and behavior may be a communication barrier for Julia. Then list some specific advice that will help Gloria communicate more effectively with Julia:

Drew Palm, Gloria Sharpe's manager, has just introduced her to Julia Hernandez, who represents a printing company in Mexico City. Gloria will be working closely with Julia in the future.

Extending her hand, Julia said, "I am very happy to meet you, Gloria." "My pleasure!" exclaimed Gloria. Speaking very quickly, Gloria went on, "I'm really looking forward to working with you, Julia, I mean really excited! You know, when Drew told me I'd have this opportunity, I really thought he was pulling my leg! I mean, I really love Mexico, and I plan to get my act together so I can take a trip to see your plant in Mexico City. I spent a few months in Spain once, so I can speak your language pretty well!"

IN BRIEF

❶ Communication takes place both through words (verbal) and actions (nonverbal). Verbal communication happens in the form of listening, speaking, reading, and writing. Nonverbal communication happens through gestures, body movements, and other actions.

❷ Communication is a process comprised of four interacting elements: sender, message, receiver, and feedback.

❸ Business communications can be described as external or internal. When communicating with a superior, the communication is upward; when communicating with peers, the communication is lateral; and when communicating from a position of authority, the communication is downward.

❹ Many verbal and nonverbal communication barriers exist and can exist at any stage of the communication process. Typical "sending" barriers include assuming too much knowledge on the part of the receiver and sending an incorrect or unclear message. Typical "receiving" barriers include not reading or listening actively and not asking for clarification on trouble spots.

❺ International business situations present unique barriers to communication because of language and cultural differences. Even though language differences are often overcome because of the prominence of English in the business world, cultural awareness, acceptance, and sensitivity are keys to productive business relationships.

WORDS OF NOTE

Define each of these terms introduced in Chapter 1.

communication
communication process
downward communication
external communication
feedback
internal communication
lateral communication
medium
message
nonverbal communication
receiver
sender
transmit
upward communication
verbal communication

CHECK YOUR RECALL

1 What are the four basic methods of communication?

2 What is the difference between verbal and nonverbal communication? What are some examples of each?

3 What are the four steps in the communication process?

4 Explain what is meant by *upward*, *downward*, and *lateral* communication. What are examples of each within an organization? What are some examples of each when communicating with people outside the organization?

5 What are three examples of sending barriers?

6 What are two examples of receiving barriers?

7 What are the guidelines for speaking, writing, listening, and reading when communicating with someone whose first language is not English?

8 What other communications barriers, beyond language, exist in international business?

SHARE YOUR PERSPECTIVE

1 Many of the rules of communication that we apply to everyday inter-actions are so ingrained that they become automatic. Take a few minutes to think about how your communication "behavior" is influenced by your relationship to the individual with whom you are communicating. Identify the different ways you speak and behave when in the presence of the following:

    a. brother or sister
    b. parent
    c. professor or instructor
    d. senior citizen
    e. police officer
    f. stranger

2 Ask someone from another culture to name three ways in which communication in the workplace differs between the person's culture and your own. Write a summary of these differences.

3 Consider the differences that you discovered in question 2 and create a situation in which one or more of these differences causes a breakdown in communication and affects work performances. Use dialogue if it is helpful.

FOCUS ON THE FINE POINTS

Read the following background information. Then follow the instructions to locate and correct grammar errors.

Background

Grounds For Discussion (GFD), a Florida-based chain of coffee houses, recently closed a deal with a British coffee broker to open ten coffee houses in Scotland and England. This is GFD's first foreign venture. Tulisa Wirthe, GFD's marketing vice president, plans to present the details of the venture at the upcoming meeting of her regional managers. Attending the meeting will be Charles Pettinger, the broker's president and international representative.

Tulisa has called on two members of her marketing team, Leo Schwalm and Lyn Pucetta, to help her prepare for both the meeting and her presentation. Lyn has prepared two documents for Tulisa's signature: a memo to GFD's regional managers announcing the meeting and inviting them to bring questions and ideas to share and a letter to Charles Pettinger. Leo has drafted Tulisa's introductory remarks about Charles Pettinger and his company, Old World Coffee Ltd.

Your Instructions

Each of the following documents contains up to 15 errors. Indicate and correct errors by circling the problem and noting the solution on a photocopy of the page or on a separate sheet of paper. In each case, you may assume the document is formatted correctly.

Note: If you have difficulty locating errors, turn to page 000 in the Appendix. There you will find additional information about the errors in Document 1.

Document 1: Memo to Regional Managers

M E M O R A N D U M

TO:　　　　Regional Managers

FROM:　　Tulisa Wirthe, Vice President of Marketing

DATE:　　　September 28, 19XX

SUBJECT:　UPCOMING QUARTERLY MEETING

The fall quarterly meeting will be held Tuesday thru Thursday, October 17, 18 and 19 at the home office conference center. Lyn Pucetta has booked a block of rooms at the Bluefin Breeze Hotel. Please call Lyn (Extension 233) by Monday, October 2, to indicate your preference for a Smoking or Nonsmoking room assignment. Lyn will do her best to accomodate everyone's preferences. There will be no smoking during meetings however ice water and complementary hard candies will be provided.

Your input has been a great help in organizing the meeting. You'll be pleased to see that the enclosed agenda allows a full morning for discussion of the new sales formulas and at the suggestion of Leo Schwalm, we've also arranged for each of you to have lunch with your home office and territory team members.

The highlight of the weeks' events will be the presence of Charles Pettinger, a principle Officer of Old World Coffee Ltd. Charles will join us for a social hour and dinner Tuesday. On Wednesday morning he will present our joint plans for introducing GFD in Great Britain. Charles is a highly respected broker. As well as an entertaining speaker. His visit is a great opportunity for you to meet him and learn more about our exciting new partnership!

If you have questions about the meetings or wish to add an item to the agenda, please call Lyn or Leo.

We're all looking foreward to what promises to be a productive meeting with an emphasis on team building.

TW/lp

Enclosure

Distribution:　K. Ardour
　　　　　　　J. Doennes
　　　　　　　A. Filipovic
　　　　　　　T. Mendez
　　　　　　　L. Schwalm
　　　　　　　M. Zeibert

DOCUMENT 2: Letter to Charles Pettinger

September 28, 19XX

Grounds for Discussion

...simply the best

Mr. Charles Pettenger, President
Old World Coffee Ltd.
72 Heathridge Lane
London NW2 5SW
ENGLAND

Dear Mr. Pettinger,

Thank you for agreeing to include time with GFD's regional managers as part of your visit to Tampa. All of them eagerly anticipate this opportunity to meet you and learn firsthand about our companies' new partnership. For your reference, I have enclosed a meeting Agenda and a list of the managers and their territories.

My assistant, Lyn Pucetta will meet you at the airport on your arrival Tuesday, look for her just outside the customs exit. (There maybe some delay in the customs area. The airport is undergoing expansion. Resulting in tightened security. Lyn will take you to the Bluefin Breeze Hotel, where she has booked a suit for you. Your mid-afternoon arrival should allow you time to get settled before the social hour, which will begin at 6:00 P.M. in the lobby lounge and dinner will follow in the hotel's Lobster Room at 7:00.

Let's plan to meet for breakfast Wednesday morning to go over the contract changes and reveiw the agenda for the November meeting in London.

Lyn can arrange for equipment, photocopying, and any other assistants you may require for your presentation Wednesday. I've asked her to call your Secretary early next week to confirm you flight arrangements. If you have any questions or concerns, please call Lyn at her direct line: (813) 555-0233. She will be happy to assist you.

Again, thank you for taking part in our meetings. I can't imagine a better way to introduce our new adventure to the GFD marketing team!

Sincerely Yours,

Tulisa Wirthe
Vice President of Marketing

TW/lp

Enclosures

12433 North West Beach Drive
Tampa, FL 33623
(813) 555-1243
1-800-555-1243

Document 3: Introductory Remarks

Yesterday we had the official announcement of a very exciting new venture for GFD: A partnership with Old World Coffee Ltd. Old World Coffee is a distinguished company, based in London, which is over one hundred years old and which presently services nearly half of the restaurants and cafes in the British isles and one-third of the Scandinavian market; a remarkable business record in a part of the world that is known to be extremely particular about its coffee.

Through an agreement with Old World Coffee, GFD is about to make its first venture outside of the United States. Ground has already been broken for three coffee houses in England; by this time next year there will be seven operations up and running in England. And another three in Scotland.

We're going to devote the whole day to learning about this venture and what it will mean for GFD and for our marketing efforts in the coming year. I know you have alot of questions, and I want to be sure they're all answered before the day is out, and if you'll take a look at the agenda, you'll see that we've set up a format of two presentations, each with a question-and-answer period. We'll begin with a presentation about Old World Coffee, it's present business in Britian, and what the relationship between our two companies will be. From their we'll take a look at a new and expanded role of the marketing organization.

To begin, it's my great pleasure to be able to formally introduce Charles Pettinger (who many of you met last night.) Mr. Pettinger is the president and international representative for Old World Coffee. He has a long and successful career in the Coffee industry, having worn the hats of entrepreneur, researcher, salesperson, buyer, and broker. I first had the opportunity to meet him at the international show in Amsterdam last spring, where he was a keynote speaker. I was very impressed with his inciteful refreshing perspective on the exploding coffee phenomena. I know you'll be both informed and entertained by the remarks he's prepared for us this morning. Please join me in welcoming Mr. Pettinger.

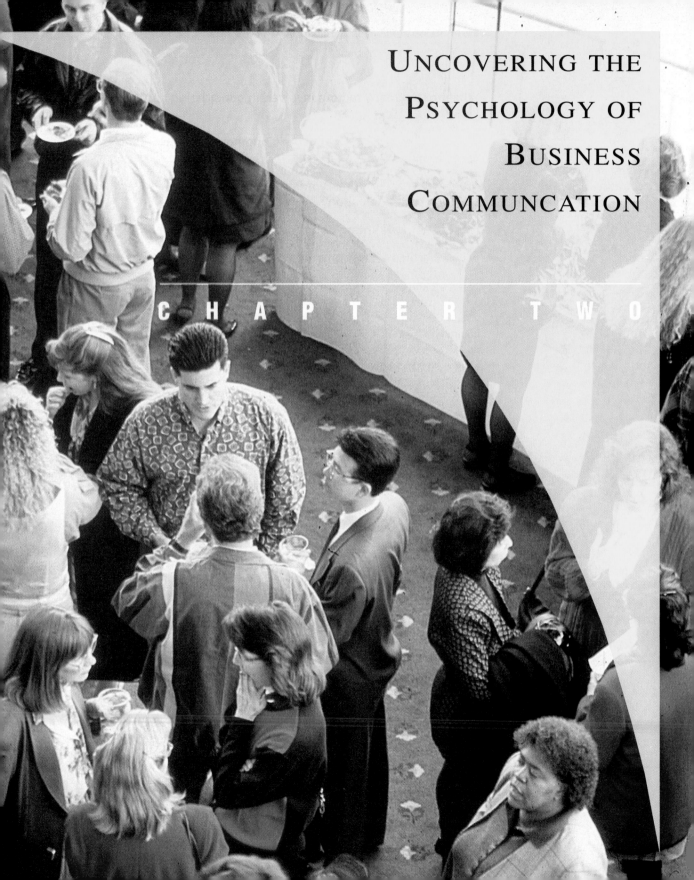

UNCOVERING THE
PSYCHOLOGY OF
BUSINESS
COMMUNCATION

CHAPTER TWO

What are the many factors involved in considering another's point of view?

What is the nature of human need and how does this relate to communication?

What are workers' primary motivations and how can these influence effective communication?

How do workers' interests and values relate to communication?

How do ethics affect communication in the workplace?

Communication does rely on words and actions, but not exclusively. Word mastery and an awareness of nonverbal cues are only part of the "equipment" needed to communicate well. An understanding of the *psychology* of communication, that is, an understanding of people's motivations, needs, interests, and values, is also vital to effective communication. These four psychological variables collectively contribute to an individual's point of view.

When you consider another person's point of view before entering into communication, you are more likely to get the results you want because you know "where the person is coming from." You can avoid offending. And your efforts might even pay off in a rewarding relationship based on mutual respect and understanding. All of these benefits are applicable to business. So let's look more closely at how point of view (each individual's motivations, needs, interests, and values) influences communication in the workplace.

MOTIVATION

incentive

a motive; something that encourages a particular action

Why are you reading this book? What is your motivation? Think of motivation as your *incentive,* your reason for behaving a specific way. You may be reading this book to improve your communication skills. You may be reading to complete a class assignment or simply because you enjoy it. Perhaps you are reading for both reasons. The point is that behavior is a direct result of motivation; you would not be reading this book *unless you had a reason.* Understanding motivation is crucial to communication because knowing what motivates people helps you communicate with them.

In business, communicating with employees in ways that acknowledge their motivations improves employee morale, cooperation, productivity, and efficiency. But what specific factors motivate employees to achieve high levels of performance? Salary? Job security? Challenging, interesting work? Regular response to work from management (feedback)? Participation in decision making? All of these may affect motivation; however, the importance of these factors probably varies among individuals.

Salary and Job Security

For most people, earning money is a major motivator. We all need money to pay our bills; therefore, we work to earn a living. In addition, we strive to perform well to keep our jobs and increase our salaries. Money and job security (the need to keep a job) are two key motivators of performance. Workers communicate their willingness to work hard, and managers communicate their willingness to pay and to allow workers to keep their jobs in exchange for hard work. This communication, which occurs both through words and actions, is based on the managers' and workers' understanding of how the other group is motivated.

Money and job security, though strong motivators, are not necessarily the most important motivators in the workplace. Today's workers, at all levels, are motivated by other things as well.

Challenging, Interesting Work

Most workers welcome tasks that are challenging and interesting and, therefore, meaningful. On the job, unfortunately, not all work tasks fit this description. Also, while job security and good pay may be easy to define for many workers, challenging and interesting work varies according to individual tastes.

C A S E   S C E N A R I O

Through the Grapevine

Greg Bishop supervises film editors for a motion picture company. The Public Relations Department often asks him to conduct tours for visitors. Last year, Greg assigned editor Maria DeCamp to conduct one tour, and according to the feedback from the tour group, she did a great job. Since then, Greg has assigned every tour to Maria. Recently, while talking with another editor, Greg learned that Maria considers conducting tours the worst part of her job. He also learned that the other editors enjoy conducting tours and wonder why Greg favors Maria.

Greg decided to ask Maria directly how she felt about conducting tours. Maria was blunt: "Frankly, I'm a little insulted. I'm a film editor, not a tour guide. Whenever I give a tour, I assume you've asked me because I'm the newest person on the staff, and the newcomer always gets the 'grunt work.'"

"That wasn't what I intended at all, Maria," responded Greg. "I assigned you the first time because you were the person who was available that day. Then you did such a great job that I thought you must enjoy giving tours. I'll be happy to ask some of the other editors to do them too. In fact, I'll schedule a meeting to discuss projects, tours, and other assignments."

"That'd be great, Greg," Maria replied.

Why was Greg unaware of how Maria and the other editors felt? What happened because of this? If he hadn't learned about everyone's dissatisfaction through the "grapevine," what might have happened as time went on? What about Maria? Could she have done something differently? What?

As a result of talking with Maria and the other editors, Greg will be able to accomplish several things. He will learn about each person's editing preferences. He'll also have an opportunity to build communication, teamwork, and trust among his staff.

Successful managers know that what one person considers challenging or interesting, another person may not. They try to discover each employee's preferences and, when possible, assign work accordingly. The communication involved in this management process motivates workers; it also allows them to better handle the uninteresting assignments they occasionally receive. If workers must perform tasks they consider boring or repetitive, these tasks will be more bearable if they know the next task is likely to be challenging and interesting.

Response from Management

Most workers value their manager's response to their work—hearing about what they do well and how they should improve. Naturally, no one wants to hear a negative report, but criticism can be productive if given wisely. Worse than criticism is lack of feedback. Hearing nothing about their work does not motivate employees.

Workers consistently communicate to their employer the kind of work they are willing to do and the level of performance they are willing to give. They communicate this through words at times but most often through their actions, that is, through their job performance.

Successful managers consider their employees' job performance a means of communication and are, therefore, aware of the need for feedback. These managers consistently reinforce employees' positive behaviors. In addition, they inform employees specifically how to change or improve their work. They emphasize how employees can become more effective, not what employees are doing "wrong." By giving regular feedback with a productive tone, managers maintain a flow of communication between themselves and their workers and, thereby, increase worker motivation.

Employee Participation

When you help to create something, you are likely to feel some sense of pride and ownership. What's more, that feeling of ownership will increase as your participation in the task increases. To illustrate this, imagine you are a master carpenter. You've been assigned a job to build a cabinet. Which do you think might be more satisfying: being told by someone exactly how to make the furniture or creating your own one-of-a-kind cabinet? Wouldn't you feel more satisfied if you were able to design the cabinet as well as build it? Isn't it ultimately more satisfying to see your own ideas through than simply to follow directions?

Perhaps this motivation—to be involved in decision making rather than simply to carry out decisions—is a mingling of self-interest with a genuine desire to apply all of our skills to a task and create the best possible outcome. Whatever the reasons, this phenomenon is evident in the workplace. Employees do not want merely to implement management's decisions; they want to participate in making decisions.

Not all decisions must be made by management. In fact, there are advantages to having the workers decide who will do what. The workers know their own strengths and weaknesses, and often each other's. They certainly know their own preferences regarding the kinds of work they like to do and the people with whom they like to work. Finally, they know as well as anyone else the process by which the work will get done. All of this knowledge makes them ideal decision makers in some situations. And making these decisions provides workers a sense of participation in the company's direction and success.

C A S E   S C E N A R I O

Decision Points

Shirley LaCrosse is Director of Marketing and New Product Development for Make Believe Software Inc. At a recent meeting, the Board of Directors decided to eliminate an entire line of game software and add to their line of educational software. This would mean much reassigning within each department.

Shirley immediately scheduled a half-day meeting with her market researchers and project managers. At the meeting, Shirley introduced her staff to the need for refocusing development efforts and explained which projects should now receive the department's emphasis. Then she said, "I'd like all of you to continue working together today to develop a proposal outlining which teams will handle which projects. Then I'd like to meet with you again to review the proposal in case I have any questions or concerns."

The next day, Shirley and her staff met to review the proposal. She found that they had not only made a sound division of labor but had also suggested some ways to co-team on certain projects to move them along more quickly. In addition, the group identified two critical questions for Shirley to take up with the Board.

What effect did Shirley's including her staff in decision making have on the members of her work team? What effect might it have on the Board's decisions? What is a more authoritarian, "top-down" way Shirley might have handled the situation? What might the result have been?

Read the following situation and consider the specific motivators. List each key motivator you find present, and briefly explain how and why it is present:

Matt Henson recently became manager of the Purchasing Department for Belleville Hospital. Matt now supervises two purchasing agents, Maureen Furniss and Darnell Wall. In his first business meeting with Maureen and Darnell, Matt asked whether they had any suggestions for changing departmental procedures or any other ideas that might help improve productivity or lower purchasing costs.

Darnell spoke first: "Right now Maureen and I handle requisitions as they come in by dividing up the work evenly. That's the way it's always been done here. But we've talked about it, and we think it would be more efficient to separate requisitions into two categories. One would be hardware and equipment, the other supplies and pharmaceuticals."

"Yes," Maureen explained. "I'm not as comfortable working on computers and medical equipment. Darnell understands that side of it so much better than I do!" Darnell added, "Maureen is just as expert when it comes to the supplies we order, the thousands of drugs with different strengths. It just seems that if we each could handle what we know best, we'd both be more productive, and things would go faster and smoother."

NEEDS: WHERE MOTIVATION BEGINS

Motivation begins when we feel a need, when we sense that something is missing. As a result of the need, we feel a drive that urges us to satisfy that need. For example, consider one of our most basic needs—food. When we are hungry and thirsty, we feel the drive to eat and drink, and we act accordingly. In this way, needs create motivation, and motivation leads to specific behavior (action).

Maslow's Hierarchy of Needs

Our needs are not limited to basics such as food, shelter, and clothing; we also have a number of higher-level needs (called "higher" because the basic needs must be satisfied first). Because human needs strongly influence our motivation and, in turn, our behavior, they are key factors in communication with others. To apply communication psychology effectively, therefore, you must understand the full range of human needs.

The most famous studies of human needs were conducted by psychologist Abraham Maslow, a pioneer in this area. Maslow grouped human needs into several levels, forming a *hierarchy* of needs known as **Maslow's Hierarchy.** By helping us under-

hierarchy

a grad*ed or ranked series or set of levels

stand human needs, this hierarchy (Figure 2.1) helps us understand human needs, motivation, and behavior.

On the lowest level Maslow placed the most basic human needs, our physical needs. These are **biological needs**—physical drives to satisfy hunger, thirst, and reproduction. On the next level are our needs for security, shelter, and freedom from danger—our **safety needs.** Together, the first and second levels make up our **deficiency needs;** they are called deficiency needs because we cannot survive without meeting them. According to Maslow, we concern ourselves with the next level of needs only as our deficiency needs are adequately met. Thus, for example, a person who is starving will focus on the need for food without concern for higher-level needs.

On the next two levels are our **growth needs.** The first level of growth needs are our **belonging** or **social needs,** basically our drives to give and receive affection and love. On the second level of growth needs are our **ego** or **esteem needs,** meaning our drives for personal worth and our need to feel valuable, to have a high opinion of ourselves. Our growth needs include our drive to achieve and to be free and independent. Again, each level of need is felt only after lower-level needs are met.

At the top of the pyramid Maslow places **self-actualization needs.** These are our drives for competence and mastery—generally, the need to fulfill our potential in all areas of our lives.

FIGURE 2.1 ▶

Maslow's heirarchy of needs.

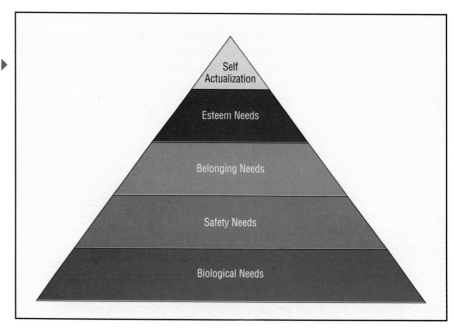

What Maslow's Hierarchy Shows

Maslow's Hierarchy can help us understand how our needs are met in work situations:

- Basic physical needs are satisfied by the availability of a cafeteria or vending machines, by the existence of convenient restrooms, and by having time throughout the workday to eat and use the restroom.

- Safety needs are satisfied by a clean environment, temperature control, and modern work stations (or perhaps private offices), company security (such as cameras and locks), as well as by the wages received, job security, health insurance, pension plans, and so on.

- Social needs are satisfied by involvement with and recognition from management and coworkers.

- Esteem needs are satisfied by choice work assignments, promotions, raises, feedback and evaluation from coworkers and management, and self-evaluation.

- Self-actualization needs are met by understanding one's own contributions to company success and from the feeling that the job one has is worthwhile and satisfying.

Because Maslow's Hierarchy shows how human needs are related to one another and how these needs affect motivation, understanding the hierarchy helps us communicate effectively in business situations. For example, if you understand a coworker's needs as well as your own, you can help organize your working relationship to meet both sets of needs. The same possibility exists among people working at different levels of responsibility. However, because everyone's needs are satisfied differently at different levels, you can only apply Maslow's Hierarchy when you have a good understanding of the audience with whom you are communicating.

C A S E   S C E N A R I O

The Job's the Thing

During her three years arranging international travel at Horizon Vacations, Elana DuPree earned a reputation for helping others learn Horizon's complex computer system. However, with news of impending cutbacks, Elana began to worry constantly about her job security. As a result, she no longer volunteered to help; in fact, she began to ignore all requests for assistance. Elana was reluctant to share her expertise, fearing that she might lose her edge as the computer expert when layoffs were made.

Elana's supervisor, Mai Vang, noticed Elana's change in behavior with concern. She approached Elana. "Elana, I can't help noticing you haven't been acting like yourself lately. Martin mentioned that when he asked you for help last week, you brushed him off. I know Lydia's feeling frustrated because she doesn't know how to input the itineraries. In the past, you've always jumped right in and offered help. What's up?"

"I've been so busy," Elana told Mai, adding defensively, "I'm just making sure that I stay on top of my own work."

Mai nodded. "I understand everyone's under a lot of pressure, especially with all the talk about cutbacks," she said. "I can't say for sure, but I think our department is safe, especially if we keep up with our work. But your resistance is only getting in the way, Elana."

Elana blushed. "Gosh, Mai, I didn't realize I was slowing things up. I'm sorry. I've been so worried about keeping my own job that I was afraid to spend any time helping anyone else."

What need was Elana fulfilling for herself by not volunteering to help others at work? As a result, what needs were going unfulfilled for Martin and Lydia? How did Mai address these needs?

C A S E   S C E N A R I O

Parking Perk

AnneMarie D'Amato is the Director of Quality Control for a computer distribution company. During the past year, the company received too many complaints and product returns, and as a result, AnneMarie decided to hold Saturday training sessions for the Order Fulfillment Department. She wanted Rita Melendez to do the training. For three years, Rita has produced the fewest complaints about packaging and shipping, the fewest product returns, and the highest productivity. Every day Rita wears her gold Employee of the Year pin, and she hopes to win another this year. However, although Rita works overtime weekdays, she generally does not work on weekends.

AnneMarie decided to offer Rita an incentive. She approached Rita on her break one day and explained the situation in detail. Then she said, "You know, Rita, everyone's complaining about the parking situation around the plant. Parking in the company lot is limited almost exclusively to management, but as a way to thank you for conducting this training, I've arranged for you to have one of the reserved spots in the company lot—you know, the ones with your name on a plaque. Now, will *that* persuade you?"

What did AnneMarie recognize as Rita's need on the job? How did this help her find a way to approach her employee? If you were Rita, would you consider doing the weekend training? Why would you feel that way?

Business involves give-and-take people giving what they are willing to give in exchange for what they want. Although some people might have found the overtime pay for weekend sessions appealing, AnneMarie recognized that Rita is motivated by something else. AnneMarie was right in predicting that Rita would consider having her own reserved parking spot even more prestigious than wearing her Employee of the Year pin.

USE YOUR JUDGMENT 2

Read the following situation and consider the specific motivators. List each key motivator you find in this situation, and briefly explain how and why it is present:

NTI Real Estate Corporation recently bought out a competitor, Glendale Enterprises Inc. Within a very brief time period the old Glendale office was closed down; all its employees moved to the newly finished 15th floor of NTI headquarters. After the first week in the NTI Building, the new employees were grumbling. They found that they had no receptionist to screen visitors and virtually no communication with the rest of the NTI staff. The security guards didn't patrol that floor, and the cleaning service did not clean it. To make matters worse, the new employees had no ID cards to get them into the cafeteria, and the coffee wagon didn't stop on the 15th floor.

Some employees of Acme Industries feel the company has been too slow to determine their honest feelings on incentives

◀ FIGURE 2.2

Business involves give and take.

INTERESTS AND VALUES

As we have seen, our needs motivate us to behave as we do. Interests also contribute strongly to our motivation and our behavior. Think of interests as your preferences, your likes and dislikes, all of which affect how well you perform. For example, psychologists found that students who worked poorly improved when using materials related to their career interests. Because these students were interested in specific careers, they were more likely to work hard in school when they saw the connection between their schoolwork and their career preferences.

Your awareness of other people's interests and the impact those interests have on motivation can help you communicate more effectively. In addition, an awareness of your own interests can help you select the best career options. Many *vocational aptitude* tests exist to help determine a person's job interests and, therefore, his or her "fitness" for specific occupations.

vocational aptitude

talent, ability, or suitability for a skill or trade being pursued as a career

Slightly different from interests, **values** are beliefs that are important to you. Perhaps you have not thought much about your values, but whether you realize it or not, you have already developed a number of them, and you express them in many ways. For example, consider your beliefs concerning such controversial topics as the death penalty, abortion, and the role of private business in government services. Where do you stand on these issues? Your answers help you and others define your values.

Yet values are not simple and often cannot be measured exactly. Helping the poor or sick, for example, is one value many people share; however, some people sacrifice greatly to help while others do little. Therefore, although you may share values with others, the degree to which you hold each value will vary. In any case, your values make up your particular **value system,** a combination of values that, as a whole, is as individual as you are.

FIGURE 2.3 ▶

Some values develop when we are very young.

Values develop as a result of lifelong interactions and relationships with other people, most notably our parents and other authority figures. If we desire love and esteem from our parents, for example, we may learn to value what they value. Other life experiences also influence our value systems, perhaps more strongly than our parents do. For example, a child who grows up very poor in a culture that emphasizes material wealth may, as an adult, have a value system that is geared to the pursuit of financial and material success. However, this adult may or may not value working hard as a means to this success, especially if a parent worked hard but did not appear to be rewarded for it.

Whatever their origin, your values will affect your career. If you value increased pay and job advancement more than free time, you might gladly spend extra hours at work; on the other hand, if you value free time more than increased pay and job advancement, you might not consider working overtime a desirable option. If you value helping others, you might find working as a teacher or health-care professional fulfilling. If you value high pay more than job fulfillment, you will probably choose a job based on its pay rate.

C A S E   S C E N A R I O

Perfect Pitch

Francis DiStefano was Director of Advertising for AtHome, a furniture manufacturer. He also volunteered at the National Literacy Center, a non-profit organization that teaches adults to read and write. His project at the center was to develop a series of magazine ads to recruit volunteers for local community reading centers. Francis knew the ideal person for this project was Leroy Morgan. Leroy was a copywriter on Francis's staff and a volunteer teacher at one of the reading centers.

To persuade Leroy to work on the ads, Francis approached him and explained his own involvement with the National Center. Then he said, "You volunteer at a reading center, Leroy. You certainly understand both the importance of these ads and the target market. And you're one of the best copywriters in the business. You could really bring some creative flair to our ads. They'll be our main effort for attracting volunteers. And we can't help people if we don't have teachers, right? By the way, Leroy, the company has approved some release time for you to work on this project. AtHome fully supports the volunteer work we do."

What did Francis believe Leroy valued? In his approach to recruiting Leroy for the ad campaign, what needs of Leroy's did Francis address?

USE YOUR JUDGMENT

Read the following two job advertisements and consider the values represented as well as the motivations, needs, and interests. Then contrast the two job ads by answering the following questions:

    a.   What motivations, needs, interests, and values does each ad represent? How?

    b.   Assuming the company wants to hire an applicant who can truly meet the goals discussed in the ads, which ad is better? Why?

**AIR QUALITY
CONTROL MANAGER**

Full-time manager needed to promote use of alternative means of transportation to and from work. Salary open, depending on qualifications. Call R. Sutherland, Human Relations Dept., X4772.

AIR QUALITY CONTROL MANAGER
"A Job That Makes a Difference!"

Concerned about our environment? Wish you could "do something" about it? Eager to find a more rewarding, more challenging job? As AQC manager, you will promote the use of alternative means of transportation to and from all our branch offices and plants. This full-time position is a great opportunity for someone who wants a challenge, a chance to be innovative, an excellent salary, and a better environment! Salary open, depending on qualifications. Call B.J. Frankel, Human Resources, X1234.

USE YOUR JUDGMENT

Revise the less effective ad in Exercise 3 in another way to make it more appealing to qualified candidates.

THE QUESTION OF ETHICS

Ethics is the widely accepted code of rules that guides our understanding of right and wrong and establishes appropriate moral conduct for business dealings. Acts of unethical behavior in the workplace can range from distorting the truth to telling bold-faced lies; from pilfering office supplies to embezzling funds; from speaking ill of a coworker to blatant harassment.

The question of ethics is a complex one. In many cases, what is or is not ethical falls in a "gray area"; that is, there is not widespread agreement as to whether the behavior is right or wrong. For example, assume that because of your religious beliefs you view the Sabbath as a day of rest: Is it ethical, then, for your employers to demand that you work on this day? Some would argue that employers have a right to expect employees to hold the value of performing for the company above any personal values.

To communicate effectively with your employers, it is helpful to know where they stand (and where you stand) on ethical issues that will affect your career. In any event, recognizing and confronting ethical violations and taking personal responsibility for your own ethical behavior in the workplace can contribute to an environment that *fosters,* rather than *impedes,* communication.

foster

to encourage; to promote the growth or development

impede

to hinder; to interfere with or slow the progress

C A S E   S C E N A R I O

What's in a Word?

When Barbara Gorski checked her "In" basket, she found a rough draft of next month's magazine ad for her company's SleepNice humidifier. The copy was well written, but Barbara noticed one problem: In small print near the end, the ad claimed SleepNice was "the *only* humidifier approved by the Association of Allergists and Immunologists." Barbara knew this was incorrect; one competitor recently received the same approval. She deleted the words "the *only* humidifier" and returned the ad to Advertising & Promotions.

A few days later, the final version of the ad came to her again for approval. Changing anything at this stage would cost money and delay the ad's appearance. However, Barbara saw that the ad still made the false claim she had corrected previously. Barbara took the ad and went personally to Advertising & Promotions, where she talked to Inez, the marketer for the humidifier. "Inez," she began, "there is only one correction needed on this proof. Sorry. I did note it on the earlier version, but somehow the change was not made. We've got to correct this."

Inez looked at the correction, frowning. "I've got to get this out today, Barbara," she said. "Otherwise we might miss the magazine's deadline. And the print is so small, no one will ever read it."

"Look, Inez, I understand your concern," replied Barbara. "The last thing I want is to miss the deadline. Actually, that's the next-to-last thing. The last thing I want to hear is a complaint from someone who thinks we're trying to mislead customers. And I don't need to tell you how strict this magazine is about ads, do I? If it receives one letter claiming false advertising and the complaint is true, they'll never accept ads from us again."

"All right." Inez sighed. "But let's get on it right away."

What do you think of the way Barbara handled herself in this situation? If she and Inez had decided to leave the ad as it was, how likely is it that their false claim would have been noticed? What would you have done in this situation? Defend your answer.

Deadlines, costs, and other business constraints can sometimes blur ethical issues. In the workplace, you can make a difference by communicating a commitment to ethical behavior. Many business situations will challenge your beliefs, values, and judgment, and some will do so in the most surprising ways. You must be aware of such situations so that you can respond effectively and within the guidelines of your own values and beliefs.

The Ethics Litmus Test

1. Does the course of action you plan to follow seem logical and reasonable? Never mind what anyone else has to say, does it make sense to you? If it does, it is probably right.

2. Does it pass the test of sportsmanship? In other words, if everyone followed the same course of action, would the results be beneficial for all?

3. Where will your plan of action lead? How will it affect others? What will it do for you?

4. Will you think well of yourself when you look back at what you've done?

5. Try to separate yourself from the problem. Pretend for a moment it is the problem of the person you most admire. Ask yourself how that person would handle it.

6. Hold up the final decision to the glaring light of publicity. Would you want your family and friends to know what you have done? The decisions we make in the hope that no one will find out are usually wrong.

From On My Honor, I Will: How One Simple Oath Can Lead You to Success in Business, by Randy Pennington and Marc Bockmon. Published by Warner Books, New York, 1992. Used by permission.

5 **USE YOUR JUDGMENT**

Write a paragraph explaining what you would do in response to the following situation and why:

In the morning mail, you receive a package from Quick Printing Company. Quick is a new supplier that recently bid on one of your large printing jobs. The package contains an expensive and attractive pen-and-pencil set. The rules in your company's operations manual specifically prohibit accepting gifts from suppliers. However, you also want to avoid insulting a business partner.

IN BRIEF

1 Good pay and job security are traditionally recognized motivators of worker performance; however, other motivators are important as well, including interesting work, positive feedback from supervisors, and participation in decision making. Good communication considers all these motivations.

2 Maslow's Hierarchy of Needs classifies human needs based on importance, showing that basic survival needs must be met before people will try to meet higher-level needs. Human needs at all levels affect communication in the workplace.

3 Workers' interests and values also affect their work. Workers and supervisors who know each others' interests and values can work together more productively; thus, open communication regarding interests and values is vital in the workplace.

4 Ethical problems can hamper communication because of differing standards and beliefs.

WORDS OF NOTE

Define each of these terms introduced in Chapter 2.

belonging needs
biological needs
deficiency needs
ego needs
esteem needs
ethics
growth needs
Maslow's Hierarchy
safety needs
self-actualization needs
social needs
values
value system

CHECK YOUR RECALL

1. What are eight factors affecting workers' motivation?

2. Which set of needs in Maslow's Hierarchy represent the higher-level needs?

   a. Growth needs
   b. Deficiency needs

3. What two deficiency needs does the chapter discuss? Explain these needs in your own words.

4. What three growth needs does the chapter discuss? Explain these needs in your own words.

5. What is a workplace example for satisfying each of the following needs?

   a. Basic physical needs
   b. Safety needs
   c. Social needs
   d. Esteem needs
   e. Self-actualization needs

6. What is the difference between interests and values?

7. What is the role of ethics in the communication process?

SHARE YOUR PERSPECTIVE

1. Examine the following three situations. List any people who may have an interest in each situation, and summarize their probable points of view:

   a. A firm that makes plastic containers considers relocating from an inner-city location to a new site in the suburbs. Good public transportation exists in the city, where most of the employees live, but does not exist in the suburbs. However, the current building needs repairs, and the company must soon install an expensive waste disposal system. The community offers tax incentives to get the business to move to the suburban site.
   b. A popular music group records a song whose lyrics are obscene, according to parents of many of the group's fans. The group's producer must decide whether to include the song on the group's new album.

    c. A group of workers learns that people hired by the company in the current year are paid more than those hired previously. They petition the company to increase the pay of all people hired earlier. If they do not receive raises, the employees might quit; if they receive raises, the company's costs will be high and could create financial problems.

Imagine that you work for a company that periodically supplies employees with tickets to popular sporting events. The tickets are distributed on a rotating basis, and you are in charge of distributing them. A good friend and coworker, who is not in line to receive World Series tickets, has suggested that you "fudge" on the list and place her name at the top so that she can take a client to the game. From your point of view, you are more interested in keeping your job than accommodating her request. Write a paragraph explaining what you would do, how you would do it, and why.

FOCUS ON THE FINE POINTS

Read the following background information. Then follow the instructions to locate and correct grammar errors.

Background

Monty Schwarz is the scheduling coordinator for the Family Fitness Center in Solon Springs, Maine. Recently Monty's supervisor asked him to conduct a survey of members regarding center activities. Monty prepared three documents: a letter, a questionnaire, and a guest coupon.

Your Instructions

Each of the following documents contains up to 15 errors. Indicate and correct errors by noting them on a photocopy of the page or on a separate sheet of paper. In each case, you may assume the document is formatted correctly.

Note: If you have difficulty locating errors, turn to page 451 in the Appendix. There you will find additional information about the errors in Document 1.

Document 1: Letter to Members

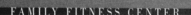

FAMILY FITNESS CENTER

602 West Coast Road Highway
Solon Springs, NH 03452
(603) 555-6767
Fax (603) 555-6890

February 12, 19XX

Dear Family Fitness Center Member:

To better serve member's needs, Family Fitness is conducting a survey to learn what activities and services members find most useful, how he or she would change activities and services, and what additional activities and services members' wanted to have available. We have enclosed a brief questionnaire and asked that you complete and return it in the enclosed postpaid envelope at you're earliest convenience.

As a thank-you for taking time to complete the questionnaire, we will send you a coupon good for one guests' visit to the Solon Springs Family Fitness Center or to one of it's satellite centers in Freeport or Rocky Crest. A member need not accompany their guest on the visit. Additionally, if your guest become a member of Family Fitness, you will be credited with two month's dues absolutely free.

Thank you for your help. Each of us at Family Fitness are eager to serve your families fitness needs and in responding to any questions.

Sincerely,

Monty Schwarz
Scheduling Coordinator

Enclosures: survey and envelope

DOCUMENT 2: Questionnaire

FAMILY FITNESS QUESTIONNAIRE

_____   _____
Name of person completing questionnaire   Date

1. In which of the following activities do someone in your family regularly participate? Check all that applies.

   ____ tennis   ____ running   ____ volleyball
   ____ aerobics   ____ karate   ____ weight training
   ____ dance   ____ swimming   ____ basketball

2. Which of the following exercise and conditioning machines does you or someone in your family use? Check all that applies.

   ____ stairclimber   ____ cross-country track
   ____ treadmill   ____ rowing machine
   ____ bodybuilder   ____ aerobic bicycle

3. Circle yes or no for each of the following statements:

   yes   no   Someone in our family use the exercise and conditioning
               equipment three or more times per week.
   yes   no   Someone in our family participated in the diet program in
               the past two years.
   yes   no   Someone in our family has used the services of Family
               Fitness' massage therapist in the past two years.
   yes   no   If it's dues were lowered by 5%, our family would be likely to
               use Family Fitness's "pay-extra" services such as massage
               and personal training more often.

4. Which of the following best describes you're families use of the Family Fitness
   Center? Check one.

   ____ We are using the center less than one time per week.
   ____ We use the center one or two times per week.
   ____ We use the center at least three times per week.
   ____ We are using the center more than three times per week.

5. Other comments? Please ask all family members for additional comments,
   writing them on the lines provided, and note who made each comment by
   marking A for a family adult or the age in years for a child under 18.

   _____
   _____
   _____
   _____

DOCUMENT 3: Coupon

Be our guest! Family Fitness Center and the _____ family invites you
to use this coupon for one free visit to the Solon Springs

FAMILY FITNESS CENTER

or for visiting one of it's satellite centers, Freeport Family Fitness Center or Rocky Crest
Family Workout World.

For making an appointment or to inquire about this offer, call **555-6767.**

Please redeem this coupon any weekday or Saturday before January 1, 19XX.

_____   _____
Name of guest   Date of visit

This coupon is nontransferable and could not be refunded for cash. This offer was good for the above-named guest only. This offer is not valid with other coupons or discounts from Solon Springs Family Fitness Center or its' satellites, Freeport Family Fitness Center or Rocky Crest Family Workout World. Guest may be required to show identification when presenting coupon and may have been asked to take a no-obligation tour of the facilities' of Family Fitness World. A member need not accompany their guest on the visit.

UNIT I
COMMUNICATE FOR RESULTS

1 Think of a scene in a movie or television show you viewed recently that portrayed a problem resulting from a communication barrier. Describe the scene, the communication barrier, and the resulting problem. Identify verbal and nonverbal cues that contributed to the problem and describe as best you can each character's point of view.

2 Given the following point of view, evaluate whether each of the following communications would be effective or ineffective. Explain your answers. For those that are ineffective, suggest ways to improve them.

Point of view: You work in an employment office. You like your job; it is especially rewarding when you find meaningful work for qualified applicants. You aspire to move into management. You value hard work, honesty, and playing by the rules. You like to give people the benefit of the doubt. You are not very fond of your supervisor but respect how he manages the office. Outside of work you are very active in sports and spend most weekends golfing, sailing, or in-line skating.

a. You have a good working relationship with the people at a local accounting firm; their management usually calls on you to find qualified accountants and secretarial staff. An executive you've worked with many times calls you on Thursday in a panic and says she needs to interview five people for an accounting position no later than Monday.

b. A new executive from this accounting firm calls to complain about an applicant you referred. You listen and respond as reasonably as you can, but the executive interrupts repeatedly and starts ranting about the lack of good help these days.

c. The executive from the accounting firm in situation *a.* above, sends a requisition for additional workers; he has attached a handwritten note requesting that all applicants be white females under 40 years of age.

d. Your supervisor invites you to attend a workshop titled "Management and the Employment Office." It falls on a weekend when you planned to go sailing.

e. Your supervisor reminds a coworker to complete some paperwork. Behind the supervisor's back, this coworker rolls his eyes at you and shakes his head in disgust.

❸ It has become commonplace to learn about public officials and business people violating accepted ethics in conduct. Often the accused either claims innocence or interprets events in a way that justifies his or her behavior. Read the newspaper to find an article that reports about a scandal or other ethical violation. Write a short analysis of how the persons involved made a communication error in word or deed. (Attach the article to your analysis.)

UNIT II

Good listeners talk silently to themselves as they process what other people say; they distinguish between listening and hearing. In addition, they consider the speaker's purpose for speaking; they relate what they already know to what they hear; and they know how to show attention, when to take notes, when to follow directions, when to comment, and when to remain quiet. They continuously evaluate what they hear to check their understanding, to keep themselves focused on the topic, and to aid their memories. Good listeners do all these things and more.

Good listening is a critical business skill. Your attention to what a supervisor or a client says can make the difference between successful and unsuccessful performance at work. The salesperson or customer service representative, for example, must listen carefully to what the customer says and does not say in order to improve sales and customer satisfaction. Also, your attention and understanding in meetings can influence your actions and reactions in significant ways.

▼ **When you finish Unit II, you will be able to**

- Evaluate what you hear based on the speaker, the speaker's purpose, and the message

- Determine when listening whether you must take notes, ask questions, or participate in discussion

- Adapt your behavior to increase what you take away from listening situations

- Adjust your listening strategies depending on the speaker's purpose and your own

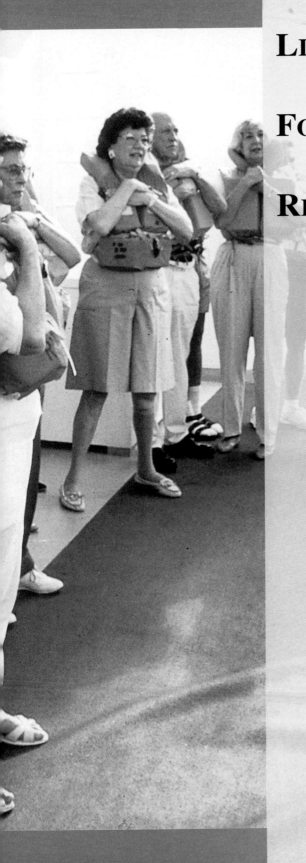

LISTENING

FOR

RESULTS

CHAPTER THREE

What is the difference between listening and hearing?

How can your knowledge of a speaker and a touch of skepticism help you improve your listening?

How can what you already know help you improve your listening?

What benefits can you derive from evaluating messages as you listen to them?

How can you improve your listening skills by changing your listening habits?

How well do you listen? If you are like most people, you have probably developed some poor listening habits. You probably know how to "tune out" a speaker, how to appear to listen when your thoughts are far away. Even when you "hear" something, you may not be "listening." *Hearing* is a physical process; when sound waves reach your ears and send messages to your brain, you are hearing. *Listening*, however, is an intellectual process that combines hearing with evaluating; in addition, listening often leads to follow-up. Consider the following situation. As you read, ask yourself, "Is Amy hearing or listening?

C A S E   S C E N A R I O

Repeat Performance

Robert Fiske's supervisor, Amy Lederer, asked him to review with her the status of the very important Carlsbad project. "Robert," she began, "I don't understand why this project is still behind schedule. Your staff has been working on it since February, yet we seem to make no progress. Your report says the project is still late. What's going on?"

"We have a number of obstacles, Amy," Robert replied. "One is approval of the marketing survey. That's still in Wendy's hands. And the Legal Department still hasn't...."

"Wait a minute, please," interrupted Amy. "These are the same things I heard at our last status meeting. Why haven't you resolved these problems?"

Trying to remain calm, Robert answered her: "As I said at our last meeting, I can't resolve these problems alone. Wendy doesn't report to me, and I don't control the Legal Department. I've done all I can do to get them to cooperate, but I'm at a loss."

Was Amy listening to Robert? How can you tell? How has Amy's listening, or lack of it, affected the Carlsbad project? How might it be affecting other projects? Her communication with other employees?

Listening, because it can and does affect business functioning in significant ways, is considered the most important management skill. But it is a skill needed by all workers, not just managers. Business people who do not listen effectively usually do not know what their customers want, what their employees and coworkers think and feel, what problems their supervisors are facing, and what their top executives expect.

Most business people spend more time listening than they do writing, speaking, or reading. Telephone conversations, informal speeches, job interviews, performance analyses, formal presentations, small-group conferences, status meetings, product demonstrations, business luncheons, and hallway chats all require careful listening. So much valuable communication is spoken that every business worker needs sophisticated listening skills to receive information and to understand it.

However, while few people argue against the importance of listening, the fact is that listening skills are often ignored, probably because they are hard to observe and measure. As children and as students, we are expected to listen, but we are never taught to listen as we are taught to read, write, and speak. In most cases, listening is assumed. How effectively someone is really listening, therefore, is often an unknown, and sometimes a costly error:

- Bill Hamilton is explaining a new procedure to his staff. The room is quiet. All 12 people are either looking at Bill or writing. Bill assumes everyone is listening. The next day, however, four people make errors in following the new procedure, costing the company hours of wasted time.

◀ FIGURE 3.1

Informal business communications require careful listening. Valuable information is often exchanged in the hallway or over the water cooler.

- In her usual quiet voice, Debbie Bradley tells Lance Kimoro that she is not satisfied with the service she receives from his company, Weber Business Services. But it's December, and Lance is preoccupied with meeting his sales goal for the year. All Lance hears is that Debbie is not canceling services now. In January, however, Lance is surprised when his manager says Debbie has not renewed her contract.

The key to improved listening is to listen *actively*. You cannot rely on the speaker to make sure you understand. That responsibility is yours. In any listening situation, **active listening** requires that you do the following:

- Consider the speaker's purpose or message before, during, and after the talk.

- Evaluate what you hear by relating it to what you already know by using prior knowledge.

- Participate fully in the situation by showing attention, taking notes, asking questions, and making comments when appropriate.

- Adopt good listening habits, such as arriving early, sitting in front, and fighting distractions.

RECOGNIZING THE SPEAKER'S PURPOSE

Whenever you speak, you have a purpose (or reason) for delivering the message you are delivering. Likewise, whenever you listen, you are listening to someone who has a purpose or reason for delivering the message you hear. Your job as listener starts by determining the speaker's purpose.

This is often easy. In many situations, the general purpose seems clear before the speaker even begins:

- The agenda for your national sales conference shows that the treasurer of your company is speaking on "The Need To Cut Sales Costs." Can you have any doubt about the purpose of her presentation?

- You have a message that Russell Coventry called and wants you to call him back. Russell, a good customer, calls every time he needs a rush order. Your prior knowledge of Russell forewarns you of this particular speaker's message or purpose!

- On the elevator Tina Powers, the Production Manager, says, "I really meant to call you to discuss your suggestion at this morning's meeting. I understand your dissatisfaction with Allied's last printing job. But I'm sure that Allied won't have that problem any more." When Tina calls, what do you think her purpose will be?

Sometimes discovering the speaker's purpose is more difficult. Speakers can have purposes or reasons that are not immediately apparent. For example, Roselyn Perrozzi is the president of a small company that will be bought out by one of two buyers.

Although her employees do not know it, Roselyn knows that one buyer would replace her as president while the other buyer would ask her to stay. When Roselyn hears that both buyers will interview the employees to get a feel for their work and their morale, she presents information about both buyers to the employees. She speaks favorably of one—the one that would keep her—and unfavorably of the other. The employees believe Roselyn is simply passing on information, yet her real purpose—to sway employees in favor of the buyer who would retain her—is quite different.

The better you know the speaker and the situation, of course, the better you can detect a speaker's real purpose. For example, if you know Jackie well and she has a history of being honest and following through on her promises, then you probably are safe to assume that Jackie will be forthright in her purpose when she speaks to you. In other words, she doesn't have a "hidden agenda." In contrast, if you know that Rochelle frequently lies to cover up her mistakes, you will be more careful when ascertaining her purpose as she communicates with you.

Keep in mind that a touch of *skepticism* can help you discern the ***bottom line*** of a message whenever speakers stand to benefit (financially or otherwise) from their statements, especially when the statements seem exaggerated. We'll look more closely at how to do this in the section on listening to persuasive talk in Chapter 4.

In short, active listening requires you to consider the speaker's motives, including those of the people you know. Even the most honest people may not admit a mistake because they would be embarrassed. They may cover up an error for fear of losing their jobs or being reprimanded. Or they may not be aware that they have a strong *bias* for or against a person or a company.

skepticism

an attitude of doubt; a degree of mistrust

bottom line

the crux, the essential point; the most important consideration (look for another meaning of this term on page 72)

bias

prejudice; a personal and/or unreasoned distortion of judgment

A Touch of Skepticism

It's always a good idea to listen with a touch of skepticism. Ask yourself:

- "Is Gary saying this to make his department look good?"

- "Is Kate making excuses for a serious error she made?"

- "Is this salesperson simply trying to get on my good side?"

USE YOUR JUDGMENT

For each of the following situations, predict what the speaker's purpose will be and explain why you predicted as you did.

a. You receive a short memo from Charles Reynolds, the Director of Advertising, inviting you to a meeting. The subject line of his memo reads "New Newspaper Advertising Rates Effective January 1."

b. Melissa Coburn, a coworker, calls you: "Hi, it's Melissa. I just received your purchase order, and . . ."

c. You receive a letter inviting you to a "Free Investment Seminar." The letter is businesslike and includes no sales brochure.

FIGURE 3.3 ▶

Even the most honest people may say things that are not entirely true in order to achieve their purpose.

As you read the following situation, consider what you would conclude about Margaret's motive for responding to Harry as she does. Explain the reason for your conclusion:

Harry Evans cannot find his copy of the requisition he sent to the Purchasing Department last month. He cannot remember whether the requisition included an order for business cards. Harry is in no rush for the cards; he has a few months' supply. But since his assistant is now reordering cards, he decides to add his order at the same time—that is, if he hasn't already placed an order. He calls Margaret DeMara, the supervisor of the Purchasing Department, and begins, "Margaret, about a month ago I sent down a requisition...." "Harry," Margaret interrupts, "last month the mail room really messed up the works. They delayed lots of requisitions, and as a result Purchasing is getting blamed. Just the other day. . . ."

EVALUATING WHAT YOU HEAR

Active listening means combining hearing with **evaluation.** Throughout any presentation, meeting, or conversation, you must assign meaning to and evaluate what you hear.

Often assigning meaning to what you hear is simple. You know the meaning of all or most of the words the speaker uses, and, like most people, you can put those words together to form meaning. When your boss says, "We will close at noon next Friday," his meaning is obvious. Or is it? The problem with assigning meaning to words arises because people do not always say what they mean. However, you can derive meaning from more than just the speaker's words.

Note Body Language and Other Nonverbal Cues

Body language and other nonverbal cues will help you interpret speakers' messages. When you watch *and* listen to someone speak (for example, when you are in the same room or see someone on television), you often understand more than when you *only* listen (for example, to a radio program).

Consider the numerous interpretations possible for this simple statement: "I must thank Bob for all his hard work." Reading this comment, you may assign the most obvious meaning to it: The speaker has sincere thanks to give Bob. However, watching the speaker say this might lead you to another interpretation.

For example, what if the speaker rolls her eyes when she says it? This probably means she is exaggerating and that Bob didn't do as much as her statement suggests. Furthermore, Bob's presence will affect how you interpret this statement. If Bob *is* in the room, watching and listening, the speaker is probably teasing Bob lightheart-edly or she is being very cruel. If Bob *is not* in the room, the speaker is probably making a joke at Bob's expense, expecting most of the audience to agree that Bob didn't really contribute much.

Other body language and nonverbal cues also help as you assign meaning to a speaker's words. What words does the speaker emphasize when she announces her gratitude to Bob? How would different emphasis on different words alter the mean-ing of the sentence? What is she doing when she makes the announcement? If she's shuffling through papers distractedly, the message can be interpreted as less sincere than if she delivers it while sitting upright and looking Bob in the eyes. In short, see-ing someone speak provides more information about the meaning of the words than simply hearing the person speak.

Consider Personality

Personality is another factor to consider when assigning meaning to what a person says. What about the boss who says, "We will close at noon next Friday"? How can those words mean anything but what they say? Well, if he's being sarcastic, his real meaning may be, "Just because it's Friday doesn't mean we're closing any earlier than normal, and I'd better see everyone hard at work up until 5:00." Employees who know this person well may fully understand what he means even though he has said just the opposite. If he's being flippant, his comment may mean nothing; he may simply have said it to get a chuckle from employees who know better. The more you know about a speaker, the easier it will be to assign meaning accurately to that person's words.

Use Prior Knowledge

Knowledge of speakers can not only help you assign meaning to their words but also help you evaluate their messages. *Evaluating* meaning means judging the accuracy and truthfulness of what you hear:

- Does it make sense?

- Does it match the nonverbal cues given by the speaker?

- Does it fit with other information you have (can you think of any reason not to believe it)?

All are important questions to ask, but the only way to answer such questions is to compare what you are hearing to your *prior knowledge* of the situation. Comparing new information to your prior knowledge means relating the new information to information you already have and believe. If new and old information match or agree, you may choose to believe what you hear. However, when new and old infor-mation contradict each other, you must question further.

For example, when you listen to candidates for political office, you know their purpose is generally to convince you that they will serve the public well if elected. They may say, for example, that they will reduce taxes, create jobs, increase access to health care, reduce crime, and so on. Do you believe them?

The only way to answer this question is to compare their claims with what you already know about the situation. Have these candidates kept most of their promises in the past? Do their political records suggest that they want to accomplish these goals? That they are able to accomplish these goals? Are the goals good ones? Are they realistic, given the current economy, political process, and power structure? Your knowledge of and opinion on all these issues (and more) will help you determine whether you believe the claims of political candidates.

The evaluative use of prior knowledge has at least three general benefits:

1. **Improved memory.** Research shows that people are better able to remember information that is personalized—that relates directly to them. By relating new information to old, you are, in effect, personalizing it, and you will remember more of that information.

2. **Improved focus.** Many people find it easy to begin thinking about other things when listening to information that has no personal connection for them. By relating new information to old information, you personalize the information, and your ability to pay attention to that information increases.

3. **Improved understanding.** Relating old information to new information means constantly checking for agreement or contradiction between the two. The mere act of checking forces you to comprehend what the speaker is saying; you cannot check it if you do not comprehend it. Beyond comprehension, this checking forces you into a critical approach to the information: "Is it true or isn't it, given what I already know?"

Use Self-Talk

There are a number of questions you can ask yourself as you sift incoming information. Silently research the topic in your mind to uncover what you already know:

*   Do the speaker's facts support what you have heard, read, or seen from other sources?

*   Do the speaker's facts agree with or contradict facts presented by the same speaker earlier?

*   Do the speaker's conclusions agree with your experience?

*   Do the speaker's suggestions and recommendations have substance?

*   Does your speaker meet the test of common sense?

This type of **self-talk** can help you to listen actively and respond appropriately.

▲FIGURE 3.4

Prior knowledge is an important part of listening to a candidate for political office. It can help you evaluate which candidate to vote for.

FIGURE 3.5 ▶

Silently research the topic in your mind to uncover what you already know.

C A S E　　S C E N A R I O

What Are the Facts?

Roland Delzer was recently assigned to manage all promotional materials for the Culver Cereal Company. He still has much to learn about this new area, but a coworker, Suzanne Werness, provided some helpful information. Yesterday, a representative from Allied Printing stopped by Roland's office to talk about printing services.

The rep told Roland, "Allied Printing is an agent for independent printers. That means we can guarantee you the lowest costs and the fastest deliveries. For example, we would charge you only 29 cents a copy for this brochure. Other printers would charge you more."

"That's not what I heard from Suzanne," Roland said to himself. "She told me that you get the best prices when you deal directly with the printer. When you deal with an agent, the agent gets a commission, and that must cost more. But I know we paid more than 29 cents a copy for the corn flakes brochure. I'd better ask Suzanne about that." To the rep, Roland said, "I believe I can get a better price by going directly to a printer. If you leave me with some information about your services and a rate sheet, I'll do some comparing on my own."

*How did information Roland had from Suzanne help him evaluate what the Allied rep had to say? What other prior knowledge came in to play here? How can Roland's careful listening affect his company's **bottom line**?*

bottom line

the line at the bottom of a financial report that shows the net profit or loss; financial considerations such as cost, profit, or loss (look for another meaning of this term on page 67)

Evaluation Takes Many Forms

Once you begin evaluating what you hear by relating old information with new information, your evaluations will take various forms. Some examples:

You recognize misunderstandings or deceptions:

- "He isn't really answering the question, is he?"

- "He knows a lot about our trading relationship with Japan but hasn't said one word about Germany."

You recognize discrepancies between old information and new:

- "Did she say 'zero point seven percent'? I've heard estimates much, much higher. I wonder which numbers are accurate."

- "Wait a minute. Didn't he say just the opposite of that last week?"

You check your own understanding:

- "Oh, I get it. To speed up the approval process, from now on we...."

- "I guess this means the budget cut will affect us sooner rather than later."

You clarify information:

- "Oh, I thought she said 70 before. She must have said 17."

- "That graph sure helps. Now I see the sales growth he's talking about."

You recognize similarities between old information and new:

- "Hmm, this agrees with what I read in the newspaper yesterday. There must be some truth in this."

- "The problems he's reporting about this project are just like those that surfaced on the Broder project. Maybe we need to revisit how we handled the Broder project."

Another way to evaluate as you listen is to categorize incoming information based on whether it is positive, negative, or questionable. Observe how this **positive-negative-questionable strategy** is applied:

C A S E   S C E N A R I O

A Clearer Picture

For a special report, John Gregus needed bids on computer equipment from two vendors. Because he needed the information by the end of the day, John called both companies. First, he called Ford Computers. After listening to what the Ford rep had to say, John had a great deal of information but no clear picture of what it meant.

On a sheet of paper, John wrote:

Positive
State-of-the-art system
Competitive price ($1,599)
Includes color monitor
2-year warranty for parts

Negative
Tower design will not fit into current work-
station
Warranty does not cover labor

Questionable
Free installation (Really necessary since I
can do it myself?)
Free software bundle (None of the programs
fit our business needs)

How did using the positive-negative-questionable model help John get a clearer picture? What other things might be questionable here? How might John use this information in listening to the bid from the second vendor?

Keep a log for one day. Identify at least five situations in which you are able to use prior knowledge to help evaluate what you hear. For each situation, record the following:

    a.   The situation
    b.   What you heard
    c.   The prior knowledge you used
    d.   How you related old to new knowledge

Read an advice column in the newspaper. Select a letter and response; then analyze the response in writing using the positive-negative-questionable strategy. Include your own evaluation as to whether the columnist really "listened" to the letter writer.

LISTENING AND PARTICIPATING

Although some business situations require only that you listen carefully and evaluate what you hear, many will require you to participate in various other ways as well. There will be times when it is both appropriate and necessary that you show attention, take notes, ask questions, and make comments.

Show Attention

One significant way in which you can participate as a listener during face-to-face communications is to convey, through your body language, that you are paying attention. Stop what you are doing and turn to face the speaker. Engage in enough eye contact to signal that you are focused on the speaker (but avoid staring, which can be both intimidating and distracting). Lean toward, rather than away from, the speaker to indicate that you are "tuned in." Be appropriately responsive—smile or laugh at a humorous anecdote, frown at bad news. Nod your head, but only when you understand an important point, and if you are puzzled by something, let the speaker know by furrowing your brow.

Apply these suggestions as they fit the circumstances, and be mindful that the speaker will be evaluating your nonverbal feedback. And take care—while alert body language communicates active listening, nonverbal cues such as roving eyes, a flat *affect,* and inappropriate facial expressions communicate indifference and even rudeness.

affect

feeling or emotion as shown by one's facial expression

Showing attention benefits you, the listener, in the following ways:

- To show attention, you actually need to be paying attention to the message. This means you are likely to receive the information you are intended to receive.

rapport

accord; relationship marked by harmony

- Your attention builds positive ***rapport*** with the speaker, which encourages further communication. Think about it, don't you want people to show interest (rather than yawn and look distracted) when you speak? How do you feel toward someone who looks bored when you have something to say?

- The discipline of showing attention makes it easier to ignore distractions. By committing yourself physically to the task of listening, you are less likely to stray from the object of your attention.

Take Notes

Writing down things a speaker says sounds easy, but it is not. First realize that the goal is not to record every word spoken. Instead, the objective is to jot down the speaker's points that are meaningful to your purpose for listening. To do this effectively requires careful, active listening.

Consider the thinking process you must go through to take good notes. You must not only *hear* what is said, but you must also *comprehend* it, *evaluate* it, and *translate or summarize* it. You then must determine if it is important enough to write down. Next, you must record it quickly but in a meaningful form, and as you write, you must continue listening because the speaker continues. Finally, you must begin the process again. And this process, as described, does not account for at least one complicating factor: You must not only record information but record it in such a way that the relationship between noted points is clear.

Given this process, you can easily see that in taking notes, less is more. For example, rather than writing down four separate statements, you may be better off writing down one slightly longer statement that encompasses and shows the relationship among those four statements. While writing down separate statements, you may not be hearing the relationship among those statements. If, however, you begin to build a summary in your head, you can write down a single statement that covers both the main points and their connection.

Here are some tips for taking good notes:

1. **Consider your purpose and be selective.** Some people take notes automatically and note everything. Avoid this. In fact, even if others are taking notes, you may not have to take notes at all. Other people may have a different purpose for listening than you have. Take notes only if you have to, and then be selective. Write down only what you need or may need. Listening carefully means, among other things, judging which information is important and which is not.

2. **Organize your notes for efficiency.** Let the format of your notes correspond to the speaker's message. For example, if the speaker is contrasting two things, take notes in two side-by-side columns. If, on the other hand, you are taking thorough notes of information arranged by main ideas and supporting details, take your notes in informal outline form, indenting details under main ideas. Also, use abbreviations and symbols—arrows, asterisks, bullets, lines, circles, and so on. As long as the notes are for you only, you can cut as many corners as you like.

3. **Use handouts to save yourself time.** Avoid rewriting information that already appears in a speaker's handout. Look at the handout as you are listening. If you see information being repeated or if your speaker refers you to a section of the handout, simply highlight it or put a check mark in the margin.

4. **Avoid recreating complex visual aids.** In most cases, the time you would spend redrawing a complex line graph or a flow chart is not worth your effort. Instead of recreating the visual, write down the main point if it's important. If a speaker uses a complex table of information you would like to recall, do not try to recreate the table; you will miss the information the speaker gives as you are drawing. Instead, write down the source of the table, or simply ask the speaker afterwards for the source or for a copy of the table.

5. **Avoid using note-taking as a substitute for active listening.** If you plan to simply take notes and then think about and evaluate the information later, you are fooling yourself. Part of the importance of evaluating what you hear as you hear it is to help put the rest of what you hear into perspective. In other words, comprehension and evaluation of one part of a presentation affect comprehension and evaluation of later parts. You are far better off listening carefully and taking no notes than you are doing the opposite.

6. **Notice other note-takers.** Since note-taking is not an exact science, everyone who is taking notes is writing down information that differs slightly from yours. Notice the other people taking notes and do not hesitate to call on them later for help interpreting and filling in your own. No doubt you will be able to help them as well.

7. **Listen until the end.** Often speakers are repeating, emphasizing, and summarizing their most important information just as time is running out and listeners are no longer paying close attention. In fact, you may be able to listen to the last ten percent of a presentation and hear every significant point. Clearly, this is a good time to be listening carefully with pen ready, if necessary.

8. **Note things you must do.** During meetings, supervisors and coworkers will ask you to do things, or the discussion will imply that you must do something. Listen carefully for any such directions, whether stated directly or merely implied, and write them down. You will often leave meetings with many things on your mind, some of which you will forget if you do not write them down.

Ask Questions and Make Comments

Active listening always means asking questions and making comments. However, it does not always mean asking questions and making comments *aloud*. Clearly, some situations call for quiet listening, but when possible and if necessary, ask questions and make comments.

Be aware, however, that questions and comments can fall into two categories, friendly and unfriendly, with some gray area between. Friendly questions and comments are those with which someone simply requests or adds clarification or further information. Unfriendly questions and comments, however, are those with which someone challenges another person.

Friendly questions and comments are usually welcomed by speakers. By asking friendly questions and making friendly comments, you show that you are listening, interested, and confident enough in the speaker to seek more information. Unfriendly questions and comments are usually unwelcome. Even if the speaker has a good response to an unfriendly question or comment, the inherent challenge may create an uncomfortable atmosphere.

This does not mean you should mindlessly ask friendly questions and make friendly comments whenever you feel like it. Nor does it mean you should always avoid unfriendly questions. There is a time and place for both.

FIGURE 3.6 ▶

Always phrase your question or comment carefully.

Friendly Questions

- "Ms. Sorenson, did your marketing questionnaire elicit any information on family income?"

- "Fred, this summary sheet says this year's sales goal is ten percent higher than last year's. Is that ten percent over last year's actual sales, or ten percent over budgeted sales?"

- "Mr. Mendoza, how much memory does this software program require?"

- "I agree. We must get that budget back on track."

- "Maybe if we give them a copy of that appendix, Ron, it will answer all of their questions. Let's do that."

Unfriendly Questions

- "Ms. Sadowski, last week you said last month's sales were up ten percent, but today you say they were down five percent. Which is it?"

- "You claim there are no problems with clear-cutting forests. How do you account for the article in last week's Forestry Magazine, which listed several problems with clear-cutting?"

- "That sounds like a very high number. Do you have empirical evidence to support that claim?"

- "I completely disagree with that. I take just the opposite view. We should . . ."

- "You always talk about Total Quality Management, but you have yet to really implement it in this department."

When asking friendly questions and making friendly comments, consider the following:

- **Timing.** Pick the best time to ask questions and make comments. Avoid interrupting a speaker, if possible. Write your question or comment down for later. In some cases, the speaker will answer or respond to your question or comment as the presentation or meeting proceeds. Furthermore, the speaker may have scheduled time for questions and comments at the end of the presentation. If you have more than one question or comment, pause between them to give others a chance to participate.

- **Relevance.** Avoid asking questions or making comments that do not relate to the topic. The speaker may not see the relevance and, therefore, may not be able to answer comfortably. Also, the other listeners will probably become impatient. If you must ask questions or make comments that are only vaguely related to the topic, wait until all other listeners have had a chance, and make the speaker feel at ease if he or she looks confused.

- **Length.** Some questions and comments are more disruptive than others. If you must interrupt, at least keep it very short.

When you wish to ask unfriendly questions, consider the following:

- **Diplomacy.** Although unfriendly questions and comments are often meant to point out discrepancies, inconsistencies, falsehoods, biases, or other problems with a speaker's message, maintain a professional tone. If you ask a good question or make a good comment in an unprofessional or sarcastic manner, your lack of professionalism is what people will remember. Always leave the lines of communication open.

- **Speaker's purpose.** Often an unfriendly question or comment suggests that the speaker has purposely misinformed or deceived the listeners. Speakers sometimes do this, of course. On the other hand, speakers sometimes make mistakes. Give the speaker the benefit of the doubt and phrase your question or comment carefully.

- **Relevance.** Avoid nitpicking. If a speaker makes a general point with which you agree but supports it with a detail or two with which you disagree, do not challenge the detail unless you foresee it being misused later. In most cases, the general point is the more important aspect of the presentation.

- **Timing.** Avoid interrupting the speaker. Ask the question or make the comment when the speaker has finished or has invited questions.

- **Audience.** If your disagreement is intense, consider approaching the speaker privately, for example, after others have left the room. Your goal should be to correct the speaker, not to publicly embarrass anyone.

5   USE YOUR JUDGMENT

Take notes of a class lecture or discussion and compare your notes with a classmate's. Discuss the following with your classmate: How do the notes compare? How do the notes differ? Whose notes are better? Why? Take notes on this discussion.

During a class lecture or discussion, write down any questions or comments you bring up or would like to bring up. After class, categorize your questions and comments as friendly or unfriendly. For each that appears in the unfriendly category, write a note next to it that describes the intended point of the question or comment.

DEVELOPING EFFECTIVE LISTENING HABITS

We all have habits—some good, some not—that affect our ability to listen. Use the Listening Checklist at the end of this unit (page 111) to evaluate your listening habits. Be as honest and objective as you can.

Although improving your listening habits takes a good deal of self-discipline, there are specific ways you can help yourself. Showing attention, questioning, commenting, and taking notes are important listening aids. In addition, when you are listening for a specific purpose—as you would be when attending a meeting or presentation—try the strategies that follow.

Arrive Early

Arriving early is not merely a courtesy to the speaker or other meeting participants; it is also an aid to your listening. It allows you time to settle in, familiarize yourself with your surroundings, greet people you know, and shuffle any necessary paperwork before the speaker begins. The beginning and end of any speaking situation are often crucial. At the beginning and end, speakers often introduce and summarize their main points. By missing the first few minutes of a presentation, you cannot benefit from the speaker's attempt to focus the discussion and introduce main ideas. Finally, arriving late is simply disruptive to all other participants.

Sit in the Front

The front of the room usually provides fewer distractions. You will not see latecomers, and you are less likely to be distracted by those sitting between you and the speaker. From the front, you can hear the speaker better and see any visuals with less effort. By sitting in the front of the room, you will more easily be able to participate in the communication process.

Fight Distractions

Good listeners fight distractions by giving all their attention to the task of listening. They concentrate on the message and ignore outside stimuli. This power to concentrate also helps to keep internal distractions—those created by one's own mind—in

FIGURE 3.7 ▶

Many times business must be
conducted amidst distractions. In
these situations, all attention must
be given to the task of listening.

check as well. When listening to a presentation, especially one that is less than stimulating, you may feel the urge to plan tomorrow's meeting or your weekend, to catch up
on your mail, to draft a letter or memo; in short, to use the time more "productively."
However, if the information you are hearing is worth hearing, listen actively. Only
when you stop listening actively will your mind look for something else to do.

7 USE YOUR JUDGMENT

If you have not already done so, use the Listening Checklist found on page 111.
How well did you do? A score lower than 7 for any of the five items suggests that
you need improvement in that area. If you focus on these weaknesses, you can trans-
form them into strengths. For each score lower than 7, make a list of specific things
you can do to improve your performance in this area. Then practice.

8 USE YOUR JUDGMENT

Most people are subject to distractions when listening. Write an essay answering the
following questions: Of the six types of internal distractions listed earlier, which are
you most often affected by as a student? How? Which are you most often affected
by in social settings? How? How do you differ as a listener in the two settings?

Six Common Internal Distractions To Avoid

1. **Laziness.** Lazy listeners stop paying attention when the information becomes too long or complex.

2. **Closed-mindedness.** Closed-minded listeners tune out a speaker because they are not interested in learning from the speaker and are uninterested in helping maintain an environment conducive to open communication.

3. **Inflexibility.** Inflexible listeners refuse to listen to a speaker who has said or implied something they disagree with, especially if the speaker has said something that contradicts their value and belief system.

4. **Insincerity.** Insincere listeners are those who listen to the words but not the message. They often avoid eye contact with the speaker and, therefore, cannot benefit from the speaker's body language.

5. **Boredom.** Bored listeners are those who find no interest in the subject. They either become impatient and hostile with the speaker or preoccupy themselves with something else.

6. **Inattention.** Inattentive listeners pay little attention to the speaker's message but may concentrate on the speaker's body language and mannerisms. They become distracted by ringing telephones, passing conversation, and other outside noise.

IN BRIEF

❶ Unlike writing or speaking, your listening skills are often overlooked. But the business world's emphasis on communication skills has drawn more attention to listening than ever before.

❷ You can improve your listening skills through active listening, which means:

    a.   Consciously considering the speaker's purpose

    b.   Consciously evaluating what you hear by considering your prior knowledge of the situation

    c.   Fully participating in speaking situations by showing attention, taking notes, asking questions, and making comments

❸ You can maximize what you hear and comprehend in formal listening situations by making an effort to arrive early and sit in front and by fighting distractions as best you can.

WORDS OF NOTE

Define each of these terms introduced in Chapter 3.

active listening
evaluation
positive-negative-questionable strategy
self-talk

CHECK YOUR RECALL

1. What is the difference between *hearing* and *listening*?

2. To listen actively, what four things must you do?

3. What are four practices that will help you evaluate what you hear?

4. What are three benefits of using prior knowledge to evaluate what you hear?

5. What are three ways to participate appropriately as you listen?

6. What are some guidelines to follow in note-taking?

7. What is the difference between a friendly and an unfriendly question?

8. What three habits can you develop to become a more effective listener?

SHARE YOUR PERSPECTIVE

1. Your company has proposed that its staff maintain a 40-hour work week but that employees put in their 40 hours in four days instead of five. Use the positive-negative-questionable strategy to evaluate this proposal as thoroughly as you can in writing.

2. Observe a speech or presentation (either live, on tape, or on television). Evaluate the presentation by mentally researching the topic against your prior knowledge. Write an evaluation of the presentation based on your answers to the following questions:

   a. Do the speaker's facts support what you have heard, read, or seen from other sources?

b. (If applicable) Do the speaker's facts agree with or contradict facts presented by the same speaker earlier?

c. Do the speaker's conclusions agree with your experience?

d. Do the speaker's suggestions and recommendations have substance?

e. Does your speaker meet the test of common sense?

❸ During a class lecture or discussion, write down any questions or comments your classmates make. After class, categorize these questions and comments as friendly or unfriendly. For each that appears in the unfriendly category, write a note next to it that describes the point you believe that question or comment was intended to make. Note also whether each student adhered to the guidelines for asking questions and making comments.

FOCUS ON THE FINE POINTS

Read the following background information. Then follow the instructions to locate and correct grammar errors.

Background

Miranda Lambert is the executive assistant to Larry Martinez, the president and CEO of a small business. Mr. Martinez is interested in learning more about a consulting company, Oscar Pratt Associates (OPA). He has asked Miranda to listen to the company's public service announcement on the radio and to call for additional information. Mr. Martinez wants a recommendation from Miranda regarding whether the company should hire OPA as an ethics consultant.

After listening to the radio spot, Miranda calls OPA and requests some literature about the company and its services. Miranda reviews the sample seminar agenda OPA sends, and then evaluates what she has learned about the company, using the positive-negative-questionable model. She plans to include the evaluation in a memo to Mr. Martinez.

Your Instructions

Each of the following documents contains up to 15 errors. Indicate and correct errors by noting them on a photocopy of the page or on a separate sheet of paper. In each case, you may assume the document is formatted correctly.

Note: If you have difficulty locating errors, turn to page 453 in the Appendix. There you will find additional information about the errors in Document 1.

DOCUMENT 1: Public Service Announcement

Public Service Announcement (PSA), 45 seconds

Dates: _____

Are you a manager that is concerned about ethics in the workplace? Are you discouraged by the many business people today for who the very idea of reconciling the bottom line with the common good has become merely "quaint" or "old fashioned"? Do you want to find a way to build a real commitment to "doing the right thing" at all levels of your organization?

Just between you and I, if your answer to any of these questions is yes, you are not alone. More and more managers are concerned about ethics in the workplace. Companies everywhere are recognizing and addressing these concerns. From the problem of an employee "borrowing" company supplies to insider trading on the stock market companies around the world are looking for ways to refocus their organizations on "doing the right thing."

We all know that ethical standards, once universally held, no longer seem evident of late. As a manager who cares about corporate integrity, there is a company dedicated to guiding them and their organization toward the highest ethical standards and practices. Oscar Pratt, author of the international best-seller *Business: Doing It Right,* has formed Oscar Pratt Associates to do just those. OPA offers businesses custom seminars in workplace ethics. OPA is in its fifth year of helping companies large and small develop solid, realistic plans to establish and maintain a company-wide commitment to integrity. For a no-obligation consultation with a professional OPA representative, take down this number now: 1-800-557-4448. That's 1-800-55-RIGHT. Join the thousands of managers whom are facing the vital issue of ethics head on and are working to make their workplace the very best it can be!

DOCUMENT 2: Agenda for One-Day Seminar

Agenda for a One-Day OPA Management Seminar in
WORKPLACE ETHICS*

Time	Topic/Plan

8:00 - 8:30   <u>Welcome and Introductions</u>
Participants introduce himself or herself and briefly explain his or her goals for the session.

8:30 - 10:00   <u>Overview of Ethical Issues in the Workplace</u>
•Four general areas, which are of ethical concern in today's workplace, are presented.
•Participants discuss how these areas of concern play themself out in the workplace.

10:00 - 10:30   <u>Break and Informal Discussion</u>
Participants are encouraged to chat informally with themselves and with the facilitator.

10:30 - 11:45   <u>Identifying Problems</u>
•The Ethics Blueprint is presented; this is a six-part foundation, from the bottom up, to building an ethical organization.
•Having reviewed the Ethics Blueprint, identifying and discussing participants' real problems comes next.

11:45 - 12:00   <u>Organizing Lunch Groups</u>
Participants are organized into lunch groups with shared workplace situations, concerns, or goals of 6-8 people.

12:00 - 1:00   <u>Lunch</u>
During lunch groups informally strategize ways to introduce a company-wide interest in workplace ethics.

1:00 - 2:00   <u>Small-Group Planning</u>
Working more formally, a list of strategies for workplace success is developed by lunch groups. During this time, group members
•Define situations in common
•Define general goals
•Identify common strategies
•Identify possible barriers and solutions

2:00 - 2:45   <u>Group Presentations, Part I</u>
Each group presents and discusses his or her strategies.

2:45 - 3:15   <u>Break</u>
Recognizing that they need time to make business phone calls, participants may use this time for that purpose and for informal discussion.

3:15 - 4:30   <u>Group Presentations, Part II</u>
Groups continue to present and discuss strategies.

4:30 - 5:00   <u>The Day's Wrap-Up</u>
•Together, facilitator summarizes the day's learning.
•The facilitator presents a variety of possible "next steps" for they and their companies to take.

*This is an example of one possible agenda for an introductory session for managers. Many other formats are available.

DOCUMENT 3: Part of Miranda's Memo to Mr. Martinez

I'm not convinced as you can see from the following notes that OPA is the ideal consultant on workplace ethics. Based on his or her radio ad and literature, here are some of my thoughts:

<u>Positive</u>
As a well-known, respected author of books on professional ethics, I have no doubt that Oscar Pratt is an expert in the field.

OPA says he is willing to customize training to meet a company's specific needs.

<u>Negative</u>
The costs, which I was quoted on the phone, are some of the highest which I have ever encountered. (See the attached price breakdown.)

<u>Questionable</u>
Their ad, that is called a "public service announcement," is really an advertisement. Why is OPA "coloring" the way they present itself in this way? Also, the radio announcement uses vague and/or trite language that does nothing to distinguish the OPA firm. Why would someone allow their name to be used in this manner—as knowledgeable and respected as Oscar Pratt?

Given the research we've already done on the topic of workplace ethics, the content (meager as they may be) of OPA's radio spot and literature does not mesh with what we know about sound practice (e.g., "Don't announce a 'company-wide ethics program'").

What can you do to make sure you get all the information you need when listening for specific information?

How is listening to a request different from listening to directions? How should your listening strategies in these situations differ?

How can you listen to persuasive talk objectively?

In Chapter 3, you learned the importance of trying to identify the speaker's purpose. Your purpose for listening is equally important. If you are listening to a sales representative trying to sell you a product, your purpose may be to learn as much as you can about the product and the company. Your purpose for listening differs, on the other hand, if you are not interested in the product but instead want to learn selling techniques by observing a professional.

Because your purpose for listening will differ according to the situation and the needs you bring to that situation, you will listen more effectively if you identify your purpose and adapt your listening behavior accordingly.

LISTENING FOR SPECIFIC INFORMATION

When you are aware that you need specific information from a speaker, you are better prepared to receive that information. And there are some things you can do as a listener to make sure you collect the information efficiently and accurately.

For example, Francine Cameron needs to call for flight information for an upcoming business trip from Minneapolis to New York. Francine knows that she will be listening for specific information: the flight number, the departure time, and the arrival time. Before she calls, Francine gets a sheet of paper and writes the following:

From Minneapolis to New York

Date: _____

Flight # _____	*Flight # _____*	*Flight # _____*
(d) _____	*(d) _____*	*(d) _____*
(a) _____	*(a) _____*	*(a) _____*

From New York to Minneapolis

Date: _____

Flight # _____	*Flight # _____*	*Flight # _____*
(d) _____	*(d) _____*	*(d) _____*
(a) _____	*(a) _____*	*(a) _____*

As she listens to the flight information, Francine simply fills in the blanks.

Like Francine, you will often need to listen for specific information—a number, an address, a dollar figure, or other statistical data. If you must listen for a great deal of data, prepare in advance whenever possible. Before you go to a meeting, attend a conference, or make a telephone call, decide what information you hope to carry away. Then start a note sheet that you can fill in as you listen, as Francine did in planning her travel. Being prepared in this way can save you time and help you get all the information you need to know.

C A S E   S C E N A R I O

Take Note!

Marion Mahabadi was preparing to attend a meeting at which the sales manager would be discussing past and current sales performance for the division. At the meeting, Marion needed to get specific information so she could determine how her department contributed to overall division performance.

Before the meeting, Marion took the time to prepare the following note sheet:

Unit Sales		*Dollar Sales*	
Last Year	*This Year*	*Last Year*	*This Year*
___ *units*	___ *units*	$ _____	$ _____

Marion took the note sheet with her to the meeting and filled in the amounts as the sales manager provided them. Toward the end of the meeting, Marion noticed that she did not yet have a figure for last year's dollar sales. During the question-and-answer period, she asked for the information she needed.

Did Marion's note sheet help her get the information she needed? How else could the sheet have been helpful?

Of course, in a listening situation you will not always need numerical information, nor will you always know in advance what to listen for. Also, you often will find that you must take notes other than those you planned to take. Each situation is different. Still, to the extent that you can plan what to listen for, you will listen more effectively.

1

Use Your Judgment

Read the following situation. Then write a paragraph in which you describe the problem and how it might have been avoided through more active listening:

Jenni Chang was annoyed. She had just received an invoice for the laser printers she purchased for her department. The total was nearly $2,000 higher than the estimated cost that her production assistant, Paula Gregorian, had provided. Jenni took the bill to Paula and asked, "Why did this invoice come in so high, Paula? It's so far over budget that I'll have to get special permission before I can approve it." Paula frowned at the invoice, then raised her eyebrows as she saw the problem. "I see what happened," she said. "They charged extra for tax, shipping, and installation."

LISTENING TO RESPONSES

When someone responds to your request or question, you probably need no special motivation to listen carefully. After all, the response should interest you since you requested it.

complex

complicated, intricate; hard to separate or analyze

If the response is *complex,* however, you may miss part of it. This is especially true if part of the response is unexpected. Always make sure you understand all parts of the response and its details. Write notes and ask questions to clarify any points that are potentially confusing.

In some situations, speakers may provide "non-answers." If you listen halfheartedly, you may not even notice.

FIGURE 4.1

A job interview is a critical time for both the interviewer and interviewee to listen actively.

Detour to a Deadline

At a press conference, Tyrone Brooks, the press secretary for a large munitions company, is taking questions about the company's downsizing. Tara Blix, a reporter, shouts her question: "Mr. Brooks, is there any chance the company will lay off any additional employees within the next year?" "As I said earlier," Mr. Brooks replied, "we have been studying our operations very closely nationwide in an effort to be sure that we are doing all that we can to keep layoffs to a minimum. At this point, we expect the next quarter to turn sales around as some of our subsidiary divisions get up and running. That's the last question, folks. Thank you for your time."

Scribbling furiously, Tara ran to the phone to call in her story before her deadline. Tara's story began: "Franklin Munitions plans no more layoffs in the coming year, according to spokesperson Tyrone Brooks."

Later the same day, Tara's editor was furious to see a front-page story in a rival paper where the reporter had presented the story quite differently. The rival story began, "Are more layoffs in store at Franklin Munitions? At a press conference today, company spokesperson Tyrone Brooks skirted the question, leaving hundreds of employees and subcontractors hanging in the balance."

Why might the two stories have been different? Did Tyrone Brooks answer Tara's question? Whose information was correct, Tara's, or the other reporter's?

In this situation, the speaker may have been deliberately dodging a direct answer because the issue was sensitive. In other instances, speakers may not know answers and may try to hide their uncertainty. Whenever you recognize that the speaker does not know, be gracious. Pressing people for information they do not have can result in embarrassment for everyone. Nonetheless, as Tara's situation points out, it can be extremely important to listen attentively to whatever information the speaker does provide.

Sometimes speakers may not understand or may misinterpret the question and provide a response that is off target. When this happens, you may wish to follow up politely to refocus the question:

"Excuse me, Ms. Vaccaro. I did not mean government regulations. My question was aimed at industry practices regarding . . ."

USE YOUR JUDGMENT

As you "listen" to the following statements, you will find that you need clarification. Compose what you would say in each situation in light of the information provided in italics.

SPEAKER 1: Effective immediately, all expense account statements must be in by the 10th of each month.

You are not sure whether the speaker is saying that your expense account must be submitted to your manager by the 10th of the month or must be in the Accounting Department by the 10th.

SPEAKER 2: If you are a vested employee, the company savings plan matches your savings dollar for dollar for a maximum savings of $100.

You are interested in this savings plan. But you need some clarification. You have been with the company for 18 months. Does that make you a "vested employee"? Also, does the speaker mean $100 per month, week, or year?

LISTENING TO REQUESTS

In your career, you will likely listen and respond to many requests of varying natures. Some will be simple and will take only a brief response. Others will be tedious and time-consuming. In most cases, your first decision must be to decide whether you can or should perform whatever is being asked. Your second decision may be to decide whether you can do so in the time allotted.

- Dan Quinn calls Marvin Hershey in the Human Resources Department to ask for a copy of Donna Foster's performance appraisal from last year. Donna has applied for a job in Dan's department. Marvin goes ahead and releases the appraisal. When Marvin's supervisor finds out, he's angry: "Marvin, I know you meant well, but a performance appraisal contains personal information that Dan has no right to see. Dan should not have asked for that, and we certainly should not have sent it."

- When Margot Weinstein was invited to join her company's Forms Review Committee, she accepted. Unfortunately, Margot never asked how much time committee work would require. Margot's manager is quite irritated when Margot says she will be attending committee meetings every Friday from 9:00 until 2:00 p.m. Margot should not have agreed to this request without receiving her manager's permission first.

To be helpful and well liked, some employees try to fill every request, including unreasonable requests. But you must always question and evaluate the requests you receive. When you are listening to a request, you must decide whether the request is reasonable and, of course, whether you should comply. Each situation will have a unique set of circumstances and will test not only your listening skills but also your judgment and your decision-making abilities.

Unlike the examples concerning Dan and Margot, most requests are reasonable. However, evaluation and judgment are still required. Listen to be sure you understand the *what, where, when, why,* and *how* of the request. Ask follow-up questions to clarify complex issues. Make comments that summarize what you are to do. Do not rely on your memory; take notes, especially for numbers, dates, and so on. Often, repeating and summarizing requests helps avoid problems, as the following situation shows.

C A S E   S C E N A R I O

Missing Pieces

Joe Burgoyne, Arne Johannson's manager, asked Arne to send a letter to Teresa Lopez of Superior Lithography. Arne took notes as Joe described the request in detail. To make sure he had the information right, Arne restated what he'd heard: "Let me be sure I've got all the information. We want Teresa to bid on printing this flier. Print run: 150,000 pieces. Full color. Include shipping charges to our mailing house. No later than Monday, August 4, for a mailing on Thursday, August 7. Is that it? Have I left anything out?"

"Did you mention the size of the flier?" asked Joe. "Oh, thanks," said Arne, making another note. "Okay, I've included the size. That should do it."

Was Arne thorough in his note-taking? If so, why did he miss a piece of information? How did taking notes help Arne in this situation?

As you can see, **summarizing** is an active listening technique that can help to ensure that you omit nothing.

Sometimes requests have special hidden meanings, forcing you to—read or in this case listen—between the lines. Listen carefully for hidden meanings:

ROY: Do you have a few minutes for me later today, Teri? I'd like to talk with you about the requisitions we're getting from your department.

Roy has not used the word "problem," but the *implication* is that there is a problem with Teri's department's requisitions. If Roy had wanted merely to exchange simple information, he probably would not have asked to meet with Teri later; instead, he probably would have initiated a brief conversation on the spot. Thus, when Teri calls or visits Roy later, she should not be surprised by the topic. His request should serve as a tip-off to Teri; and it might be worthwhile for her to review the department's requisitions before heading to his office later in the day.

implication

something implied; the implied or suggested meaning; a statement exhibiting a relationship of implication

FIGURE 4.2 ▶

In listening, as in all business communication, always be prepared.

Apparently Cummings misunderstood that this was
to be a working retreat.

3   USE YOUR JUDGMENT

Read the situation that follows. Then write a short paragraph in which you explain why you think Sherry failed to respond correctly to Bethany's fairly simple request and what Sherry might have done differently to avoid her mistake:

Bethany Moss is a guest speaker at a computer services convention in Chicago. Somehow, Bethany has misplaced one of the transparencies she needs for her presentation tomorrow afternoon. She calls her office to ask her assistant, Sherry Yackle, to send a duplicate by overnight delivery to her hotel. "Thanks for handling this for me, Sherry," Bethany concludes. "Just send it to my hotel, please. I'll look for it tomorrow morning."

Proofreading a letter on her computer screen as she speaks, Sherry replies, "No problem, really. I'll take the envelope to the mailroom myself when I leave for lunch." Before she goes to lunch, Sherry prepares the transparency, but she addresses the envelope to the convention center instead of Bethany's hotel.

LISTENING TO DIRECTIONS

A major challenge when writing and speaking to direct is to make others understand and follow your directions. Thus, when others are directing you, help them out. Accept the responsibility of listening actively to what you must do, when you must do it, where, why, and how.

If you can predict that you will be given directions and know what they relate to, be prepared. Find out as much as you can about what you are to hear at the meeting or the presentation. Bring the catalog, report, manual, budget, or whatever other materials will be discussed. Having this prior knowledge will give you something to which you can relate your new knowledge. At the meeting or presentation, apply all the techniques you learned earlier: Talk silently to yourself, ask follow-up questions that clarify key points, and make comments that summarize and clarify key points. Ask questions and make comments along these lines:

- "You said this software can be networked, but does that apply both to IBM and to Apple networks?"

- "In other words, our 10 percent discount is on the wholesale, not the retail, price. Now I understand."

- "Must we submit both forms to Human Resources?"

- (to yourself) "Did I miss something here? She suddenly jumped from first-quarter expenses to third-quarter expenses! I'd better ask." (then aloud) "Excuse me, Ms. Borg. Are there any changes in second-quarter expenses? Or are only first- and third-quarter expenses affected here?"

If you are listening to a complex process, take notes that clearly define and differentiate each step. Review the steps to make sure you understand them and have not overlooked any. Politely ask the speaker to slow down or repeat a point, if necessary. In short, if the information is worth getting, make sure you do not leave without it.

Also, as you listen to directions, try to anticipate your future needs. Will you need any help or further directions later, after the meeting? Find out when and where you can get help if a problem should arise.

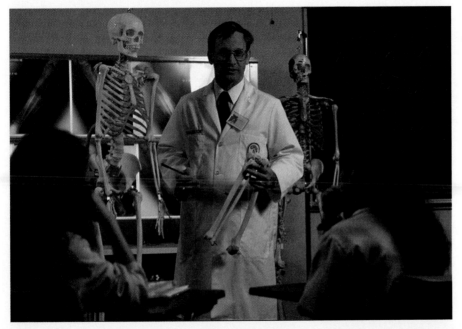

◀ **FIGURE 4.3**

When listening to directions, be sure you get all the information you need. Careful listening will help you avoid costly mistakes.

```
C  A  S  E        S  C  E  N  A  R  I  O
```

A Change of Plans

Just before leaving on a business trip, Edward Winthrop asked Jana Frost to arrange travel and hotel accommodations for a number of staff who would be attending a large conference out of town. When she met with Edward, Jana listened attentively and took careful notes. As their meeting ended, Jana thought to ask Ed, "Everything seems clear . . . but if something unexpected comes up, should I call you, or talk to someone else here at the office?"

Edward nodded. "Good thinking, Jana. If anything comes up, talk to Kurt. He's in charge of the booth *and* the budget on this, so he's got the last word."

In making the arrangements, Jana discovered a special, but non-refundable, air and hotel package that could save the company considerable money. Kurt was delighted. But two days later, after she'd made all the plane and room reservations, Jana received phone calls from two of the reps who were to attend the conference. JoBeth Follett needed to change her arrival date; Rich Woessner wanted to reroute his flight so he could make a sales call en route. Jana took the questions to Kurt, who okayed JoBeth's request and said he'd discuss Rich's situation directly with Rich.

How did Jana's foresight help the company? How did it help Jana's standing with Edward? What might have happened if Jana had not known whom to check with in this situation?

4   USE YOUR JUDGMENT

Recognizing that it is your responsibility to figure out what you need will improve your ability to respond efficiently and effectively to directions from others. After reading the following situation and dialogue, write a paragraph in which you explain how Mark's listening skills affected the situation and how Mark might have listened to follow directions more effectively.

Beverly West asks her assistant, Mark Angstrom, to arrange a meeting for her with Andrew Edward, the executive vice president, for next week. Mark calls Mr. Edward's office and reaches Pat, Mr. Edward's secretary. "Hello. This is Mark Angstrom, Beverly West's assistant. She'd like to schedule a meeting with Mr. Edward for next week." "Hi, Mark," Pat returned. "No problem. I've got his calendar in front of me. Just tell me briefly what the meeting is about and who'll be there so we can estimate how much time to allow and where to meet." "Hmm," said Mark, "I, uh, guess I'll have to get back to you about that, Pat."

LISTENING TO PERSUASIVE TALK

When a speaker is trying to **persuade** you to do something, that speaker has a purpose: to change your attitude or behavior.

Identifying the speaker's purpose will help you to listen critically. When you know what the speaker wants, you will be better able to analyze whether the speaker's information is self-serving or accurate.

Sometimes you can recognize **persuasive talk,** but the speaker's motives may not be obvious. In this type of situation, try to determine the speaker's purpose by asking yourself:

- What's in it for the speaker?

- Whom does the speaker represent?

- What does the speaker want me to do or believe?

- What are the pros and cons on this issue?

A corporate executive who is addressing employees about poor sales and the need to control expenses may have no hidden message. On the other hand, if he is addressing employees with whom he does not ordinarily discuss sales and expenses, then perhaps he does have a secondary purpose. He might, for example, be trying to convince all employees—not just management—of the need for belt-tightening. Or he may be laying the groundwork for a later announcement that salary increases will be lower than anticipated this year. If you listen carefully and evaluate what you hear within the context of the entire situation, you will be an effective judge of persuasive talk.

It is also useful to be aware of your own needs and motivations when listening to persuasive talk. Persuasive speakers will try to determine what drives you and direct their arguments with your "weaknesses" in mind. For example, if you are a cost-conscious manager, an employee proposing a new incentive program may emphasize its cost-saving features and downplay other characteristics. However, without evaluating these other characteristics, you might agree to a program that is inappropriate because all you've thought about is how it will save your department money. *Astute* listeners recognize when their own needs and motivations are getting in the way of the whole picture; they try to listen "above" their preferences so that they make rational, rather than emotional, decisions.

astute

having or showing shrewdness; clever, shrewd, wily; intelligent

The Bottom Line

Reuben Patrikas purchased a photocopier from Deluxe Products for his employer's graphic design business. Reuben traded the old copier in because it kept breaking down; the repairs were expensive and inconvenient. With this in mind, Ron Ahola, the Deluxe sales representative, says to Reuben, "This service and maintenance contract covers you for a full year. If *anything* goes wrong with the copier, just pick up the phone and we'll be out in no time at all. Plus the maintenance schedule keeps the machine in optimum shape."

Reuben thought about it only briefly. He knew how important it was to have a reliable copier. "That sounds great, Ron," he said. "Where do I sign?"

A few days later, the bill for the copier and service contract arrived. Reuben's boss, the owner of the company, called him in to discuss it. "Ron," he began, "I'm a little surprised by the bottom line on this copier deal. Why did you agree to a service and maintenance contract? Isn't there already a one-year factory warranty? Is there some reason this new state-of-the-art machine shouldn't be reliable?"

Why do you think Reuben was so quick to sign the agreement? What are some things he should have thought about? What questions should he have asked? How did not thinking critically about the sales rep's pitch affect Ron and his company?

Evaluating as you listen means weighing the *validity* of the information you hear. A touch of skepticism is a good thing. For example, in all situations, persuasive or not, do not automatically accept "facts" as accurate. Use silent self-talk to question incoming information. If you doubt the accuracy of what you hear, you may politely ask the speaker to support questionable statements. For example:

validity

logical correctness, justifiability; soundness

SPEAKER: According to experts, the best tools for marketing consumer goods are free samples.

YOU: (During the question-and-answer session) Ms. Northrup, I'm interested in knowing more about the use of free samples. Can you tell me, who are the experts you referred to?

Don't make the mistake of being a *passive* listener, especially when you're the target for a persuasive argument. Recognize that effective persuasive speakers carefully prepare and adjust their arguments to obtain the results they want. As a listener, you should just as carefully prepare your mind to analyze incoming arguments in light of the speaker's purpose and your own needs and motivations so that you come away from the interaction with results you can live with as well.

passive

acted upon by an external agency; receptive to outside influences; not active

USE YOUR JUDGMENT 5

Listen to a television or a radio talk show on the subject of your choice. Then use the positive-negative-questionable strategy described in Chapter 3 (page 74) to categorize and clarify the arguments the speakers used. As you listen, consider the items you will list in each category. When the show is over, revise and finish your lists, and in three or four sentences, describe how this strategy helped you listen and how it helped you draw conclusions about what you heard.

IN BRIEF

❶ Even when you are listening, you are participating in the communication process. In each circumstance you have a specific purpose, and identifying that purpose helps you focus on what you should be listening for.

❷ When listening for simple information, try to anticipate what you need and prepare a checklist or note sheet to ensure that you get it.

❸ When listening to responses, you are already motivated to listen; however, you can make sure you understand by writing notes and asking questions to clarify information.

❹ As you listen to requests, you must decide if you are willing and able to perform the task within the time allowed. An active listener will also evaluate the request for its reasonableness and to determine possible hidden meanings.

❺ You can prepare to listen to directions by finding out as much as you can about what you are going to hear. Active listeners also try to anticipate any problems they might encounter when they have the chance to get answers or further directions from the speaker.

❻ When listening to persuasive talk, you must continuously evaluate the speaker's motives and message. Also be aware of your own needs and motivations, as they can influence you to "hear what you want to hear."

WORDS OF NOTE

Define each of these terms introduced in Chapter 4.

persuade
persuasive talk
summarize

CHECK YOUR RECALL

1 What can you do to prepare to get the information you need when listening for specific information?

2 How can you tell when a speaker's message is not clear? What can you do during the listening situation to get the information you need?

3 What might you do differently when listening for directions than when listening to a request?

4 What are some examples of persuasive talk?

5 When listening to persuasive talk, what four questions should you ask yourself to determine the speaker's purpose?

6 Why is it important to be aware of your own purpose, or needs, when listening to a persuasive speaker?

7 What is passive listening? How is it different from listening actively?

SHARE YOUR PERSPECTIVE

1 Read the following situation. Then write a paragraph in which you (a) identify Craig's purpose for listening, (b) explain how Craig's listening skills led to his problem, and (c) discuss what Craig could have done to avoid the problem.

> Craig Burbach has an emergency. He has to send a check to a bank, and the check has to arrive at the bank tomorrow. He rushes the approval through the Accounting Department and receives the check. Now he has to find out about overnight delivery services. He decides to call the Post Office to ask about overnight mail.

CRAIG: So, you said I can drop the envelope in any drop-off box? And I have until 4:00 p.m.?

CLERK: Yes, 4:00 p.m. at any drop-off box.

CRAIG: And it's guaranteed delivery the next day, right?

CLERK: Yes, that's true for most ZIP Codes. I can check that for you. What....

CRAIG: Thanks, but I already know the ZIP Code.

Craig quickly hangs up the phone, prepares the envelope and the label, and personally carries the package to a nearby Express Mail drop-off box. The next day, Craig is surprised and angry when the bank calls to say that his check has not arrived.

2 Choose a simple everyday task such as tying shoes, putting on a coat, or sharpening a pencil. Write clear, thorough step-by-step instructions for accomplishing this task. Next, choose a classmate to follow your instructions. Read the instructions step by step as you wrote them and have your listener do exactly as instructed. You may repeat but may not adapt or modify your instructions or help the listener in any way. Your listener must follow your oral instructions exactly as they are given and may not ask questions. Discuss the difficulties you had and how, in a normal situation, you and your listener might have avoided the problems.

paraphrase

to restate a spoken or written idea, giving it meaning in another form or other words

3 Choose a social or political issue that is highly controversial. Find a classmate who disagrees with you on the issue. Ask your classmate to explain his or her position to you. **Paraphrase** each point your classmate makes, using neutral language. Then trade places. When you and your classmate have both paraphrased each other's arguments objectively, discuss any difficulties you had doing so.

FOCUS ON THE FINE POINTS
Read the following background information. Then follow the
instructions to locate and correct grammar errors.

Background

Joel Mahoney is the office manager and secretary for CedarRest, an arts
retreat center in Seattle, Washington. Joel acts as the recorder for meetings
of the workshop committee, which meets once a month to discuss and select
summer workshops for upcoming years. Joel's duties include preparing the
meeting agenda, writing up the minutes, and creating catalog copy that
describes the workshops.

Your Instructions

Each of the following documents contains up to 15 errors. Indicate and correct errors by noting them a photocopy of the page or on a separate sheet of
paper. In each case, you may assume the document is formatted correctly.

Note: If you have difficulty locating errors, turn to page 455 in the Appendix.
There you will find additional information about the errors in Document 1.

DOCUMENT 1: Meeting Agenda

MEETING OF THE CEDARREST WORKSHOP PLANNING COMMITTEE

July 10, 19XX

AGENDA

1. Call to order: 1:00 p.m.

2. Approval of minutes from June 12 meeting:

    a. Note that since Joel had been ill on the meeting day, the June minutes were a group effort.

    b. Before we meet, please read the rough notes from that meeting (which is presently circulating). We will hopefully be able to approve the notes without extensive discussion.

3. Old business:

    a. Report on search for new workshop possibilities:
    •Yvonne will be recommending which of the two native dance people look best.
    •Gregor will report on his interviews with four journal workshoppers.
    •Paul will present a wide array of potentially good music workshops.

    b. Report on progress with kitchen coordination. The issues are:
    •Doing the daily cooking for guests.
    •Accommodating the herbal remedies group.
    •How to work side by side with the canning/preserving group.

4. New business:

    a. Unanticipated, unexpected registration overload for outdoor meditation and primitive camping:
    •What to do about it this year?
    •How can we handle it in future years?

    b. Decisions on music, fine art, and dance workshops. Come prepared to:
    •Evaluate both this fiscal year and next—the farther we can look ahead (particularly for musical workshops), the better off we will be.
    •Consider simultaneous presenters and topics.
    •We will consider the best site for each workshop.
    •Vote on our final choices in all three categories.

    c. Other.

5. The meeting will adjourn at 4:00 p.m.

DOCUMENT 2: Minutes

MEETING OF THE CEDARREST WORKSHOP PLANNING COMMITTEE

July 10, 19XX

MINUTES

APPROVAL OF MINUTES	Notes from the June 12 meeting was approved in lieu of formally having minutes. Gregor Menz noted that many workshop titles and names of presenters are misspelled. All agreed to attach to the July minutes a list of workshops and presenters (with accurate spellings).
KITCHEN COORDINATION	Yvonne Selaca next reported that she and Mary McCormick have agreed upon the better dates for both kitchen-based workshops. Mary is preparing a list of instructional procedures for kitchen workers and workshoppers; Yvonne will present the list at the August meeting.
RECOMMENDED WORKSHOPS	The committee voted to recommend 18 workshops (5 music, 9 fine art, and 4 dance) to the executive committee. A list of the workshop titles, descriptions, and presenters are attached.
NEW BUSINESS	Bill DeNorio and Kate Bathke, the husband and wife scheduled to present four marriage encounters, has requested that their contract should be canceled. Gregor and Yvonne will meet next week with the Executive Committee to decide how best to handle this.
	The executive committee has again reconsidered our April request for additional funds for the ecology workshops and will be agreeing to increase our budget. Krista Ozolins from Accounting will present the new budget at the August meeting.
	Paul Volber announced that Rauel Pozel died July 9. Rauel led yoga workshops for CedarRest for many years and has to take early retirement precipitously three years ago due to illness. CedarRest is sending flowers and will be collecting funds for a memorial. We agreed to send a special card from the committee. Joel will purchase and will then circulate the card.
ADJOURNMENT	4:15 p.m.
NEXT MEETING	Tuesday, August 4, at 1:00 p.m.

DOCUMENT 3: Page of Workshop Descriptions

June 2-8
George C. Quist, countertenor
Alan Benowicz, trumpeter
Merging Gregorian Chant and Jazz
Discover the joy of blending the time-honored harmonies of chamber music with the soulful song of the jazz saxophone, clarinet, trumpet, and piano. Join a group of twenty singers and players who will listen together to recordings in this new genre, singing and playing existing works, improvising, and be composing music as well. Before the workshop participants are asked to become familiar with "Gregory Revisited" (the most recent musical offering from the vocalist group Chant and trumpeter Alan Benowicz) and to read "New Souls for Old" by Marietta Moon-Pierce in the Fall 19XX edition of *Chamber Singer's Quarterly*. Singers of all abilities and styles are urged to enroll, as is jazz musicians who plays saxophone, clarinet, trumpet, or piano.
7 days   **Tuition: $655**

June 4-9
Marjorie Wolfman, dancer
Paulette Maurer, psychologist
Dancing the Dream
First, we will share our most cherished and meaningful dreams—those that both disturb and pleases us. Secondly, we will bear witness to the dream dances of Marjorie Wolfman, which embody ritual, drumming, storytelling, and music. Thirdly, we will be creating our own visions for dances that give expression to our deepest and most rich personal experience—our dreams. Lastly, we will all leave the workshop feeling refreshed in our sense of self and of community.
6 days   **Tuition: $610**

June 7-8
Steven Julliard
Art on the Internet
Be part of CedarRest's very first on-line art project—even if you don't own a computer! If you have a creative flair, if you love the idea of a group "art-venture," and if spending an intensive weekend with people from around the country are exciting to you, read on! Do you have access to a computer? If so, you'll be able to just log on. If not, you can participate by using one of the computer centers we've lined up in twelve West Coast cities. Sound interested? Use the toll-free number or the e-mail address on the back cover of this catalog to request detailed information.
2 days   **Tuition: $325**

UNIT II

COMMUNICATE FOR RESULTS

❶ Create a grid or recording sheet to record how often a person listens during a given period of time.

	Monday	Tuesday	Wedne
9:00 - 9:15	L	R	
9:15 - 9:30	L / W	R	
9:30 - 9:45	L	R	
9:45 - 10:00	S	N	
10:00 - 10:15	N	L	
10:15 - 10:30	R	L	
10:30 - 10:45	R	W	
10:45 - 11:00	S	N	

- Divide each day into 15-minute segments.
- Use L, S, W, R, and N to stand for listening, speaking, writing, reading, and not communicating verbally.
- After each 15-minute time period, insert the letter that stands for the communication activity that dominated that period.

    a. Spend one or two typical days recording your communication activity to see more precisely how much time you spend listening.

    b. Contact someone who works in a job you are interested in (or a similar job). Ask if the person is willing to do this same activity for a day or two while at work; supply a clean copy of your recording sheet. Compare the worker's time spent listening (and other communication activities) with your time spent listening as a student.

❷ Brainstorm with your classmates new or controversial ideas that have arisen locally or nationally. Select one idea and analyze that idea in writing, using the positive-negative-questionable strategy.

③ Listen to and tape a local or national radio or television talk show. Then listen to the tape and listen well for all five purposes (you should listen more than once). Then explain in writing how your listening behavior changed as your listening purpose changed.

Listening purposes:

a. Listening for simple information
b. Listening to responses
c. Listening to requests
d. Listening for directions
e. Listening to persuasive talk

Behaviors:

f. Estimating the speakers' purpose(s)
g. Making ongoing evaluation of the messages (i.e., silent self-talk relating old to new information)
h. Focusing on specific content based on your purpose
i. Note-taking, questioning, and commenting (assuming you are part of the audience)
k. Avoiding or giving in to distractions

LISTENING CHECKLIST

Evaluate your habits

● Whenever possible, you prepare for listening situations.

Always									Never
10	9	8	7	6	5	4	3	2	1

● For scheduled meetings or presentations, you generally arrive early.

Always									Never
10	9	8	7	6	5	4	3	2	1

● You usually sit in the front of the room

Always									Never
10	9	8	7	6	5	4	3	2	1

● You tune out distractions when you are listening.

Always									Never
10	9	8	7	6	5	4	3	2	1

● You take notes to make listening more effective.

Always									Never
10	9	8	7	6	5	4	3	2	1

● As you listen, you are aware of your purpose for listening and use that purpose to determine how to take notes, make comments, and ask questions.

Always									Never
10	9	8	7	6	5	4	3	2	1

● As you listen, you continuously evaluate spoken messages as you hear them by using prior knowledge of the speaker and the topic to understand what you hear and judge its accuracy.

Always									Never
10	9	8	7	6	5	4	3	2	1

● You listen "skeptically" to hear the speaker's underlying motive.

Always									Never
10	9	8	7	6	5	4	3	2	1

UNIT III

To speak effectively, you need to know your own purpose and the purpose of your listening audience. You also need to consider what information will accomplish these purposes. You must prioritize the information, and determine what approach will deliver your message most favorably. Each of these elements is essential when planning to speak under formal or informal circumstances in the workplace.

In Chapter 5 you'll learn how to prepare for formal speaking situations. You'll also learn ways in which you can polish your presentation skills and speaking ability. Next, in Chapter 6, you'll find out how to plan for informal speaking situations with specific purposes.

▼ **When you finish Unit III, you will be able to**

- Understand the importance of analyzing your purpose, audience, approach, and other communication factors to plan and prepare formal oral communication

- Control your use of visual aids and handouts, voice, body language, and other factors to effectively complement your message

- Evaluate and improve your presentation skills

- Plan and prepare informal oral communication based on your purpose, audience, and other factors

SPEAKING

FOR

RESULTS

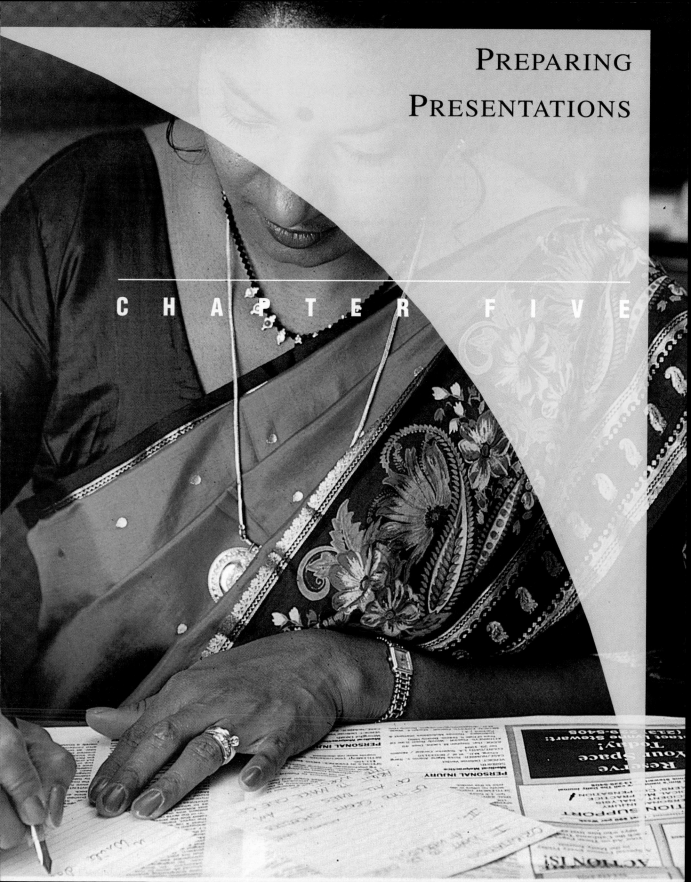

PREPARING
PRESENTATIONS

CHAPTER FIVE

How much planning goes into a presentation before listeners actually hear it?

What elements can add to the interest level and effectiveness of a presentation?

How can you polish your presentation skills to improve your speaking success?

Oral communication is an essential element of business. Although you may not have an opportunity to speak formally early in your career, you are likely to do so often when you advance to a supervisory level, regardless of your other duties. Because your time will be limited and because you will often have only one chance to present your points well, planning will be *imperative.*

Your first talk may be a fifteen-minute product demonstration to a few potential customers, a one-hour speech to a large convention, a ten-minute sales report to the Executive Committee, or a three-hour workshop on management techniques. While they can vary in length, topic, and audience, most presentations and speeches are:

imperative

necessary; not to be avoided; of utmost importance

- Tightly scheduled to start and end at specified times

- Formal in tone

- Given to a group

Sometimes one speaker does all the talking. Sometimes two or more people share the responsibility, as in a panel discussion. Often the presentation includes a question-and-answer session, allowing the audience to participate more fully. The audience may be coworkers, customers, professionals from other companies, or some other group with a shared interest in the topic. Clearly, presentations vary as much as business situations.

Perhaps you're thinking, "I won't need to give presentations. I'm not going into sales or public relations." You may be right. But presentations have become a routine part of the information age. Accountants, architects, designers, computer operators, nurses, paralegals, administrative assistants all are likely to give presentations or make speeches as part of their work.

- Paralegal Kara Flenoy never thought she'd give presentations. One day she was invited to speak at a high school's Career Day. She had 30 minutes to tell an audience of students and teachers about her company, her training, and a "typical" day in her job. Kara prepared carefully and thoroughly for her presentation and was very well received. Now she participates in all Career Days, and company executives value her contributions.

◀ FIGURE 5.1

Presentations have become a routine part of the information age.

- Presentations were the furthest thing from Brad Rodriguez's mind when he was learning to be a computer operator. One day Brad's manager asked him to speak at the annual computer convention in San Francisco. At first, Brad's main interest was the trip to San Francisco. Then Brad discovered additional benefits, such as meeting many interesting people in his industry. And he found that, by speaking at the conference, he was able to meet and talk with a variety of people in his field. Now he enjoys giving presentations.

- Danielle Kiluti works as a nurse in the Medical Department of a large firm. There she became involved in the company's Drug-Free Workplace Program. When asked to speak to employees about the program, she accepted because she was committed to the program. That was three years and twelve presentations ago. Now Danielle presents all over the country.

The ability to make effective, informative presentations is an acquired skill. It is definitely an asset and certainly required of leaders in any field. If you possess this skill, you improve your chances of being promoted. And, at a minimum, you open yourself up to exciting, challenging opportunities.

PLANNING ACTIVITIES

As a rule, the longer and more formal the presentation, the more detailed your planning will be. But whether your talk is short or long, formal or informal, your first task is to figure out what you want to say and how you will say it. This aspect of planning a presentation is similar to the writing process. As with the writing process (discussed in Unit Four), when preparing a presentation, you need to identify:

1. **Your purpose.** Ask yourself why you are speaking and what you want to accomplish with your talk. Identify both your general and your specific purposes.

2. **Your audience.** Think about who will be listening to your talk. Will the group be friendly or skeptical? Do you know them? Will they know much about your topic? Let your answers guide the approach you take, the information you cover, and your overall delivery.

3. **The ideas you want to communicate.** As with writing, you need to identify what ideas support your purpose. What does the audience need to know? Do you need to do some research to strengthen your presentation?

4. **The order in which you will present each idea.** Decide whether the direct or indirect approach suits your topic. Then choose the best way to present the information, piece by piece. Do you need to define terms before you discuss an idea? Can you introduce a policy first and then explain why it is being implemented?

The Outline

To plan your presentation, you will *read, research, and think* along the same lines you would follow in a writing process. (Chapter 9 in Unit Five describes the RRTWRP process: Read, Research, Think, Write, Revise, Proofread.) Your **outline,** in which you have identified the ideas you want to communicate and the order in which you will present them, is the "backbone" of your presentation. It may be all you need to write or it may be the starting point for a full draft of your talk.

Depending on the topic and your comfort level with public speaking, you may decide to speak from your outline. If this is the case, you need only include enough information on your outline to help you remember each point; the exact phrasing you keep in your head. If you are a beginning speaker, or if the topic is sufficiently complex, it is better to draft your presentation word for word. Once you have written and practiced the entire presentation, you may find that you can revert to speaking from your outline. In either case, the less you can rely on your notes during your talk, the more natural and relaxed your presentation will be to your audience.

Words Aloud versus Words on Paper

Before you write your presentation, think about how spoken language differs from written language. We tend to be less formal in our speech than in our writing. Sentence constructions are less complex. In fact, over the past several decades, the printed word—in everything from newspapers to textbooks—has become more and more like speech; that is, more plain and natural. Let this trend guide your presentation writing. Keep your sentences short and use words and phrases that will increase comprehension rather than interfere with it.

If you write out your presentation, you may catch some wordiness as you revise your copy. Proofreading your talk is unnecessary unless you plan to publish your presentation or make it available to the audience. The best way to evaluate what you have written is to say it aloud. When you practice your presentation, and you'll learn about how to do that later in this chapter, you'll notice the words and phrases that sound awkward. Then you can change them to improve the flow of your talk.

C A S E   S C E N A R I O

Expert Words

Rex Haley was a scientist in the environmental lab of a chemical processing plant, ChemRite. He was asked by the town council to explain the company's pollution reduction activities and how these efforts conform to local, state, and national regulations. The council called on Ray because he was known as an authority on the subject of pollution control and reduction.

Rex was very comfortable with this topic, so he readily outlined the information he would cover in his talk. Because he was rarely called on to speak in public, he decided to write his presentation in full. Here's an excerpt:

```
With regard to national regulations, I
will, if you please, expound upon the
exemplary record of ChemRite. No other
company of similar size or stature has
maintained the stringent effluent
regulatory standards that are the
hallmark of ChemRite's environmental
policy. The polemic of certain
strident environmental groups aside,
we at ChemRite do care deeply about
preserving our earth and our future on
this planet.
```

How do you think Rex's speech was received by the town council? Why do you think Rex chose to speak in this style? What constructive criticism would you give him? How would you rewrite the excerpt to better get the point across?

1 USE YOUR JUDGMENT

Write an outline for a short talk on why you are for or against one of these topics: welfare reform, handgun control, women in combat. Tape-record yourself speaking from your outline. If you have difficulty doing this, write down what you want to say. Analyze which method worked for you. Hand in your outline, taped or written presentation, and analysis to your instructor.

2 USE YOUR JUDGMENT

Take a newspaper or magazine article, or a paper you have written for another class, and explain how you would "translate" it for an oral presentation, using words and phrases that are more natural for speech. Be sure to decide first who your audience will be. Be specific as you describe how your wording or approach might change from the printed original.

PREPARING CONTENT

Two common temptations can be present when making speeches or oral reports. If you have a flair for drama, you might err in one of these areas. You might exaggerate, which can taint your credibility. Or, you might rely too much on humor, or use the wrong kind of humor, either of which can drown out your message. Use data and humor in presentations with respect to the following guidelines.

Facts

Facts and figures can impress an audience. But for the very reason that they can influence opinion, they must be used responsibly. Consider this example:

> "Used-home sales rose almost 6 percent in March—that's up 18 percent over last year's sales during the same period."

What if the percentage of used-home sales in March included for-sale-by-owner homes, when previous calculations did not? Would the statistics cited reflect an actual difference in overall sales, or just more accurate reporting? It is helpful to know how data was gathered and analyzed before using it to make a point. Cite only data that comes from reliable sources, and never inflate or alter figures to support your position.

If you are using statistics in your talk, there are ways you can increase your listeners' attention to and comprehension of them. Try to relate your "facts" to a common experience or understanding. Consider how each of the following analogies help you understand the speaker's point:

- "You can eat a bacon-and-egg breakfast, a burger and fries for lunch, and a steak with all the trimmings for dinner and still not consume as much fat as there is in a medium-sized buttered popcorn from your local movie theater!"

- "A pack-a-day smoker spends at least $14 per week on cigarettes. Over a year, that's enough pocket change to purchase a year's membership at the local health club."

Humor

Depending on your purpose for speaking, there may be occasions when it is appropriate to inject humor in your presentation. A short, funny story is often a good way to open a talk or provide "comic relief" during a presentation. If a secondary purpose is to entertain, or when the topic would not be diminished by a touch of humor, consider how you might weave a joke or an anecdote (related to your topic) into your speech. You may find good jokes or stories in books available at your local library or bookstore.

When and if you do decide that humor will help you achieve your purpose, be careful about what type of humor you use. Humor is extremely **subjective;** what's funny to one person may not be equally funny to another. In all cases, use no joke or anecdote that could offend someone—not just someone in the audience, but *anyone*. A joke in poor taste or at the expense of someone else is in bad form and will ruin your rapport with the audience. And, of course, make sure the joke is *funny* which often has as much to do with delivery and timing as it does with content.

── C A S E   S C E N A R I O ──

Lunch, Anyone?

Clarice Peterschick worked in human resources at a progressive manufacturing company. Her company was implementing an employee suggestion system and Clarice decided to make a presentation to inform employees about the program and encourage them to participate. She knew that in her audience of 500 there were workers who would be *skeptical.* She really wanted to reach the workers who were not yet convinced the company was willing to help them make their jobs easier and more pleasant.

An important idea that Clarice wanted to get across was about employee ownership. She believed the suggestion system was a powerful way for

skeptical

doubtful, mistrusting

employees to "own" the conditions under which they worked. Somehow, she wanted to stress the idea that "if you don't like it, don't grumble change it." However, she wanted to say it in a way that wouldn't leave any listeners feeling defensive. She settled on using a humorous anecdote to amuse and inform her audience at the same time. She included the story in her talk right after her introductory remarks:

> A friend of mine told me a story about one of his coworkers. It seems that every day this fellow would bring a sack lunch, and every day he would complain to my friend about what was in the sack. "Peanut butter again," he would groan, or "A lousy apple. I wanted grapes." My friend usually played along, but one day it got to him. He turned to the guy and said, "If you never like your lunches, why don't you make them yourself?" "Gosh," the fellow replied, "I already do."

Clarice's audience howled with laughter. She had won them over and kept their attention and interest for the rest of her talk.

What made Clarice's anecdote successful? Did you find it funny? Do you think it could offend anyone? Why do you think it was more effective than it would have been to lecture about not grumbling and doing something? What do you think Clarice might say after the anecdote to tie it into her overall message?

3   USE YOUR JUDGMENT

analogy

a resemblance in some particulars between things otherwise unlike; a comparison or parallel made about two unlike things based upon a particular aspect they have in common

Do one of the following:

a. Use a fact or statistic to create an ***analogy*** that would help a listening audience understand an idea.

b. Identify a cartoon, joke, or anecdote that could be applied to a business situation.

In either case, explain the idea or situation that applies.

Humor and International Communications

Humor is both personal and cultural. In international business, it is treacherous territory indeed. Irony, sarcasm, and innuendo risky in domestic business relations are outright dangerous in the international arena.

Consider, for example, how the foreign recipient might understand this:

I missed my latest deadline, and it's all your fault! Instead of working on the project last weekend, I completely lost track of time reading the excellent report that you sent.

A variation of humor that relies on idiom or local color is also to be avoided. Again, consider the foreign perspective on:

As nervous as a long-tailed cat in a room full of rocking chairs

A memorable way to make your point? Perhaps, unless your contact has never seen a rocking chair!

Word pictures we Americans paint are often seen by others as a jumble of foreign objects:

Flat as a pancake	Safe as Fort Knox
Old as Methuselah	Flying by the seat of your pants
Keep a low profile	Run it up the flagpole
Dog and pony show	100K (for 100,000)
It will never fly	Don't make waves

Remember, too, that foreign contacts use the telephone. Make it a practice not to tell jokes, play weird music, or be flip in your recorded message.

And a final word about humor: Ethnic jokes are never acceptable.

Adapted from Mary A. De Vries, *Internationally Yours* (Boston: Houghton Mifflin, 1994); The Parker Pen Company, *Do's and Taboos Around The World* (Elmsford, NY: Benjamin, 1985); and Letitia Baldrige, *Letitia Baldrige's New Complete Guide To Executive Manners* (New York: Macmillan, 1993).

ENHANCING YOUR SPEECH

Up to this point we've focused on how you can use spoken words to get ideas across in a formal presentation. There are other "tools of the trade" that you should not overlook when assembling your talk. **Visual aids, handouts,** and **demonstrations** can help you make your point and can add variety and interest to your presentation. Their use can have a big impact on how well a message is received.

How Visual Aids Help Your Audience

- They help listeners understand concepts and related items by presenting information graphically.

- They help listeners remember information by providing visual images.

- They allow listeners to check their understanding by relating what they hear to what they see or do.

- They provide a diversion from listening to a single voice for a long period of time.

How Visual Aids Help You When You Speak

- They allow you to further listeners' understanding without the burden of relying solely on words to explain.

- They provide an organizing structure as you use visuals, handouts, and demonstrations to remember the order of delivery and important information that must be discussed.

- They provide a means of emphasizing and dramatizing important information.

- They allow you to affect listeners even after they have left the presentation.

- They help you inject interest and motivation into your presentation.

Even in short presentations, visual aids, handouts, and demonstrations can be important and useful tools. It may take some effort to develop a transparency or table to reinforce or clarify a key point or to coordinate a demonstration of a complex procedure, but it is likely to pay off with success in getting your message across. You will want to consider the wide choice of materials available and guidelines for their use before selecting the items or activities that will complement your presentation.

Visual Aids

Think of all the visuals you have seen in books and magazines—graphs and charts of all kinds, photographs and line drawings, cartoons and caricatures, words and sentences in enlarged type, flow charts and blueprints, illustrations and sketches. What do they do? What are they for?

Visuals can simplify concepts, clarify relationships, illustrate steps, emphasize principles, dramatize differences, highlight features, accentuate details, break the monotony, add variety and interest, or create a mood. Equally important, visuals can help your audience remember what they hear. Research confirms that people quickly forget most of what they hear. After three days, most listeners remember about 10 percent of what they hear *but as much as 65 percent of what they hear and see*. By including visuals in your presentation, you can increase the likelihood that listeners will retain key information.

You have a wide variety of visual equipment to choose from, including (but not limited to):

- **LCD units** to project computer screens to a large audience

- Slide projectors to show 35-millimeter slides

- Overhead projectors to show **transparencies**

- VCRs to show videocassettes

- Chalkboards, whiteboards, or flipcharts to outline ideas, write notes, highlight thoughts, show the flow of processes, or list questions or concerns

- 16-millimeter projectors to show films

Common Visual Aids

Some of the most common visual aids include horizontal bar graphs, vertical bar graphs, pie charts, photographs, cartoons, diagrams, flow charts, and word charts.

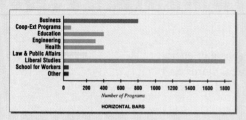

Horizontal bar graph

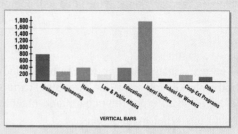

Vertical bar graph

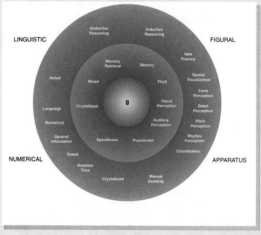

Diagram

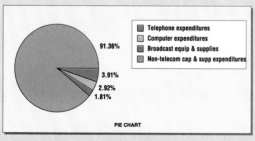

Pie chart

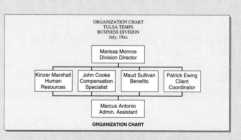

Organizational chart

Obviously, the best visual aid for a presentation varies with each presentation and is, in any case, a matter of opinion. Choosing between a diagram and a pie chart, for example, will depend on the information you want to convey. A diagram or a flow chart is excellent for illustrating a technical process. A pie chart immediately conveys the relative difference in values for each sector within the pie. A cartoon provides a break in the monotony and summarizes a main point.

Here are some tips for using visual aids during a presentation:

1. **Use only visual aids that help you pass on or emphasize the information you are presenting.** Visuals that add unnecessary complexity, that overemphasize unimportant points, or that do not relate will only confuse listeners.

2. **Explain to listeners the purpose of each visual aid.** For example, say "The graph you see here shows that . . ." or "As you can see from this graph. . . ." Don't leave listeners wondering what they are looking at or why.

3. **Use visual aids that everyone can see clearly.** The bigger the audience, the bigger the visual aid must be to project to people in the back of the room.

4. **Use visual aids that enhance your professional image.** This means *planning and preparing* visual aids so they appear professionally done.

5. **Practice your use of visual aids so that you incorporate them smoothly as you go along.** If you are not familiar with the equipment, find someone who can help you before you start your talk.

6. **Allow time to check all equipment before your presentation to ensure that it works properly.** Even if the equipment works, you may have to make adjustments, such as moving an overhead projector further from the screen to increase the size of the image or moving the podium so it does not block the screen. If the equipment does not work properly, you will have to arrange to replace it or reorganize your presentation without the benefit of the visual aids. So be sure to give yourself enough time to troubleshoot *before* the audience arrives.

Handouts

Handouts are materials that the speaker distributes to the audience. The nature of the materials will vary depending on the topic, the technical level of the information, the audience, and the speaker's purpose. Handouts may be professionally developed brochures, pamphlets, or manuals provided by your company. They may be copies of visuals you show during your presentation or notes highlighting your key points. They may be copies of related articles. Or they may simply be an outline of your presentation. Generally, handouts help your listeners understand the presentation, provide additional information, or both. They are a means of affecting listeners long after your presentation is over.

Tips for Using Handouts

- **Present any important information orally.** Do not rely on people to read your handouts to get key information.

- **Keep handouts as short as possible.** Most people will not read a large amount of material.

- **Plan when and how you will use them.** Planning how you will use your handouts within your presentation will help you know when your audience must have them. If listeners need the handout during the presentation, you may pass it out before you begin. If, however, you fear the handout will distract listeners from your presentation, you may pass it out only when listeners need it. In this case, have a plan for distributing materials quickly and unobtrusively, and do not continue your presentation or your discussion of the handout until everyone has a copy and is ready to begin. If listeners do not need the handout during the presentation, you may wait until you finish.

- **Make sure you have a copy for everyone.** If for some reason you end up not having enough for every person in attendance, offer to mail the handout at your cost.

- **Use handouts that enhance your professional image.** This means planning and preparing handouts so they appear professionally done.

Demonstrations

Is there a way to *show* your audience exactly what you are talking about? If so, work it into your presentation. For example, if you are explaining how to operate a piece of equipment, demonstrate its operation for your audience if you can. If the equipment cannot be moved to where you are speaking, consider videotaping someone operating the equipment and show that tape during your presentation. In doing so, you give the audience the benefit of hearing about a procedure and then seeing that procedure "live."

Consider also that your demonstrations can involve the audience. For example, why not try role-playing a customer service approach? Audience participation makes an impact on listeners and often adds to the interest level of your talk.

Discuss the kinds of visual aids and handouts the speakers in the following situations might plan to use to help their audiences.

a. Poa Xiong, a county department of transportation official, must speak to the state transportation board for approximately 30 minutes. His purpose is to pass on information about the number of people in his county who take driver's tests (both first tests and retakes) and who renew licenses each month. He must compare this information to similar information for the past ten years and project the information for the next five years. Poa knows the state board wants this information because it is considering widening several of the county's highways.

b. Lorraine Guiterrez, sales manager for the local branch of a large warehouse grocery outlet, has noticed a huge increase in customers over the past several months. She has also noticed that the store's layout is causing bottlenecks in a few key places because of the increased traffic. Lorraine believes the solution is to change the store's layout, but to do this, she must have the approval of the chain's vice president. She has scheduled a one-hour meeting to persuade the vice president to approve this change.

c. Warren Roll, information systems specialist for a small company, must train the company's other 20 employees to use the newly installed local area network. He can get all 20 people together for the first two hours (without computers) to introduce the network's capabilities and basic operations; after that, he must work with each person as needed at individual work stations.

◀ FIGURE 5.2

Audience participation makes an impact on listeners and often adds to the interest level of your talk.

PRACTICING YOUR PRESENTATION SKILLS

Presentation skills refer to your speaking ability, your body control when speaking, your comfort level with your material, and your ability to plan for and handle problems that may arise during a talk.

You can work on your presentation skills before you even have a speaking assignment. By analyzing and adjusting how you use your voice, words, and body language as you speak, you can improve the delivery of your message. The benefits of sharpening your skills extend beyond formal speaking situations; you will become more effective in the daily interactions that require you to speak.

Once you do have an assignment and know what you are going to say, practice is essential. When you are relaxed and confident, both byproducts of good planning and sufficient practice, you put your audience at ease. You lend credibility to what you have to say.

Your Voice

Naturally, your voice is your most important tool in speaking situations.

The first step toward improving your voice is to become aware of how you sound to others. Only then will you know what, if anything, needs improvement. Fortunately, you can significantly improve your voice quality by concentrating on a few simple techniques.

Self-Evaluation

Tape yourself reading a few paragraphs from a book, magazine, or newspaper, using your normal speaking voice. Then use the Speaking Checklist at the end of Unit III (page 172). Try to listen objectively to the voice you hear as if it were someone else's voice. How does that voice sound?

- Is the volume appropriate?

- Is the rate of speaking too fast? Too slow?

- Do you pronounce words correctly?

- Do you slur words, drop word endings, or add syllables?

- Do you say "um" frequently?

- Do you emphasize enough? Too much? Too little?

If you cannot be objective, ask someone for help—a coworker or a friend, for example. But be sure to select someone who has excellent speaking skills, who understands your objectives, and who can give you constructive criticism.

Volume and Rate

When you speak too loudly, your listeners become more aware of your **volume** than of the content of your message. When you speak too softly, you force listeners to strain to get your message. In either case, your audience will soon tune out. Be aware that you must adjust your volume to the room and the audience.

How do you know whether your volume is appropriate? Ask a friend or coworker to sit in the back of the room where you will be presenting and provide cues. Or ask the audience: "Can you hear me clearly in the back?" If audience members respond "No," then by all means speak louder. You may need to use a microphone when speaking in a large auditorium; if this is the case, practice using it before your presentation to increase your comfort level. When you begin your presentation, ask for feedback to find out if your voice is amplified to the right volume for your listening audience.

You also can work at controlling the **rate** at which you speak. If your rate of speech is too fast, your words will run together and listeners likely will miss much of what you are saying. If your rate of speech is too slow, you risk losing the listening audience to distractions.

There will be times when it is necessary to slow down your speech. When you want to get the audience's complete attention and provide emphasis for a statement, pause for a few seconds. When you present something technical or something you know your audience will write down, speak more slowly and repeat the information. In general, however, maintain a consistent, normal rate, a speed at which your listeners can comfortably keep up.

Bob is slow to learn that the approach that works on the West Side doesn't necessarily work everwhere.

◀ **FIGURE 5.3**

When you speak too loudly, your listeners become more aware of your volume than of the content of your message.

Pronunciation and Enunciation

Perhaps the most common reason for "mispronouncing" words is not the difficulty of making particular sounds but the reality of our speaking most often in informal situations—situations in which listeners are not evaluating our speech. Often, too, we may have learned certain words through reading and do not know the correct pronunciation. Another reason, of course, is that correct pronunciation is relative to geographic location. People in different parts of the country (and certainly in different parts of the world) pronounce sounds and sound combinations slightly differently.

Though mispronouncing words can be a problem, a bigger problem for many speakers is not enunciating clearly—not pronouncing syllables and sounds clearly. No matter what the reason, you can change speech habits and learn to say words differently (and in some cases, more accurately).

Pronunciation Checklist

Use the following categories to discover the kinds of pronunciation and **enunciation** errors you tend to make:

- **Do you drop sounds at the end of words?** For example, do you drop the *g* in *-ing* words and say, for example, "runnin'," "eatin'," "workin'"? Do you drop the final *t* when you say words such as *list* and *tourist*? Do you drop the final *d* in words such as *field* and *build*?

- **Do you omit some letters and sounds?** Do you omit letters (that is, sounds) from words such as *interest*? The correct pronunciation is "IN-ter-est," not "IN-trest."

- **Do you add sounds?** Do you add sounds when you say certain words, such as "ATH-*a*-lete"? The correct pronunciation is "ATH-lete."

- **Do you alter vowel sounds?** For example, do you say "GEN-you-*in*" (correct) or "GEN-you-*ine*" (incorrect)? "NU-*clee*-er" (correct) or "NU-*cue*-ler" (incorrect)? "REAL-ter" (correct) or "REA-*la*-ter" (incorrect)?

- **Do you stress the wrong syllable?** For example, you should say "in-COM-pa-ra-ble" (not "in-com-PAR-a-ble") and "in-SUR-ance" (not "IN-sur-ance").

- **Do you mispronounce words?** Many people make the mistake of pronouncing words just as they appear in writing. For example, do you pronounce *epitome* "ee-PIT-i-me" (correct) or "EH-pi-tome" (incorrect)? Another common mispronunciation is "aks" (incorrect) instead of "ask" (correct).

- **Do you use different forms of the same word correctly?** For example, for the verb form of *orientation*, do you say "orient" (correct) or "orientate" (incorrect)?

You can heighten your awareness of appropriate pronunciation and enunciation by paying attention to the speech patterns of national newscasters and radio announcers. These people are paid very well to articulate carefully. Another help is the dictionary; use it when a question of pronunciation comes up.

Emphasis

When you are writing, you can emphasize a word by underlining, italicizing, or using capital or bold letters. The word is emphasized because the other words are not underlined, italicized, capitalized, or bolded. How do you provide emphasis when you are speaking?

When speaking, you can stress a word to make it stand out from the others by simply raising the volume of your voice.

- "I repeated it clearly: NO!"

- "NEVER have I heard of ANYTHING so silly!"

You can also provide emphasis by raising the **pitch** of your voice. Pitch describes how high or low a sound is. You have learned to raise the pitch of your voice to show surprise, most often in questions such as these:

- "I don't believe she said that, do *you*?"

- "You mean he didn't *know* that the procedures had been changed?"

FIGURE 5.4

Paying attention to national television and radio newscasters will give you a good example of clear articulation and how it helps a listening audience.

Another effective technique for emphasizing words is simply to pause; the word or words following the pause receive extra emphasis. You also can "introduce" the words you want to emphasize. The words preceding the pause prepare listeners to attend to important information:

- "Now here is the key to increasing profits: (pause) We must all work harder."

When speaking, you cannot emphasize everything you say, and the opposite, emphasizing nothing, is equally ineffective. Speech that is **monotone** is delivered with the same *intonation,* stress, pitch, and volume. It offers no variety and, worse, no emphasis. From it we derive the adjective *monotonous*, meaning "tedious, dull, boring" the last characteristics you want for your presentation!

intonation

the rise and fall in pitch of the voice in speech

Body Language

In Unit Two you learned about nonverbal messages and how body language—gestures and facial expressions, for example—communicates feelings. We mentioned that effective communicators control their body language to coincide with and complement their messages. Here are some tips to help you do just that:

1. **Make eye contact with your listeners.** When you deliver a talk to an audience, make eye contact with someone in front, then someone to the left, someone to the right, and so on, one person at a time. By shifting your focus every so often you connect with more audience members and avoid making any one individual feel uncomfortable.

2. **Keep unnecessary body language to a minimum.** Do not twirl a pencil or a pointer, play with a ring on your finger, tap the microphone, look annoyed, read your notes, stare at the podium or the floor, or otherwise distract your audience. If you do, your audience will start paying more attention to what you are doing rather than what you are saying.

3. **Stand erect with your feet comfortably apart.** Do not shift your weight from foot to foot; doing so shows discomfort and nervousness. Slouching is distracting; good posture "heightens" your credibility.

4. **Smile as appropriate.** If the topic is laying off employees, of course, there may be nothing to smile about. But, in most situations, smiling is helpful. Show some enthusiasm for what you have to say and it is likely to be contagious.

5. **Dress appropriately.** Clothing is a form of body language; your clothing communicates feelings as much as your gestures or facial expressions do. Be aware that both overdressing and underdressing for a speaking situation can communicate more than you'd like—either "I'm better than you" or "I don't really care about this topic."

Body Language and Stage Fright

Your body language can give you away if you experience stage fright. If you find that you are nervous about speaking in front of others, you can work to improve your comfort level. First know that if you are not prepared, you *do* have something to be nervous about. Preparedness will give you confidence, but even with this insurance some people will still have the jitters. If this is the case for you, try these tips:

- **Breathe in and breathe out.** Before you stand up to speak, take three deep breaths. Then when you stand before your audience, regulate your breathing to help you slow down your speaking rate and feed oxygen to your lungs and brain.

- **Use visualization.** Before your presentation, close your eyes and visualize yourself making your presentation. See yourself as a confident presenter in front of a friendly, receptive audience. Address your fears by visualizing how you would handle problems— a difficult question or a missing visual aid, for example. Often we are afraid of the unknown, so by preparing for the worst you can lessen your fear.

- **Take a sip of water.** Bring water to the podium so that you can take sips. Stage fright can cause a dry mouth and make speaking difficult.

Remember, in most cases the audience is rooting for you. It is as uncomfortable for them to watch you break into a cold sweat as it is for you to stand before them. You may even want to admit how you feel, just to free yourself from the terror of being "found out." Your fear—and the physical signs of it—can distract listeners from your message. By addressing the stage fright and dismissing it, you can put the focus back where it belongs—on your topic.

Practice, Practice, Practice

Effective presentations are the result of careful planning, preparation, and plenty of practice. As we mentioned before, you can start by practicing your presentation skills long before you have an assignment. Then when you receive an assignment, you can work on specific aspects of the presentation.

You'll need to become familiar with the sequence of topics in your presentation. Practice by making key points over and over again. Experiment with pausing, emphasizing a word, lowering or raising your voice, using visual aids and handouts, looking at your audience, standing straight, and so on. As you practice, you refine, revise, and improve both the content and delivery of your message.

Here are some guidelines that will help you to make your practice effective:

1. **Read your speech aloud.** Do this just as if you were in front of your audience. Stand in front of a mirror if you can, and always dress professionally when you practice so you can project confidence.

2. **Practice in the place you will speak.** Try at least once, if possible, to practice your speech in the room where you will actually deliver it. You increase your own comfort level by being familiar with your surroundings. You can also correct problems, for example by locating missing markers if you plan to use a writing board.

3. **Practice using equipment.** Rehearse as often as necessary how you will coordinate audiovisual equipment. Basically, you want the audience to stay focused on what you are saying, not what you are doing.

4. **Ask friends to be your "practice audience."** They can provide feedback about your volume, rate, clarity, tone, rhythm, pronunciation, eye contact, use of visual aids, posture, hand motions, and body movements. If possible, select someone who is an effective, experienced speaker. You would be surprised how willing (and flattered) coworkers and others will be to help. Review the suggestions and criticisms you receive as objectively as possible. How can the recommendations or comments improve your talk?

5. **Time yourself.** It's essential to determine the length of your presentation. If you are allotted 20 minutes for your speech but in practice you are running 30 minutes, you need to trim your presentation.

6. **Work on improving transitions.** Use your voice, body movements, or visual aids in addition to words to tell the audience you are introducing a new thought.

7. **Get away from your notes.** Try presenting by referring only minimally or not at all to your notes. Commit some of your presentation to memory so that you can look at your audience and move with ease.

You may want to join Toastmasters International, an organization devoted to public speaking. Through membership you will have the opportunity to listen to other speakers and prepare and give speeches of your own. Members provide valuable feedback to help one another. Attending Toastmasters or a group with similar goals is a satisfying way to gain confidence in your public speaking ability and meet interesting people from a variety of work backgrounds.

Troubleshooting: What If . . . ?

Experienced speakers can share horrendous stories of what can go wrong in speaking situations. Knowing some of the potential problems can help you to prepare for—and possibly avoid—disaster:

1. **What if my handouts do not arrive?** Speakers often ship their handouts to the hotel or conference center in advance. Sometimes the handouts are lost or late. One solution is to carry the handouts with you. Another is to keep at least one good copy with you. If necessary, you can find a local print shop and quickly run off as many copies as you need. If you have not taken these precautions, as a last resort you can simply announce to the audience that your handouts have not arrived but that you will mail a copy to each person who gives you his or her name and address.

    It is best to avoid shipping your slides, transparencies, computer software, or other visuals. They are often irreplaceable, particularly at the last minute, so keep them nearby at all times.

2. **What if someone asks a question in the middle of my talk? What if I don't know the answer?** If you have planned a question-and-answer session for a certain time, ask the audience to save questions for that time. If not, ask the interrupter to see you at the end of your talk. Best of all, if you can work in the answer without jeopardizing the effectiveness of your talk in any way, do so. In a situation where you do not know the answer, just say so. Offer to find the information later and get back to the individual.

3. **What if the audiovisual equipment does not work?** Your best insurance is to check equipment before you give a presentation to make sure it is in working order. If it is not, ask the hotel or meeting director for back-up equipment. If none is available, check the phone book for a local rental shop. The person charged with providing this equipment, often a conference official, should be willing to help you and cover any expense.

FIGURE 5.5 ▶

Checking equipment ahead of time
can save the speaker and the
audience a lot of headaches.

Luckily Dankins discovered during his practice session that there were technical
problems with his laser pointer.

4.   **What if the speaker before me speaks overtime?** Sit patiently and wait.
     While you're waiting, revise your plans. For a number of reasons, some
     speakers will not end their presentations on schedule. Perhaps they did not
     plan and time their talks as carefully as you did. Perhaps the previous
     speakers spoke too long. If another speaker immediately follows you, then
     you must end on time.

Do not pass on the discourtesy of the previous speaker. However, if a break or inter-
mission follows your talk, you might be able to take a few minutes (but not all) of
that break time. If you are the last speaker at the end of the day, you may more comfortably go over your time limit. But be aware that some people will leave.

5   **USE YOUR JUDGMENT**

Tape yourself for 10-15 minutes giving a presentation or reading a passage from
an article or essay, or even from this textbook. Trade tapes with at least two other
classmates (one at a time) and evaluate your classmates' speaking skills based on
the Speaking Checklist on page 172 at the end of Unit Three.

Return the checklists to the people whose voices you rated. Once you receive
your checks from classmates, make sure you understand their comments. If you
do not, ask for clarification. Use this feedback to improve your speaking skills.

USE YOUR JUDGMENT 6

As a class, brainstorm as many words as possible that are often mispronounced or incorrectly used. Review how these words should be pronounced and used. Keep a list for yourself.

IN BRIEF

❶ The secret to successful presentations is planning. Like the writing process, planning a presentation begins with a thorough understanding of your purpose for speaking and the audience to whom you are speaking.

❷ Once you understand your purpose and audience, you must gather information, select an approach, and organize your information into an outline. At this point, you may choose to speak from your outline or create a draft from which to speak.

❸ When writing your presentation, your writing style should reflect spoken language.

❹ Data (facts and figures) and humor must be used carefully in presentations but can add to the interest and acceptance of a spoken message.

❺ Visual aids and handouts help listeners by giving them information in another format and by allowing them to take something away from the presentation that summarizes key points. They also can help speakers organize their presentations.

❻ Demonstrations, by either the speaker or audience members, are a valuable teaching tool in presentations.

❼ You can improve your presentation skills before you get an assignment. By listening to yourself speak, you can learn to adjust your volume, your rate of speech, and your emphasis. Also, by focusing on language use and pronunciation, it is possible to improve and correct the way you pronounce and enunciate words.

❽ You can learn to control your body language to complement your speaking, even when stage fright is a problem.

⑨ By practicing your presentation before you give it, you can catch organizational problems, time yourself, plan voice quality and gestures, correct problems manipulating visual aids and handouts, smooth out transitions between main points, and commit difficult parts of your presentation to memory.

⑩ Knowing in advance what can go wrong in your presentation and planning how to avoid or fix these problems is a good defensive strategy.

WORDS OF NOTE

Define each of these terms introduced in Chapter 5.

demonstrations
enunciation
handouts
LCD units
monotone
oral communication
outline
pitch
rate
subjective
transparencies
visual aids
volume

CHECK YOUR RECALL

❶ What three characteristics do most business presentations and speeches share?

❷ When planning a presentation, what four things do you need to identify?

❸ What is the "backbone" of a presentation?

❹ How does spoken language differ from written language? How does this affect preparing and giving an oral presentation?

❺ What should you consider in deciding to speak from an outline or a fully written speech?

❻ What are two pitfalls to avoid when speaking?

7 How do visual aids, handouts, and demonstrations help the audience? How do they help the speaker?

8 What are some examples of visual aids? What are some guidelines to follow in using visual aids?

9 What are some guidelines to follow in using handouts?

10 What two means of using demonstrations does the chapter discuss?

11 The chapter discusses four techniques for improving voice quality. Name and explain each technique.

12 What are five tips for controlling body language and making it effective?

13 What can you do to help alleviate stage fright?

SHARE YOUR PERSPECTIVE

1 Select a common product and outline a 15-minute presentation in which you persuade your audience (your classmates) to purchase the product. Include visual aids and/or handouts.

2 Using the same product you chose above, outline a 15-minute presentation in which you persuade your audience (your classmates) *not* to purchase the product. Include visual aids and/or handouts.

3 In writing, explain how your presentations in items 1 and 2 differed and why.

4 Give one of the two presentations, practicing all of the following before the presentation:

- Content and organization
- Visual aids and/or handouts
- Voice
- Body language

5 Plan (in writing) and give another presentation in which your purpose is to pass on information. Here are some possible topics:

- Research a local, national, or international company and report to your audience what you learned.
- Research a business topic and report to your audience what you learned.

- Describe and demonstrate a hobby.
- Read about a current political or social conflict (national or international) and explain to the audience the nature of the conflict and the parties involved.
- Research cultural differences and considerations for doing business in another country and report what you have learned.

FOCUS ON THE FINE POINTS

Read the following background information. Then follow the instructions to locate and correct grammar errors.

Background

Gerri Toensing is the director of her county's Young Children's Education Coalition (YCEC), a nonprofit organization. Gerri is working on a project for a preschool center that will be a model for helping "at-risk" children prepare for school. At her state's annual Preschool Education Association meeting, Gerri plans to speak to a group of executives representing toymakers, school suppliers, and developers of educational materials. Gerri's goal is to persuade the businesses to contribute money and products toward the center's development.

Several weeks before the convention, Gerri sends a letter to corporate registrants inviting them to her presentation and telling them a little about the YCEC project. Three of the many documents Gerri needs to prepare for this event include that letter, a chart showing the benefits of a similar venture in California, and a handout that highlights parent responses to the California program. Gerri's assistant, Sue Ellen Mason, has prepared the three documents for Gerri's review.

Your Instructions

Each of the following documents contains up to 15 errors. Indicate and correct errors by noting them on a photocopy of the page or on a separate sheet of paper. In each case, you may assume the document is formatted correctly.

Note: If you have difficulty locating errors, turn to page 457 in the Appendix. There you will find additional information about the errors in Document 1.

DOCUMENT 1: Letter

Y O U N G
C H I L D R E N ' S
E D U C A T I O N
C O A L I T I O N

Febuary 12, 19XX

Dear _____:

You are invited to attend a special presentation hosted by YCEC at this years' Preschool Education Association meeting. At the meeting I will be addressing executives from the education industry about an exciting demonstration project the Story County YCEC has initiated to improve the odds for at-risk children.

No doubt you are aware of the acclaimed New Generation Preschool in California's La Linda County. In its' six years of operation, New Generation has had measurable success in improving childrens' skills acquisition and in raising there parent's level of involvement. Eight seperate studies have documented the results of New Generation's program.

One of the most important factors in La Linda Counties' success has been the assistance of private secter businesses in building and maintaining their program. Contributions from the education industry, in money and in kind, continue to sustain New Generation in her ongoing service to the children and families of La Linda. The ultamite benefit, of course, is to us all.

With that background, I invite you to join other education professionals and I for a social hour and presentation:

Thursday, April 5
Geneva Hotel, New Amsterdam Room
Social Hour 4:00-5:00 P.M.
Presentation 5:00-6:00 P.M.

I hope you will come to hear about the progress many of we in Story County are making in its effort to help New Yorks' children and families.

Best regards,

Gerri Toensing
Director

sem

7500 WEST ELM STREET SUITE 1001 HILL CITY NEW YORK 10123
914-555-1237 TOLL FREE 800-555-7722 FAX 914-555-1248

DOCUMENT 2: Chart

**Selected Results from a Study of Children and Families of the
LA LINDA COUNTY NEW GENERATION PRESCHOOL
1988-1994**

The study was conducted over a six-year's period. By design, children and families came from three groups: New Generation (NG), Control A (CA), and Control B (CB). Children in the CA group were funded to attend the private Mertz Day Preschool. Children in the CB group also attended the Mertz Day Preschool; there tuition was payed by his or her families. Racial and ethnicity backgrounds for each group were 25% Hispanic, 25% African-American, 25% Caucasion, and 25% Other.* Groups NG and CA represented family groups of dissimilar socioeconomic status: at or below poverty level. Group CB came from middle-class families (income $32,000- $52,000). In group NG, 65% of families were single-parent; 45% were duel-parent families. In group CA, 52% of families were one-parent; 58% were two-parent. In group CB, 43% were single-parent, 57% were two-parent.

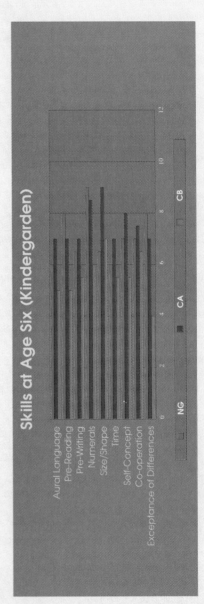

Skills at Age Six (Kindergarden)

*Other included Native American, Asian/Pacific, and nonspecific others.

DOCUMENT 3: Parent Comments

Comments from Parents of New Generation Preschool
1988-1994

"My little girl is a changed child! I can't beleive how she opened up."

Mother of Sasha (age 5, two years in program)

"Both my kids are so good about cooperating now . . . suppertime is the best time of the day now—what a change!"

Mother of Dante (age 6, three years' in program) and Nikia (age 4, one year in program)

"The teachers showed so much patience to both Brendan and I—it's them in the 'trenches' I really respect! Brendan can hardly wait to leave for school these days. Some days he's all ready got his coat on at breakfast!"

Father of Brendan (age 5, two years in program)

"It's just so hard for children these days, and the (New Generation) school is better then home to them. They feel safe there, and they're minds and hearts just open up. If you had asked me three months ago if my daughter was going to learn all her numbers and letters so soon, I'd never have believed it. Now it's 'Mama, can we read?' all the time."

Mother of Maria (age 5, three months in program)

"Mamaru goes to the school, but our whole family is learning from them every day. He sits in the car with his little sister and teaches her the name of everything we drive by! A huge thanks to New Generation from we all!"

Grandmother of Mamaru (age 4, one year in program)

"New Generation has effected everyone in our family. I wish all children could have them the same experience. My advise is to start preschools like this one all over the country. Thank you for all you've given to my daughter and I."

Mother of Frannie (age 6, three years in program)

"Thank you New Generation! Our childrens' future is bright because of you!"

Father of Joey (age 6, two years in program), Marco (age 5, two years in program), Linda (age 4, one year in program), and Danny (age 3, two months' in program)

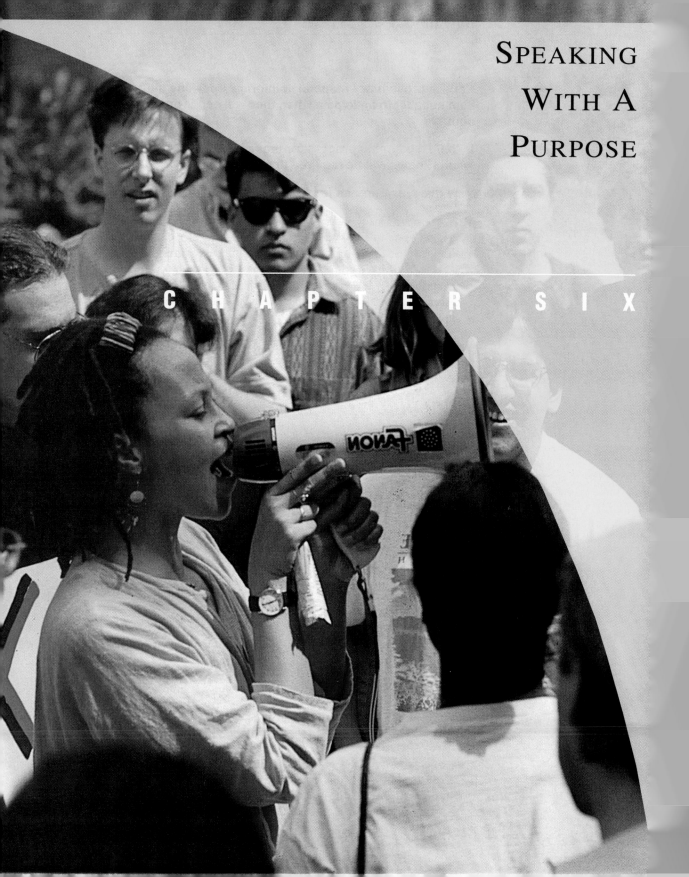

Can I improve how I respond in informal speaking situations even when I am not able to anticipate when they will occur or what they will be about?

Is there a planning process for those informal business situations when I know I will be required to speak?

How does my purpose for speaking affect my planning process?

There are many instances during the typical business day when you will be required to speak to achieve a business objective. Although most of these situations will be informal, you can still benefit from having a plan. The primary benefit of having a plan is efficiency. In general, a plan will enable you to accomplish what you set out to accomplish. The secondary benefit of having a plan is enhancing your professional image. When you are organized and know what you want, you project a businesslike attitude.

C A S E   S C E N A R I O

Telephone Tag

Janice Diener, a sales assistant at Vernon Industries, spends a lot of time on the telephone. On one particularly frustrating day, she tried three times to reach Andy Parker in Accounting. Each time she called, she got Andy's voice-mail message; each time, she asked him to call her back. After three rounds of "telephone tag," Janice finally got through. "Hi, Andy," she said. "Thank heaven I finally reached you! I checked on the payroll information you needed: Jenny Royko, Karen Fauve, and Rico Munro all started in March of 1995. Bill Mathies started in June of 1987. Sarah Wendt started in July of 1993. And Mark Holmgren and Bernie Malkowicz started in April, 1990."

"Thanks, Janice," said Andy. "The only person missing is Juanita Fruela. Now, what about their social security numbers?"

"Oh, darn!" Janice exclaimed. "I forgot to check on that, Andy. I knew I was forgetting *something,* but I couldn't put my finger on it."

"That's okay, Janice," Andy replied. "You can call me back with the numbers and the info about Juanita too. Why don't you just leave the information on my machine."

Hanging up, Janice sighed to herself, "What a crazy day I've had on the phone! All these problems connecting with Andy—and then I forgot the social security numbers—*and* Juanita! And this morning I had to call Roy Dykstra twice because I forgot when I first called to tell him I got the credit approval on his CompuQuick sale. My memory is getting worse every day!" Janice felt discouraged. She was working long hours, and she knew she wasn't accomplishing as much as the other sales assistants. How did they do it?

What could Janice have done to make her telephoning go more smoothly? How might the other sales assistants be managing to accomplish so much more than Janice?

Just as you can plan your spoken communications, you can plan for telephone calls and short face-to-face conversations. Whether the purpose of these communications is to pass on information, to respond to questions or requests, to make requests, to **direct,** or to **persuade,** you can improve your effectiveness and productivity by planning ahead.

You may not realize that you can plan your spoken messages *even when you do not have advance notice about the speaking situation.* With practice, planning your verbal messages "on the spot" will become second nature; essentially you become *intentional* about your oral communication. Before you open your mouth, you stop and think: What do I want to communicate here? What information do I need? Has there been any misunderstanding that I need to clear up? Is it necessary for me to say anything, or is it best that I remain quiet? The more you think before you speak, the less speaking you will need to do.

intentional

purposeful; to do by design, by planning

◀ **FIGURE 6.1**

A friendly telephone manner is essential, but take care not to confuse "friendliness" with "chattiness."

Be Prepared!

While Erica LeTendre walks down the hallway with her manager, Dorothy Trainor, Dorothy asks Erica to call the Security Department. "Let Security know that we plan to have all twelve East Coast sales reps in the building for a meeting next Saturday," Dorothy instructed. "Oh, yes, be sure they know that three are new employees who don't have ID cards yet. We'll be meeting in the large upstairs conference room. Oh, Erica, find out which door to the building will be open. I don't want the reps to waste time running around outside looking for an open door. Then you'll need to call the reps and tell them. While you're calling, please make arrangements to have Saturday service for breakfast and for refreshments at break time. We won't have lunch in the building. We'll finish up by 12:30, because most of the reps will be running to the airport. Hmm . . . I wonder if the air-conditioning will be on?"

Erica had worked for Dorothy long enough to know she should carry a small notebook and pencil anytime she went anywhere with her manager. As Erica listened to Dorothy's request, she jotted down the key items Dorothy mentioned. Then Erica read the list back to Dorothy to make sure she'd noted the essential details. When she got back to her desk, Erica added other key facts she knew she would need to make the calls.

After rechecking her list carefully to make sure she had included everything, Erica's list looked like this:

```
call Security
          reps here Sat
          3 no ID (how get in?)
          lg up conf rm
          which door?
          call/tell reps
          air condtng?
brkfst a.m. break
```

Erica called Security to get the information she needed. Then she made a copy of the phone list of the sales reps, circled the twelve invited to the meeting, and systematically called each one, leaving complete messages for those who did not answer in person. She checked each name off the list as she completed the calls. All Erica had left to do was arrange for the food for the morning break.

How many different ways did Erica ensure that she could handle all the details Dorothy brought up thoroughly and efficiently? Are there other things she could have done?

PASSING ON INFORMATION

When you are required to relay information to someone else, the best planning technique is to make a list.

Anytime you have a number of issues to discuss, questions to ask, or items of information to provide, develop a list. Apply this principle to phone calls and meetings and you will find that you save a great deal of time—not just your own, but other people's too.

USE YOUR JUDGMENT 1

For each of the following situations, list all the information you would need to have ready:

a.   Your manager wants to meet with you this afternoon at 3:30 to discuss your computer needs and expenses. He agrees that you need a laptop computer to take with you on the road and to work at home, but he knows little about computers. You know that he acts quickly and may even want you to order the computer after his approval at the meeting.

b.   You have persuaded a guest speaker to come to your school and make a presentation for your class two weeks from today at one o'clock. Your guest speaker lives next door to you but does not know where your school is. She will call you at five o'clock today to confirm all the details of her visit and presentation and to get directions to your school and your classroom.

RESPONDING TO QUESTIONS AND REQUESTS

When you are posed a question or asked to provide information or a service, it is worthwhile to give a thoughtful response. Simple planning techniques can help you to respond in the way you would like.

Take Note!

At a time-management workshop, Dan West picked up on this bit of advice about responding to questions and requests: "People often write the list for you. For example, when someone sends you a letter requesting information, that letter is a list, a list that you can use as your plan when you respond."

When he returned to his office after the seminar, Dan found the usual assortment of memos, letters, brochures, ads, and other messages. One memo invited him to attend a meeting to discuss ways to handle regional space ads more effectively.

MEMORANDUM

TO: Dan West

FROM: Sue Vincetti, Marketing

DATE: September 8, 19XX

SUBJECT: REGIONAL SPACE ADS MEETING
                Wednesday, September 19, 10:30 - Noon
                Conference Room B

Please plan to attend the above meeting. We will discuss ways to make ads for each of the five regions more effective.

In preparation for the meeting, please review all ads for all regions for the months of May, June, and July of last fiscal year. Bring sales records (June-September) for your region. Be prepared to discuss what's worked, what hasn't, and other possible approaches. This is your opportunity to present any new ideas your team has come up with.

The attached ads were run in the summer issue of *California Quarterly*. As part of our discussion, Rico Martinez wants us to look at these ads and consider what they tell us about what the competition has in store for us. (This discussion should also shed some light on our new agency selection process.)

SV/llt

Attachments

> *How could Dan use this memo to prepare for the meeting? How could he use it at the meeting? What other information might he need to take with him to the meeting?*

Whenever you must respond orally to written questions and requests, write notes directly on the requests or questions, and let this combination of information become your plan. Then refer to your plan as you make your call or attend your meeting. Doing this will provide you with accurate and thorough information. You can then focus on speaking well instead of trying to remember facts and statistics or thinking up answers to questions.

USE YOUR JUDGMENT   2

You receive a letter of request as (illustrated on page 156). Because the potential customer asks for a fast response, you decide to call her immediately to answer her questions. Prepare your call to Ms. Paulson, using the product information provided below. If possible, photocopy Ms. Paulson's letter and write your notes directly on her letter. Then ask a classmate to play the role of Ms. Paulson while you call her. Also, ask "Ms. Paulson" to evaluate your response to her questions. Finally, switch roles and play the role of Ms. Paulson for your classmate.

Product information:

a. PageOne is a state-of-the-art paging system.
b. PageOne is compact; it weighs only 2.5 ounces.
c. To page you, someone simply dials the PageOne 800 number (free) and then punches in your code number.
d. Within seconds, the PageOne satellite system relays a signal to your paging unit.
e. PageOne reaches more than 250 cities; a complete list is available.
f. A price list is available; it includes competitor comparisons.
g. PageOne Messaging system is also available; it allows callers to leave voice messages.
h. A free booklet explains all details.

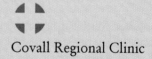

Covall Regional Clinic

7775 South Inland Road
West Duluth, Minnesota 55097
(218) 555-0880
Fax (218) 555-0890

November 5, 19XX

Customer Service Department
PageOne
P.O. Box 17999
Duluth, MN 55099

Dear Customer Service Representative:

The Covall Regional Clinic needs to convert to a state-of-the-art paging system. We are experiencing several problems with our current paging system.

Elevation variations and Lake Superior air currents seem to interfere with the signal. Some brands of cellular phones also seem to interfere. The clinic serves clients over a ninety-mile radius; doctors and practitioners often travel to four different satellite clinics in a single day. At times it is necessary for a doctor to carry two different pagers to receive signals across this broad geographic area.

If your paging service can readily accommodate our needs, I would like to hear from a customer service immediately. We want to set up a new service as soon as possible. Please call me at 555-0883.

Thank you.

Sincerely,

Juliette Paulson, Office Manager

MAKING A REQUEST

Routine requests—that is, those not requiring persuasion—are simple and direct. Most often they will not require much planning.

Consider Karen Von Hoffman. She was asked to prepare sales projections for her region. She recalled that Jim Doherty presented the findings of several studies projecting *demographics* at a planning meeting not too long ago. At the meeting, Jim had presented the data in charts on overhead transparencies. He had offered photocopies of the charts to anyone who needed them.

Is it appropriate for Karen to ask Jim if she may use his data? Certainly. How might she approach him? Even when a request is routine, it is essential to follow these "rules" of making requests:

1. **Be polite.** Even when information has already been offered, as it was in Jim and Karen's case, this does not mean that anyone can simply demand the charts. Business etiquette requires courtesy.

2. **Be direct.** Make the request in a straightforward manner. Avoid elaborate explanation or justification. And there is rarely a need to be subtle. *Subtlety* can lead to misunderstanding.

3. **Be specific.** Use clear, direct language so there can be no mistake. In Karen and Jim's case, Jim may frequently give presentations and may get requests for any number of other charts, so it would be important for Karen to specify what she wants. It is your responsibility to ensure that your listener knows what you want.

4. **Be informative.** Tell the person when you need the information and how you will use it. Why? There may be some reason, unknown to you, that the information requested is not suitable for your intended use. By explaining how you plan to use the material, you give the person an opportunity to share additional information with you. If you have a short deadline, be straightforward and polite about it. If the person cannot comply, he or she will tell you.

5. **Be reasonable.** Don't ask the person to deliver something immediately. Don't ask for 100 copies of each item. Rather, put yourself in your listener's place: Make sure your request is reasonable.

6. **Be helpful.** Consider the reasonableness of your request, and offer the listener help when appropriate. Karen might have said to Jim, "Jim, if you don't mind, I'll have my assistant drop by to pick up the master copies. I can do the photocopying and return the originals to you. I need 100 copies of each chart, and I don't want to tie up your assistant. By the way, I plan to make a handout to go with the charts. I'll give you a copy of the handout when I return your master copy."

demographics

the statistical characteristics of human populations (such as age and income) used to identify markets

▲ FIGURE 6.2

People are more inclined to agree to your request when you are courteous and helpful.

subtlety

indirectness; the quality of being obscure, difficult to understand or distinguish

3 USE YOUR JUDGMENT

For each of the following situations, list the information you must have to make your requests and the information you must request:

a. You need to hire an additional office assistant to lighten the workload of the other two assistants. You need to talk to someone in Human Resources about running a want ad; it is the first time you have coordinated this type of activity.

b. You have an appointment with a benefits counselor to discuss your choice of medical and dental benefits.

DIRECTING OTHERS

At times you will speak to direct others, as Pauline does in the following situation.

C A S E   S C E N A R I O

A Hasty Word

Pauline O'Hara was just finishing up her monthly meeting with the 15 sales representatives she managed. They were packing up their notes and discussing their dinner plans when Pauline interrupted: "Oh, one last thing before we go. I almost forgot. From now on please be sure to write each distributor's code number on the top right corner of each order you send in to the Order Department. And print neatly. It's got something to do with a new system over in the Order Department. I guess that wraps it up. See you next month."

In the next few weeks, the representatives in her district received many complaints. Distributors called to say that their orders were late, that they

hadn't received catalogs they ordered, and that their monthly statements were billed for merchandise they had not received.

Pauline decided to call Miguel Espada, the vice president of sales, to explain the problem and ask for his help. Miguel was surprised. "It's funny," he told her. "I've talked with all the other district managers yesterday and today, and no one else has mentioned this kind of problem. Well, you can be sure I'll check into it right away. Thanks for letting me know."

About an hour later, Miguel called Pauline back. "Remember that meeting we had three or four weeks ago? About the temporary system for handling order fulfillment and billing—where the reps fill in the code numbers?" "Sure," said Pauline. "Well," explained Miguel, "I'm told that your region is the only one where the reps haven't been coding their orders correctly."

"That's funny," Pauline frowned. "I told them about it at our last meeting."

Why do you think Pauline's reps were not coding the orders correctly? What could she have done to avoid this problem?

When your purpose is to direct others to action, you need to be sure they understand exactly what they must do, when they must do it, and why. Put yourself in the listener's place and try to answer the listener's possible questions:

- What exactly must I do?
- Why must I do it?
- What will happen if I don't do it?
- How must I do it?
- When must I do it?

◀ FIGURE 6.3

If your directions are important, give them the emphasis they need.

Also, give your directions the emphasis they deserve. If they are not important, you may work them in hastily at the end of a meeting. If they are important, however, include them as a meeting agenda item; use visuals as needed to present the information and provide a written reminder or summary of the information. Also, provide an opportunity for workers to discuss the information. You may discover unexpected questions, and workers will appreciate the opportunity to talk about any directions they have concerns about.

4   USE YOUR JUDGMENT

Read the following situation and consider how George directs employees to handle calls from customers and potential customers. Evaluate George's approach, giving specific examples. Then write a brief presentation showing how George could have better directed his listeners. Practice this revised presentation and give it to other students. Ask for their evaluation.

unscrupulous

unprincipled; not acting in strict regard for what is considered right or proper

Recent television and newspaper reports have discussed a few ***unscrupulous*** construction companies that do not honor service commitments to home buyers. As a result, many companies are getting calls from concerned or angry customers. Wentworth Construction, a very reputable builder, is now receiving a few calls a day.

Ken Hanover, Wentworth's public relations manager, knows the calls will increase as the news reports continue. He is concerned that employees will not handle such calls effectively, especially if they are unaware of the problem. Ken asks George McCormick to prepare a brief presentation to employees. Ken says, "It's important to remember that most of our employees have not yet received such calls, so they may not understand why we're making such a fuss. But if these news reports continue, we *will* get calls, lots of them. Show them how to explain to customers that we are 'different.'" Here is how George begins his presentation:

In a monotone voice, George says, "I wanted to meet with you to help you handle any calls you might get from customers who are worried about whether we are going to back up our warranties and continue to provide the excellent service we are known for. I assure you that we are. First of all, our business is booming. We have no financial problems. That's important for customers to know. Many construction companies are going out of business and not honoring their contractual agreements.

"Also, you might want to tell them that we've been in business for more than 50 years and that the Buyers' Association rated us the Number One Builder of private homes for the last seven years in a row. Those companies going out of business, of course, are just making the rest of us look bad. Anyway, if a caller . . ."

PERSUADING OTHERS

Many business situations require you to persuade others. You may want to persuade your supervisor to approve an equipment purchase, a customer to purchase your products, a coworker to help you complete a project, a supplier to speed up delivery, or your assistant to put in extra time on a special project.

C A S E   S C E N A R I O

A Plan to Persuade

Ben Erickson, Inventory Manager for the B&J Exporting Company, needed a minicomputer. In the past year, B&J had doubled the number of products it inventoried and added 100 customers and a second warehouse. Ben and his two assistants processed all their information on only three small personal computers. To keep up the present pace and future growth, they needed a more powerful computer. But the senior vice president, Linda Jefferson, recently announced that she was cutting all equipment budgets for the rest of the year.

Ben asked his assistants, Christine Rodgers and Mike Gorham, to meet with him right away. He explained the situation, adding, "Linda is a very reasonable person. But she'll need to be persuaded. We need to figure out the best way to go about this."

Mike offered, "I think it would be good to talk to her about how the company will benefit you know, how we'll save money and improve inventory control."

"Mike's right," said Chris. "We really need a plan. If we just go in there and say, 'We need a $12,000 minicomputer,' she'll laugh us out of her office!"

"That's for sure," agreed Ben. "We *do* need a plan to persuade her."

"Why don't we make a list of the benefits for the company," Mike suggested.

Ben, Christine, and Mike completed the following checklist. In the process, they discovered an excellent option: leasing rather than buying. They agreed that leasing would be better for the company, and Linda would surely prefer the lower monthly cost.

Cost of computer: $12,000 (tax, service contract?)

Benefits: Processing speed will greatly improve
                   (How much?)
                   Can handle current inventory x 100 (good
                   for far into future)

Problems: Moratorium on purchasing equipment

Other options: Hire additional people on temporary
                   basis when needed? (What will the down-
                   time be for training? How efficient would
                   this be?)
                   Hang in there until end of fiscal year
                   (Can we realistically do this for 7
                   months?)
                   Lease? ($375 per month x 7 = $2,625.
                   Can continue leasing next year at same
                   cost or reevaluate computer needs for
                   next fiscal year.)

Ben was able to use the list to prepare a persuasive talk to use when bring-
ing the matter up with Linda. As a result, he won Linda's approval for leasing the minicomputer.

What did you notice about how Ben went about dealing with his problem?
Did he get what he'd originally wanted? Why was he effective?

Speaking for the purpose of persuading someone is one of the most difficult communication processes. Each situation requires a different approach—and probably several different approaches. Moreover, the listener's response to one approach often
forces you to take another approach, making perfect planning impossible.
Nonetheless, with careful planning, you will be comfortable approaching your topic
from several different angles. For example, if Linda had become intrigued with the
minicomputer's capabilities, Ben should have been able to elaborate. Otherwise,
Linda may not have been convinced that a minicomputer, purchased *or* leased, was
necessary.

The Keys to Preparing a Persuasive Talk

Whatever the situation, the keys to preparing a persuasive talk are:

1. **Understand your goals clearly.** Know which of your goals are most important and which you are willing to compromise—and to what extent.

2. **Understand your listeners' needs and goals.** Anticipate how your listeners will respond to each of your arguments. Use your best arguments first and be ready to give something in return for meeting your goals.

3. **Focus on your listeners' counterarguments.** Understand their reasons for accepting or not accepting your arguments, and use their arguments to direct your own.

4. **Be prepared.** Have at your command all the facts, statistics, and arguments that might persuade your listeners. Consider how you might use data to strengthen your position and address your listeners' questions and concerns.

As you can see, being persuasive requires planning and control, even in the least formal situations.

Bill is determined to be able to defend his decision to order 2% milk with his lunch

◀ **FIGURE 6.4**

Being persuasive requires planning and control.

5 **USE YOUR JUDGMENT**

Discuss the information and arguments you might use to be persuasive in the following situations. Talk about all the possibilities for negotiating an agreement:

a. You can use vacation time only when your colleague Jane Wilcox is at work. At the last minute, you feel you must request a vacation day for this Friday due to a family situation you must handle, but Jane has been planning that day off for weeks and has already submitted the request. When you explain the situation to Jane, she says, "I'm sorry. I've been planning this day for weeks. I don't get enough time off as it is, and I'm swamped with work right now. I really need the time."

b. To try to be fair in improving the company's cash flow, your vice president trimmed 15% off each department's budget. Because of this, your company has two people, you and a coworker, assigned to do what four people should be doing in the production department. Your work is getting done; however, it is getting done late, and customer complaints about quality and promptness have increased. The sales staff is even complaining about production's slowdown. What's worse, the research and development department has introduced two new products in the past two months, products you have to learn about and produce on top of your other work. You set up a meeting with the vice president to see if there is some other way to handle the budget cuts.

IN BRIEF

① Many speaking situations—phone calls, meetings, discussions, and so on—can be planned and controlled for increased effectiveness and efficiency.

② You can plan for passing on information and making requests by listing and organizing your information ahead of time.

③ You can plan for responding to questions and requests by allowing specific questions and requests to direct your research and organize your response.

④ You can plan for directing others by listing information ahead of time, by including an explanation of the need for the directions, by giving directions their proper emphasis, and by following up to see whether people are following directions.

⑤ You can plan to persuade by considering all the information and arguments that might persuade your listener and by preparing counter-arguments to those your listener might use, showing how your point of view benefits your listener.

WORDS OF NOTE

Define each of these terms introduced in Chapter 6.

direct
persuade

CHECK YOUR RECALL

① What are two general benefits of planning for informal speaking situations?

② What are some questions to ask yourself in order to be intentional about your oral communication?

③ What is the best planning technique to use when you need to relay information to someone?

④ What are some simple planning techniques you might use for responding to questions or requests?

⑤   What are some guidelines to follow when making a spoken request?

⑥   When your purpose is to direct others, what questions should you keep in mind to help your listener?

⑦   What are the keys to preparing a persuasive talk?

SHARE YOUR PERSPECTIVE

Plan your conversations in the following situations. Be ready to discuss why you planned as you did. When you have finished planning, choose a classmate and role-play these conversations. Be ready to evaluate your planning based on the role playing.

❶   Your new assistant came highly recommended. Shortly after he started, however, he had some personal problems that interfered with his work. As far as you know, he has gotten his personal life back on track, but his work has never returned to the level you saw when he started. He is sometimes late for work and sometimes leaves early. He sometimes extends his breaks and lunch hour. Routine tasks such as filing and mailing seem to take longer to finish. And he seems to work less independently now, relying on you for many simple, routine decisions that he used to make. You decide to talk with him to try to improve his performance.

❷   You're swamped at work, and your boss asks you to respond to an unusual request made by a client. The client has numerous questions about your local area computer network because she is considering networking her office as well. Your boss hands you the client's letter and says, "Try to get a response in the mail by tomorrow afternoon." You know you are not the best person to handle this request because you will simply have to go to the on-site computer coordinator to get the information. Maybe the computer coordinator would be willing to write this letter, or at least a rough draft, for you.

FOCUS ON THE FINE POINTS
Read the following background information. Then follow the instructions to locate and correct grammar errors.

Background

Alternatives Inc. is an entertainment company with many divisions, including its own nonalcoholic night club called Neo-Bar which features bands, dancing, and comedy acts. Alternatives also has a fund-raising division that helps raise money for "Clean Night Out," a once-a-month social event for high school students. All proceeds from "Clean Night Out" go to the high school's drug prevention curriculum.

Glenda McGhonegal works in the Alternatives communications department. Recently she has had three different assignments: preparing guidelines on using voice mail for the company handbook, fashioning an upbeat recorded telephone message for Neo-Bar, and developing a script for telemarketers to follow in soliciting donations for "Clean Night Out."

Your Instructions

Each of the following documents contains up to 15 errors. Indicate and correct errors by circling the problem and noting the solution on a photocopy of the page or on a separate sheet of paper. In each case, you may assume the document is formatted correctly.

Note: If you have difficulty locating errors, turn to page 459 in the Appendix. There you will find additional information about the errors in Document 1.

DOCUMENT 1: Page from Company Handbook

Page: 4.1
Date: 03/03/XX

Voice Mail Procedures
The use of voice mail has become widely-accepted. The technology of voice mail helps us all manage our jobs efficiently. However Alternatives Inc. does want to sacrifice courtesy in its efforts to work as efficient as possible. It is Company Policy to return calls promptly, to provide callers the option of speaking to a "live body" and to ensure ready access to an operator, a customer service representative, or a secretary. To ensure that this will happen, the following guidelines are to be strictly observed:

1. Each Department will designate one full-time clerical employee as "telephone clerk." Employees are to program their telephones to go to the telephone clerk's extension *immediately* if the line is busy or *after the second unanswered ring.*

2. The telephone clerk will screen all calls and will route them into department members' voice mailboxes at callers' requests.

3. All employees *not* designated "telephone clerks" are to begin their voice-mail messages with this statement; "Hello. My name is _____. I (am/am not) in the office today."

4. Next of all:

    a. If you are out of the office, state the date you will return. If you are not on vacation, state that you will check your messages each day. *Follow through by checking your messages, returning your calls and referring any inquiries to the appropriate person.*

    b. If you are in the office, state the following: "I'm not able to take your call right now, but I will call you back as soon as possible. Please leave a message at the tone, or press 0 for an operator."

5. Being closed between 5:00 p.m. and 8:00 a.m., all telephones must be programmed to switch to the message for before-and- after-hours calls. For programmable instructions, see page 5.2.

6. Always keep in mind that, as an Employee of this company, the telephone customer's first impression is up to you.

DOCUMENT 2: Recorded Message

Whoa! You've called Neo-Bar—where "alcohol-free" doesn't mean "country" or "mainstream pop-rock." Featuring local talent only, this is the week all you "Neo-ites" have been anxiously-awaiting: Neo-Bar's fourth annual "Hangin' on the Edge" extravaganza! Tuesday through Friday we'll feature four hot, alternate, groups. Then hold on to your high tops for Saturday Night's "Battle of the Bands"!

Here's the full scoop: Tuesday, rap and romp to K.C.'s own 90-Second Minute, featuring three never-before-performed cuts from the group's upcoming album, "Fast Forward." On Wednesday, welcome back CityCyncoRama, fresh from the "Twelve Cities, Twelve Steps" tour. Thursday features the girl group Blue to Black and Back. Then, about ready to take their gig to the International stage, Friday, stomp to Heavy Boots! Saturday, it's "Hangin' on the Edge," where all four bands will be revved and ready to rock and roll in the fourth annual battle of the bands. Coming early, folks, this one always sells out!

On Sunday, join us for "Change of Pace." This week mellow out with comedienne Jeannie Jones, who'll be trying out material for her new show.

Neo-Bar is open weekly, six nights a week: Tuesday through Saturday from 8:00 p.m. to 1:00 a.m., Sundays 5:00 p.m. to midnight. There's a $5.00, cover charge.

DOCUMENT 3: Telephone Fund-Raising Script

Hello, is this _____? My name is _____ and I'm calling on behalf of Alternatives Inc. Alternatives Inc. works with Central High School's Drug Prevention staff to plan, and host, monthly "Clean Night Out" parties. These parties are held one Saturday night a month during the school year. They provide enjoyably safe evenings for students in grades nine through twelve that are free of charge. Each "Clean Night Out" features popular music (with no pro-drug messages), movies, video games, sports activities and refreshments.

As concerned adults, the use of alcohol and other drugs by teenagers in our community is something we all want to eliminate. Alternatives Inc. has established a nonprofit division, CNO, to raise money for "Clean Night Out," and to work with the school and community in planning and hosting this event.

We ask that you consider supporting "Clean Night Out" with a donation of: money, food, or time. What more better use could you make of your time and resources? Would you be willing to help? Your donation, which is tax-deductible, will go even farther if you save us the cost of mail and paperwork by charging it on a major credit card.

UNIT III
COMMUNICATE FOR RESULTS

1 Select a company (real or fictional) and a job you would like to hold at that firm in the future. What do you think are the firm's priorities in hiring someone for that job? What are your priorities in wanting that position? Decide which of your characteristics and capabilities you would mention in an interview for that job, and explain why you would do so.

2 Your school is considering an internship program for students. Clearly, internships provide students with valuable guided work experience. On the other hand, internships can be costly for schools to establish and maintain. Consider these and other pros and cons, and prepare for a discussion you might have with the school committee that will recommend or not recommend the program.

3 You are making a presentation to a stubborn city council to attempt to persuade them to provide free downtown parking. What factors might you include in your talk? Which are most important? Prioritize them in order of their importance. Would you present them in that order, or would another order be more effective? Why?

4 Using all you have learned about preparing and making a persuasive presentation, plan how you would ask for a raise. If you have a job, use your real work situation as the framework for your request. Then role play asking for the raise; have one classmate take the role of the boss and a second observe and rate your presentation using the Speaking Checklist on page 172.

SPEAKING CHECKLIST
Use the following checklist to evaluate your or a classmate's speaking skills.
As you work on speaking activities, try to do them all as appropriate.

You prepare thoroughly for formal speaking situations by doing the following:

_____a.   Knowing your purpose

_____b.   Knowing your audience

_____c.   Knowing the message you want to communicate

_____d.   Organizing information according to your selected approach

_____e.   Outlining and/or writing out presentations

_____f.   Checking your facts

_____g.   Thinking carefully about humor

_____h.   Preparing appropriate visual aids and handouts

_____I.   Practicing

You work to polish your presentation skills by doing the following:

_____a.   Adjusting your volume as needed

_____b.   Adjusting your speaking rate as needed

_____c.   Pronouncing words correctly and clearly

_____d.   Providing appropriate emphasis in your speech

_____e.   Controlling your body language

_____f.   Troubleshooting before formal presentations

You prepare thoroughly for informal speaking situations by doing the following:

_____a.   Knowing your purpose

_____b.   Knowing your audience

_____c.   Knowing the message you want to communicate

_____d.   Organizing your material and information as your purpose and situation demand

_____e.   Practicing as needed

UNIT IV

Reading skills—your ability to get meaning from written symbols and evaluate their accuracy and validity—are applied every day in most careers. You will have to read various documents related to employment, benefits, and financial and legal matters. Your company's policies and procedures, which you must follow, will be available to you only in writing. In addition, you will transact much of your business through letters, memos, reports, and forms. Finally, reading is a major mode through which you can continue learning, making you even more valuable to your company.

Have you ever read something and found yourself halfway down the page, wondering how you got there and what you missed along the way? You probably were not attending to the material; your eyes moved across the text but your mind did not *actively* process the words, phrases, and sentences. So you see, reading is more than a passive activity; it requires the reader to be involved and *to do something in response to the written material.* You *can* learn how to get the most from what you read.

▼ **When you finish Unit IV, you will be able to**

- Evaluate what you read based on the writer, the writer's purpose, and the message

- Consider ways in which you can improve your reading behaviors and skills

- Adjust your reading approach including skimming, scanning, and reading for detail depending on your purpose for reading

READING

FOR

RESULTS

READING
ACTIVELY

CHAPTER SEVEN

How can you use what you already know to read more effectively?

What benefits can you derive from evaluating messages as you read them?

What is the difference between skimming, scanning, and reading for detail? When is it best to use each of these approaches?

What can you do to improve your reading habits?

The business world produces more paper today than ever before. Letters, memos, reports, manuals, policy statements, brochures, pamphlets, fliers, reference guides, order forms, shipping labels—these are just a few of the documents that flow into and out of today's offices and plants in a steady stream. You will find many of them in your mailbox. Some will be unimportant, many will be important, and a few will be critical to your success.

How well do you read? Do you apply **active reading** techniques? Are you able to handle a large volume of daily reading? Do you know how to "read between the lines"? Your answers to these questions will reflect how prepared you are for today's workplace.

You know effective listening is an active process. Reading, too, is a complex task, and good reading must be done actively. To read actively, you must:

- Consider the writer's purpose for writing

- Anticipate what the material will say

- Relate what you read to your prior knowledge

- Evaluate reading material as you read and after you read to ensure understanding and to form judgments

- Use one or more of the three reading approaches: skimming, scanning, and reading for detail

CONSIDERING THE WRITER'S PURPOSE

Sometimes you can determine the writer's purpose before you start reading. You might know what to expect as soon as you see the name of the writer: "An envelope from Horizon Industries—must be Jack DeLorenzo's reply to my request for costs."

Seeing the Horizon Industries return address on an envelope, for example, suggests to you that the letter contains the estimate you are waiting for from Jack DeLorenzo. In other cases, you may read only a few words to identify the writer's purpose—the subject line of a memo, the title of a report, the return address or first sentence of a letter:

- The envelope says "Automobile Club of America." Two weeks ago, you requested information about membership benefits and dues; therefore, you can predict what this envelope contains.

- The interoffice envelope from headquarters is addressed to you, and it is from Marion Wilson, the person managing the United Way campaign. You collected for United Way in your department last year. What do you think this envelope contains?

- A memo is clipped to a small booklet. The subject line reads "Training Courses for Fall." Before you even look at the booklet, you know it is a catalog from Human Resources listing all the upcoming training programs.

- The letter before you is from Glendale Mail Services. You've never heard of that company. But the handwritten note scribbled on the letter is from your manager: "This is the firm I was telling you about—the one that handled the mailing for Ted Hampton." You remember the conversation with your manager and Ted. That is your purpose for reading the letter.

How can you identify the writer's purpose before reading much, if any, of the document? Your prior knowledge of the writer and of the specific situation allows you to make sense of whatever written document is before you. You can ask yourself:

- Who is the writer?

- What is the writer's purpose?

- Does the writer have a known bias? If so, what is it?

- How might **bias** appear in the writing?

◀ FIGURE 7.1

Many advertisements will caim unbelievalbe things in order to persuade people to buy a product.

Of course, you almost automatically ask such questions when you read a sales letter, an advertisement, or a marketing brochure. Whenever the writer has a financial motive, you must look for bias. In other situations, a bias may be less obvious.

C A S E   S C E N A R I O

Consider the Source

Mark Brandenauer was a new marketing manager for a magazine publishing company. A coworker sent him a newspaper clipping with a few words highlighted in yellow:

> The current status of the pulp industry, affected by developments in the environmental protection area and the scarcity of natural resources worlwide, leads to the conclusion that paper prices must rise up to 32 percent next year alone.

Mark's company purchases millions of dollars' worth of paper each year. The projected increase would be a financial disaster for the magazine. Somewhat frantic, Mark rushed to see Elena Mateo, Director of Purchasing. "Elena!" he exclaimed, waving the article in his hand. "Do you know about this 32-percent increase in paper prices? This is really bad!"

Looking worried, Elena reached for the clipping. "Where did you read this?" she asked. "Who's the source?" Quickly, she scanned the article. Her face relaxed. "Ah, look at this, Mark. The source is a spokesperson for the Federal Lumber Association. I'm not ready to get too worried yet."

"You're not?" Mark was puzzled. Elena explained: "When environmental protection groups talk about stopping a logging operation, the lumber companies and paper manufacturers have to react. They often consider a worst-case scenario. And it often gets presented in the scariest terms possible."

What bias did Elena identify? Do you think she was right not to be very worried? Why or why not? How do you think Mark and Elena should proceed from here?

Biases may be purposeful or accidental, conscious or unconscious. The more you know about the writer, the better you will be able to determine bias and assess intent:

- Harry Track submits his estimate for computer maintenance and repairs. He missed last month's meeting, at which it was announced that maintenance costs would decrease by 12 percent this year. Did he ever get that information? Maybe not. You wonder: Does his figure account for this 12 percent decrease?

- The entire marketing department evaluated a report you wrote to submit to the board of directors. Some of your colleagues' evaluations were fairly negative, suggesting significant revisions. One evaluation was extremely positive. It came from a long-time coworker who is also your best friend. Is there some reason your friend might not have been completely honest?

- Megan Silberman's request to attend a computer conference is very convincing. Most of her memo is devoted to the advantages to the company if she gets approval to attend. However, Megan does not say that the conference is in Hawaii, that it will cost twice as much as most conferences, and that the same computer companies will exhibit at a second conference one month later in a nearby city.

As with listening, it helps to have a touch of skepticism as you interpret a message.

ANTICIPATING WHAT YOU WILL READ

Anticipating what you are about to read helps in more than one way. It helps you focus and expect certain information. If your expectations are correct, you have a head start on comprehending the written material. If your expectations are incorrect, they help you identify your error quickly and adjust to the new material.

- Donna Alvarez is out of breath as she walks back to her office from her mailbox. The letter from headquarters finally arrived. She applied three weeks ago for promotion to Senior Account Executive. Everyone she knows in the company, including her supervisor, is sure she will get the promotion. She herself is certain. When she opens the letter and begins reading, she is not surprised:

    Congratulations, Ms. Alvarez. I am happy to inform you that you have been promoted . . .

  But what she reads next surprises her so much that she reads it twice and wonders if it's a mistake:

    . . . to Assistant Senior Account Executive.

- Brian Hanson came back from Los Angeles quite disheartened. He and Mr. Sween, his supervisor, had hoped the trip would lead to a sale nearing one million dollars. Brian wrote a note to Mr. Sween on Monday morning with the bad news: The Los Angeles firm had bought only $250,000 worth of goods. On Tuesday, Brian notices something in his mailbox a note from Mr. Sween. He knows his supervisor's reactions will be negative, so he decides to wait until after lunch to read it. After lunch, Brian takes a deep breath and unfolds the note:

> *From the desk of Al Sween*
>
> *Congratulations on your sale, Brian. I know we were hoping for more, but that's before I knew our biggest competitor was also meeting with the Los Angeles group. You did well to sell what you did. Keep it up.*
>
> *Al*

Similarly, anticipating what you are about to read helps you to define *your* purpose for reading. Reading with a purpose is important; it allows you to read more efficiently. For example:

- When you open a sales letter or a marketing flier, you prepare to read with a skeptical eye, to question whatever you read. You know the writer is trying to sell you something.

- When you receive a letter from your best customer, you assume before you begin that it is a request and you begin reading, ready to consider how you will respond.

- When you receive your new fax machine and open the box, you take out the papers and sort through them, ready to read and follow the instructions for installation.

But knowing the *writer's* purpose does not always help you determine *your* purpose for reading. You often read directions to follow them, of course, and you often read requests to decide how you must respond. However, you are just as likely to read a persuasive marketing brochure merely to find a piece of information, if that is what the situation requires. Or you may read a specific customer request to learn how you can make general improvements in your customer service department. In short, the writer's purpose for writing does not necessarily determine your purpose for reading.

◀ FIGURE 7.2

In the computerized world of business communications, it is often necessary to read instructions.

USE YOUR JUDGMENT 1

Select an article from the front page of your local newspaper. Consider the writer and the sources of information (people quoted or paraphrased in the article). What are these people's connection to the article's subject? What are their motives related to this subject? Do their responses and comments on the subject correspond with their motives? Explain the connection.

USE YOUR JUDGMENT 2

Select another document—a newspaper article, letter, or textbook section—and do the following:

a. Read the heading information (titles, headings, etc.) and predict from that information what the document will be about and what, more specifically, the document will say. Write down your predictions, and explain why you predict as you do.

b. Now read the first few sentences and make the same predictions in writing, explaining why you predict as you do.

c. Finally, read the entire document and evaluate your predictions. How close were you to being right? If you were very close, what information most helped you predict accurately? If you were incorrect, what information mislead your predictions?

USING PRIOR KNOWLEDGE TO HELP YOU UNDERSTAND

When you walk in at the end of a movie, you do not know the characters or understand the plot. As a result, understanding who is doing what to whom, and why they are doing it, is difficult. When you read a business document, however, you often have prior knowledge of the situation. This prior knowledge allows you to make sense of the new information: "What's this all about? Gourmet Events? Oh, that's right, that's the company who'll be catering our stockholder luncheon."

When you receive a piece of reading, and as you read it, try to draw this knowledge to consciousness by using **self-talk,** asking questions such as:

- "What do I already know about the writer?"

- "What do I already know about the situation?"

- "What do I already know about this subject in general?"

- "Did I request this information?"

- "Have I said or done something recently that prompted this information?"

- "Am I receiving this information because it relates to my job? How does it relate?"

- "How can I use this information?"

This recall of prior knowledge to aid your reading works at all levels of your thinking process, from the situation level down to the word level. At the **situation level,** you must attach new knowledge of the situation to prior knowledge of the situation and, if necessary, act accordingly.

C A S E   S C E N A R I O

What's the Rush?

Dorine Sykes entered her associate Raul Santino's office after opening the morning's mail. "Raul," she said, "here's an order from Mr. Watts. It looks urgent."

Raul knew almost immediately how he would respond to the letter. Skimming it, he remarked, "I can take care of this tomorrow."

"But Mr. Watts wants this done immediately. Yesterday you got a standard order from Julie Peterson and you rushed it through. Today you get a rush order from Barry Watts and you don't even react. I don't get it."

"I've worked with both Barry and Julie before," explained Raul. "When Julie says she needs something by a certain date, she's not kidding. But Barry writes "rush" on every order and tells us he needs it at least a week before he really does."

How did Raul use prior knowledge in deciding how to handle this matter? In the future, should Dorine automatically assume that any rush order from Mr. Watts needn't be handled immediately? Explain your answer.

A similar use of prior knowledge in reading takes place at the **word level** or **concept level.** We derive meaning from single words or from groups of words by recalling usage in other contexts.

C A S E   S C E N A R I O

User-Friendly

Ramona Avery had little experience using computers when she started her first job. When her supervisor showed her her work station, Ramona realized she would learn in a hurry. She began browsing through her software and hardware manuals and read this sentence: "You will find this word processing software very user-friendly."

"'User-friendly'?" she thought to herself. "I've heard that term before, but I'm not sure what it means." Ramona silently analyzed the word: "How can a computer program be 'friendly'? And to whom? The user? Hmm, friendly to the user. That must mean it's easy to use. Well, I'll soon find out!"

Did Ramona's prior knowledge have anything to do with computers? Why was it still helpful to her?

Like Ramona, good readers use prior knowledge every time they read something. Some do it subconsciously, automatically; others must do it more consciously until it becomes a habit. You will never learn *all* the words and concepts you need to know to be a good reader; thus, having the skill of applying prior knowledge to new words and concepts is important to your success as a reader.

EVALUATING WHAT YOU READ

Once you have assigned meaning to what you read, you must evaluate it. This evaluation must take place both as you read and after you read. The need to evaluate after you read should come as no surprise. Your common sense tells you this must be done in many cases. To evaluate something *as you read* is not as "natural," yet it is central to active reading and total comprehension.

Using Self-Talk to Evaluate As You Read

As you read, talk silently to yourself:

- "Am I understanding what the writer says?"

- "Where am I confused by the message? Why?"

- "The writer talks about topic X here. I'll bet he talks about topic Y next."

- "I wonder why the writer used the word *peddle* instead of *sell*. Is he suggesting something negative about sales?"

- "I'll bet all this is leading to the conclusion that the company has no choice but to cut staff."

- "I don't agree with this point. I'll have to remember that in case it's important later."

- "Oh, here are the four steps I need to follow to complete this report. I'd better highlight all four."

- "So what is being said here? What's the point?"

- "What are the 'three key items' she mentions here?"

C A S E   S C E N A R I O

Short Notice

On Friday, Clark asked to use vacation time to take the following Friday off. On Monday he found a short memo in his mailbox. As he read the memo, Clark talked silently to himself:

SUBJECT: VACATION TIME RECENTLY REQUESTED

As you know, Clark, December is a very busy time for us. The sales staff is rushing to meet quotas. The accounting staff is trying to get yearly records in shape. And we're all preparing for January's annual meeting. Also, the holidays are right around the corner. Therefore, although I can approve the vacation day you requested for Friday, December 17, I must ask that you try to give us at least three weeks' notice in the future.

"Oh, great if they had approved the vacation, I wouldn't be getting a memo. I must not get the day off."

"Just what I thought. This is how all bad news messages start by justifying the bad news."

"Quotas are too high. They raise them every year."

"Is it in Palm Springs this year?"

"But I can't wait until then. I need the day now."

"Oh, thank you what a relief!"

"Yes, okay! In fact, I think I remember something about three weeks' notice at a meeting a few months ago."

How did Clark react to the subject of the memo? As he read, what early conclusions did he draw? How was it valid to assume he would not be granted vacation time? Why was it important that he evaluate both as he read and after he read?

This interaction with the written word is one of the most important behaviors of an active reader, but an active reader will also evaluate after reading by asking questions such as:

- "Do the writer's facts support what I have heard, read, and seen?"

- "Do the writer's facts support the writer's conclusions?"

- "Do I accept what the writer is saying?"

Although you must evaluate each reading situation based on your own needs, you may find general evaluation systems useful in many instances. Two simple methods for evaluating your reading are to **consider all factors** and to use the **information in/information out** system.

Considering All Factors

The goal of this system is to help you systematically focus on all factors related to what you are reading. To consider all factors, simply do the following:

1. Listen to your self-talk as you read the material, and write down any questions or comments you have.

2. Use your prior knowledge and new knowledge of the situation, and list any information the writer did not include or discuss.

3. Gather all the remaining information.

C A S E   S C E N A R I O

A Co-op Considered

Denise Triston was a product manager in the Marketing Department of a sports equipment company. Today she received this memo from the company's National Sales Manager:

MEMORANDUM

DATE: May 3, 19XX

TO: Denise Triston

FROM: Margie Gooden

SUBJECT: CO-OP ADVERTISING FOR SMALL STORES

Bart Jennings, our sales representative in Orlando, recently recommended that we consider developing a cooperative advertising program on a local level. Bart is convinced that many small stores would increase their local newspaper advertising if they could share the expense with a manufacturer like us. They have always resented the attention we give to the major chains.

I've discussed this with my four regional managers, and they also believe this idea is worth pursuing. After all, our national co-op ads with major store chains are very successful, so maybe we should give this some serious thought. Perhaps we're missing a good opportunity. What do you think?

Denise wanted to consider all factors. Here is part of the list she made:

- What is the estimated cost of this co-op advertising?

- Should we explore it for all our products or for just one product line? If just one, which?

- How many stores would participate?

- What have we learned from our national co-op advertising that will help us evaluate this local program?

What did Denise do to systematically evaluate all factors? What kinds of questions did she ask? What else might she have asked?

Information In/Information Out

Another useful evaluation system encourages you to focus on what information is missing. The information provided in your reading is the *information in*—information that is included. The information not included is *information out*. Considering all factors, this system helps ensure that you do not overlook **relevant** data as you evaluate. To use this system, simply do the following:

- As you read the document, list all the information that is relevant to the decision you must make.

- Also, as you read the document, listen to your self-talk and list questions and comments you have.

- Based on the list you developed in point 2 and on your prior knowledge of the situation, list any additional information that should be provided in the document but is not. Items on this list will probably appear as questions.

- Seek answers to any questions that remain.

relevant

significant; related to the topic of interest, having significant bearing on the matter at hand

Calendar Info

Paul Eisner received the following memo from his assistant, Sheila LaBlatt.

MEMORANDUM

DATE: July 10, 19XX

TO: Paul Eisner

FROM: Sheila LaBlatt

SUBJECT: DayCal CALENDARING PROGRAM

Paul, here are the instructions I'm going to send our salespeople along with DayCal, the computer calendaring program they asked for at our recent sales convention. Of course, we have written permission from DayCal to copy and distribute this program to all our sales reps.

First, create a DayCal directory on your hard drive.

Second, copy all the DayCal files on the enclosed minidisk to your DayCal directory.

Third, once DayCal is installed, you can access the program by:

1. Keying CD\DayCal (to get into the DayCal directory)

2. Keying DT (to run the program)

That's all there is to it! Once the program is installed, refer to the *DayCal Users' Manual* for any questions you may have.

As soon as you approve this copy, Paul, I'll start shipping the minidisks and manuals to our 56 sales representatives.

Paul decided to use the information in/information out evaluation system. He started his list as follows:

Information in:

- *We have permission from DayCal to duplicate disks.*

- *Program is available on minidisk.*

- *Sales reps have requested this calendaring program.*

Information out:

- *What about those salespeople who don't have a hard drive on their computers?*

- *Will all reps know what a "directory" is and how to create one? Some are computer novices.*

- *Is the program available in both Mac and PC? Not all our salespeople have the same computer system.*

- *Are we providing copies of the DayCal Users' Manual for each person? The memo doesn't say.*

- *What if they encounter some problems? Whom do they call?*

What did Paul do to systematically evaluate all factors? What else might he have asked about the "information out"? How might his list help Sheila revise the copy to the sales reps?

3 USE YOUR JUDGMENT

Ask a friend or family member to write you a letter of at least one page. Read the letter and number each place in it where you use prior knowledge—of the writer, the subject the writer discusses, or the words the writer uses—to help you understand the letter thoroughly. For each number you put on the letter, provide a short explanation of the prior knowledge you used and how it helped you.

4 USE YOUR JUDGMENT

Select a news article or another short document. Read the document, and *as you read*, write down any silent self-talk that comes into your mind. Do this by placing a number in the text and quickly writing your comments or questions on a piece of paper. Be sure to stop and write any questions or comments that come to you before you read further.

Before you start, recognize that you may do this silent talking so automatically that you do not even know you are doing it. Try to make yourself aware of it. If you find that you *do not* talk silently in response to the material you read, try to react to the material by asking questions or making comments throughout your reading.

5 USE YOUR JUDGMENT

Evaluate the following situation either by considering all factors or by using the information in/information out system. Write a memo to Andy with your response.

You agree with your coworker, Andy Benson, that he must hire someone to handle the desktop publishing on a special project estimated to take six months. Andy has an office and a laser printer for his new employee, but he needs a computer. You and Andy agree that he could either lease or buy one, depending on costs. Read the memo Andy sends (page 193).

MEMORANDUM

DATE: June 4, 19XX

TO: (Your Name)

FROM: Andrew Benson

SUBJECT: COMPUTER LEASE FOR DESKTOP PUBLISHING

As you know, Scott Thomas, our new employee, will report to work on the first of next month. We have an office and a laser printer for him. All that remains is renting a computer.

I've checked with the three computer dealers we work with. Lance Business Systems had the lowest price for the computer we need: $180 per month. (The other two bids were $185 and $189.) With your permission, I'll order the computer from Lance for delivery next week.

Let me know if you have any questions or concerns.

USING DIFFERENT READING APPROACHES

There are three general approaches to reading—skimming, scanning, and detailed reading—which good readers select, and sometimes combine, based on their reading purpose. You can learn to use them to become a more efficient reader.

Skimming

Skimming means glancing quickly through a document, noticing key words and phrases. The goal of skimming is often to determine the main ideas or main content. By skimming a document and combining that new information with prior knowledge of the writer and subject, good readers can usually develop a sense of a document's general content.

Skimming is especially useful in the following situations:

- When you read for general information

- When you read simple responses and requests

- When you want to know the general coverage or content of a document

- When you want to preview a document you must read in greater detail

- When you want to locate a specific section of a long document that does not provide specific headings or other organizers

FIGURE 7.3 ▶

The goal of skimming is to determine the main ideas or main content.

Even though it seems that you must "do" a lot when skimming, it is actually a fast process. You will be able to check for most of the items in the list simultaneously. With practice, you will be able to skim most short documents (one- or two-page memos and letters) very quickly. Longer materials, such as books, manuals, or long reports, require slightly more time to skim through, of course. Figure 7.3 highlights what a reader might read when skimming.

Checklist for Skimming Memos and Letters

- For memos, look first at the DATE, TO, FROM, and SUBJECT lines. The subject line should tell you the purpose of the message. For letters, check the letterhead to see whether you know the company. Check the signature block to see whether you know the writer. Read the first sentence or two; usually they are enough to tell you what a letter is about.

- Check whether anyone received a copy of the memo or letter.

- Check for enclosures.

- Skim the body of the document.

- Glance down the page, looking for words that are <u>underlined</u>, *italicized*, **boldfaced**, or CAPITALIZED.

- Look for numbered, lettered, or bulleted lists and determine their purpose.

Checklist for Reading Books and Reports

- Read the title.

- Skim section titles and headings in the table of contents. Note elements such as glossary, bibliography, appendix, and index.

- Flip through pages, spending no more than 10–15 seconds on each page.

- As you turn pages, read the headings, look at the graphs and charts, and be on the alert for any words that are <u>underlined</u>, *italicized*, **boldfaced**, or CAPITALIZED.

Scanning

Scanning means glancing quickly through a document to find something specific. The goal of scanning is often to find a specific word, number, phrase, or sentence. Unlike skimming, which readers often do because they are not sure what is in a document, scanning is something readers do when they know information is in the document and their goal is to find it. Figure 7.4 highlights what a reader might read when scanning.

Scanning is used in many, many reading situations. You scan when you want to find:

- A phone number in a telephone book

- A word in a dictionary, index, or other list

- An order number (or any other specific piece of information) on an order form

- A conference hotel's address in a memo you received and read previously

- A new client's business title in the return address of a letter

- A number within a table of data

- A memorable quotation you once read in the transcript of a speech

While skimming means looking quickly at text to get a feel for a document's contents, scanning is more specific. You can scan by doing the following:

1. Identify as specifically as possible the information you must find (for example, a word in a dictionary or a phone number in a memo).

2. Determine clues or characteristics of that information that will help you locate it within the document you are scanning. For example, say you need to find a definition of the word *probate*. You know this word begins with a *pr*, so you go to the *pr* section of the dictionary and scan for *probate*. Similarly, if you are scanning for a phone number in a memo, you probably search for numbers (as opposed to words).

3. When you find something with characteristics for which you are looking (for example, a number), analyze it quickly to see if it is what you need. For example, is it a *phone* number? If it is not, continue scanning.

4. When you find something that matches the characteristics for which you are scanning (for example, a phone number), you may have to quickly read around it to determine if it is the one you need. For example, is this the phone number needed, or is it someone else's phone number?

Like the description of skimming, this description of scanning is misleading because of its length. Scanning often happens very quickly.

Reading for Detail

Reading for detail is what people often think of when they hear the word *reading*. Reading has been defined in various ways, but generally it means "taking meaning

▲FIGURE 7.4

The goal of scanning is to find a specific word, number, phrase, or sentence.

from written symbols, usually words." If this is true, then reading for detail means reading with attention to the details as well as the main ideas. Generally, reading for details means reading all words or phrases to consider their meaning and the ways in which they combine with other elements—words, phrases, sentences, graphics—to make up the document's main ideas and total meaning.

Reading for detail is necessary in many situations, such as when you must read:

- A textbook chapter to learn the concepts it teaches

- A proposal to help determine whether your company will accept or reject it

- A budget report to recommend to your supervisor how your department could cut its budget for next year

- Political position statements to determine which policies will more effectively cut taxes in your district without cutting important services

- A company's annual report to decide whether you should accept a job offer from the company

The process of reading for detail is not completely describable, for two reasons. First, it is an extremely complex interaction between the words on the page and the way those words are manipulated and processed by the reader. This **reader processing** involves many factors, including:

- The reader's prior knowledge of words and other language symbols, such as spacing and punctuation

◀ FIGURE 7.5

The process of reading for detail differs with each reader.

- The reader's interpretation of aspects of the document, such as the writer's tone, personality, and truthfulness

- The reader's prior knowledge of the situation and all that prior knowledge suggests, including related emotions and biases

- The reader's general prior knowledge—that is, the general experiences the reader brings to the document

As Figure 7.5 shows, the second reason the process of reading for detail is difficult to describe is that it probably differs with each reader. Also, it probably differs for all readers depending on the document or type of document they read. Generally, however, the process of reading for detail can be summarized as follows. Notice how it incorporates elements of active reading introduced earlier in the chapter:

1. Once documents are received, readers may anticipate document content based on their prior knowledge.

2. If readers do not possess enough prior knowledge of documents to determine a reading purpose, they may skim documents to help determine a reading purpose.

3. Assuming the reading purpose warrants it, readers will (now or later) begin reading for detail by reading word by word or, better, phrase by phrase, connecting concepts to form larger concepts.

    - While reading, readers talk silently to themselves, questioning and commenting on the writer's statements and generally checking their understanding and comprehension of the document. If readers have difficulty comprehending, they reread until they understand, or they read ahead to see if later text helps clarify earlier text.

    - If readers get stuck on words or concepts while reading, they either use their prior knowledge to work through the problem areas or they seek outside help, such as a reference book or a coworker.

4. When readers finish their detailed reading of a document, they evaluate what they have read, considering the purpose for which they read and the situation in which they read. They draw conclusions about the reading based on this purpose and situation.

Notice that reading for detail often uses the other two approaches, especially skimming, to accomplish its goals. Good readers allow the specific situation to determine the level of detail at which they will read and the general approach they will use. If the best approach is a combination of skimming, scanning, and reading for detail, good readers will combine these approaches.

USE YOUR JUDGMENT **6**

Select a textbook or other nonfiction book with fairly short sections (about 150 words per section). Choose a section at random, and do the following:

a. Skim the section until you can write one sentence that states its general subject and main idea. Note how long this takes you.
b. After you write down the main idea, write down the things you saw in the document (words, phrases, etc.) that were most helpful to you.
c. Repeat this activity with three or four more sections.

USE YOUR JUDGMENT **7**

Select a newspaper or magazine article or some other two- or three-page piece of writing, and do the following:

a. Imagine you have to scan the material for the following five items: numbers, proper names, quotations, questions, the word *you*. What characteristic of each item will you look for to help you locate it? (*Hint:* The characteristic should be something you can spot quickly that also distinguishes the item from other text as much as possible.)
b. Scan for each of the items (one at a time) and write down the number you find.
c. Consider whether you used characteristics of these items other than those you listed (in point a.) to find the items. If so, write down those other characteristics as well.

IMPROVING YOUR READING HABITS

Your reading skills and habits, good or bad, were probably set years ago. If your skills are good, you should have no problem applying them on the job and will only get better by applying some of the strategies in this chapter and the next. If your reading skills are weak, you can strengthen them by practicing. Read as much as you can and challenge yourself to apply the principles of active reading as they are incorporated in the suggestions for business reading that follow. If you strive to read actively, the more reading you do, the better you will get at it.

Prioritize Your Reading

Spend a few minutes each day skimming the documents you have to read. Skim each one only enough to decide whether you must read it immediately, whether you can wait and read it later, or whether you need to read it at all. Separate that material into three groups:

• Read Now

• Read Later

• File or Throw Out

Read Now

The material in this group should be read as soon as possible. This should include material addressed to you by name (other than obvious mass mailings from sales organizations). It should also include material you recognize as important to your job duties and current priorities. For example, if you are the assistant manager on the Wilcox account and you receive a memo on the Wilcox account from your supervisor, you should read that memo right away.

Read Later

The material in this group should be material you have to read but which you do not have to read today. This may be a schedule of next week's meetings, information about new policies effective the first of next month, or information about the company picnic.

File or Throw Out

This is information you do not need now or will never need. Information on completing the new expense account form may not be useful to you right now, but it might be someday. File it appropriately. Information on a bridge group that plans to meet after work in the company cafeteria may never be useful to you. If this is the case, throw it away.

Prioritizing your reading will ensure that you have all the time you need for reading important documents and that you do not waste your time reading unimportant documents.

Mark Your Reading Materials

Do not approach your business reading empty-handed. Always read with a pencil, a color highlighter, self-stick notes, or any other tools that help you focus on and mark key information. Unless there are specific reasons for not marking the document, do the following:

- Write notes, questions, or comments in the margins

- Highlight or underline important text

- Attach paper clips or self-stick notes to important pages

- Use stick-on tabs to mark manual pages you will use repeatedly

What you write, highlight, underline, clip, note, and tab depends, of course, on the reading situation and your purpose for reading. It also depends on your very individual evaluation of what is and is not important. In any case, this process helps you focus on and remember what you read, and the marks themselves will help when you must refer to those materials in the future.

▲FIGURE 7.6

It is important to prioitize your reading.

prioritize

to list or rate in order of priority; to rank beginning with what is most important

Read Phrases, Not Words

Practice reading groups of words rather than individual words. Reading word by word is slow, reduces your concentration, and reduces your ability to connect concepts to form meaning. Read the following sentence one word a time:

> One of the companies that submitted a bid for this project is Dean & Brown Contracting.

Now read the same sentence in meaningful phrases:

> One of the companies / that submitted a bid /
> for this project / is Dean & Brown Contracting.

Many words—for example, *of*, *he*, *that*, *for*, *is*—have significant meaning only when combined with other words. Also, some words, though they have meaning on their own, acquire new meaning when attached to other words. In short, words combine to make meaning, so read sentences in meaningful phrases.

If you find that you do not already read this way, this technique requires particular concentration and steady practice. A change in reading behavior like this results from effort and experience.

Build Your Vocabulary

To build your vocabulary, make a point of looking up words you do not understand when you come across them. If it is inconvenient to check a dictionary, write down unknown words and look them up later. Work especially hard at understanding words and terms that are commonly used in your industry or business. You might consider buying an inexpensive paperback vocabulary-building book. Many are on the market. As illustrated in Figure 7.7, many computerized dictionaries are avail-

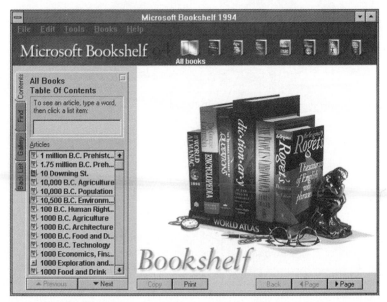

◀ **FIGURE 7.7**

Computerized dictionaries are available in software programs and on-line in many networks. They are also included in most word processing programs.

able as well. In addition, be aware that the best way to improve your vocabulary and your reading in general is to read a great deal.

A large vocabulary not only makes your reading easier and your writing more exact, it also makes you a better thinker. Because we think in concepts, the more concepts you know, the better you will be able to think.

Control Reading Conditions

Do you read in a noisy area or at a poorly lit desk? If so, try to find a quieter place or seek out better lighting. Are you interrupted often as you read? If your answer is yes, consider what you can do to reduce or eliminate these interruptions. If you don't have a quiet office, perhaps you can do your reading in an unused conference room or in a colleague's office, anywhere in which you find it easier to concentrate. Perhaps you'll find it necessary to arrive at work early so you can address the day's reading before the phone begins to ring.

Be Ready To Read

downtime

time during which work is stopped, often due to unanticipated waiting periods, scheduling problems, or mechanical breakdowns

Keep your workplace reading in a folder, and have the folder with you whenever you anticipate *downtime*—that is, whenever you expect to be without something to do. As busy as they are, many business people seem to waste time waiting: on subways, in cabs, at the airport, in traffic, in waiting rooms. You will be surprised how much work you can get done if you use this time for extra reading.

FIGURE 7.8 ▶

You can catch up on reading in almost any waiting situation.

Wilson believes in taking full advantage of his mixed-doubles partner's dominance at the net.

Enroll in a Course

Take a speed-reading, reading-comprehension, or time-management class. Many companies provide free training for their employees. Also, many local colleges and universities offer classes or minicourses in these areas. While "speed-reading" claims tend to be highly exaggerated (you can't really read a whole novel in two minutes!), you can learn techniques to increase your reading rate without losing comprehension.

Review Your Reading Habits

By reviewing your reading habits, you can look for those areas where your skills are weakest and then work to improve those particular areas. Here's how you can assess how effectively you read:

- Time yourself. How long does it take you to read and understand a letter or memo? Can you improve on that time without sacrificing comprehension?

- Pay attention to how often you interrupt yourself before you finish one letter or memo or article.

- Pay attention to your use (or nonuse) of silent talk.

- Consider whether you use different reading approaches for different kinds of reading.

- Consider whether you allow your reading purpose to help determine your approach.

- Try to recognize whether you read word-by-word or in phrases.

- Count the number of times you read a page and find, when you finish, that you do not really know what you have read.

If you notice a weakness in one or more areas, use the information in this book to improve your reading habits.

USE YOUR JUDGMENT 8

Review your reading habits as just discussed. Select one area in which you could use improvement and work on improving that skill during a one-week period. Write a paragraph describing what you learned about this specific reading behavior during the trial period.

IN BRIEF

1 You can read actively by doing the following:

- Considering the writer's purpose for writing and your own purpose for reading
- Anticipating what the material will say
- Relating what you read to your prior knowledge
- Evaluating reading material as you read and after you read to ensure understanding and to form judgments

2 Understanding the writer's purpose will often help you improve your reading by allowing you to anticipate the message; however, the writer's purpose for writing and the reader's purpose for reading do not always correspond.

3 Anticipating the contents of a document, both before you read and as you read, is vital to active reading because it forces you to constantly consider the message by encouraging you to check your predictions.

4 Using prior knowledge is an important aspect of active reading because you can use old information to assign meaning to new information. Good readers use their prior knowledge at both the situation and the word/concept level.

5 Active readers evaluate reading material at two points. First, they evaluate what they are reading as they read it by questioning and commenting on the material silently. Next, they evaluate reading material after they've read it, particularly when they must make a decision or follow up. In any case, it is often helpful to evaluate material systematically.

6 The three general reading approaches are skimming, scanning, and reading for detail.

7 Skimming means reading quickly through material, relying on key words and phrases to determine the main ideas within a document.

8 Scanning means reading quickly through material, searching for clues or characteristics to find a specific piece of information.

9 Reading for detail means reading words and phrases closely, attending to details to gain full understanding of a document.

10 Reading habits can be improved by understanding and following the guidelines for active reading, including suggestions for changes in behavior such as prioritizing and marking what you read, reading by phrases instead of words, building a larger vocabulary, controlling time and reading conditions, and enrolling in a course or other formal study.

WORDS OF NOTE

Define each of these terms introduced in Chapter 7.

active reading
bias
concept level
consider all factors
information in/information out
reader processing
reading for detail
scanning
situation level
skimming
word level

CHECK YOUR RECALL

1 What is active reading? What must you do to read actively?

2 What kinds of prior knowledge can help you consider the writer's purpose?

3 What are two ways in which anticipating what you are about to read can help serve your purpose?

4 What are some questions to ask yourself as you read to draw on your prior knowledge?

5 How can recalling prior knowledge aid your reading at the situation level? The concept or word level? Give an example of each.

6 To evaluate what you read, what are some questions to ask yourself as you read? After you read?

7 What two systems are suggested in the text for evaluating what you read? Explain each.

8 What three reading approaches are described in the text? How is each different from the others?

9 What eight habits can help you improve your reading skill and comprehension?

9 How can you prioritize your reading?

10 What are some things you can do to thoroughly review your reading habits?

SHARE YOUR PERSPECTIVE

1 Evaluate the following situations in writing either by considering all factors or by using the information in/information out system.

    a. You read the following notice in your local newspaper:
State Assemblyman Jack Mann will introduce a bill that, if passed, would increase auto insurance for students by as much as 25 percent.

    b. You read the following excerpt in your school newspaper:
Effective immediately, the school bookstore will no longer accept checks and credit cards. All purchases must be paid in cash.

2 Create a grid on which you can record the reading you do each day. Each time you read something, record an SK for "skim," an SC for "scan," and a RD for "reading for detail." If you use a combination of these three, record both or all abbreviations.

Monday		Tuesday		Wedne
Item Real	*Purpose*	*Item Real*	*Purpose*	
Copier Manual	D			
Catalog	C+E			
Memo	D			
Letter	SI			
Letter	C+E			
Report	SI			
Magazine	SI / C+E			

Note: Record all your reading—not just books, articles, and letters but also signs, menus, and other incidental reading you do throughout the day.

❸ Find a newspaper or magazine article. Read it from beginning to end, then answer the following questions *in the alphabetical sequence in which they appear.*

a. What is the main point of the article?
b. Were any statistics or facts cited to support the information in the article?
c. Was anyone quoted in the article to support the story? If so, did the quote(s) help you understand the topic more clearly? How?
d. Did you have to reread all or part of the article to answer any of the questions a, b, or c? If so, what approach did you use to find the information? How did that reading differ from the way in which you first approached the article?

FOCUS ON THE FINE POINTS
Read the following background information. Then follow the instructions to locate and correct grammar errors.

Background

Micki Estrada is learning to write programmable ready materials (PRMs) for a computer company called DataSmart. It's her first day on the job, and her supervisor has given her a copy of DataSmart's style guide. Micki scans the section summaries until she comes to the information about her first assignment, writing review questions for tutorials. She then reads more about her topic, relying at times on the glossary to define terms for her.

Your Instructions

Each of the following documents contains up to 15 errors. Indicate and correct errors by circling the problem and noting the solution on a photocopy of the page or on a separate sheet of paper. In each case, you may assume the document is formatted correctly.

Note: If you have difficulty locating errors, turn to page 461 in the Appendix. There you will find additional information about the errors in Document 1.

DOCUMENT 1: Section Summaries

DataSmart Style Guide

PAGES IN A TUTORIAL

This section begins by listing and defining the different pages in a tutorial. And explaining the use of each (Parts 1, 2, and 3). Parts 4 through 9, respectively, moving beyond these fundamentals. Covers the following pages: title, name, introduction, practice, question, and glossary.

You should not neglect to read this section if you have written PRMs for other computer programs, they will not necessarily have followed the same page style.

GRAPHICS ON A PAGE

This section define the different types of graphics that is available: line art, full-color art, and logos and icons.

- Line art (including horizontal and vertical bar graphs, pie charts, flow charts, and loop charts) which is typically used in higher-level tutorials and for line art the writer should include a rough sketch using the writing software's "draw" function.

- Full-color art includes any kind of art that can be generated by a computer artist.

- Logos and icons includes those that can be generated by the computer. And if any those that can be created by a programmer.

Page 6

DOCUMENT 2: Questions for Tutorials

DataSmart Style Guide

QUESTIONS
Questions can be either true/false or multiple choice.

True/False
The Base
- Ending with a period, each base must be a full sentence.
- Each base must use the full screen, be centered beginning on line 3, and have a length of no more than 2 lines (38 characters per line).
- At the end of the base, on line 5, use this instruction: "Select T or F:"

  Example:
  Brett needs to check with the credit
  department before filling the order.
  Select T or F:

The Feedback
- Not to repeat the same response for each question is important when writing feedback. Particularly when you have written two or more true/false questions.
- True/false questions do not allow a second try and an incorrect answer automatically send the user back to the section of the tutorial that he or she need to review.

Multiple Choice
The Base
- Each base must be a full sentence that end with a question mark.
- Each base must use the full screen, be centered beginning on line 3, and have a length of no more than 2 lines (38 characters per line).
- At the end of the base, on line 5, use this instruction: "Select a letter:"
- Highlight key words in red.

The Choices
- Multiple choice questions work best with four choices, the rules, however, is: Provide no less than three and no more than five choices.
- Begin the first choice on line 7. The choices can cover a minimum of three lines and seven lines are the maximum.

The Feedback
- When writing multiple choice feedback, write all five messages that might possibly apply:
  1. Very good. The correct answer is __.
     (Note: Use the correct letter here.)
  2. No. Select another letter.
     (Note: For the first incorrect response.)
  3. No. Reread the question and select another letter.
     (Note: This is for the second incorrect response.)
  4. Yes. Go on to the next question.
     (Note: Use this after either the second or third correct response.)
  5. No. Press Enter to review this section.
     (Note: Use this after a third incorrect response.)

Page 16

DOCUMENT 3: Glossary

DataSmart Style Guide

base
The stem of a question.

choice
One of the options the viewer may selects to answer the base question. In answering a true/false question, the choices is F or T. Depending upon the number of choices in answering a multiple-choice question, the viewer can choose a letter A-C, A-D, or A-E.

feedback
The answer or answers the computer gives in response to the key the viewer have selected.

multiple choice question
A question for which the viewer can select a possible answer from a set of no more than five choices. And no less than three.

PRM
Programmable ready material. PRMs is the text, instructions, and simple codes from which the programmers develop the design, images, and complex codes that becomes a computer program.

true/false question
A statement for which the viewer can select one of two possible responses: T or F. (If the statement is true or if they are not true.)

tutorial
A program that teaches something. For example, if a person wants to learn how to ensure quality in a manufacturing setting, using a tutorial called "Quality at Work."

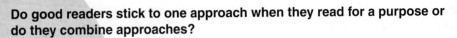

Do good readers stick to one approach when they read for a purpose or do they combine approaches?

Is there a general strategy you can use when you need to find specific information within a document?

What's the best sequence of reading approaches when you need to follow written directions?

What reading behaviors will help you respond carefully to persuasive writing?

Do you read a job application the same way you read a novel? Do you read a newspaper article the same way you read a textbook? Do you read a dictionary or a book's index the same way you read the instructions for changing the battery in your watch? Good readers will answer no to these questions. They know that the reading approach they use should depend on their purpose for reading the material.

Few documents that cross your desk at work demand that you read every word of every sentence. Perhaps you need to read only a portion of that document in detail; you will skim or scan until you find that important part. The best overall method for reading is to combine the different approaches as necessary to accomplish your reading purpose. In this chapter we discuss how you might combine approaches when you encounter these common reading situations: reading for specific information, reading to follow directions, and reading persuasive writing.

READING FOR SPECIFIC INFORMATION

When **reading for specific information**, no matter what the writer's purpose, readers often *skim* or *scan*, depending on the nature of the information they need. In general, they will skim until they find the portion of a document that is likely to contain the desired information. Then they scan this section to locate the specific piece of information. This strategy is used whether the document passes on information, responds to a question or request, makes a request, or gives simple directions.

As discussed in Chapter 7, readers skim for general information about a document's main ideas and contents, and they scan for specific, identifiable pieces of information. Naturally, how the reader combines these approaches to perform a specific reading task will vary depending on the individual's prior knowledge.

─── C A S E   S C E N A R I O ───

What's in a Memo?

Doris Lozar, a veteran warehouse employee, and Kyle Ranch, a new employee, received the following memo:

MEMORANDUM

TO: Warehouse Staff

FROM: Management

DATE: October 5, 19XX

SUBJECT: WAREHOUSE CLOSING FOR ANNUAL INVENTORY

Each November we must close the warehouse for ten business days to take our annual inventory. This year, we will close from Monday, November 4, through Friday, November 15. As always, we will notify all customers by enclosing a flier with their October statements.

We also notify all our employees so the warehouse closing does not adversely affect business operations. If you need any supplies or products, we urge you to note the above dates and submit your requisitions as early as possible to avoid the end-of-October rush. Please try to anticipate your needs as best you can.

Doris and Kyle read the memo to themselves. Each of them applied a different "history" to the memo as they evaluated its contents.

As a veteran employee, Doris was used to the warehouse closing in early November. Once she saw the subject line ("WAREHOUSE CLOSING FOR ANNUAL INVENTORY"), she knew what the memo was about. She skimmed the memo for new information—information that was different this year than it was last year—but found none. Then she scanned the memo once to note the closing dates and mark them on her calendar. The whole process took about one minute.

Kyle, on the other hand, had no prior knowledge of this situation; the memo and its contents were completely new to him. When he received the memo, he skimmed it to see what it was about. The subject line did not tell him enough, so he read the entire memo more closely. His reading left him with many questions.

What are some of the questions Kyle might have? What might he do as a first step to organize his questions? How can he find the answers? Regardless of questions, what should Kyle do with the information he has?

Notice that both Doris and Kyle skimmed and scanned as part of their reading approaches:

- Doris skimmed to identify the general contents of the memo and to assure herself that there were no surprises in the memo. She scanned to find what she identified as the one piece of information worth saving: the inventory dates.

- Kyle skimmed at first for the same reason Doris skimmed: to identify the general contents of the memo. However, because Kyle had no prior knowledge to bring to the memo, he found he had to read for detail.

Because of prior knowledge, Doris and Kyle defined the situation above differently. For Doris, the situation was routine, and she approached it accordingly. For Kyle, the situation was new, and he had to approach it with more caution, which forced him to read with greater attention to detail.

protocol

a code prescribing strict adherence to correct etiquette and precedence; custom or etiquette which is strictly followed

Many times, business documents contain words, phrases—even entire paragraphs— that are there for reasons of ***protocol***. For example, a standard business contract will define the parties entering into the contract over the course of one or two paragraphs. If you deal with these contracts on a routine basis, it is unlikely that you will

FIGURE 8.1 ▶

The language in a business contract can be mind-boggling at first. Over time, you'll learn to recognize which parts contain the details you need to read carefully.

Snyder misses the old days when all that it took to get the executive wash room painted was to tell someone to do it.

read the opening paragraphs word for word each time you review a new contract. Similarly, over time you will learn to recognize what you can "overlook" when you read familiar types of documents at work, particularly when your purpose is to find specific information.

C A S E   S C E N A R I O

Lowest Bidder

Danielle Blank received a letter from Bob Dennison. As she read the return address, she said to herself, "Oh, this must be Bob's response to my request for an estimate for installing the new phone system." Because Danielle made the request, she was expecting Bob's letter.

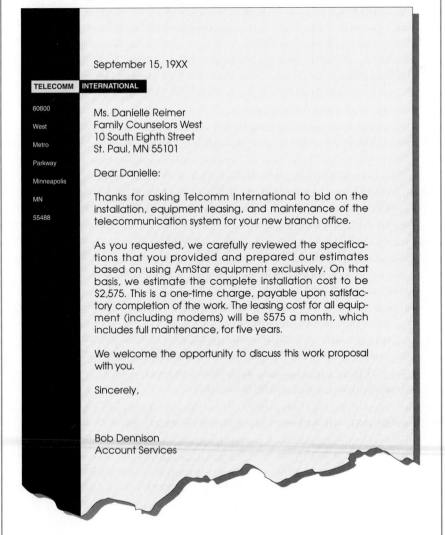

September 15, 19XX

TELECOMM INTERNATIONAL

60600
West
Metro
Parkway
Minneapolis
MN
55488

Ms. Danielle Reimer
Family Counselors West
10 South Eighth Street
St. Paul, MN 55101

Dear Danielle:

Thanks for asking Telcomm International to bid on the installation, equipment leasing, and maintenance of the telecommunication system for your new branch office.

As you requested, we carefully reviewed the specifications that you provided and prepared our estimates based on using AmStar equipment exclusively. On that basis, we estimate the complete installation cost to be $2,575. This is a one-time charge, payable upon satisfactory completion of the work. The leasing cost for all equipment (including modems) will be $575 a month, which includes full maintenance, for five years.

We welcome the opportunity to discuss this work proposal with you.

Sincerely,

Bob Dennison
Account Services

The first thing Danielle did was scan the memo for numbers—dollar amounts. She was curious about Bob's offer. Once she located specific dollar amounts, she skimmed the text around those dollar amounts to make sure she understood what they related to.

Danielle was surprised: Bob's bid was significantly lower than two other bids. His bid for installation was about $500 less than either of the other two estimates, and his monthly lease fee was $125 less. Danielle concluded that Bob's bid was the best, but she knew she was being a little hasty.

What questions did Danielle probably need to answer for herself? What could she do next?

1 USE YOUR JUDGMENT

Assume Danielle received another bid from Connections Inc., one of Telcomm International's competitors (see example below). Read it to determine how it compares to the bid from Bob Dennison. Then answer these questions: Is the bid lower or higher? Does this bid offer the same level of service?

CONNECTIONS, INC.

1700 Ridgeway Lane
Suite 770
Plymouth, MN 55422
612.555.1390
Fax 612.555.1397

September 14, 19XX

Ms. Danielle Reimer
Family Counselors West
10 South Eighth Street
St. Paul, MN 55101

Dear Danielle:

Connections Inc. is pleased to submit the following bid for services. The bid is based on the specifications provided by you during our meeting last week.

For installation of 18 AmStar phones, we charge a one-time fee of $2,840. Leasing and maintenance of the equipment is $540 per month on a 24-month contract.

Once you approve this proposal, we can schedule the installation within 48 hours.

Sincerely,

Susan Brink
Account Executive

Name several types of reading materials that you regularly read to find specific information (for example, a bus schedule). Name what it is you read to find.

READING TO FOLLOW DIRECTIONS

Reading to follow directions is a common workplace reading task and often calls for reading for detail. You read to follow directions when you:

- Read to complete complex forms, such as IRS forms

- Read to follow step-by-step processes, such as instructions for accessing electronic mail on your personal computer

- Read to learn a procedure, such as a new hiring process approved by management

- Read the company operations manual to learn how to complete an expense report

When reading to follow directions, sequence is important. Most directions must be followed in a certain order to obtain the desired result. A set of directions might also call for materials or special circumstances or may be quite complicated; it is best to read through a set of directions at least once *before* attempting to complete them. It is not uncommon for readers to reread items within the directions several times to fully understand what must be done. As the following situation illustrates, reading to follow directions is a difficult task because it requires concentration, yet frequently involves interruptions in the reading process.

◀ **FIGURE 8.2**

Reading to follow directions often requires intense concentration.

Consider the situation of Martin Erickson, a new sales representative for the consulting firm Financial Solutions Inc. (FSI). FSI has just installed TCSys, a telecommunications system that connects computers linked to the system. Using telephone lines and modems, TCSys connects all sales reps with one another and with coworkers at the company's headquarters. Martin has just received his TCSys manual and software in the mail. He now needs to read the manual so that he can learn how to install the software and use the new program. Here is the reading approach Martin uses:

1. Martin skims the entire TCSys manual, paying special attention to the table of contents and pausing at the section headings within the manual. His goal for doing this is simply to familiarize himself with the manual.

2. Martin returns to the table of contents and skims for any section that might tell him how to get started. He finds a section called "Setting Up the Equipment."

3. By thumbing through the manual and scanning page numbers, Martin locates the section. Once he finds the page, the section heading quickly catches his attention. (See example on next page.)

4. Martin next skims the section to see how long it is and what parts it contains. (Like most readers, Martin wants to have some idea of how long his reading and setting up will take.)

5. Finally, Martin returns to the beginning of the section and begins reading more closely. Since he knows little about installing software and nothing about modems, he thinks he should read closely for detail.

   As he reads, however, Martin realizes that the information on modems might not be important. He knows his goal is to get the system working, not to learn about modems. He skims through the information on modems, looking for the actual set-up instructions. He knows he can return to the modem information if necessary.

6. He reaches the subsection called "Connecting the Modem" and reads the first step. After reading the entire first step, he reads it again, this time stopping at the word *and*. He then sorts through the equipment he needs: the phone line and the modem. He finds what he thinks is the correct slot on the modem to attach the phone line, and he turns to Figure 2.A in the manual to confirm this. He attaches the phone line to the modem.

7. Then he rereads the second half of the first sentence. He finds the equipment he needs and moves between the equipment, the written instructions, and Figure 2.A until he completes step 1.

8. He follows the subsequent steps similarly until he has the system working. The entire process takes him about 45 minutes.

Setting Up the Equipment

To install the TCSys system on your computer, you must have a modem, a telephone line, and communications software.

Modems. A modem is a special device that connects your computer to another computer by way of a telephone line. The modem converts the signals it receives from your computer to telephone signals, transmits those signals across the telephone lines, and at the other end converts the signals back to computer signals once again. The process is reversed when data is sent from another computer to your computer.

The speed with which a modem transmits data is measured by its baud rate. Typically, a modem will have a baud rate of 300, 1200, or 2400. These baud rates identify modems that transmit 30, 120, and 240 cps (characters per second), respectively. The faster the modem, the faster it transmits data, and faster transmission means less telephone time and lower operating costs. If you must buy a modem, we recommend a 2400-baud model.

There are two kinds of modems:

1. An internal modem is one that is installed inside your Central Processing Unit.

2. An external modem is connected to your Central Processing Unit by a cable and is plugged into an electrical outlet.

Connecting the Modem. To connect an external modem to your computer, follow these directions:

1. Attach one end of the phone line to the modem in slot A (see figure 2.A), and attach the other end of the phone line in your phone jack. (Note: A phone jack adaptor is enclosed, allowing both your modem and your regular phone line to be serviced by the same phone jack. See figure 2.A.)

Note the complexity of Martin's reading process. He skims until he is comfortable with the manual. He scans to find the sections he needs. Then he begins reading for detail. However, after he begins reading for detail, he realizes that this particular detail is not what he currently needs, so he reverts to skimming until he finds what's needed. Then he begins reading for detail again.

Even when Martin finally finds what he needs, he does not read for detail—the way you might now be reading for detail or the way people read most books and newspaper articles, for example. His reading purpose is to follow directions to help set up computer equipment. So, instead of reading all the instructions and learning them in order to set up the equipment, Martin constantly alternates between reading and setting up the equipment until the job is done. Further, he not only alternates between reading and setting up equipment but also between two types of reading—reading the words and reading the figure, which provided help in the form of a diagram.

As this example shows, reading—especially reading for detail—can be quite complex. Reading tasks often combine skimming and scanning with the more complex reading for detail to achieve the goal of the reading situation.

3   USE YOUR JUDGMENT

Apply what you have learned about reading to follow directions as you read the steps below. First read the steps. Then respond to items a and b.

1. Write down the names of two authors you enjoy reading.

2. Under each author list a favorite title.

3. Under each title, write a paragraph describing the story line of that particular work.

4. Underline all of the adjectives within each paragraph.

5. Circle the nouns within each paragraph.

6. Ignore steps 1 through 5; instead, put your feet up and relax. (Note: If you followed our advice for reading to follow directions, you did not waste your time performing steps 1 through 5 because you read all of the steps before attempting to complete them!)

    a. What did you learn about your own reading habits through this exercise? Did you jump right into the task or did you read through all the steps first?

    b. If you didn't do steps 1 through 5 prematurely, do them now. Be aware of how you read and reread to perform the required tasks.

READING PERSUASIVE WRITING

Reading **persuasive writing** to evaluate its merit is another situation that usually requires reading for detail. Some might argue that reading persuasive writing requires the highest degree of detailed reading because it requires readers to constantly evaluate what they are reading. When you read to follow instructions, for example, you generally do what the instructions tell you. That is, while you must read for detail and do a certain amount of interpreting, you accept the instructions as accurate and valid. When reading persuasive materials, however, you can make fewer *presumptions* about the accuracy and validity of the writer's details and arguments. In short, you must evaluate everything, and this affects your reading strategy.

You will find yourself reading persuasive material when you have before you:

- Letters of application to recommend which four candidates your department will interview for an open position

- A report that concludes that the company must shift its emphasis to sell to a different population

- A form letter from a charitable organization asking you to donate time or money

- A sales letter or a marketing brochure

- A memo from another department asking you to be on a committee with the purpose of evaluating that department's operations

- A position announcement encouraging you to apply for a promotion to this new position in the company

Remember that reading for detail is an approach that relies heavily on anticipating what will be read, using prior knowledge, and evaluating through self-talk. Without these efforts, the reader cannot hope to make a solid judgment about the material's validity.

To illustrate this type of situation, consider Frances Candela. Frances is the managing partner for Del Mar Electronics, a wholesaler specializing in audio equipment. Frances receives a memo from her partner. Frances needs to evaluate the memo's message and determine how she wants to respond:

▲FIGURE 8.3

In business, persuasive reading material is a daily reality.

presumption

something that is assumed or believed without question; a belief based probable or assumed reliability

MEMORANDUM

TO: Frances Candela

FROM: Bea Walsh

DATE: November 25, 19XX

SUBJECT: MONTHLY BILLING AND CLERICAL TIME

Sending out our monthly statements now occupies our three assistants full time for two full days each month. When vacations, holidays, or sick days interfere with this process, statements go out late, resulting in late payments and serious cash-flow problems. The more our company grows, the bigger this job will get, and the greater the problem.

I recommend that we use Clancy & Ramsey Billing Services to handle all our monthly statements. I've talked with Jill Clancy and Jason Ramsey, and both are reputable, knowledgeable, and dependable. They now handle billing services for nearly 50 clients, and I have personally checked some of their references. I have also compared C&R to other firms, both for services and costs. Please see the attached comparison chart for details.

Clearly, the costs are reasonable, especially when you consider the fact that we can then free our assistants for six workdays a month.

When you have had an opportunity to review the attached comparison chart, please let's meet to discuss this.

Here's how Frances reads the memo. Notice her silent self-talk, shown by the marginal callouts:

1. First, Frances skims the subject line, which leaves a question in her mind:

SUBJECT: MONTHLY BILLING AND CLERICAL TIME

"Hmm, does Bea see a problem with this?"

"Yes, I can see her point we do use a lot of our clerical time on billing, but using an outside firm? I don't know if I like that idea. Maybe we could hire a fourth assistant cheaper, maybe part time. What details does Bea include?"

2. Next, Frances skims the memo to answer her own question.

3. Because her skimming leaves her with some questions and possible disagreement with Bea, Frances reads the memo for greater detail, hoping to evaluate it more carefully:

Sending out our monthly statements now occupies our three assistants full time for two full days each month. When vacations, holidays, or sick days interfere with this process, statements go out late, resulting in late payments and serious cash-flow problems. The more our company grows, the bigger this job will get, and the greater the problem.

I recommend that we use Clancy & Ramsey Billing Services to handle all our monthly statements. I've talked with Jill Clancy and Jason Ramsey, and both are reputable, knowledgeable, and dependable. They now handle billing services for nearly 50 clients, and I have personally checked some of their references. I have also compared C&R to other firms, both for services and costs. Please see the attached comparison chart for details.

Clearly, the costs are reasonable, especially when you consider the fact that we can then free our assistants for six workdays a month.

When you have had an opportunity to review the attached comparison chart, please let's meet to discuss this.

"It does? Doesn't one of these assistants just help out a little when the others are running late?"

"Yes, I've noticed this."

"Yes, I've definitely noticed this."

"True, but can't we figure out a way to handle this growth in-house?"

"I wonder how well Bea knows these people how she found them?"

"I wonder how many? Looks like she's put in a lot of time on this."

"She's certainly done her homework!"

"I wonder how they compare to hiring a part-timer?"

"But billing is one of their major jobs. Do we want them freed from this or from some other duties? If we need to have something done outside, maybe it should be something else."

"Yes, this idea is worth pursuing. I think we need answers to additional questions. I'll talk with her tomorrow about this."

4. After thoughtfully reading Bea's memo in detail, Frances decides to meet with Bea to discuss the idea. So she skims through the memo once more, locating every point at which she has questions and writing her questions in the margins to prepare for a meeting with Bea.

Frances combined skimming with reading for detail to accomplish her reading purpose. She particularly gave attention to detail as she read this memo. Almost every sentence (certainly every main point) invited some question or comment from Frances.

While all reading requires readers to talk silently as they read to check comprehension, silent talk is most important when reading persuasive writing because of the need to question the accuracy of details and the validity of the writer's arguments.

4 USE YOUR JUDGMENT

Imagine yourself as the manager in the following situation. Read the letter that follows as you would in that situation. Before you read and as you read, be aware of the reading approaches you use, and describe this process step by step when you have finished:

You manage a small motel that is several miles from the nearest restaurant or business district. You do not have full kitchen or dining facilities, but you do have some room in the office area to add some fast-food preparation facilities (such as a refrigerator/freezer, a microwave oven, and so on). You believe your guests would use this fast-food service and that it would increase your customer base. You receive this letter:

Dear Business Owner:

You are no doubt aware of the popularity of pizza. But are you familiar with the fine line of quality frozen pizzas made by Mama's Pizza Company? Please let me tell you about us.

A few people experienced in fine food preparation opened Mama's Pizza in 1982. The company started with two styles of pizza and a goal of selling 25,000 pizzas in its first year. People liked Mama's pizzas, and the business grew quickly. We now offer ten styles of pizza and expect to sell over 100,000 pizzas this year. According to a recent study by the AMPA, "Mama's Pizza is a shining star in the frozen pizza market. From the beginning, the company has maintained the highest quality."

Here are comments from some other happy customers:

"I always have Mama's pizzas in my freezer section. They go very quickly."
—Tate Halliday, National Manager, Quick Stop Shops

"We have fussy customers. If we run out of Mama's pizzas they let us know right away."
—Walter Wendel, East Coast Buyer for S&N Markets

At Mama's Pizza, we are proud of our record. We look forward to serving you with our fine products.

Sincerely,

IN BRIEF

❶ To be an effective reader, you must adapt your reading approaches to conform to the specific reading situation.

❷ When reading to find specific information, you can first skim for general information or to get an "overview" of the document's contents, then scan for specific information by looking for clues or characteristics of the information you need.

❸ Reading to follow directions requires reading for detail. You probably will reread the steps several times before completing them. A suggested technique is to read, then stop to complete a step, then read further, then stop again, and so on.

❹ Reading persuasive material also requires reading for detail, yet with more evaluative effort than reading to follow directions. To weigh the validity of the document, you need to anticipate what you read, and continuously consult prior knowledge and evaluate by using self-talk.

WORDS OF NOTE

Define each of these terms introduced in Chapter 8.

persuasive writing
reading for specific information
reading to follow directions

CHECK YOUR RECALL

❶ What techniques are typically used when reading for information? How and why might prior knowledge affect this type of reading?

❷ What are some examples of reading you might do to follow directions?

❸ When reading to follow directions, why is sequence important? What are some reasons that reading to follow directions can be an especially difficult task?

❹ What are some examples of persuasive reading material?

❺ What specific techniques are especially helpful when reading persuasive material?

SHARE YOUR PERSPECTIVE

1 Using a recording grid similar to the one used at the end of Chapter 7 (page 206), record the purposes for which you read throughout an entire week. Use the following categories:

- To find specific information (SI)
- To follow directions (D)
- To consider and evaluate persuasive writing (C&E)

2 Use questions a, b, and c as your guide to determine your reading purpose. Then read the letter in below and answer the questions.

    a. What is the cost of owning a Business Executives SuperCard?
    b. How can you earn 10,000 miles on Northeast's Flyer program?
    c. How do you apply for a card?

Business Executives, Inc.

P.O. Box 75000 Louisville, Kentucky 40222
(502) 555-3506 Toll Free (800) 555-1900 Fax (502) 555-3355

April 5, 19XX

Dear Executive:

As a member of the local business community, you are invited to apply for the new Business Executives SuperCard, now offered at an introductory rate of just 7.9% with no annual fee.

The Business Executives SuperCard helps you to support a local charity of your choice at no additional cost to you. Each time you use your card to make a purchase, a donation will automatically be made to the designated group.

When you use the Business Executives SuperCard, you can also earn mileage on the Northeast Flyer's Program. Each dollar spent is equivalent to one mile under this program.

Here are some other advantages to owning a Business Executives SuperCard:

- Free cards
- 28-day interest-free grace period
- International charge privileges
- Toll-free cardholder service number

Don't delay! You too can enjoy the prestige and convenience that comes with the Business Executives SuperCard. Plus, you can feel good about helping the charity of your choice. Simply complete the enclosed application and mail it within 30 days.

Sincerely,

Deanna Goodhue
Membership Director

Enclosure

FOCUS ON THE FINE POINTS
Read the following background information. Then follow the instructions to locate and correct grammar errors.

Background

Marquetta Lopez works as the communications assistant for a very large company headquartered in a large Midwestern city. It is the responsibility of the communications department to publish a monthly company newsletter. Recently there have been several requests for restaurant reviews. Marquetta, her boss, and two friends visited the Mix It Up Grill on three occasions; then Marquetta wrote a review. To add interest, she included with the review a portion of the restaurant's menu and a recipe for one of its desserts.

Your Instructions

Each of the following documents contains up to 15 errors. Indicate and correct errors by circling the problem and noting the solution on a photocopy of the page or on a separate sheet of paper. In each case, you may assume the document is formatted correctly.

Note: If you have difficulty locating errors, turn to page 463 in the Appendix. There you will find additional information about the errors in Document 1.

DOCUMENT 1: Restaurant Review

Mix It Up Grill gets mixed review

If you've got a group of people with widely differing tastes, you may want to try the Mix It Up Grill. Billed as a restaurant "where no two meals are ever alike," the Mix It Up Grill lived up to its promise on two out of three recent visits.

The first visit was for Sunday brunch. One member of our group of four opted for the design-your-own omelet (choosing olives, pimientos, basil, and goat cheese with a side of fried potatos) for $6.95. A second chose a seafood pizza--a typical mix of seafoods (shrimp, scallops, and clams) in a nontypical presentation-- for $7.95. Both declared their meals excellent. My other dining companion and I tried our luck at the buffet ($8.50). Her selection of vegetarian lasagne turned out to be a case of false representation, unless sausage has recently been categorized as a vegetable. My peppered walleye brushed with lemon-thyme butter in a white wine sauce was dry, and my palette could discriminate no hint of lemon or thyme. On the plus side, the coffee is rich, the unusual selection of fresh juices (papaya, grapefruit, kiwi, carrot, mango) delightful, and the service more competent.

Our second visit, for a weekday lunch, proved disastrous. Having told our server that we had exactly one hour, we found ourselves waiting thirty-five minutes for our entrées, one of which almost didn't arrive at all. When three of us were finally served, the eggplant parmigiano ($8.95) and poached halibut in wine sauce ($10.95)--both billed as "light" and "very low in salt"--were so salty that one of our party could not even eat hers; my Waldorf salad ($8.95) included cashews rather than walnuts and a blend of pears and apples. Our other dining companion had to take his entire Monte Cristo sandwich in a doggie bag and found it unedible by the time he got it back to the office.

Surprisingly, visit number three proved more enjoyable of all. The skewered lamb appetizer (six kabobs for $7.95) included a pungent, spicey mint sauce. Miniature Cape Cod crab cakes (four for $6.95) are crispy on the outside, light and flavorful on the inside. The black bean soup with sour cream ($3.75 a cup) was shear heaven. Of our four entrées--peppered rib eye in a hearty burgundy sauce ($21.95), lamb a la Provençal ($22.95), nutty wild rice with artichoke-stuffed mushrooms ($15. 95), and swordfish baked with apples and mustard ($18.95)--only the latter was mildly disappointing, due in larger part to the fact that the burgundy sauce is less hearty than it was skimpy. The specialty desert of the house, an orange poppy seed cake, was exquisite.

The verdict on the Mix It Up Grill: Give it a try, but be willing to experiment and come prepared for a few disappointments along with the happy surprises!

DOCUMENT 2: Menu

Appetizers

● ●

Skewered Lamb Kabobs—six grilled slices of tender lamb and purl onions
with our special ginger mint sauce $7.95

Miniature Cape Cod Crab Cakes—four cakes stuffed with lump crab and spices
and grills to crispy perfection $6.95

Smoked Turkey Quesadillas—with fresh cilantro tomato sauce $7.95

Salads

● ●

Waldorf Salad—served traditionally New York style with plenty of
fruit and nuts...$8.95

Ceasar Salad—romaine lettuce tossed with anchovies and fresh croutons
topped with a classic Ceasar dressing $8.95

Southwestern Surprize—for the adventuresome palette, a firey array of
seasoned black beans, jalapeños, chili peppers, onions, corn, cilantro,
and shredded pork, topped with chocolate-chili salsa the most exotic
dish eastern of the Mississippi $9.95

Soups

● ●

Black Bean Soup with Sour Cream—a smoothe, heartily blend of premium
black beans and sour cream seasoned with cumin and cilantro, and we
serve it in an earthen crock

         cup $4.95
         bowl $6.95

Chilled Cream of Vichyssoise—traditional soup of creamed potatos and
onion with a hint of dill, served over ice

         cup $4.95
         bowl $6.95

Document 3: Recipe

Mix It Up Grill's Orange Poppy Seed Cake

2 cups sifted, all-purpose flour   2/3 cup canola oil
1 3/4 cups confectioner's sugar   1/2 cup orange juice
1/2 teaspoon salt   1/2 cup plane yogurt
1 tablespoon baking soda   zest of 2 oranges
2 eggs   1/8 cup poppy seeds

Preheat oven to 350 . Butter and have floured two round 9" pans.

Sift together the first four ingredients twice. Mix the eggs, oil, orange juice, and yogurt on low until well blended. Careful fold dry ingredients into wet. Add orange zest. Beat on high for one minute; do not overbeat. Gently stir in poppy seeds after beating.

Pour the batter into the pans. Bake 40-45 minutes, until the center sprung back when you touch it and a toothpick inserted into the middle of the cake comes out clean. Turn the cake rounds onto wracks and let them cool.

Frosting

3 tablespoons flour
1 cup milk
1 cup granulated sugar
1/2 teaspoon vanilla exact
2 tablespoons orange juice
1 cup butter
zest of 2 oranges
1 cup poppy seeds
3 tablespoons heavy grated orange peel

Cook the flour and milk over medium heat, stirring constant, until thick. Set aside.

Beat the sugar, vanila, orange juice, and butter on medium until fluffier, about 10 minutes. Add the cooked mixture and beat it again until very fluffy, about 10 minutes. Gently stir in the orange zest and poppy seeds.

Place one cake round on a plate. Frost the top. Place the second round on top of the latter. Spread the top and sides of the cake generously with frosting. Sprinkle the orange peel over the top and serve.

UNIT IV

COMMUNICATE FOR RESULTS

1 Read the following situation and the letter below. As you read the letter, use self-talk to question, comment on, and generally respond to what you are reading. Write any questions, comments, and responses down before moving on. Then, after reading the letter, evaluate it using either the "consider all factors" or the "information in/information out" system.

You are the distribution manager of a computer software distribution service. Your company distributes thousands of software programs produced by other companies. The following request came in this morning's mail:

Dear (Your Name):

Recently some of our sales representatives requested that we provide them with a computerized calendaring system. All of our representatives have personal computers.

We would like to find the least expensive way to provide all of them with your DayCal calendaring software. Also, we would like to install some of your other software on the local area network here in our office.

Will you please provide me with information about your licensing arrangements? Also, please let us know the hardware requirements for your latest version of DayCal, and send me all the literature you have on your other software.

Sincerely,

② Imagine yourself in the following situation and read, as you would in that situation, the memo below. Describe in writing your detailed, step-by-step reading approach as you read.

You find the memo in your mailbox. It is from Louise, who is one of your assistants in the advertising department of your company. You know she is an excellent worker but also that she is very defensive when her work is questioned for any reason.

M E M O R A N D U M

TO: (Your Name)

FROM: Louise Taylor

DATE: October 1, 19XX

SUBJECT: HOLIDAY CATALOG MAILING SCHEDULE

I've attached the revised mailing schedule for the Holiday Catalog. The Marketing Department submitted complete copy three weeks late. This made it impossible for us to meet our deadline. Fortunately, I was able to cut one full week from our production schedule, so the final date for delivering printed catalogs to our mailing house is November 15. This is not bad when you consider how late we received the final copy.

---

③ Select one area of reading weakness and do the following:

a. Research the ways in which you can realistically work on improving that aspect of your reading, and make a list of these methods.

b. Then write a one-year plan to correct this reading weakness. Be as specific as you can; for example, if your plan includes taking a course, name that course and its dates, and if your plan includes self-study using books, give the titles of those books. For each activity, include dates that commit you to starting and finishing at certain times.

READING CHECKLIST

Use the checklist below to assess your own reading skills and behavior.

You read actively by doing the following:

_____a. Considering the writer's purpose

_____b. Continuously anticipating what will come next

_____c. Continuously using prior knowledge to assign meaning to new information

_____d. Continuously evaluating messages during and after reading, using self-talk to assign meaning and judge accuracy.

_____e. Identifying your purpose for reading and tailoring your reading approach to accomplish your purpose.

UNITY

Writing is required in business for many purposes and in diverse forms. Yet there is one common aspect to all business writing: It is results-oriented.

Think about it. Business is all about action. So more than any other form of writing, the primary function of business writing is to produce action—to get someone to buy, sell, agree, or respond in a desired way. Workers—and consumers, too—do not have the time to produce or digest writing that rambles on or digresses from the main point. The writer needs to write only enough to get the job done. So, when writing for business—even more so than when you are listening or reading in the workplace—your purpose should "drive" what you do.

▼ **When you finish Unit V, you will be able to**

- Follow a process for preparing business documents that includes a planning stage, writing stage, revising stage, and proofreading stage

- Be mindful of style as you create business documents to produce concise, effective, and professional written communications

- Write in the appropriate format according to the situation—whether it be a letter, memorandum, or report

- Use format elements that attract your reader and enhance your message

- Write to inform, to request, to respond, to sell, and to report with attention to the guidelines for each type of document

WRITING

FOR

RESULTS

WRITING AS A
PROCESS

CHAPTER NINE

How much planning goes into a business document?

What should you achieve with your first draft?

Why is it important to revise and proofread your work before it is seen by your readers?

How can following a writing process help you to achieve your business goals?

You could say that there's more to good writing than meets the eye. The words on the page do not get there without some forethought—and probably a fair share of afterthought. Good writing comes about when writers approach each of these "phases"—pre-writing, writing, and post-writing—methodically and rigorously. They do this by following a writing process.

When you use a process to guide your business writing, you are more likely to keep your message on track. Your written communications will be crisp and clear because you know what you want them to accomplish; and you plan, create, evaluate, and revise them from these standpoints. You take the time to check each revision for any new or previously unnoticed mistakes. With practice, the writing process will become second nature to you as you produce notes, memos, forms, charts, letters, and reports in response to business needs.

In this chapter we define the writing process as the **RRTWRP** plan: **R**ead, **R**esearch, **T**hink, **W**rite, **R**evise, **P**roofread. In the pre-writing stage, we've identified three tasks: Read, Research, and Think. These tasks make up the first half of the RRTWRP process. Once you have defined your purpose and gathered your facts through these activities, you can sit down and tackle the writing stage. With a draft in hand, you are ready for post-writing activities—revising and proofreading. These three tasks—Write, Revise, and Proofread—comprise the second half of the RRTWRP process.

As you read about the writing process, consider that it is useful, too, in some speaking situations. With formal presentations, you must prepare what you are going to say and how you will say it. Oftentimes it is useful to write down what you will say so that you can perfect it, both on paper and in your delivery. (Formal presentations are covered in Chapter 5.)

Without having tried it, the RRTWRP Plan may seem as though it makes more work for the writer. Actually, because the plan breaks each step of the writing process into manageable activities, it yields more productivity with less strain. Approaching a blank piece of paper without a plan can be very intimidating, and often causes writer's block. Putting the RRTWRP plan into action is more likely to result in a satisfactory finished product.

READING, RESEARCHING, AND THINKING

Before you write, you have some "homework" to do. The extent of this homework will vary depending on the importance and complexity of your topic. If you put in the time at the beginning to explore your topic completely, you're less likely to backtrack for supporting data. *Writer's block* will pose less of a problem, too, when you are prepared. Certainly, it is easier to write when you have a good grasp of your purpose and all the relevant information at your fingertips.

writer's block

a psychological inhibition preventing a writer from proceeding with a piece

To read, research, and think in an ordered fashion, first ask yourself the following questions:

- Why am I writing?

- Who is my audience?

- What ideas do I want to communicate? What do I want my reader to think and do?

- Where can I find the information I need?

- When do I need the finished document?

- How should I organize my information?

With these questions answered, you can go about the *how* of the pre-writing stage. Gather your information, research your ideas, organize your thoughts, and choose

◀ **FIGURE 9.1**

At one time or another, every writer experiences writer's block.

your medium: note, chart, brochure, memo, letter, report, etc. The box below shows these questions applied to a writing task. Whether or not you write down your answers as shown here, you should be able to answer each question before you move to the writing stage.

Al Ferris, a group leader in Human Resources, has a writing assignment. To plan his message, he answers each question identified in the pre-writing stage.

Purpose: To pass on information re: status of search for new Research Department administrative assistant

Audience: Collette DeNares, HR Supervisor

Ideas: • What has been done to date

• Plans for continuing search

• Want Collette to see we are moving forward and approve our activities

Sources: Talk to coworkers in HR to confirm activities related to search (how many interviewed to date?)

Deadline: Tomorrow (12/7) noon

Approach: Direct, chronological

Medium: Interoffice memo

Why Are You Writing?

Just as when you listen or read, when you write you have a specific purpose or reason for doing so, related to the situation. Your specific purpose will usually fall under one of the following broad purposes:

- To pass on information

- To respond to questions and requests

- To request

- To direct

- To persuade

For example, perhaps you are writing to your assistant to detail work that must be completed in your absence. In this situation, your broad or general purpose for writing is to direct. Your specific purpose is to list the three projects that must be completed (for example the Banforth merger, the Carter acquisition, and the Plenary contract) as well as any pertinent information. Identifying both the general and the specific purposes for writing will help you to write appropriately.

Who Is Your Audience?

What you write in business may be read by many people. Your **primary readers** are those to whom you direct your writing. However, you may also want to consider any **secondary readers** of your communication. These are readers who need to know that the communication took place or what information is contained in the communication. In either case, after reading your writing, both sets of readers should be satisfied that you considered their point of view and addressed their concerns.

How do you determine another's point of view? Sometimes you will know your readers personally; this enables you to tailor your message to their likes and needs as well as their background and knowledge base. If you do not know your readers personally, try to identify the common characteristics of the group to which they belong and the values and point of view those characteristics suggest. For example, if you are communicating with someone who has a scientific background, this person will probably be responsive to facts and figures. An individual in public relations may be concerned with how a business activity is perceived by others and may judge your communication from this perspective. Use these insights to guide your writing.

You also will want to consider your audience with regard to the classifications we discussed in Chapter 2 of this text. Is the communication internal or external to the organization? Are you writing to a superior, a subordinate, or a peer? Your answers to these questions will influence the format and tone of your document.

What Do You Want Your Reader to Think and Do?

For the most part, if you want your reader to do something in response to your message, you need to be intentional about it. So it is necessary to identify as best you can what actions should result from your communication. Essentially, your answer to this question expands on your purpose for writing, i.e., you are not just writing to inform your drafters about the CAD training session, you want them to *attend* the session. In this case, it might be wise to mention the benefits of attending the session.

What Ideas Do You Want to Communicate?

By asking this question, you help yourself focus on the essence of your message. What do you want your reader to come away with? The ideas, like purposes, can be both specific ("There is no way we can support the Remmington deal") to general ("We are still very interested in doing business with you"). The list you generate in response to this question will help you determine which ideas need to be supported by facts and figures and which ideas you already have sufficient information about. Keep in mind that as you research your topic, new ideas may surface that you will want to include in your presentation.

C A S E   S C E N A R I O

Costly Catalog

Trevor Hawkins worked in the art department of a direct mail marketing firm. He wanted to propose a new catalog design that would feature four-color art on better-quality paper than previously used. He was confident from focus group data that the target market would order more if the company switched to this new, more expensive format. However, he needed to convince the operations manager (who was working on tightening the budget), and the art director (who had a goal of winning an award for the company at the next marketing awards ceremony) that the added expense would benefit the company. Trevor had two memos to write: one to the operations manager, Meghan Burns, and one to the art director, Elliot Cashman.

Before writing, Trevor jotted down the features of the new catalog design, how it improved upon the current catalog, a cost comparison between the two catalogs, and relevant focus group data. Next, he prioritized the material. As he did this, he realized his purpose for writing to Meghan and to Elliot was the same: to convince them that the new catalog design was worth the added expense. He decided to draft just one memo. After reviewing what he'd written, fixing a few sentences, and correcting typos, Trevor

attached samples of both the new and the old catalog to each memo to help his readers judge for themselves.

Do you think writing one memo was a wise decision? Why or why not? If Trevor had written two memos, how might the memos have been different? Would the same information be necessary for each? Explain your answers.

Where Can You Find the Information You Need?

Your topic will dictate where you must look for source material. For example, if you are writing about a competitive product, you may need to obtain brochures and other literature from the manufacturer. There will be instances where you need information from colleagues; from existing memos, letters, and reports; from databases; from the library; from newspapers or trade magazines—the list goes on. Be prepared to go where your topic takes you so that you can write a message with substance to it.

As you gather information, always check your facts to be sure you are working with accurate data and productive ideas. Are your names, dates, prices, and statements accurate? Does your idea agree with company policies and procedures? Should you include a sales brochure or other advertising material? If you have a question about your information, how can you verify it?

Gathering information takes time, and once you have all the data you think you need, you must review, analyze, and organize it. You will discard some information, and you may return to sources to check facts or find additional information. You may need to develop a survey or questionnaire and send it to coworkers or customers, for example. The complexity of your topic will dictate how much time you must spend on research.

▲FIGURE 9.2

In business, good writing is critical. It is very important to plan the extra time good writing requires. With practice, the time necessary for each step will probably become shorter.

When Do You Need the Finished Document?

In business, deadlines are an important consideration. A letter that is poorly timed may not accomplish what you thought it would. A late proposal, no matter how brilliant, is essentially worthless. Establishing priorities and managing your time to accommodate all stages of the writing process will help you meet your deadlines.

Use deadlines to help you determine what you can accomplish within the available time, given the specific circumstances. If you need to turn around a message in several hours, you obviously won't have time to go to the library and do extensive research. On the other hand, if you have a month to get a report together, you can plan to do a thorough study of your topic. If you do not have any specific deadline for sending a letter or submitting a sales proposal, setting one for yourself is likely to help you get it done.

How Should You Organize Your Information?

Once you have the information you need, you must determine the approach of your document as well as the order of the information within the document. The *former* is a global decision; it means deciding whether you want to dive into your topic or take a more subtle approach. The *latter* entails a number of specific decisions; for example, it requires determining whether Statistic A should come before or after Statistic B.

Approach

Most houses have a front door and a back door. This provides a good analogy for the two ways in which you can approach a topic. You can either come in "the front door" by using a **direct approach** or in "the back door" by using an **indirect approach.**

The direct approach is generally desirable for most written communications—particularly when the reader is expecting the message and wants *hard data.* To use a direct approach, organize and present the information in the clearest and most logical way, beginning with a statement of your main idea and moving on to support that main idea.

Note how these individuals use the direct approach to organize their materials:

- To train new order-takers and teach them the steps in billing a client, Bette Furnace organizes a training manual in step-by-step sequence, explaining the actual order process from start to finish, beginning with receipt of the order ("Step 1") and ending with customer payment ("Step 12").

- When Jack Thompson writes a proposal of his five-year plan for increasing sales, he decides to organize his materials chronologically, showing how the plan will unfold year by year.

- When Alexandra Ford prepares a report summarizing personnel changes and key events in her company's branch offices, she organizes the information alphabetically by city—first Albuquerque, then Atlanta, Birmingham, and so on.

The indirect approach can work well when the message is harsh—meaning the reader needs to be primed for it. Use it when you must convey negative information (plant closings, employee layoffs, decreases in employee benefits) or when you need to persuade your readers (to increase a budget, sign a contract, or change a policy). With an indirect approach, you will want to begin your document with information that prepares your readers to respond to your message in the way you want them to respond.

Here are three situations that call for an indirect approach:

- Cameron Klingensmith knows his production team is not going to like the news that everyone must work overtime for the next two months. He decides to begin his memo to the team by emphasizing the benefits

former

of, relating to, or being the first of two things mentioned, referred to, or understood

latter

of, relating to, or being the second or the last of two things mentioned, referred to, or understood

hard data

definite, factual information used as a basis for reasoning or discussion; firm measurements or statistics used as a basis for calculation

Duncan thinks his luck is finally changing when the judge tells him he has just won an all-expenses paid vacation.

◀ **FIGURE 9.3**

An indirect approach works well when the message is harsh.

everyone will realize from the overtime—bonus pay and higher profit sharing. Then he will go on to detail how they will meet a difficult production deadline.

- To announce the new Employee Safety Program in the company's internal newsletter, Chris DeLorenzo begins her article by citing the current accident rate. Then she explains how the new program has been developed to curb the frequency of accidents and to conform to OSHA regulations. Lastly, Chris lists each new safety procedure, mentioning first those that offer the most protection to workers.

- To handle customer accounts more efficiently, Dave Feinberg has ordered a sophisticated new software program for use by office staff. To learn the program, the staff must attend training seminars held on four consecutive Saturdays. To get the staff excited about the program and willing to forfeit several weekends to learn it, Dave starts a memo by emphasizing its time-saving features. After he has convinced the staff that the program will benefit them, he explains the training schedule.

Use of an Outline

There will be times when you must write a simple note or electronic-mail message and you already know everything you need to communicate without doing research or outlining. In these situations, perhaps all the preparation you need do is take a few minutes to brainstorm and jot down the two or three points you want to make. However, when you are writing any type of document that will convey several ideas, it is useful to create an outline as a guide.

C A S E   S C E N A R I O

Positively Put

Carla Cohen wanted to persuade the Executive Committee to spend an additional, unbudgeted $125,000 a year. The committee chair agreed to review her written proposal. Carla knew the chair and the committee would not be excited about spending more money. Her proposal had to be very convincing.

Carla sat down to prepare her proposal. She listed statistics and background data that supported her stand. Once she had identified the information to include, Carla began her document:

> This proposal will convince you that we need to hire three additional telemarketing representatives as soon as possible. The cost to our organization will be about $125,000 annually. However, once you consider our needs and weigh the benefits, there will be no doubt that this action is desirable.

What approach did Carla choose to take for her proposal? Do you think it was likely to work? Why or why not? What would you have done if you were in her place?

An outline can help you to organize the information you want to present and determine the relationship between one piece of information and another. Start by selecting the best information—that is, the information that will help you achieve your purpose for writing. Then consider your approach and the order in which you want to present the information.

One way to produce an informal outline is to list the information you will include in your written message and number each item on the list. Later, when you write your first draft, the numbers tell you in what order to present the information. To create a more formal outline, list the most general ideas you want to present in the order you want to present them and then list more specific ideas under those general ideas (the outlines below illustrate both methods). Neither type of outlining takes long, and both will help you write your first draft with more ease and efficiency.

Too many people labor unnecessarily over their outlines. They waste time and become frustrated trying to develop a perfect outline. They may struggle over how to word the opening, strain to find the right words, or grapple with the order of topics or ideas. Remember: Your outline is only a tool, a temporary list that allows you to organize your document, find direction, and start writing.

To create an informal outline, list the information you will include in your message. Number each item to reflect the order in which you will present the information as illustrated below.

> Subject: Status of search for new Human Resources administrative assistant
> 8   Plan to continue our efforts aggressively
> 7   Plan to evaluate the job description—is the job bigger than its title?
> 2   Five candidates interviewed for position but none met criteria
> 1   No new hire to date
> 3   No further response from ad
> 4   HR staff are contacting search firms for referrals
> 5   HR staff are evaluating the wage/compensation package now offered
> 6   HR staff are contracting with a temporary agency until the position is filled

This following outline is more structured than the illustration above. Here, main ideas are listed followed by information that supports each main idea.

> STATUS OF SEARCH FOR NEW HUMAN RESOURCES
> ADMINISTRATIVE ASSISTANT
>
> I.   The position is still open
>   a. No new hire to date
>   b. Five candidates interviewed but none met criteria
>   c. No further response from advertisement
> II.   The HR staff has stayed on top of the situation
>   a. Contacting search firms for referrals
>   b. Evaluating wage/compensation package
>   c. Contracting with a temporary agency
> III.   The HR staff has a plan for filling the position
>   a. Continue an aggressive search
>   b. Evaluate job description—is the job bigger than its title?

1 USE YOUR JUDGMENT

In the following situation, Phillip's list is incomplete. Consider what other information Phillip might add in an effort to address the feelings of other plant workers, their families, executives, the community, and the press. Then outline Phillip's announcement as it should have been outlined, and explain why you changed it as you did.

Phillip Jenkins, Public Information Director for a public utility, must write a press release regarding an accident at one of the utility's plants. Three men and one woman received minor injuries, were treated at the local hospital, and are in good condition. They will return to work in two days. The utility for which Phillip works has been criticized in the past for allowing unsafe working conditions, but these are the first injuries reported in many years. Phillip outlines the release as follows:

1. Explain what happened, the time the accident occurred, and describe the cause of the accident.
2. Tell how many employees were injured.
3. Announce that the families have already been notified.

2 USE YOUR JUDGMENT

Read the following situation. Describe Harold's approach, stating whether you believe it is direct or indirect. Explain why you consider his approach effective or ineffective.

Harold Anderson must prepare a memo in which he announces the closing of the company's Gary, Indiana, warehouse. He plans to present the following information in the order shown:

1. Summarize the company's losses during the past two years.
2. List key actions the company had taken to protect its workers.
3. Describe how the economy (and specifically foreign competition) has hurt the company.
4. Explain what the company is doing to resolve the present dilemma.
5. Announce the warehouse closing and the effective date.

Read the following situation and perform the activities that follow:

You have been promoted and are planning to move from Denver, Colorado, to Toledo, Ohio. Your company's personnel department has given you a relocation plan that includes the names and addresses of real estate agents in the Toledo area. You decide to contact one of these agents to help you in your house hunting.

a. Define your purpose and audience.
b. Brainstorm a list of all the information you must include in your letter. Include the things you and your family need and want to help your realtor select the best homes for you to view.
c. Organize your list into an informal outline of your letter.

WRITING

Pre-writing should prepare you for the task of writing. You know the action you want your message to elicit, the facts that support each idea you will present, and the order in which you plan to present the information. The goal of the writing stage, then, is simple: Get your ideas on paper in sentence form. Doing so allows you to move quickly to the next stage of the process to shape your work into an effective piece of communication.

With notes or outline in hand, you are ready to write your **first draft.** Since your reader will not see your first draft, it does not matter where you begin. You can begin at the top of your outline and work to the bottom. Or you may decide to start somewhere in between. In many cases, opening and closing paragraphs of business correspondence are especially difficult to write because they are vital in setting the tone and focus of your correspondence. Because of this, you may be more comfortable drafting those sections last.

Do not expect your first draft to be your final draft; expect to revise later. As you write, do not worry yet about the organization of your document. Include as much information as possible; it is easier to remove sentences later than to add them. Do not worry about format elements such as dates and addresses; they also can be added later. Do not stop to ponder whether a certain sentence sounds good or whether some grammatical aspect of the sentence is correct; there will be time to evaluate and polish in the revision stage. Just maintain your train of thought and get it all down. The more you derail your thinking to make unnecessary decisions, the longer it will take to get it all on paper and the harder it will be to get back on track after each decision.

Writing Checklist

This writing checklist capsulizes both the pre-writing and writing steps. Use it as a guide each time you plan and write a first draft.

- Have you identified your purpose?

- Do you know who your audience will be?

- Have you clarified the ideas you need to communicate?

- Have you identified your sources of information?

- Do you know when your deadline is? Have you planned how to meet it?

- Have you considered and selected an approach?

- Have you considered and selected your medium?

- Have you drafted your main message?

- Have you drafted an introduction?

- Have you drafted a closing?

- Did you write with your purpose and audience in mind?

Given the freedom you have to meet the one goal of the writing stage, drafting should not take long. You may create the first draft of a one-page memo in five minutes. The reason you can do this so quickly is that you are not yet making decisions about the effectiveness of your writing; you are simply getting it on paper or on the computer screen. A first draft (based on the outline on page 249) is demonstrated on page 253.

This first draft still needs revising and proofreading, but the writer has successfully put all of the ideas of the outline in sentence form.

Human Resources staff have been working hard to fill the Research Department administrative assistant position vacated last month by Lynette Meyer's retirement. To date, no one has been hired to fill the position, although five candidates have been interviewed. None was qualified. Currently, we have no further leads from our advertisements
Human Resources staff have recently been in contact with several employment search firms with the hope of obtaining referals. In addition, we are evaluating the wage and compensation package mentioned in our ad to determine if we are offering a salary that is commensurate with the experience this position requires. Until the position is filled, we are contracting with a temporary agency. To find a good candidate, we plan to continue an aggressive search. We think it is possible that the job is bigger than its title so we plan to evaluate the job description. Perhaps a different ad will attract the right person.

USE YOUR JUDGMENT 4

Using your outline from the third "Use Your Judgment" exercise (page 251), write a first draft of the letter you would send to the realtor. Follow the advice on drafting you have learned in this section. See how quickly you can create a first draft in which all of the ideas are expressed in sentence form. Remember, do not worry about the quality of your first draft; just get it down.

REVISING

Once you have all of your ideas in sentence form, the next step is to improve the quality of your message. This aspect of the writing process is called **revision,** and it involves many levels of decision making. Revising means editing your document for clarity, coherence, and consistency as well as technical correctness.

Editing for technical correctness demands that you have a good command of the English language. If your skills are not as good as you'd like them to be, take time to review the rules of grammar. Consult a reference manual to check questions of usage, and keep a dictionary and *thesaurus* on hand to verify and tighten meaning. Chapter 10 reviews aspects of writing **style** that guide revision decision making.

thesaurus

a book or computer program of words and their synonyms

Start the revision step of the RRTWRP process by considering aspects of your writing that affect the whole piece: content, organization, and formatting. Once those aspects of your document are sound, work from the next-largest units to the smallest—from paragraphs to sentences to words and finally to punctuation. After all, it makes no sense to struggle to find just the right word for a sentence when you might later remove the entire paragraph. (You will learn more about style at the sentence and word levels in Chapter 10.)

Good writing results from careful revision. Learn to ask yourself questions about your first draft. Learn to answer those questions honestly from your reader's point of view. Finally, learn to make changes in your writing when they are needed. The document below shows how each line of questioning can help you refine your writing.

Most writers go through several revisions of their first draft before achieving an acceptable final draft document. Here you can see how questions at each level—whole document, paragraph, sentence, and word—help identify ways to improve the message.

Whole Document:

Break second paragraph into two paragraphs to differentiate ideas?

Paragraphs:

Second paragraph is choppy; needs more transitional statements.

Sentences:

Add date to clarify opening statement?

Check subject-verb agreement here.

Tone inconsistent?

Words:

More specific?

Human Resources staff have been working hard to fill the Research Department administrative assistant position vacated last month by Lynette Meyer's retirement. To date, no one has been hired to to fill the position, although five candidates have been interviewed. None was qualified. Currently, we have no further leads from our advertisements

Human Resources staff have recently been in contact with several employment search firms with the hope of obtaining referals. In addition, we are evaluating the wage and compensation package mentioned in our ad to determine if we are offering a salary that is commensurate with the experience this position requires. Until the position is filled, we are contracting with a temporary agency. To find a good candidate, we plan to continue an aggressive search. We think it is possible that the job is bigger than its title so we plan to evaluate the job description. Perhaps a different ad will attract the right person.

Whole Document Level Questions

Once you have a first draft of your document, ask the following questions. Does your document as a whole

- Present the information and ideas fully and clearly?

- Address the specific audience you are supposed to be addressing?

- Employ the style and tone most suitable for the situation?

- Employ the format most suitable for the situation?

Paragraph Level Questions

Once you have considered your document as a whole, consider each of the paragraphs. Does your first paragraph

- Suggest quickly to your reader what your main points are going to be?

- Start the document with a "you" attitude (focusing on the reader's point of view)?

Does your concluding paragraph

- Reinforce your main point briefly?

- Leave your reader with a clear view of how to react or respond to your writing?

Does each of your middle paragraphs

- Employ a clear organizational structure so your reader can follow your ideas easily?

- Include that information, and only that information, that best allows you to make your points and cause your reader to respond in the desired way?

- Include that information, and only that information, that will most affect your reader?

- Support your main ideas with specific supporting details?

- Consider and respond to possible objections your reader might make to your main points?

- Clearly relate to the paragraphs before and after it?

Sentence Level Questions

Once you are satisfied with each paragraph, consider each sentence. Does each sentence

- State its point clearly and completely?

- Support the main idea?

- Work with the sentence before and after it to form a smooth, easy-to-read paragraph?

- Contain strong nouns and verbs when possible instead of too many modifiers?

- Contain modifiers that are placed next to the words they modify?

- Express agreement between sentence parts such as subjects and verbs?

- Express ideas in parallel construction?

- Avoid unnecessary words and phrases?

- Employ a style and tone consistent with the rest of the document?

Word Level Questions

Once you are satisfied with each sentence, consider the words.   Is each word the best choice, considering

- Your reader's knowledge of the topic?

- The situation's level of formality?

- The level of specificity you are trying to achieve?

- The tone you are trying to achieve?

- The emotional impact you are trying to make or trying to avoid?

Your Reader's Point of View

Once again it's time to consider the reader's point of view. Does your written document reflect it or ignore it? You may think your document is very good. However, if your reader finds it unclear, insulting, or simply unconvincing, then it will fail. For the most part, it does not matter what you think of your writing, only what your reader thinks. This is why you must know your audience as well as possible.

Distance

One way to help yourself read your own writing from your reader's point of view is to distance yourself as much as possible from your work. After you have produced a first draft and perhaps made some revisions, take a break from your writing. Go to lunch, go to a meeting, do some other work, let the draft sit overnight or, better still, over the weekend. The longer you stay away from the draft, the newer it will seem to you when you finally look at it again. This allows you to consider the writing a little more ***objectively.*** You will better evaluate what it actually says with less interference from what you thought it said or wanted it to say.

objectively

fairly; undistorted by personal feelings, prejudices, or interpretations

Second Opinions

Another way to check your writing is to get other opinions. A friend or coworker can read your letter, for example, to help you judge whether it will have the intended impact on your reader. In business, it is not unusual for important documents to be reviewed by several people, even by a committee, before distribution. This suggests that business people know the importance and impact of good writing, as well as the cost of bad writing.

When you are lucky enough to have individuals willing to review your writing, help them give you what you need. Make sure they understand the situation in which the document is written or the problem it is intended to solve. Also, do not hesitate to direct their review by asking questions. For example, ask "What do you think of the tone of this memo?" or "Are you able to follow my argument in the third paragraph?"

FIGURE 9.4

If you are defensive, you will have difficulty persuading people to review your work.

Eventually the director came to understand the critics' questions concerning his interpretation of the Tiny Tim character.

Finally, be a good listener. When a reviewer suggests a change, many writers feel offended and immediately leap to their own defense. This is unproductive. An oral explanation does not strengthen the writing; you will not be able to defend your work when your intended reader sees it. Therefore, if a reviewer suggests a change or has difficulty with something you have written, try to understand why the reviewer had trouble. Ask questions to help you solve the problem; you may even ask for revision suggestions. In short, recognize that your reviewer is criticizing the writing, not the writer. If you are defensive, you will have difficulty convincing people to review your work.

The Editing Checklist on page 261 capsulizes the revision step of the writing process. Use it as a guide each time you evaluate your work.

PROOFREADING

Your document will often be judged by its correctness and its appearance. Errors can distract from your message and suggest to some readers that you were careless in preparing your communication. For this reason, proofreading is an important last step in the writing process. It involves checking the final copy for accuracy of information, spelling, punctuation, formatting, and for *typographical* errors.

typographical

of or relating to letters or characters that have been typed, keyed, or typeset

When writing on a computer, use all of the computer's capabilities. Most word processing programs have spell checking software. However, this does not relieve you of the task of proofreading! The computer will not pick up errors that occur when you type the wrong word, such as when you type *you* instead of *your* or *is* instead of *as*. "Style checker" and "grammar checker" software are also available. These programs will identify various potential problems with your writing. With both types of software, you still have to make decisions about how to correct your writing, but these computer writing aids will help you get started.

Follow these guidelines when proofreading your copy:

1. Generate a **hard copy** to proof and mark changes on the text *or*, if you must proof **soft copy** (on the computer screen), advance the copy line by line and make corrections as you go.

2. Proofread for content by reading the copy slowly, concentrating on the accuracy of the message.

3. Read the copy aloud.

4. Enlist a coworker to be a proofreading partner. Read aloud from your copy while your partner checks against the final document. It is easier to catch subtle mistakes with another set of eyes.

5. Try to put some time between the task of revising and proofreading and making final changes. Again, you will be more objective if you've allowed some time to elapse between readings of your document.

As you proofread, be on the lookout for these types of mistakes:

- Repeated words or parts of words, especially at the end of one line and the beginning of the next line

  George just left to meet with a finan-
  nancial planner.

- Substitutions or omissions, especially those that change the meaning of the sentence

  The courts have ruled that this type of business activity is now legal. (The intended meaning: The activity is not legal.)

- Errors in names, titles, addresses, dates, numbers, amounts of money, time

  Project costs have exceeded the $10,000.000 budget.

- Errors of **transposition**

  The meeting be will held next Friday.

- Errors in fact or logic

- The company's fiscal year runs from December through January.

- Errors or problems in formatting (see Chapter 11)

Figure 9.5 shows standard proofreaders' marks. Use these to note errors and changes. You save yourself time using a standardized system, and the marks can be interpreted by anyone (in case someone else will be keying your changes). When you mark your copy, use a red pen so your notations will be easy to spot.

The document on page 262 shows that you can catch several more problems within a document through proofreading. This is the same document that has been demonstrated throughout the chapter. The final revised and proofread memo as shown on page 263 is ready for interoffice mail.

Proofreaders' Marks

Proofreaders' Mark		Example	Revised
#	Insert space	lettertothe	letter to the
ℰ	Delete	the commands is	the command is
lc /	Lowercase	he is Branch Manager	he is branch manager
cap ≡	Uppercase	Margaret simpson	Margaret Simpson
#	New paragraph	The new product	The new product
no #	No paragraph	the meeting.	the meeting. Bring the
		Bring the	
∧	Insert	pens, clips	pens, and clips
⊙	Insert period	a global search	a global search.
⊐	Move right	With the papers	With the papers
⊏	Move left	access the code	access the code
⊐⊏	Center	Chapter Six	Chapter Six
∩	Transpose	It is raesonable	It is reasonable
sp	Spell out	475 Mill Ave	475 Mill Avenue
• • •	Stet	I am very pleased	I am very pleased
	(do not delete)		
⌣	Close up	regret fully	regretfully
ss	Single-space	The margin top	The margin top
		is 1 inch.	is 1 inch.
ds	Double-space	Paper length is	Paper length is
		set for 11 inches.	set for 11 inches.
ts	Triple-space	The F8 function	The F8 function
		key contains commands	key contains commands
bF	Boldface	Boldface type	**Boldface** type
		provides emphasis.	provides emphasis.
ital	Italics	Use italics for terms	Use *italics* for terms
		to be defined.	to be defined.

FIGURE 9.5

Standard proofreader's marks.

Editing Checklist

This editing checklist capsulizes the revision and proofreading steps. Use it as a guide each time you evaluate your work.

- Did you use the correct approach? (Direct for good news; indirect for bad news)

- Is the message effective? (Is the reader likely to respond in the desired manner?)

- Has all necessary information been included? (Who? What? Where? When? Why? How?)

- Is your document reader-oriented?

- Do the paragraphs flow logically?

- Does each paragraph have a clearly identified topic sentence?

- Do sentences flow logically?

- Are all sentences complete?

- Do subjects and verbs agree?

- Is the verb tense consistent?

- Have you defined terms where necessary?

- Have you eliminated jargon, clichés, and pompous words?

- Have you verified dates, amounts, or other data?

- Have you eliminated needless repetitions?

- Is the punctuation correct?

- Is the spelling correct?

M E M O R A N D U M

TO: Collette DeNares

FROM: Al Ferris

DATE: May 26, 19XX

SUBJECT: STATUS OF SEARCH FOR NEW RESEARCH DEPARTMENT
             ADMINISTRATIVE ASSISTANT

Since April 1, Human Resources staff have been working to fill the Research Department administrative assistant position vacated last month by Lynette Meyer's retirement. To date, no one has been hired to fill the position, although five candidates have been interviewed. Unfortunately, none of these candidates met the specific criteria for the job. Currently, we have no further leads from our advertisements.

Human Resources staff have recently been in contact with several employment search firms to obtain referals. In addition, we are evaluating whether the wage and compensation package mentioned in our ad is commensurate with the experience this position requires. Until the position is filled, we are contracting with a temporary agency.

To find a qualified candidate, we plan to continue an aggressive search. We also plan to evaluate the job description; it is possible that the job is bigger than the title we have given it. We may need to alter the wording of our ad to attract the right person.

At this point, the document has been revised several times, but the writer still catches and corrects several errors by proofreading.

The final version of the memo (shown on page 263) accomplishes the purpose.

MEMORANDUM

TO: Collette DeNares

FROM: Al Ferris

DATE: May 26, 19XX

SUBJECT: STATUS OF SEARCH FOR NEW RESEARCH DEPARTMENT
ADMINISTRATIVE ASSISTANT

Since April 1, Human Resources staff have been working to fill
the Research Department administrative assistant position
vacated last month by Lynette Meyer's retirement. To date, no
one has been hired to fill the position, although five candidates
have been interviewed. Unfortunately, none of these
candidates met the specific criteria for the job. We have no
further leads from our advertisements.

Human Resources staff have recently been in contact with
several employment search firms to obtain referrals. In addition,
we are evaluating whether the wage and compensation
package mentioned in our ad is commensurate with the
experience this position requires. Until the position is filled, we
are contracting with a temporary agency.

To find a qualified candidate, we plan to continue an
aggressive search. We also plan to evaluate the job description;
it is possible that the job is "bigger" than the title we have given
it. We may need to alter the wording of our ad to attract the
right person.

USE YOUR JUDGMENT 5

Produce a **mailable letter** by revising and proofreading the first draft you produced in "Use Your Judgment" exercise 4 (page 253). Use the revising and proofreading questions from pages 255-256 as your guide.

6 USE YOUR JUDGMENT

Interpret the proofreaders' marks in the following press release and write a corrected version.

COMPUTE WITH EASE PLANS TO MERGE WITH KEY LEARNING

BELLE PLAIN, August 2 Compute With Ease of Belle Plain plans to merge with Key Learning of Detroit, Michigan next month to form a large company specializing in developing and publishing computer education products and services. Both companies are are privately held and will remain so.

The new company, which will operate under the Compute With Ease name, will offers schools computer education products in such areas as mathematics, statistics and programming. It will support a base of 19,000 current customers representing over 2 million students worldwide.

The new Belle Plain-based firm will have 89 employees and offices in Chicago, Los Angeles, New York, Quebec and London The company will continue selling through out Europe, Japan, Australia and the Middle East.

"The company will be bigger and better," says Anastasia Previn, president and CEO of Compute With Ease. "We will be better able to meat the needs of our customers and deliver state-of-the-art, cost-effective educational products. We will continue to expand our role in the global market place

IN BRIEF

1 Good writing is more than words on a page. It requires careful planning, reviewing, revising, and proofing.

2 The best way to get your message across is to follow a process. We suggest the RRTWRP plan: Read, Research, and Think; Write a draft; and then Revise and Proofread.

3 The goal of the writing process is to produce a well-written document that effectively addresses the situation for which it is written. Rather than making more work for writers, it breaks writing activities into manageable tasks.

4 In the pre-writing stage of the RRTWRP plan, writers identify why they are writing and to whom. They then determine what information they will include and how they will organize that information. They also consider deadlines in their planning.

5 Writers use outlines as a reference tool when they write. An outline can help a writer to delineate the relationships between ideas and establish the approach to the topic.

6 After planning thoroughly, writers following the RRTWRP plan quickly create a first draft to get their ideas into sentence form. At this point, they do not waste time trying to perfect the document.

7 The post-writing stage of the RRTWRP plan requires writers to make final decisions about content, organization, paragraphs, sentences, words, punctuation, and other mechanics.

8 Proofreaders' marks offer a standardized method for marking changes to copy.

WORDS OF NOTE

Define each of these terms introduced in Chapter 9.

direct approach
first draft
hard copy
indirect approach
mailable letter
primary readers
revision
RRTWRP
secondary readers
soft copy
style
tone
transposition
usage

CHECK YOUR RECALL

1 What are the six tasks of the RRTWRP process?

2 What questions will help you decide how to approach your topic?

3 What two types of readers do you need to keep in mind when considering your audience? What other things should you consider about your audience?

4 What does it mean to be intentional about your message? How can you do this?

5 Depending on your topic, what might be some sources of information?

6 When might you want to take a direct approach in writing? An indirect approach?

7 How is making an outline helpful? What information should an outline contain? What do you do to create an informal outline? A formal outline?

8 What is your goal in writing your first draft?

9 What is your goal in revising your first draft? What writing aspects do you need to attend to in your revision?

10 In revising, what are the four levels of questions you need to address? What questions should you consider at each level?

11 How can you help yourself read your document from your reader's point of view? Why is this important?

12 What are the guidelines for proofreading your document?

13 In proofreading, what six types of mistakes do you need to be alert for?

SHARE YOUR PERSPECTIVE

1 Use the writing process described in this chapter to produce a document as follows:

    a. Read an opinion piece in a newspaper or magazine and write a letter to the editor supporting or disputing the position presented.

    b. Write a press release that expresses the opinions of your peers regarding a current event or hot topic. (*Note:* You will need to do an informal survey to obtain the data for this document.)

    c. Write a one-page report that summarizes current job opportunities in the health care field and general qualifications. (*Note:* Use local want ads to obtain data.)

2 Evaluate the first draft of a want ad based on the situation. Photocopy the ad below and then, using proofreaders' marks, revise the ad at the document, paragraph, sentence, and word levels. Then interpret your marks and rewrite the document.

You are a buyer with TechTools Inc., a leader in the tool industry. The company has an opening for an assistant buyer—someone who is good at math, has experience buying in large quantities, knows how to deal with customers, and can operate a computer. The assistant buyer will place orders and put a price on products. TechTools Inc. is a young company that wants to employ enthusiastic and friendly people. You have been asked to revise the ad for this position written by your department manager.

Assistant Buyer

Join a progressive company commited to excellence!

We are TechTools Inc. and have an opening for Assistant Buyer in our construction division. Are you the person were looking for?

You have experience in a large-volume buying environment if you're qualified. You are both quick and accurate with with numbers. You know also how to work with customers and can operate word processing and spreadsheet software on a pc!

Your responsibilities in this exciting job will include but are not limited to placing orders and confirming price and quantities with suppliers, and pricing products.

If you fit the bill for this exciting job, submit your credentials to: TechTools Inc. Attn: H. Miller, P.O. Box 847, Minneapolis, MN 99439. We're looking forward to meeting you!

FOCUS ON THE FINE POINTS
Read the following background information. Then follow the
instructions to locate and correct grammar errors.

Background

Peter Auglund is the recreation coordinator for the Fairfield County
Recreation Department. During the past year his office has received several
requests for organized sports activities for single adults. Peter believes these
requests represent only a portion of the number of single men and women
who might be interested in team sports. At a regional conference last month,
Peter noticed that many communities were having success with volleyball
leagues. Recreation workers from Sweetwater, a town in the southern part of
the state, gave a presentation explaining how they had enlisted the help of a
large local employer in funding and organizing their teams. Peter made a
special note of this, because Fairfield County was the home of CompuTec, a
leading computer company Peter thought he could approach.

Peter meets with several colleagues, including a vice president from
CompuTec, to discuss his idea and brainstorm ways to recruit participants.
Then he sits down to make an outline of a plan, drafts a letter to community
leaders who work with single adults, and roughs out a classified ad to run in
local newspapers.

Your Instructions

Each of the following documents contains up to 15 errors. Indicate and correct errors by noting them on a photocopy of the page or on a separate
sheet of paper. In each case, you may assume the document is formatted
correctly.

Note: If you have difficulty locating errors, turn to page 465 in the Appendix.
There you will find additional information about the errors in Document 1.

DOCUMENT 1: Outline

PLAN FOR RECRUITING VOLLEYBALL LEAGUE PARTICIPANTS

I. Use direct mail to inform and motivate the community.
   a. Send a letter to all singles, (using the list developed through cooperative market research with CompuTec) inviting him or her to participate.
   b. Send a letter to every CompuTec manager inviting his participation and requesting financial support.
   c. Send a letter to Directors of adult singles groups, in local churches and synagogues, asking for their support and requesting an opportunity to speak to its group in the near future.

II. Use print media to get the word out and further motivate the community.
   a. Invite a local sports columnist to write an article for their newspaper about the league in Sweetwater and explains why such a league would be a great idea for Fairfield County.
   b. Running classified ads in the local newspaper to support the article and recruit participants and coaches.
   c. Run an article and ad in CompuTec's company newsletter inviting interested people to call.
   d. Carry out a poster campaign using donated services and materials. Display the posters in churches, in synagogues; at CompuTec and at other places of business such as stores, restaurants etc.

III. Using television and radio to further motivate the community and neighboring towns.
   a. Seek free radio and television time for public service announcements.
   b. Consider running an ad or announcement on electronic mail. (To do this, explore whether public service announcements can be made in this way, and, if so, finds a person who knows how to take advantage of this mode of communication.)

DOCUMENT 2: Letter

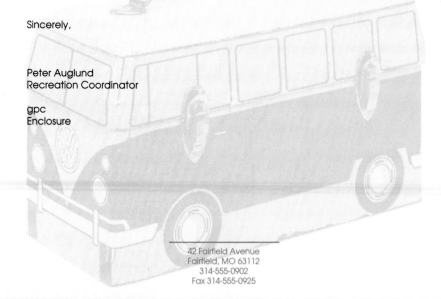

Fairfield County Department of Recreation
County Administrative Building

August 5, 19XX

Dear Adult Singles Director:

The Community of Fairfield County is experiencing phenomenal growth. As you and me both know, activity for adult singles in our community are limited. Us at the recreation department are interested in building sports and social programs for single women and men. As a part, of this effort, we invites your help in recruiting participants for a mixed singles volleyball league.

A recent article (enclosed) in the *Sweetwater Gazette* profiled a volleyball league in the southeastern Missouri city of Sweetwater. It's our belief, that Fairfield County, has a large enough pool of single adults, due, in part, to CompuTec Industries' move to the area, to support similar activities. Volleyball provides healthy, enjoyable activity for men and women alike.

If you believe members of your group would like to learn more about this idea, I would welcome an opportunity to make a brief presentation to you and they. You may, also, be interested to know that we seek qualified volunteer coaches.

I'll plan to contact you within the next week to see if you and me can arrange a time. In the meantime, please call me at 555- 0925. Thank You.

Sincerely,

Peter Auglund
Recreation Coordinator

gpc
Enclosure

42 Fairfield Avenue
Fairfield, MO 63112
314-555-0902
Fax 314-555-0925

DOCUMENT 3: Classified Ad

Classified

505 General

▲▲▲▲▲▲▲

Attention All You Single Guys and Gals

Are you tired of the Singles Scene in the bars?

Are you looking for fun and physical challenge?

Do you want to get back in shape?

Do you want a healthy, pressure-free way for meeting, and getting to know, other Singles?

If any of these describes you, why not join the Fairfield County Community Volleyball League today!

The process of setting up teams have already begun. Games will begin January 3. Men and women alike are invited to call now to reserve his or her space on a team. If you want to join other people who wants to be both physically, and socially, active; don't wait, call today!

555-0902

▼▼▼▼▼▼▼

515 Help Wanted - General

Management

MANAGEMENT TRAINEES

We are a service-oriented company with opportunities for management trainees. These hands-on positions involve customer service, sales, deliveries, and account collections. Good attitude and strong communication skills a must. Mon. - Fri. days. Degree not required; we prefer experience. Expect to make $25,000+ your first year.
Excel Appliances, Inc.
961 City Blvd.
Suite 444

Management

...MENT
...r in the
...work
...ced
...ar.

...train
...nce

515 Help Wanted - General

Management

MANAGER

Convenience store seeking energetic and responsible individual for evening management position. Pay range in the low thirties if degreed.

Superior Shopping
"Open Around the Clock"
555-2951

Mail

MAILROOM ASSISTANT FULL-TIME WEEKDAYS START AT $28,000

We are a leader in business applications software. If you are detail oriented and dedicated, we want you to help us prepare packets for shipments, perform data entry, and operate our mail machines. Degree not necessary, but helpful.

OCS
Office Computer Systems

...ainee
...achines
...directed
...nce
...ange

515 Help Wanted - General

Management

MANAGER - SPORTING GOODS
1st Year $22,000-$26,000
2nd Year $30,000-$34,000

Entry-level retail career. You can train for store management with complete operational responsibility.
Degree and interest in management required; strong interest in sports a plus. Must be willing to work nights, weekends - but reward will be great!

SPORTS WORLD
SuperStores
1200 State Ave. 5th floor

Management

MANAGEMENT OPPORTUNITY

Due to expansion we have an immediate need for assertive, degreed individuals to start our paid management training program. Upon completion you will work Monday through Friday days in our fast-paced distribution warehouse. We offer a competitive salary, beginning range $26,000 - $30,000 depending on qualification. What are you waiting for - APPLY NOW!

XYZ Industries
809 University Place

WRITING WITH STYLE

CHAPTER TEN

What constitutes writing style?

What elements of style will contribute to the effectiveness of your business messages?

What elements of style can detract from your messages?

Style refers to the way a writer strings words together to convey an idea. It reflects the numerous decisions the writer must make regarding word choice and the construction of sentences and paragraphs. The best writing style for business is one that enhances readability and advances the writer's purpose.

Writers achieve effective style by selecting more specific words, eliminating jargon or clichés, varying the length of sentences, changing passive voice to active voice, improving transitions between ideas or paragraphs, and tightening the logic of their messages.

You can strive for effective style as you draft your business documents. However, if you are a beginning writer, it may be easier to get your ideas on paper first and concentrate on the style of your document during the revision stage.

Because there are many ways to express an idea in writing, there are no formulas for creating a perfect sentence, paragraph, or document. However, there are elements of style that contribute to crisp, effective business documents. In this chapter, you'll learn about these elements as they apply to choosing the words, sentences, and paragraphs that form your messages.

CHOOSING THE RIGHT WORDS

Words should be handled with care. Words have exact, definite meanings according to the dictionary, but sometimes they convey even more. Word meanings can vary within different contexts and can conceal or reveal your point of view.

In business writing, you must think carefully about the words you use. The real meaning of a word resides in the mind of the user, not in the word itself or in its dictionary definition. If your communication is to be results-oriented, you must be sensitive not only to your intended meaning but also to the various meanings your words might call up in the mind of the receiver. There are choices you can make at the word level that will increase the likelihood that your readers will respond as you want them to.

Precise Language

Words vary with regard to how precise they are. When you use precise language, your readers will be better able to "get" what it is you are trying to communicate. Notice how much easier it becomes to create a mental picture as words become more specific (see Figure 10.1):

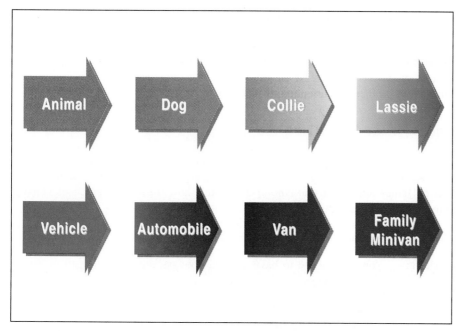

FIGURE 10.1

The more specific the word, the easier it is to create a mental image.

There are times when you want to write in general terms before you get more precise. For example, if you are writing about office technology, you may need to define a bubble jet printer before referring to it by its model number.

Personal Pronouns

The words *I, you, he, she, it, we, they, me, my, your,* and so on are **personal pronouns.** We use them constantly when we talk, but sometimes writers adopt a style that avoids them. Their writing ends up sounding stuffy and distant. You can personalize your message by using personal pronouns, particularly those that are reader-oriented: *you* and *your*.

Euphemisms

The trend in language today is to remove any negative connotation from our communications. In many ways this trend is good, because it helps us to think differently about people and things that have been judged negatively and often unfairly. We adapt our language and use **euphemisms** that express unpleasant ideas in more pleasant terms. For example, in our changing language the *complaint department* is now *customer service*; one who once was called *handicapped* is now *physically challenged*.

Sometimes the person who uses a euphemism is trying to be sensitive; in other instances, the person is trying to express a negative thought without having to pay the price for it. For example, a senior executive might describe a young female business associate as "assertive"—but does the executive mean that she is confident and bold, or pushy and overbearing? This use of euphemisms should be avoided.

Some business people are reluctant to use euphemisms at all. However, business writers should be sensitive to the opinions of the dominant culture regarding language use—or they risk offending their readers.

Negative and Positive Words

In business writing, it is easier to influence people and get results with words that express positive feelings. For example, it is always better to emphasize what you *can* do rather than what you *cannot* do. Notice how these two sentences convey information in contrasting styles:

Negative: We *cannot* mail your package by overnight express mail.

Positive: You *can* choose to have us send your package by 2-day air or 3-day ground service.

There are many words that tend to provoke negative reactions; similarly there are words that generally have a positive effect on readers. A letter containing several of the following words is likely to elicit good feelings:

advantage	comfort
deserve	enjoy
help	pleasure
satisfaction	success
thoughtful	valuable

However, you won't always be able to avoid the negative in your written business communications. There will be times when your message is far from pleasant. When a business topic deals with a touchy situation, search for neutral words to convey your message. For example, consider how a message can be weighed down by the words on the left; on the other hand, the words on the right are neutral or positive equivalents:

Negative	**Neutral/Positive**
cheap	affordable
defective	malfunctioning
fault	responsibility
misinformed	unaware
neglect	forget
regret	apologize

Shades of Meaning

With carelessness, **shades of meaning** between words can cause miscommunications. For example, if you describe an office facility as "adequate for our needs," one reader may interpret adequate as "sufficient" and another may interpret it to mean *"marginal."* Each will each have a different impression of the facility.

marginal

close to the lower limit of qualification, acceptability, or function

Or consider the words *defective* and *broken*. Both are used to describe something that does not work properly. But when a customer claims a product is defective and the manufacturer claims it is broken, the shades of meaning that distinguish the two words clash. After all, *defective* implies manufacturer responsibility, while *broken* implies user responsibility.

Use the dictionary, a thesaurus, and your own experience to distinguish shades of meaning and choose the most appropriate words for your document. If you are concerned that your message may be misunderstood, define your terms. Then there can be no confusion regarding what you really mean.

Redundancies

Redundancies occur when two or more words are used where one would do. The "extra" words are just that; they add no value to the sentence. Some redundancies are commonplace, others we craft ourselves. To make your document concise, be on the lookout for redundancies such as these when you write, and choose the concise alternative:

Redundant	Concise
above and beyond	above
best interests	interests
both alike	alike
check into	check
exact same	same
first and foremost	first
past experience	experience
repeat over	repeat
switched over	switched
telltale sign	sign

▲**FIGURE 10.2**

A thesaurus can help you find alternatives to euphemisms or to terms that may have a negative connotation. Once you settle on a word, however, check its meaning in the dictionary. This will give added insurance that your reader won't interpret the new term in a way you do not intend.

Familiar Words

The words you choose to express your ideas should be strong and vigorous to attract and hold your reader's attention. They should be simple, everyday words. Long words "look" difficult to the reader and sometimes they are. In contrast, short, familiar words have more force and clarity than long ones. So, when a short, familiar word will convey your message quickly and clearly, use it instead of the longer or unfamiliar one. Especially if your message will go out to the public, it is best to create a document that is easy to read and understand.

Long/Unfamiliar	Familiar
utilize	use
terminate	end
endeavor	try
demonstrate	show
ascertain	find out
query	ask
initiate	begin
procure	get
peruse	read
converse	talk

Clichés

One challenge to writers is to find fresh, new ways to express common or everyday objectives. That is why it is tempting to use **clichés** (overused phrases) in our messages. But each shortcut can cost you in terms of your readers' attention and trust level.

You'll recognize these clichés from everyday speech, television, and even the newspaper:

- Easy as pie

- A needle in a haystack

- Quick as a wink

There are also clichés that show up almost exclusively in business writing:

- Dear *Valued Customer*:

- *Enclosed please find* a free sample of our new . . .

- *Per your request* the shipment is scheduled . . .

- Your mail will be *hereinafter* delivered to . . .

Because clichés are commonplace, they do not have the ability to compel your reader to act. In fact, readers may not even get a cliché-ridden message since they are likely to skip over or block out clichés as they read!

With a little imagination, it is possible to find new ways to express old ideas. Instead of the cliché, "We appreciate your business," you might consider ending your letter with a more personal remark: "As one of our best customers, you have helped Jetson Markets reach our sales goal of $1,000,000. Thank you!"

Jargon

Jargon is "insider" language—words and phrases that communicate ideas, processes, or equipment in an abbreviated form. Jargon is usually specific to a line of work or area of expertise. For example, sports car dealers categorize cars according to the shape they are in; an outsider may not know the specific requirements for a card labeled "mint" or "near-mint." Similarly, stockbrokers talk about "bull" and "bear" markets; again, the uninitiated will have no idea what this jargon implies.

Because it is exclusive language, jargon can turn off readers. It does have its place in internal communications, when you know your reader will understand the terminology and the jargon speeds up the communication process. However, if readers are unfamiliar with the technical terms you use, they will feel left out. And even if they know the words, they may feel as though you are trying too hard to impress them with your insider vocabulary. Use jargon carefully, or not at all.

Trendy Words

Trendy words are not a good choice when writing because they date your material. For example, during the 1992 Presidential election, words such as *sound bite* and *politically correct* became trendy. Like jargon, trendy words can make it look as though you are trying to impress your readers. There also is a chance that a reader will not be familiar with a trendy word or phrase, which can result in a communication breakdown. And like clichés, trendy words will give your writing a tired, unimaginative flavor.

Trendy Words Then and Now

Vogue words, catch words, buzzwords—over the years even slang itself has been renamed and reinvented. When, in 1828, Noah Webster called it "low, vulgar unmeaning language," slang had already been a part of American life for more than 200 years.

A Century of Slang

- In the early 1900s, the hip cats were into jazz and everyone else was excited about the talkies.

- By the 1920s, unchaperoned flappers flocked to the flicks.

- During the '30s while Roosevelt's New Deal sought to put an end to Hoovervilles and flacks were busy trying to boost the Big Board, neighbors met at the nabe for movies in Technicolor.

- By the end of the 1940s, most of the nation's snafus had been deep sixed. Big bands were boffo; the baby boom had begun.

- The going was good in the '50s—whether you were cruising the dragstrip, hanging out at the drive-in, or heading home on the expressway for a night with the idiot box. Beatniks were with-it, cats were cool. "Modern" was rediscovered and redefined.

- The '60s were a groovy happening. Hippies turned on, tuned in, and dropped out. The exchange was bullish on America. Families bridged the generation gap by watching "Laugh-In." Computerniks talked computerese. Far out, man.

- 1970 ushered in a decade of inflation. The stock market had turned bearish. Buzzwords were "oil," "microwave," and "bicentennial." Valley Girls thought the whole thing was like, you know, totally awesome—unless it was grody to the max. "The Mod Squad" was mod and "The Brady Bunch" was blended. Computerphobia was on the rise. For sure.

- Along came the '80s. Technologies were converging. "Stress" took on a new meaning. Our phones went cellular. Our notebooks became machines. Our televisions hooked up to cables. We listened to sound bites. Overnight air delivery business soared. Inflation gave way to stagflation. We communicated via voice mail. We sought MBAs and quality time.

CASE SCENARIO

The Price Is Right

Dane Kravitz worked at Robertson Press. On Monday he received payment for a mail order from Ms. Dorothy Greco. Ms. Greco sent a check for $27.95, the full amount listed on the invoice. She also included a note questioning the price of the book. Apparently the Robertson catalog lists the price as $24.95, and she questioned this discrepancy. Dane knew why the price was higher—the catalog was printed before a price increase was instituted. Before filling Ms. Greco's order, he wanted to respond to her question. Dane explained the situation to Ms. Greco in the following letter:

One Publishers' Place
Columbia, South Carolina 29201
803/555-1373
Toll Free 800/555-7788
Fax 803/555-1348

Robertson Press

August 2, 19XX

Ms. Dorothy Greco
1777 East Whitcomb
Apt. 2A
Middleton, WI 54042

Dear Ms. Greco:

This letter will acknowledge receipt of your inquiry of August 2 concerning the price of *Modern Home Renovation*, by Levitt and Sommers. The price in our catalog is $24.95; the price on our invoice is $27.95.

With regard to this matter, please be informed that it is common practice in the publishing industry to raise book prices in subsequent printings after the initial publication as a result of increases in manufacturing costs. The price of $27.95 is, therefore, correct.

Sincerely yours,

Dane Kravitz
Customer Service Representative

What do you think of Dane's letter-writing style? What word choice problems exist? To improve his message, what words could Dane eliminate or find substitutes for?

USE YOUR JUDGMENT 1

Identify ten words or phrases that are jargon or trendy, then define them, using familiar words. Use both versions in a sentence.

USE YOUR JUDGMENT 2

Think of a simpler word or phrase for each of the following:

a.	acquiesce	k.	equitable
b.	aggregate	l.	equivalent
c.	apparent	m.	interrogate
d.	approximately	n.	modification
e.	ascertain	o.	preclude
f.	assist	p.	predisposed
g.	commensurate with	q.	procure
h.	conclusion	r.	remit
i.	demonstrate	s.	subsequent to
j.	disseminate	t.	verification

EXAMINING SENTENCE STRUCTURE

We use the sentence to express our ideas in understandable units of thought. As a business writer, you must arrange your words so that your sentences will convey a meaningful unit of thought in your reader's mind.

Length and Balance

Short, simple sentences are more understandable than long, involved ones. In a short sentence the reader can identify the main idea immediately without having to wade through unnecessary words. Short sentences highlight their contents; longer sentences give less importance to their contents.

Short: The company hopes the plant will open next spring.

Long: With much anticipation, the company hopes the plant, which will cover 200 square acres, will open next spring.

Reserve long sentences for generalizing and summarizing, when it may be necessary to use 20 to 30 words to capsulize your ideas.

Short sentences, interspersed with slightly longer sentences for variety, make your messages crisp and clean. There is less clutter—fewer *modifiers,* phrases, and *clauses* to sidetrack the reader. Try to say what you need to say in as few words as possi-

modifier

a grammatical qualifier; a word, phrase, or clause that affects (changes, restricts, enlarges) the meaning of another word or group of words

clause

a group of words that contains a subject and a related verb and that is part of a sentence ble. You'll find that some sentences will still require more words, but this discipline will help you tighten your writing.

Active versus Passive Voice

Verbs are the heart of the sentence. As the action words, they tell us what is happening. In the **active voice,** the subject (the noun) is doing the action. In the passive voice, the subject is acted upon.

Active Voice	Passive Voice
He explained the policy.	The policy *was explained.*
The company approved the plan.	The plan *was approved.*

Most of the time, we talk using the active voice. We use personal pronoun and noun subjects to identify the doer of the action in our sentences.

- *She* joined the company in 1989.

- *First Mutuals Inc.* offers financial planning services.

- *The union* objects to nonunion hiring.

The active voice emphasizes immediacy and adds vitality to your writing.

While we seldom talk in the **passive voice,** many people consistently write in it. But writers should reserve the passive voice for very specific situations. Here are some appropriate uses of the passive voice:

- When the doer is unknown:
  The building was constructed in 1984.

- When the doer is unimportant:
  Your order was shipped on Thursday.

- When the doer of the action should not be mentioned out of tact or diplomacy:
  An error was made in the computation of your taxes.

- When the action is more important than the doer (as in formal reports):
  Forty charge-account customers were surveyed regarding their spending habits.

When you use passive voice in these situations, your writing will be effective. In other situations, choose the active voice.

Fred would probably get significantly better results from his memos if someone would tell him that there is no Pulitzer Prize awarded for memos

◀ **FIGURE 10.3**

Effective business writing is concise and gets to the point immediately.

No Frills

Good business writing has "no frills." Every sentence—and every word within the sentence—contributes to the overall message in a meaningful way.

Executives who read business letters, memos, reports, and brochures are busy. They must be able to identify the issue immediately so that they can make productive decisions. When you write for business, it is your job to get your point across as *succinctly* as possible.

succinctly

precisely, exactly; without wasted words

Consider how "frills" in the first paragraph detract from the message. The second paragraph is concise:

Frills: While I was away from my desk for a few short moments today, your package arrived. It was shortly before lunch. Imagine my surprise when I opened it to find the transparencies for the meeting I attended at 9 A.M.!

No Frills: The package of transparencies arrived today at 11:30 A.M. Unfortunately, I needed them for a 9 A.M. meeting.

When your writing is concise, you don't waste time explaining every detail of the day or using every descriptive word that applies. Subsequently, your reader does not waste time either.

Identify the passive voice and rewrite those sentences that would be better in the active voice.

a. The site for the new company headquarters was selected by the committee.
b. Our chemist tested the perfume samples.
c. The quota was not met by the sales department last month.
d. The amendment was approved by a majority of the Board members.
e. Last week, the Department of Health inspected the restaurant.
f. Several steps are being taken by our staff to improve customer service.
g. Smoking is prohibited in the entire building.
h. This shipment should be examined for damage.
i. For some reason, the manager believed that we had punched out early.

EXPLORING PARAGRAPH DEVELOPMENT

Good paragraphs are a series of well-written, coherent sentences arranged in a meaningful order and joined by **transitional words and phrases.** Within the paragraph, the writer should establish the sequence of sentences to carry the reader from one topic to the next in a logical manner. Good paragraphs function to:

• Force you, the writer, to think in terms of general statements or main ideas and the specific statements that support them

• Help your readers to identify each new main idea and supporting ideas so that they can follow your message more closely

• Break the monotony of a long document, making the material more visually attractive to the reader

There are three parts to a paragraph: the introduction or **topic sentence, developmental sentences,** and the **closing sentence.** One effective test of a paragraph is to ask whether you can reduce its content to a single topic statement. Everything else in the paragraph should relate to this statement.

Most paragraphs contain from three to five sentences. The length of your paragraphs will vary according to subject matter and according to sentence construction. As a general guideline, a paragraph should not be longer than six to eight lines. Of course, quality is more important than length.

In business writing, you will find that paragraphs are usually shorter than in scholarly or technical writing. Sometimes the paragraph may consist of only one sentence. The one-sentence paragraph serves as a link between the preceding and the following paragraph or it may be used effectively as the opening or closing of the message.

Paragraphs may be constructed in a **direct order** or an **indirect order.** With the direct approach, the topic sentence is followed by descriptive details. It is a very readable format and is the most widely used in business writing. With the indirect approach, details precede the topic sentence. The indirect approach is useful when you must give your reader bad news. Such an arrangement allows you to present reasons before giving a bad news message.

Style Guides

The following books are excellent resources on writing style and usage:

Bernstein, T.M. *The Careful Writer: A Modern Guide to English Usage.* New York: Atheneum, 1978.

Condon, G., and F. Andera. *The Paradigm Guide to English Essentials.* St. Paul, MN: Paradigm, 1991. (check date)

Dumond, V. *The Elements of Non-sexist Usage: A Guide to Inclusive Spoken and Written English.* Englewood Cliffs, NJ:Prentice-Hall.

A Manual of Style. 14th rev. ed. Chicago: University of Chicago Press, 1993.

Maggio, R. *The Dictionary of Bias-Free Usage: A Guide to Nondiscriminatory Language.* Phoenix: The Oryx Press, 1991.

MLA Handbook for Writers of Research Papers. 3d ed. New York: Modern Language Association of America, 1988.

Seraydarian, P.E. *Proofreading & Editing Business Documents.* 2d rev. ed. St. Paul, MN: Paradigm, 1995.

Seraydarian, P.E., and M. Longyear. *The Paradigm Reference Manual.* St. Paul, MN: Paradigm, 1993.

Skillin, M.E., and R.M. Gay. *Words into Type.* 3d rev. ed. Englewood Cliffs, NJ: Prentice-Hall, 1974.

Strunk, W., Jr., and E.B. White. *The Elements of Style.* 3d rev. ed. New York: Macmillan, 1979.

Two computer programs on style and usage are:

Grammatik

RightWriter

Logic

Your writing is logical when you have presented and connected ideas so that they make sense to the reader. Logic is tied to how you arrange your thoughts on paper—are your points clearly made? Does each paragraph build upon the last? Following the writing process will help you to establish logic in your documents.

Transitions

Transitions are certain words, phrases, and sentences that give direction to your flow of ideas. They clarify the relationship between two or more thoughts.

- The promotion will begin on September 15. *Consequently,* sales should be brisk during October.

- Your account is seriously past due. *As a result,* your charge privileges are temporarily suspended.

- Let's examine the reasons for the new procedure.

Transitions prepare readers for what is coming so that they are in a better position to understand the message. As the box on page 287 indicates, transitions serve a number of purposes.

Writers are so close to their subject matter that they frequently omit these useful links in their writing. Without transitions, your writing will sound choppy, the relationship among ideas will be unclear, and your readers will be confused. When these connectors are overused, your writing will sound stilted and overly formal. Moderate use of connectors, within and between paragraphs, adds to the clarity of your writing.

Useful Transitions

Purpose	Transitions
To introduce a topic	in the first place in addition and besides
To review a point	in other words that is in conclusion to summarize
To compare items	likewise in the same way
To show examples	for example namely including for instance
To contrast	however on the other hand but yet in contrast on the contrary
To show cause	consequently because therefore accordingly as a result
To concede a point	granted of course to be sure certainly
To guide a reader through time	after several weeks again eventually earlier later next now ultimately
To guide a reader through space	above below nearby
To conclude	all in all finally in conclusion to summarize

C A S E   S C E N A R I O

Deposit Dispute

Kia Timmons works in the customer service department of the First Groverdale Bank. Yesterday she spoke with a client, Marshall Hall, about a discrepancy in Mr. Hall's checking account. Mr. Hall believed he had deposited $125.00 in his account Friday, but he had no proof since it was a cash deposit. The teller's records showed that he deposited $75.00. Kia told Mr. Hall during their meeting that she would look into the matter. Today, she learned that there was no overage with the teller's cash bank last Friday; in addition, the teller located the deposit slip Mr. Hall had filled out by hand for $75.00. Kia wrote the following letter:

Telephone (813) 555-9811
Fax (813) 555-9827
Toll Free (800) 555-3566

April 22, 19XX

First Groverdale Bank

319 East Main Street
Prescott, CO 80022

Mr. Marshall Hall
534 James Avenue
Prescott, CO 80022

Dear Mr. Hall:

Thank you for stopping by to see me yesterday to clear up a question about your checking account. I know that you have been a faithful customer of the First Groverdale Bank for over 30 years, and I want to make sure that your banking experiences here continue to be pleasant.

I was able to talk to the teller who helped you last Friday, Kelly Henderson. Kelly showed me her cash reconciliation for the day, which indicated no overage. In addition, she was able to locate your deposit slip dated April 18, 19XX, handwritten by you, for $75.00. I have enclosed a photocopy for your information.

This type of error happens to all of us at one time or another, so please do not feel embarrassed. Certainly if we had made the error, we would correct it immediately. Please let us know if you have any other concerns in the future.

I hope this clears up any questions you have about your checking account.

Sincerely,

Kia Timmons
Customer Service Liaison

How well did Kia use strong sentences and effective paragraphs to convey her message? Are there frills that you would remove? Are active and passive voice used appropriately?

IN BRIEF

1 Style is the way in which a writer chooses words and forms sentences and paragraphs to create a message.

2 Writers can make a conscious effort to improve their writing style, which should be crisp and concise for business communications.

3 Writers need to consider how the words they choose will be interpreted by their readers.

4 Precise language adds clarity to your message.

5 Personal pronouns, particularly *you* and *your*, make your message more reader-friendly.

6 Writers can use euphemisms to express a negative idea in more positive terms; however, they should not be used if the intention is to insult or degrade others.

7 Some words are more likely to evoke positive feelings and therefore are desirable choices for business communications.

8 Writers improve their style by being aware of shades of meaning and eliminating redundancies.

9 Short, simple words as opposed to long, complex terms usually are the better choice in business writing.

10 Clichés, jargon, and trendy words should be used carefully or not at all in business communications.

11 The best recipe for a sentence is to keep it short, in the active voice, and devoid of frills.

12 A good paragraph conveys an idea through a group of well-conceived sentences. Paragraphs within a document should relate to one another logically.

13 Transitions serve to move the reader from one idea to the next within a message.

WORDS OF NOTE

Define each of these terms introduced in Chapter 10.

active voice
cliché
closing sentence
developmental sentence
direct order
euphemism
indirect order
jargon
passive voice
personal pronoun
redundancy
shades of meaning
topic sentence
transitional words and phrases
transition
trendy word

CHECK YOUR RECALL

1 At what step in the RRTWRP process do you work on your style?

2 What is style? In what ways can writers achieve effective style?

3 What are some of the issues surrounding word choice? How can you decide what words to use?

4 How can using euphemisms and neutral or positive words help make your messages effective?

5 In business writing, why should you avoid redundant language and long, unfamiliar words?

6 What do clichés, jargon, and trendy words have in common? How are they different? When is it appropriate to use jargon?

7 What is the difference between active and passive voice? Why should you use active voice in most cases? When is passive voice a better choice?

⑧ What are the three parts to a paragraph? What should everything in the paragraph relate to?

⑨ What two sequences can you use in developing a paragraph? Which is more useful for giving bad news?

⑩ What are transitions? What are several different uses for transitions?

SHARE YOUR PERSPECTIVE

① Clip an article from a newspaper or magazine. Analyze the style and critique it regarding word choice and sentence and paragraph construction.

② Prepare a 50-word paragraph (or several related, shorter paragraphs) on any of the following themes:

    a. Personalize your writing
    b. Words have the power to influence people
    c. There's too much information available through today's media
    d. Why the art of personal letter writing has died out
    e. Why I chose a career in _____
                      (fill in the blank)

③ Rewrite the following draft of a letter to improve word choice and sentence and paragraph construction:

> Dear Craig:
>
> We received an order of 50 luminescent bulbs yesterday from your outfit. Needless to say, we cannot ship it until we receive a cashier's check because of your questionable credit rating.
>
> Indubitably, we want your business. We're sure you have a good excuse for your credit history, but a bird in the hand is worth two in the bush. In other words, we need the greenbacks before we release the goods.
>
> No hard feelings, just send the check in the enclosed envelope.
>
> Have a grand day!
>
> Sincerely,

FOCUS ON THE FINE POINTS
Read the following background information. Then follow the
instructions to locate and correct grammar errors.

Background

Paul Archer, founder of the architectural firm Archer, Feldman, Archer, &
Moroni, will retire soon. LeAnn Metzger, his assistant, is a member of the
committee that is planning a dinner in his honor. At the dinner, Mr. Archer will
be presented with a memory book created by employees. The book will
include a biographical sketch about Mr. Archer and his firm and pages created by employees. LeAnn prepares a confidential memo about the dinner and
the book.

Your Instructions

Each of the following documents contains up to 15 errors. Indicate and correct errors by noting the solution on a photocopy of the page or on a separate sheet of paper. In each case, you may assume the document is formatted correctly.

Note: If you have difficulty locating errors, turn to page 467 in the Appendix.
There you will find additional information about the errors in Document 1.

DOCUMENT 1: Memo

MEMORANDUM

CONFIDENTIAL

TO: All Employees

FROM: LeAnn Metzger

DATE: June 12, 19XX

SUBJECT: RETIREMENT DINNER FOR PAUL ARCHER
            FRIDAY, JULY 3, 6:00 P.M.

The retirement dinner for Paul Archer will take place Friday evening, July 3, at 6:00 p.m. In the Fern Room of the Garden Court Hotel.

As you know, while Mr. Archer is aware of the dinner, he is not aware of some of the activities we are planning in his honor. Having said this, please take care not to accidentally give away any of the surprises!

Besides the multimedia tribute that long-time client Barbara Mulligan of Stratford Films is planning, all employees are invited to create a page for a memory book that we will present to Mr. Archer. What you do with your page is entirely up to you. Some suggestions might include writing about a past event (using the format of a paragraph, short personal note, or poem), providing a photograph with a caption, or incorporating a small souvenir along with a brief description of the occasion remembered.

As the founder of Archer, Feldman, Archer, & Moroni, we all owe it to Mr. Archer to give him a memorable send-off. As well as one that is respectful and in keeping with his stature and dignity. I mention this because, in planning how you will present your memory, the end result should be something Mr. Archer will treasure.

Should you wish to contribute to the book, please turn in your page to me or to Sandra Blake on or before Friday, June 19 and Sandra and I will assemble the book and arrange for printing and binding.

If you are able to come to the dinner, plan to arrive <u>no later than</u> six o'clock; if not, you are still welcome to create a page for the book.

Please let either Sandra or me know. We need an exact head count by June 26. If you have questions. Call me at extension 333 or by calling Sandra at extension 338.

<u>Remember: Mum's the word!</u>

DOCUMENT 2: Page from Memory Book

The Mistake of a Lifetime

Thinking about the many years I've spent with Archer, Feldman, Archer, & Moroni, Mr. Archer's compassion and wisdom are probably no better illustrated than by his handling of a terrible mistake I made on one of my first projects with the company which was in 1978 when Mr. Archer assigned me to a project for Stratford Films. Even back then Stratford was one of the firm's most important clients. For their Sacramento complex, in designing a branch studio and editing suites, I was the lead architect. It wasn't until the construction was well underway that it became clear that the measurements for three of the editing suites. Each was off by 22 inches, so one wall of each suite was shorter than it should be!

I'll never forget the moment when I had to tell Mr. Archer what I had done. I was sure he'd either kick me out the door or I would have my pay docked. Believing this, imagine how I felt as I walked into his office that day! But in true Paul Archer style, when I confessed my mistake, practically in tears, he said to me: "Redraw the plan. Find out how it can best be corrected and what it will cost. Then fix it. Have the contractor bill any additional costs back to us."

"Thank you, Mr. Archer," I stammered. "I'm very sorry."

"Son," Mr. Archer told me, "we all make mistakes, please don't make another one this big."

I can assure you, I didn't! Mr. Archer's handling of that mistake left a lasting impression. On me and on how I deal with problems every day.

Terrance Moroni

DOCUMENT 3: Biographical Sketch

The history of Archer, Feldman, Archer, & Moroni is the history of its founder. Paul Ernest Archer. Mr. Archer has often been heard to say, "I was born wanting to be an architect." And it's true. From the age of six, Paul Archer whiled away his time by drawing pictures of homes, churches, and other buildings. After only a few months in college, in 1929 the city of Chicago added another architectural firm to its roster: Archer Architecture. The depression was on, but Paul Archer was off and running, masterfully combining his visionary talent for design with the skill and savvy of a super salesman. With the formation in 1939 of a partnership with Jasper Feldman, the Archer Feldman Company had already carved a niche for itself as a premier design house. In the Frank Lloyd Wright/Prairie style.

With his son's graduation from the University of Minnesota School of Architecture in 1969, Shawn Archer joined the firm, becoming a full partner in 1975. Having worked with Shawn on a project in Sacramento, in 1978 the firm added another young architect, Francis Moroni, to its ranks, later becoming the fourth partner.

From the beginning, Paul Archer wanted his company to enrich all its employees. Its profit-sharing program set the industry standard for years, and in converting to an ESOP (employee stock ownership plan) in 1989, the employees of Archer, Feldman, Archer, & Moroni became equal owners and decision makers. What a difference this one man made for the future for us and for our families!

Integrity is, and has always been, the hallmark of Archer, Feldman, Archer, & Moroni. The fruits of this are evident throughout the company and are evidenced in the industry as well. The loyalty of its employees, its reputation with its clients—even with its competitors. All of these point to Archer, Feldman, Archer, and Moroni's founder, Paul Ernest Archer: our steward and our friend.

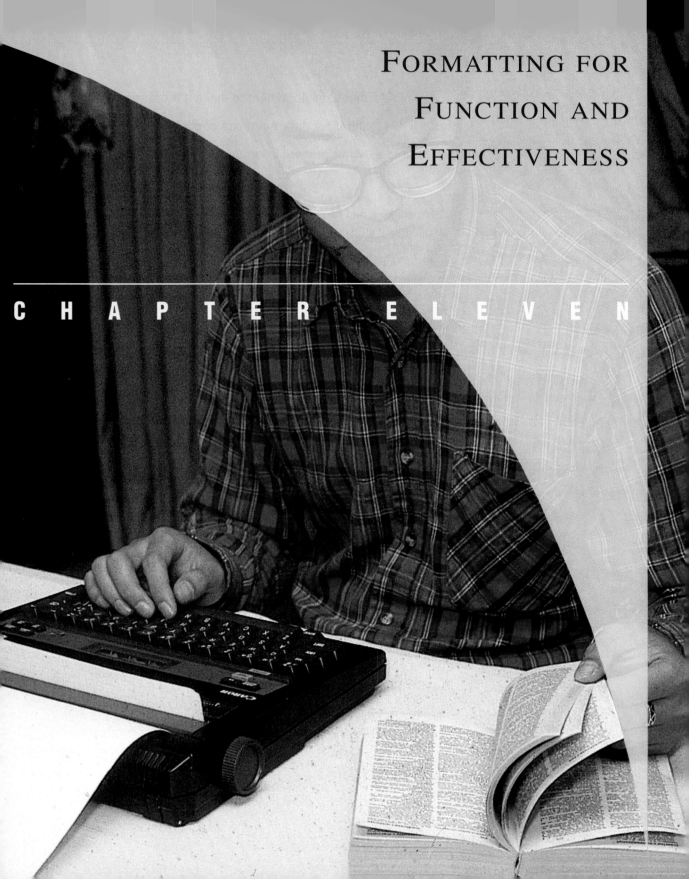

FORMATTING FOR FUNCTION AND EFFECTIVENESS

CHAPTER ELEVEN

How can you format your document to make it more readable?

How do formats differ for different types of documents?

When should a writer present information in a table or other alternative format?

If you open a book and it does not have a title page, chapter titles, page numbers, margins, and paragraphs to break up the text, what would you think? You might not even recognize it as a "book," since many of a book's standard elements would not be present. Each of these elements, which together make up the **format** of a document, provides readers with cues that influence how they receive written material. Without format elements, or with poorly selected ones, the reader can easily get lost.

Basically, format is how written information is presented on the page. It determines how the page "looks" to a reader. You may think, "What does it matter how I place the words on the page, as long as I get the message right?" Well, the appearance of your document is the first impression you make. That first glance at your message should be an open invitation to the receiver. Without **eye appeal,** your message may be discarded before it is even read.

There is another reason to consider format as you craft your message. In business, there are guidelines for formatting memos, letters, and reports as well as for formatting information that might be attached or within those documents. You will want your business messages to conform to these guidelines so that your reading audience can readily recognize and understand them.

FORMATTING FOR READABILITY

Writing has the greatest degree of readability when it is presented in small segments with lots of white space. Information presented in long paragraphs and sentences is visually cluttered and intimidating. It is also physically tiring to read, since the eyes are given few breaks. The following techniques should help to give your words visual impact:

1. **Always start your message with a short paragraph.** No one likes to sort through a long paragraph right at the beginning of a document. Instead, start with a short paragraph to introduce your main idea.

2. **Use headings.** Headings are guideposts that alert the reader to what is coming; they show organization for blocks of information in your document.

3. **Use parallel structure.** For example, when creating headings, start all your headings with a verb. **Parallel structure** gives your document consistency that will help the reader see quickly and easily how the document is organized.

asterisk

a star-shaped character * used in writing as a reference mark or in formatting to highlight or set off important information

4. **Use formatting and organizational symbols.** Use bullets, hyphens, *asterisks,* numbers, underlining, or boldface type to highlight important information or to set off related items. Use numbered lists when the order of the items is especially important.

While a poor format is full of long paragraphs and has little white space, a good format appears open and inviting. Consider the examples below.

This excerpt from a style manual is difficult to read because of its poor format. The reader sees a mass of text without formatting elements to help identify important information.

> Figures must have captions that explain the contents. It is not necessary to start by saying, "This figure shows . . ." or "The graph contains. . . ." Simply begin by stating the significance of what the reader will see. In most circumstances, the caption appears below rather than above the illustration. The list of figures, which appears on the preliminary pages of the document, must contain each figure's number and the caption as it appears on the figure. With figure captions, always use Arabic numerals. In addition, it is standard to capitalize the first letter of all words except prepositions or articles appearing in the middle of a title. Follow the rules of punctuation as with narrative text.

▲**FIGURE 11.1**

Junk mail must have eye appeal to catch the reader's attention; otherwise it will be discarded.

The excerpt is much easier to read and understand when it is formatted using a heading, paragraphs, boldfacing, underlining, and a bulleted list.

> **Figure Captions**
> Figures must have captions that explain the contents. It is not necessary to start by saying, "This figure shows . . ." or "The graph contains. . . ." Simply begin by stating the significance of what the reader will see.
>
> In most circumstances, the caption appears below rather than above the illustration. The list of figures, which appears on the preliminary pages of the document, must contain each figure's number and the caption as it appears on the figure.
>
> These guidelines apply to the format of figure captions:
>
> • Always use Arabic numerals.
> • Capitalize the first letter of all words except prepositions or articles appearing in the middle of a title.
> • Follow the rules of punctuation as with narrative text.

```
┌──    C  A  S  E        S  C  E  N  A  R  I  O    ──┐
```

Policy Change

Drew Fitzgerald, manager of a fast food restaurant, was responsible for seeing that his employees followed the policies established by company headquarters. Recently he was informed of several changes in hygiene policy.
To relay the information to his employees, Drew reviewed each policy
change at an employee meeting. He also planned to write a notice and post
it on the employee bulletin board. Drew drafted the following notice:

> NOTICE: CHANGES IN HYGIENE POLICY
>
> Effective August 15, all employees will wash their hands prior to
> the start of a shift and following any breaks using a new hand
> washing procedure. Workers are to use the new disposable
> scrub brushes along with anti-bacterial soap for no less than five
> minutes of washing. Use the foot-operated sinks and air dryers
> for washing and drying, respectively. For those whose hands are
> sensitive to repeated scrubbing, use the anti-bacterial lotion in
> the wall dispenser. Also, food handlers must wear disposable
> gloves for all stages and phases of food handling. This includes
> preparing soft drinks, which formerly was handled by cashiers.
> These new procedures will increase our overall level of cleanli-
> ness and the safety of our food products. We appreciate your
> compliance.

*What do you think of the format Drew used? What format elements would
you recommend to improve the readability of this message?*

1　**USE YOUR JUDGMENT**

Choose a textbook and examine how the publisher has used format to organize
and present the material. Consider in your analysis all the different aspects of format discussed to this point.

FORMATTING FOR PURPOSE

In business, document types are characterized not only by their different purposes
but also by their different formats. By using format appropriately, you tell your readers immediately what type of document they are receiving.

The Letter

Letters are those messages sent to business associates outside of the organization. Most business people use one of two standardized letter formats, block or modified block, for presenting information.

The full **block style** (Figure 11.2) takes the least amount of time to set up because all lines start at the left margin.

The **modified block style** is frequently used because of its well-balanced appearance. It is formatted to look like a framed picture and emphasizes readability. Figure 11.3 shows a letter formatted in the modified block style.

As you can see, both formats provide ample white space (following the date, the inside address, the salutation, the paragraphs, and the complimentary close). The reader can isolate each block of text and read without strain.

For maximum efficiency and consistency, most companies select and use one format for letters. This is particularly true if the written communications are produced by administrative personnel rather than managers or executives. If you are in charge of preparing your own letters, it will be important to find out which style your company prefers and then use it.

The essential elements of a letter are described next. Refer to Figure 11.2 to see each of these elements within a business letter.

Date

The date line consists of the month (written in full, without abbreviation or figures), the day (written in figures and followed by a comma), and the complete year.

> December 18, 19XX

Inside Address

Here is an example of the format that has been in use for the past several years:

> Mr. Angelo Costanzo, Manager
> Griffin Plumbing Supply Co.
> 1987 Susquehanna Avenue
> Wilkes-Barre, PA 18701

However, to save reformatting time, you can format the **inside address** in the same way it will appear on the envelope. The U.S. Postal Service uses electronic sorting equipment that operates more cost effectively when the address information is presented in all capitals with no punctuation:

> MR ANGELO COSTANZO MANAGER
> GRIFFIN PLUMBING SUPPLY CO
> 1987 SUSQUEHANNA AVENUE
> WILKES-BARRE PA 18701

FIGURE 11.2 ▶

The block letter style.

Return Address   *Western Distribution, Inc. • 740 North Main St • Santa Ana • CA • 92701 • (310) 555 1600 • Fax (310) 555 1699*

Date line   November 12, 19—   **5 returns**

Inside address   Ms. Rochelle Andia
800 Susquehanna Lane
Bryn Mawr, PA 15221   **2 returns**

Salutation   Dear Ms. Andoian: **2 returns**

1-inch margins   You are right! The correspondence your firm prepares sends its own message. Thus, you will want to send a clear message of efficiency as illustrated by this block-style letter.

Left justification (ragged right)   Double space

All lines begin at the left margin. This date begins approximately 12 lines from the top of the page. The inside address begins four lines below the date. Margins of 1" are used. The letter is single-spaced with double spacing before and after the salutation, writer's name appears on the fourth line below the closing. Reference initials and a file name are placed two lines below the sender's name.

Closing   Double space

Sincerely,   **4 returns**

Sender's name and title   Teresa Gomez, Account Executive
Accounting Department   **2 returns**

Reference initials/filename   wg/block.ltr

Recommended letter styles: block style.   From: *The Paradigm Reference Manual,* 1993, Paradigm Publishing Inc.

F R A N K E L
T H O M A S
P A I N E

SIMPSON BUILDING
500 WESTERLY BOULEVARD
LOUISVILLE, KENTUCKY 40202
606 555 2000

◄ **FIGURE 11.3**

The modified block letter style.

Date line begins
at center

November 15, 19—   **2 returns**

Refer to line

When replying, refer to : File 592   **2 returns**   FAX: 606 555 2999

Administrative Secretaries Association   **2 returns**
P.O. Box 5500
Austin, TX 78710

Dear Colleagues: **2 returns**

Your recent inquiry regarding letter styles endorsed by Frankel Thomas & Paine was very
timely. Our group is in the process of assembling a business letter style guide for office
support persons. This letter is the first sample for the guide.

Left justification
(ragged right)

This letter illustrates the modified block style. Default side margins of 1" are used. The date
begins approximately by 12 lines from the top of the page at center. The inside address
begins four lines below the date line. A double space line precedes and follows the
saluatation. The message of the letter is single-spaced with double spacing between
paragraphs.

The complmentary close begins a double space below the body at center. The writer's
name and title appear four lines below, aligned with the closing. The reference notation is
positioned two lines below the signature line at the left margin.   **2 returns**

Sincerely yours,   **4 returns**

Closing and key of
signature begins at
center

Theodore A. Gullman
Corresponding Secretary   **2 returns**

trw/modblock.let

Modified block style, showing 1-inch margins,
left justification, and *Refer to* line.

From: *The Paradigm Reference Manual*,
1993, Paradigm Publishing Inc.

FIGURE 11.4 ▶

The block style is the preferred
letter style.

Salutation

In your **salutation,** greet the reader by name whenever possible. It may take a phone call to find out to whom you should direct your letter, but it is worth the effort to personalize your message. Always double-check the spelling of the receiver's name. Use *Dr.*, *Mr.*, or *Ms.* as appropriate and based on your relationship with the receiver. If you are on first-name basis with the individual, then use the first name only.

It is no longer desirable to greet readers with "Dear Sir" or "Gentlemen" since this language excludes the many women in the workplace. If necessary, "Ladies and Gentlemen" is more inclusive. However, if you do not know the name of the person who will read your letter, your best course is to use words that describe the role of the person to whom you are writing:

> Dear Customer:
> Dear Circulation Manager:
> Dear Editor:

Body of the Letter

Format the **body** of your letter according to the modified block or full block style. Single-spaced type is standard. In addition to paragraphing, use underlining, bold-face type, italics, justification, and other technical devices available through word processing software to emphasize important information.

Complimentary Close

The **complimentary close** is considered the "goodbye" of the letter. Only the first word is capitalized, and the word or phrase ends with a comma. The most commonly used closings today are:

> Sincerely,
> Sincerely yours,
> Cordially,
> Cordially yours,

When you have a close working relationship with a customer or business associate, you may end your letter more informally:

> Best regards,
> Warmest regards,

Signature Line

For most business letters, the writer's name is typed on the fourth line below the complimentary close. The writer's job title and department appear beneath the name, unless the writer is using a letterhead that contains this information.

> Sincerely,
>
>
> Margaret Shaw
> Coordinator
> Business Development Division

When it is important to emphasize that the message represents the views of the company as a whole and not just the views of the writer, the company "signature" appears in all-capital letters on the second line below the close:

> Sincerely,
>
>
> TAYLOR-BRADFORD REALTY

Closing Notations

Many letters include **reference initials, enclosure notations,** and **copy notations.**

The trend today is to use only the initials of the person who types or keys the document. There is no need to use the writer's initials if that person is identified in the signature line. The first initials of the typist's first, middle, and last name are typed in lowercase on the second line below the signature line:

> Sincerely,
>
>
> Margaret Shaw
>
> smb

Enclosure notations alert the reader to materials that are included along with the letter. Spell out the entire word (Enclosure) rather than using the abbreviation (enc.). This brings attention to the enclosure and helps decrease oversights. If there is more than one enclosure, you may indicate the number or name them in vertical order. This *latter* method serves as a clear identification of what the reader should expect to find with the letter.

> Enclosures: 3
> Enclosures: Statement
>   Check
>   Letter

To indicate to the receiver when you have sent copies of a letter to other individuals, use a copy notation below the enclosure notation or the reference initials if there are no enclosures. Use "c" or "cc" (for "courtesy copy") to identify copies sent to others. Name the individuals to whom copies have been sent.

> cc: Tina Ricco
>   Gary Kowalski

FIGURE 11.5 ▶

FAX cover sheet.

Fax

To:

Fax #:

From:

Date:

Subject:

Pages:

Notes:

Occasionally, writers use a **postscript** as a device to emphasize or personalize an idea. Sales letters often use postscripts for special effect.

> P.S. Remember, our sale ends this Thursday. Don't miss the wonderful savings in store for you!

In business letters, the postscript is no longer used to represent an afterthought (such as, "P.S. I forgot to tell you we're moving. After June 1, you can reach us at. . . ."). If you discover that something important was omitted from the body of your business letter, rewrite the letter.

In today's office, letters are frequently sent by **facsimile, or fax.** Letters sent by fax differ from letters sent by mail only in that the sender uses a cover page (Figure 11.5) rather than an envelope.

C A S E   S C E N A R I O

Is the Meeting On?

Jeanine Flanders was the assistant manager of Greenway West, a resort in Tampa, Florida. Jeanine regularly corresponded with clients who planned to visit Greenway West for both business and pleasure.

In September, Corey Bingham inquired about holding a meeting at the resort in December. By mid-October, Mr. Bingham had not responded to the letter and information packet that Jeanine mailed the day after receiving his inquiry. As of October 16, the dates in question were still open. Jeanine decided to write to Mr. Bingham once more:

Greenway West Resort and Conference Center

585 Greenway Boulevard St. Petersberg, FL 33612
Telephone (813) 555-9811 Toll Free (800) 555-3566 Fax (813) 555-9827

October 16, 19XX

Mr. Corey Bingham
Director of Sales and Marketing
Hot Dog Diners Inc
St. James, MI 49666

Dear Mr. Bingham:

When you wrote me in September about accommodations for
your December 3-7 meeting, I tentatively reserved a block of
meeting and residence rooms for your group. Although you did
not ask me to do so, I wanted to make certain I had an appropriate record in case you decided to choose Greenway West.

If you are still thinking about being with us (and I certainly hope
you are), I suggest that you let me hear from you by October
25. This is the latest date on which I can <u>guarantee</u> accommodations.

Since I last wrote you, we have been building a solarium with an
indoor pool plus a very spacious sauna. I've enclosed a colorful
brochure to let you see for yourself! I hope yours is one of the
first groups to use these new facilities!

Sincerely yours,

Jeanine Flanders
Manager
Conference Division

Enclosure

*What do you think of the format of this letter? Did Jeanine do a good job of
using the elements of a business letter properly? How would you improve
the format of the letter?*

Occasionally the "business" being conducted is primarily social or personal. The format for social-business and personal-business letters varies slightly from the standard business letter.

Social-Business Correspondence

Social-business correspondence is executive correspondence addressed to high-level company officials and/or dignitaries. It does not deal with day-to-day business matters but rather with

- Praise, concern, or condolence to someone within (or without) the organization

- Corporate policy or social responsibility

The format of social-business correspondence differs from regular correspondence in the following ways:

1. The inside address is keyed at the bottom of the letter, aligned at the left margin, and started on the fifth line below the writer's signature or title (whichever comes last).

2. The salutation is followed by a comma rather than a colon.

3. Reference initials and notations pertaining to enclosures, copies, and mailing are typically omitted.

Personal-Business Letters

A **personal-business letter** is one written by a private person (perhaps a consumer) to a business organization about a business matter, such as a billing error or an incorrect shipment of faulty merchandise. The writer uses plain paper and positions the return address in the upper portion of the letter. The return address consists of the following items:

> Street Address
> City, State ZIP
> Date

No reference initials are necessary since it is assumed that the signer of the letter also prepared the letter.

The Memo

Memorandums (memos) are written communications that business people send to others within their organization. For example, memos are sent by supervisors to employees (located within the same building) as well as by district managers to sales representatives (located in different states). As long as the sender and receiver work for the same company, the memorandum is the technically correct format for written communications.

Memorandums can be used with some flexibility with an organization. They can be addressed to a single individual or to a group of individuals. They can be distributed by interoffice mail or through an electronic mail system. They can be prepared with preprinted forms or with plain paper. Preprinted forms can be purchased in office supply stores or a standard format can be programmed into your computer.

Generally the content, language, and tone of business letters and memos are quite similar. In many instances, aside from the nature of the relationship between the sender and receiver, the only difference between a letter and a memo is in the format of the message.

The standard format for a memorandum consists of a title and four informational lines. The title, centered over the top of the page, serves as a quick identification for this type of message. The informational lines identify the receiver, the sender, the date, and the topic of the memo.

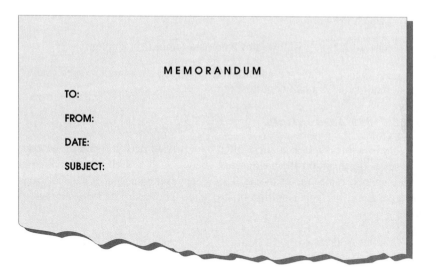

MEMORANDUM

TO:

FROM:

DATE:

SUBJECT:

Sometimes companies add other informational lines such as DEPARTMENT and LOCATION, which aid in distribution.

Courtesy titles such as Mr. or Ms. are usually omitted in the TO and FROM lines. A courtesy title may be used if the addressee is in a position of higher authority than the writer. However, position titles generally are used to identify status within the business organization.

The subject line presents a concise, concrete identification of the topic of the memorandum. It is not necessary to use articles (a, an, the) or possessive pronouns (my, our, your, etc.) in a subject line. Often, the subject line is keyed in all capital letters.

e-mail

electronic mail: messages keyed and sent from one computer terminal to others on the same computer network

> **SUBJECT:** STATUS OF NEW PRODUCTS

Figure 11.6 shows a memorandum created and sent through electronic mail, also called *e-mail*. It contains the standard formatting elements of a memorandum, but will be read by the receiver on a computer screen.

USE YOUR JUDGMENT 2

Choose a suitable subject line for the following memos:

a. A memo written to your supervisor requesting two personal days to attend your sister's graduation in another state
b. A memo written to you approving your leave
c. A memo from the vice president of sales asking the sales staff to work overtime to complete the end-of-year inventory
d. A memo from you to your executive asking for the June travel vouchers
e. A memo from your supervisor asking members of the accounting department to attend a computer software demonstration

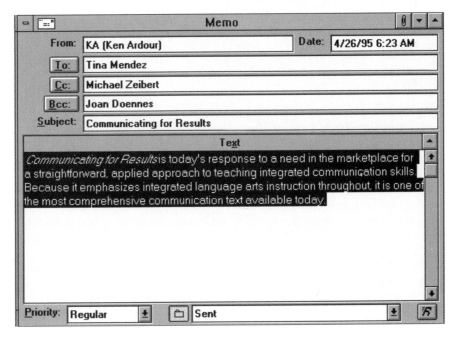

◀ **FIGURE 11.6**

E-Mail.

The Report

Business reports generally are of two types: the memorandum report and the structured report.

The **memorandum report** is formatted as a memorandum. It may be quite long and it may contain one or more tables of data, but it is constructed in the same way as a standard memo.

The **structured report** can be short or long, but it is likely to contain a number of distinct elements. The parts of a formally structured report vary according to the needs of the writer. In general, they will include a title page, a summary (for those who want a quick overview of the report), an introduction (with background information), the body of the report (with various headings and subheadings), and a closing section containing conclusions and recommendations. You'll learn more about elements of reports in Chapter 16.

The memorandum report and the structured report are both used frequently in business today. Generally, the importance and complexity of a topic, as well as who the readers will be, determine which format a report will take.

USING TABLES AND GRAPHS

When writing a report, tables and graphs will help you organize information in a clear, readable way.

Tables

If your document contains a lot of numerical data, it is best, when you can, to arrange it in table form. Readers often skip over narrative that is full of numbers because it is hard to read. Your data will stand out and be easy to read and understand when it is carefully presented in a **table.**

It can be both frustrating and time-consuming to create a table using a typewriter. Thankfully, computers and various software programs have made the task of creating tables much easier. A typical table with introductory text is shown in Figure 11.7.

Data in table form is much easier to read and understand than when it is presented within narrative:

◀ **FIGURE 11.7**

Simple table with
introductory text.

The policy of paying overtime to supervisory personnel varies widely.
Often the rate of overtime pay is based on the salary range. A typical
overtime pay provision for supervisory personnel is shown in the table
below.

TABLE 1. OVERTIME PAY RATES FOR SUPERVISORS

Salary Range	Overtime Rate
$ 9,000-$12,000	1.50
$12,000-$15,000	1.25
$15,000-$18,000	1.00
$18,000-$20,000	0.75
$20,000-$22,000	0.50
$22,000-$25,000	0.25
Over $25,000	0.00

Note that the table in Figure 11.7 is very simple and contains no rules (vertical or
horizontal lines). If you have one that is fairly complicated, you may wish to separate the data with vertical and horizontal rules as in Figure 11.8.

◀ **FIGURE 11.8**

Complex table.

This table contains vertical and horizontal rules which help the reader
separate the information within each column and row.

PROJECTED WORK STOPPAGES IN AUTOMOTIVE AND
RELATED INDUSTRIES OVER A 10-YEAR PERIOD

Year	Number of stoppages	Number of workers involved (roundedidle off to nearest thousand)	Worker-days
1	2,968	840,000	4,183,000
2	3,752	1,981,000	13,501,000
3	4,956	2,116,000	8,721,000
4	4,750	3,470,000	38,000,000
5	4,985	4,600,000	116,000,000
6	3,693	2,170,000	34,600,000
7	3,419	1,960,000	34,100,000
8	3,606	3,030,000	50,500,000
9	4,843	2,410,000	38,800,000
10	7,112	3,276,000	22,580,000

Graphs

In some business documents various types of graphs can be used effectively. The three most popular graphs for business use are the line graph, the bar graph, and the circle graph.

The **line graph** is especially effective to show patterns, trends, and changes (for example, company profits earned over a ten-year period). The **bar graph** is best to show comparative data (for example, the net sales and profits of six retail chain stores during the past year). The **circle graph,** often called a **pie chart,** is best for showing the relationship of the parts of something to the whole (for example, the percentage or amount spent for each employee benefit based on 100 percent or $1.00). The box below shows examples of these three types of graphs.

If you have the right software, a microcomputer may be able to create graphs automatically on the basis of your data. It may even be able to produce them in several vivid colors. If you are preparing graphs without a computer, however, you should

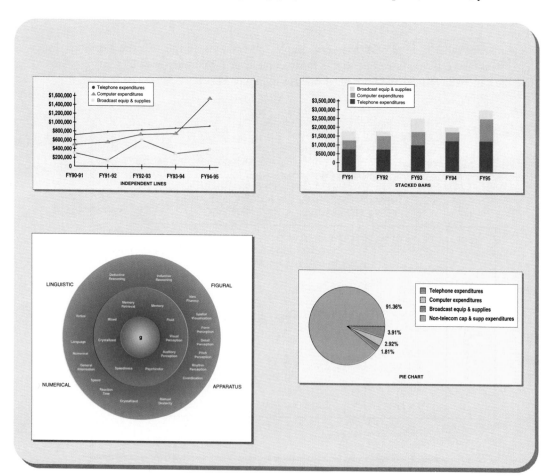

be acquainted with special techniques required to set up effective graphs. A good textbook on statistics, available in most business libraries, will include the illustrations you need.

CASE SCENARIO

Data Maze

Layne Baldwin was the assistant marketing manager of Permatrax Corporation. H.C. Simank, the marketing manager of Permatrax, asked Layne to prepare quarterly reports of bonuses earned by the seven regional managers during the year. Simank wanted figures for the current quarter and for the same quarter last year, the amount of increase or decrease, and any comments that Layne thought appropriate. Layne drafted this document:

MEMORANDUM

TO: H.C. Simank

FROM: Layne Baldwin

DATE: July 16, 19XX

SUBJECT: Quarterly Report of Bonuses Earned by
Regional Managers

Following is a report of the bonus earnings of the seven regional managers for the period April 1 through June 30 (second quarter).

This year, L. Berman earned $4,238 (her first full quarter as a regional manager). C. Burke earned $5,657 as compared with $5,046 last year, which is an increase of $611. L. Carey earned $6,617 this year and $6,958 last year, a decrease of $341. W. Dorr's second-quarter earnings this year were $3,986, and last year they amounted to $6,456. (Note: Dorr's territory was split off on April 1, which accounts in large measure for the decrease of $2,470). R. Espinoza earned $7,566 this year as compared with $6,437 last year, an increase of $1,129. B. Walthrup's earnings amounted to $3,320 (his first full quarter as a regional manager). T. Yerian had a bonus of $4,286 in the second quarter of this year and $7,706 last year. (Note: Yerian's territory was split off on April 1, which accounts in large measure for the decrease of $3,420.)

Did Layne include all the information in his report that H.C. requested? Was it hard for you to determine this? How would you format the report differently to make it easier to read and understand?

3 USE YOUR JUDGMENT

What type of written communication letter (standard business, social-business, or personal-business), memo, memorandum report, or formal report—would you select to respond in each of the following situations? Explain your answers.

a. You need to convince your supervisor to increase the advertising budget by 10 percent.
b. You want to tell your customers about a new credit policy.
c. The company's stockholders want a detailed analysis of last quarter's income statement.
d. The manufacturing arm of the Tyler Company in New York City wants to tell the marketing division, located in Boston, the specifications of a new product.
e. You want to congratulate a recently promoted coworker.

IN BRIEF

❶ The reader's first impression of your letter depends on how it looks. If the appearance is neat and attractive, the reader's initial reaction will be favorable.

❷ Too much text on a page can burden the reader. You can improve the readability of your business documents by allowing ample white space in the margins and between paragraphs.

❸ Headings and subheadings are useful organizing tools. Use parallel structure to make your document consistent.

❹ Use bullets, hyphens, asterisks, numbers, underlining, and boldface type to emphasize important information.

❺ Different document types are formatted differently. The standard formats for letters, memorandums, and reports help the reader identify the type of correspondence.

❻ Tables and graphs are effective means of showing numerical data within a business document.

WORDS OF NOTE

Define each of these terms introduced in Chapter 11.

bar graph
block style
body
circle graph
complimentary close
copy notation
enclosure notation
eye appeal
facsimile (fax)
format
inside address
line graph
memorandum
memorandum report
modified block style
parallel structure
personal-business letter
pie chart
postscript
reference initials
salutation
social-business correspondence
structured report
table

CHECK YOUR RECALL

1 What formatting techniques can help give your document eye appeal?

2 What are the two typical formats for business letters? What elements are the same in both formats? What elements are different?

3 When would someone use social-business correspondence? A personal-business letter? How is each formatted?

4 In what situations would you choose to use a memorandum rather than a letter? How are the two documents different?

5 How is a memorandum report different from a structured report?

6 When might you use a table or graph? Explain how a line graph, bar graph, and circle graph are different. How might you use each one?

SHARE YOUR PERSPECTIVE

❶ Rewrite the following draft of a social-business letter so that it is formatted properly and adheres to readability guidelines.

Ms. Genevieve LeMond   June 1, 19XX
7214 Mulberry Street
DeKalb, IL 61616

Dear Genevieve I am sorry I cannot be at the PER meeting for the final, official goodbye to you as a fellow pollution-control champion. I personally want to communicate how strongly I feel about you as a mentor. No one can prepare better waste-containment strategies, rally support for earth-friendly activities, or use her knowledge more effectively to make changes at the community level! I've also admired your ability to communicate with officials at large corporations who generally snub their noses at our grassroots efforts. Personally, you adjusted to my inexperience and patiently wove CLEANUP and PER together to create a meaningful coalition in 1992. That had to be a trying year for you and I appreciate deeply your grace in action. Now, as you enter a new life phase of your career, I hope you find new challenges to attack with your talents. And whatever you choose to pursue next, may it bring you satisfaction.

Sincerely   Minerva Harvet Executive Director

---

❷ Write a memo based on the following situation. Within the memo, use formatting helps such as bullets, hyphens, asterisks, numbers, underlining, and boldface type to emphasize important information.

You work at the Woodlake History Center. Each year the center hosts an employee family picnic; this year you are the picnic committee chair. Write a memo to your committee members to tell them the date, time, menu, and activities planned for the picnic (you supply the details).

FOCUS ON THE FINE POINTS
Read the following background information. Then follow the instructions to locate and correct grammar errors.

Background

In the spring, Boris Murlowski, an employee in a magazine publishing house, will represent his publisher at meetings in Japan. He has decided to go to the International Business School to take a course on doing business in Japan. Boris refers to the school's bulletin for information about courses and registration and to decide which of the school's campuses will be most convenient for him.

Your Instructions

Each of the following documents contains up to 15 errors. Indicate and correct errors by circling the problem and noting the solution on a photocopy of the page or on a separate sheet of paper. In each case, you may assume the document is formatted correctly.

Note: If you have difficulty locating errors, turn to page 469 in the Appendix. There you will find additional information about the errors in Document 1.

DOCUMENT 1: Registration Information

REGISTRATION INFORMATION

Deadlines for Spring Classes

February 14:	Registration begins
February 28:	Registration ends
March 1:	Late registration begins
March 12:	Late registration ends

We will except registrations beyond the late registration date only for classes that are not filled. This year we are not accepting registrations for audited classes.

How to Register

To register by mail Use the registration form on page 7. Complete the form and mail (or have it faxed) it to the main registration office.

For registering in person If you are interested in particularly popular courses (denoted by an asterisk * in the course descriptions), we advice you to use this method. Many of our most popular courses fill to capacity on or before the second day of registration. *Registrations that we have received by mail or fax will be applied at the close of business on the day recieved. Those recieved after 3:00 p.m. will apply at the opening of the next business day.*

How to Pay

To pay by check Make you're check payable to "International Business School." Include your invoice number, course number, and telephone number on you're check.

If paying by credit card We can accept tuition charged on VISA, MasterCard, or Discover. Sorry we are not accepting American Express.

Additional Services

Devises for hearing impaired individuals are available for all classes. Call at least three business days ahead of your first scheduled class to arrange for this assistants.

Child care is available at the East Shelby cite only.

The International School of Business is an equal opportunity school. For a copy of it's bylaws, call the information office at 555-0101.

DOCUMENT 2: Map with Directions to Different Campuses

To get to East Shelby:

From the north, follow Hiway 172 south to Division Street. Go left at the top of the ramp and you will be taking a right onto the service road, Barranca Drive. The East Shelby Branch of the International Business School is two blocks ahead on the right. Park in their student parking lot.

From the south, follow Hiway 172 north to Division Street. Turning right at the top of the ramp, take another quick right onto the service road, Barranca Drive. The East Shelby branch is two blocks ahead on the right. Park in its student parking lot.

To get to West Shelby:

From the east, exit Interstate Highway 85 at the Highway 80 interchange, heading east. Taking a left at the first stoplight, Juneau Drive, follow the signs for the West Shelby Racetrack, turning left *immediately* before the racetracks' entrance.

From the west, follow Interstate Highway 85 past the Highway 80 interchange to North Juneau Drive. The road will curve around. Follow its signs for the West Shelby Racetrack, turning left onto West Shelby Road *immediately* before the racetrack's entrance.

Please note: There is heavy construction on West Shelby Roads' westbound lane; procede with caution.

To get to Charles City:

State Highway 22 goes right thru Charles City. Turn off Highway 22 on Main Street and head north .3 miles. The Charles City branch is housed in the Community Activity Wing of Charles City Hall. Park in the lot or on the street.

DOCUMENT 3: Course Descriptions

DOING BUSINESS IN JAPAN

JINT001   Introduction to the Japanese
This class will give historical background about Japan and her social traditions, setting a context for understanding modern Japan. Students will also be learning some basic vocabulary for communicating in Japanese business circles. Topics include family and their role in society, personal space and it's impact on intrapersonal communications, education, and the younger generations' interest in the West.

JB101   Japanese Business: Part I
This class will look at the corporate philosophy of the Japanese business person. Students will be role playing typical business situations and will explore topics such as teams and work ethics, loyalty, responsibility, quality control, and service orientation. *Prerequisite: Introduction to the Japanese or the instructor's approval.*

JB102   Japanese Business: Part II
Students will be looking more closely at the Japanese business organization and their many faucets. Leadership and worker heirarchy, social-business customs, concensus in decision making, womens' roles, and the Japanese market are all to be covered. *Prerequisite: Japanese Business: Part I or the instructor's approval.*

WRITING TO

INFORM

CHAPTER TWELVE

What circumstances in business will require you to write to inform?

What is the standard approach when writing to inform?

What is the best approach when the message is bad news?

Are there guidelines for writing documents that confirm oral agreements?

What is a transmittal document?

What is the best way to give instructions and directions?

Company executives, managers, and other staff members frequently write to inform. They send needed information to each other and acknowledge its receipt. They write letters and memos to confirm meeting times and appointments or simply to remind each other of scheduled events. They write instructions and directions that tell individuals how and when to perform business tasks.

In this chapter, you will learn how to organize messages that inform. You will learn how to write confirmation and transmittal documents as well as instructional memorandums.

ORGANIZING A MESSAGE THAT INFORMS

When you write, you must make various decisions based on your situation. Whenever you write to inform, however, you may find yourself approaching situations similarly. There are two general plans when writing to inform, and you will select your approach depending on the nature of the news you must give.

Good News

When you write messages that contain good or neutral news, a **direct approach** is usually called for. You can use the following organizational plan:

1. **State your purpose.** Begin by stating your main idea or your reason for writing. Doing this will orient your readers and prepare them to receive the information.

2. **Inform and explain.** Provide the information your reader needs, with any explanation necessary to make the information clear.

3. **Close.** Be courteous. Offer more help, if you wish. If you want your reader to do something, ask.

Consider the following example, a note from LuAnne Phenow to Mike Roanoke:

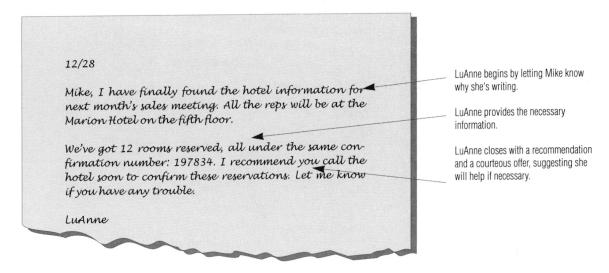

12/28

Mike, I have finally found the hotel information for next month's sales meeting. All the reps will be at the Marion Hotel on the fifth floor.

LuAnne begins by letting Mike know why she's writing.

We've got 12 rooms reserved, all under the same confirmation number: 197834. I recommend you call the hotel soon to confirm these reservations. Let me know if you have any trouble.

LuAnne

LuAnne provides the necessary information.

LuAnne closes with a recommendation and a courteous offer, suggesting she will help if necessary.

LuAnne's message flows logically and naturally. This **direct approach** is best when you are delivering good or neutral news.

Bad News

Unfortunately, you will sometimes find yourself passing on information that upsets your reader. When this is the case, use an **indirect approach**. Using the direct approach to inform someone of bad news makes the impression that you are uncaring.

You can soften the blow of bad news by using a variation of the "good news" organizational plan. Rather than inform first and then explain, give the explanation first to buffer the remainder of your message. Try this:

1. **Explain.** Begin with the positive. Provide reasons for your message by explaining the situation.

2. **Inform.** Give the bad news as positively as possible. Be honest but omit information that will unnecessarily offend your reader.

3. **Close.** Be as courteous and positive as possible. Offer help, if you can.

The key is to use tact when the message is harsh. Starting with an explanation will help your reader prepare for the negative information, especially if it is something that will seriously affect the person.

This memo from LuAnne to Mike illustrates effective use of the indirect approach:

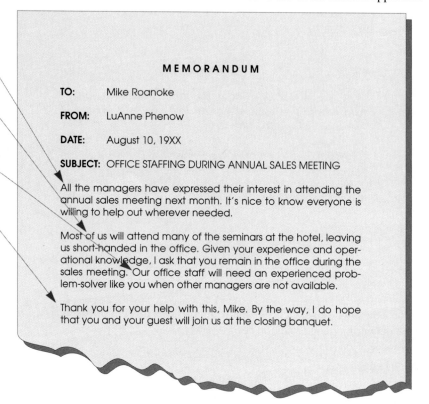

LuAnne begins positively. She compliments Mike for his interest in helping.

LuAnne explains why all the managers cannot attend the meeting.

LuAnne explains why she wants Mike to stay at the office. In doing so, she emphasizes Mike's strengths as a manager.

LuAnne closes positively. She reminds Mike that she looks forward to seeing him at part of the event.

> **MEMORANDUM**
>
> **TO:**   Mike Roanoke
>
> **FROM:**   LuAnne Phenow
>
> **DATE:**   August 10, 19XX
>
> **SUBJECT:**   OFFICE STAFFING DURING ANNUAL SALES MEETING
>
> All the managers have expressed their interest in attending the annual sales meeting next month. It's nice to know everyone is willing to help out wherever needed.
>
> Most of us will attend many of the seminars at the hotel, leaving us short-handed in the office. Given your experience and operational knowledge, I ask that you remain in the office during the sales meeting. Our office staff will need an experienced problem-solver like you when other managers are not available.
>
> Thank you for your help with this, Mike. By the way, I do hope that you and your guest will join us at the closing banquet.

In this memo, LuAnne uses the indirect approach to inform Mike of her decision because she believes Mike will be disappointed with the news. If Mike had wanted to remain in the office during the sales meeting, LuAnne would have used a direct approach. By considering her reader's feelings, LuAnne chooses the most effective approach.

There will be times when you choose the direct approach even when you must deliver bad news. Your message may involve a routine matter and may not seriously disappoint your reader. The direct approach is also a better choice when communicating an urgent message to which the reader must respond immediately. As always, the requirements of the situation must be your guide when you write.

WRITING CONFIRMATION DOCUMENTS

Business people use **confirmation documents,** memos or letters that verify dates, times, events, and other information. For example, a sales representative might write a letter to verify a meeting with an out-of-town client. A free-lance artist might write to a corporate client to confirm a business deal before starting work on a project. A manager might write a memo to remind coworkers of a meeting time.

C A S E   S C E N A R I O

Abruptly Speaking

Last month Charlotte Innez agreed to serve as the keynote speaker at the opening banquet for the annual meeting of the Women in Management Association. She accepted the speaking engagement in a telephone conversation with Vicki Crawford, WMA President. Last week Charlotte realized she would be unable to attend the banquet. She needed to write a letter to Vicki and send it by fax immediately. Charlotte quickly drafted the following letter:

Hatfield's Outlet Stores
Corporate Headquarters
9757 Broomstick Boulevard
Columbus, OH 43211

December 3, 19XX

Ms. Vicki Crawford
Crawford Industries
1212 Skyline Boulevard
San Diego, CA 95010

Dear Ms. Crawford:

Thank you again for your invitation to speak at the Women in Management meeting on January 15. Because of the influence your group has had on the business community, particularly in management training programs, I consider your invitation an honor.

Unfortunately, I have just learned that our national sales meeting has been rescheduled for mid-January and that I appear on the agenda every day, including January 15. In short, I am afraid I will be unable to speak at your meeting. Please accept my apology. I know the frustration these kinds of scheduling changes can cause.

Rita Short, our speaker's bureau coordinator, has your name and will call you this afternoon. I've asked her to work with you to line up another speaker for your meeting. Please ask Rita for whatever you need.

Again, I regret that I cannot accept your invitation. I was looking forward to meeting you and your colleagues in person. Good luck.

Sincerely,

Charlotte Innez
Vice President for Research and Development
Hatfield's Outlet Stores

What approach did Charlotte use to deliver her news? Did she use it effectively? Can you differentiate between statements that explain and those that inform? How did Charlotte buffer the bad news in this message? What else might she have done?

The general purpose of a confirmation letter or memo is to inform the reader of your understanding of some business arrangement. Business people often arrange and agree on events and relationships orally—by telephone or over lunch. Confirmation memos and letters acknowledge these arrangements and agreements. Confirmation letters and memos may also clarify the details of the arrangements.

As always, the level of formality depends on the reader and other aspects of the situation. A manager writing to coworkers to confirm a meeting would probably write a short, informal memo. On the other hand, an executive writing to a client to confirm a business agreement would write more formally.

▲FIGURE 12.1

Many business discussions take place over breakfast or lunch. Always confirm in writing any agreements made during a business meal.

Guidelines for Writing a Confirmation Memo or Letter

- When confirming an oral agreement, be very specific about the details agreed on. If documents are available to support the details, send them.

- When you are the person who stands to gain most from the oral agreement, use the opportunity to build goodwill.

- When confirming receipts, say specifically what has been received and, if you think it is important, when it was received.

- Express appreciation when confirming receipts, if appropriate.

The letter in Figure 12.2 does a good job of confirming an oral agreement. It is both detailed and congenial.

Austin Convention and Conference Center

October 3, 19XX

Mr. Phillip Paxton
The Bookfinders
17 East Arden Street
West Lafayette, IN 47907

Dear Mr. Paxton:

As agreed in our telephone conversation yesterday, I have reserved Exhibit Space K for you at the convention of the Association of Rare Book Dealers, which will be held December 27- 31. The enclosed diagram shows the exhibit area layout, and I have checked Space K in red so that you will know precisely where you will be situated in relation to the other exhibits. This is an excellent location—in the mainstream of convention traffic—and I am sure you will be happy with it.

Details concerning electrical outlets and other facilities are described on the back of the exhibit area layout. The cost for the four days is $2,400, and I will be pleased to have your check for half that amount ($1,200) to hold your space. The remainder is to be paid when you arrive at the convention.

I extend a warm welcome to Austin and hope the convention will be a very successful occasion for you and your company.

Sincerely yours,

Audrey Mix
Exhibit Manager

Enclosure

1200 First Street Austin, TX 73221
Phone [512] 555-1499 Toll Free [800] 555-0080 Fax [512] 555-1752

◀ FIGURE 12.2

Letter of confirmation

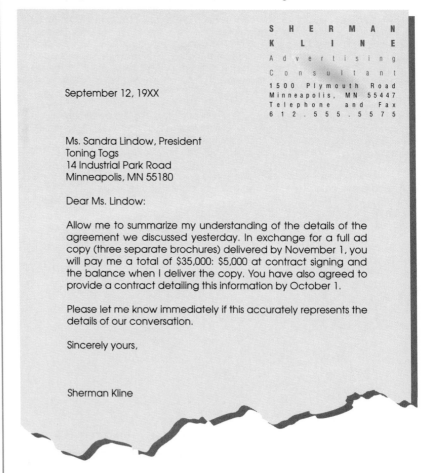

C A S E   S C E N A R I O

Clothes Line

Sherman Kline, an independent advertising consultant, was having lunch with Sandra Lindow, a clothing designer. Sandra wanted Sherman to handle the advertising for her new line of exercise clothing. During lunch, Sherman agreed to coordinate the advertising for the line and to provide finished copy within ten weeks. Sandra would pay Sherman $35,000, $5,000 when they signed a contract and the rest when Sherman finished. Sherman agreed to begin immediately.

The next day, Sherman mailed Sandra the following letter:

> **S H E R M A N**
> **K L I N E**
> A d v e r t i s i n g
> C o n s u l t a n t
> 1 5 0 0   P l y m o u t h   R o a d
> M i n n e a p o l i s ,   M N   5 5 4 4 7
> T e l e p h o n e   a n d   F a x
> 6 1 2 . 5 5 5 . 5 5 7 5
>
> September 12, 19XX
>
> Ms. Sandra Lindow, President
> Toning Togs
> 14 Industrial Park Road
> Minneapolis, MN 55180
>
> Dear Ms. Lindow:
>
> Allow me to summarize my understanding of the details of the agreement we discussed yesterday. In exchange for a full ad copy (three separate brochures) delivered by November 1, you will pay me a total of $35,000: $5,000 at contract signing and the balance when I deliver the copy. You have also agreed to provide a contract detailing this information by October 1.
>
> Please let me know immediately if this accurately represents the details of our conversation.
>
> Sincerely yours,
>
>
> Sherman Kline

What is your impression of this message? Did Sherman relay all the important information to Sandra in this letter? Do you think it could be improved in any way? If so, how?

Read the situation and letter that follow and discuss how you might improve the document:

Nancy Lee is the sales manager at Colormate Business Equipment Company. She has lunch with Daniel Stankowski, during which they discuss his company's need for new copying equipment. At the luncheon, she arranges to demonstrate a new line of laser printers and color copiers for Mr. Stankowski. When she returns to her office, she writes the following confirmation letter:

Colormate Business Equipment

7200 Metro Boulevard
Dearborn, CT 06077
203/555-8222
Fax 203/555-8239
Toll Free 800/555-3232

October 4, 19XX

Mr. Daniel Stankowski
Beacham Industries
5531 East Orange Road
Stafford, CT 06076

Dear Mr. Stankowski:

Yesterday at lunch, we agreed to a meeting in your office on Wednesday, April 6, at 1 p.m. so that I can demonstrate our new line of laser printers and color copiers. The demonstration will take about two hours.

Sincerely,

Nancy S. Lee
Sales Manager

List the information you would include in a memorandum confirming arrangements for an overnight, out-of-town business meeting.

WRITING TRANSMITTAL DOCUMENTS

A **transmittal document** is a memo or letter that accompanies an important document or other material. For example, a manager sending a formal report to a supervisor would include a transmittal memo. A financial consultant sending checks, policies, warranty deeds, or stock certificates to a client would use a transmittal letter. A mail order shoe company sending out an order would include a transmittal letter.

The general purpose of a transmittal letter or memo is to inform the reader that the writer has sent something—a document, for example. It serves to acknowledge and verify that the document was sent. You may also use such letters and memos to provide additional information to the reader. This additional information might be something you would tell the reader if you were to deliver the report by hand.

The level of formality of a transmittal document usually depends on the reader and other aspects of the situation. Letters to customers or memos to employees are often cordial, informal messages, adding little important information. On the other hand, a report writer might use a more formal transmittal letter to introduce the report to the reader. In this case, the report writer would probably include the transmittal as part of the formal report.

Transmittals that accompany official business papers (proposals, bids, legal contracts, or formal reports) may have legal implications and, therefore, must be carefully worded.

FIGURE 12.3 ▶

Transmittal documents can help prevent communication problems that might otherwise occur.

I thought I only ordered 1 box of paperclips.

Guidelines for Writing a Transmittal Document

- Identify what is being sent. If it is a check, state the amount and, if you prefer, the check number.

- Tell why the check or other document is being sent if you think that the recipient will be puzzled.

- Explain anything about the transmittal that you think is important for the recipient to know.

- Unless you need to provide full details about what you are sending, make the message brief.

The memo below from Amanda Beaulieu is an example of a transmittal document where the writer identifies the enclosed materials and explains relevant information. It is both brief and congenial as it accomplishes these tasks.

MEMORANDUM

TO: Rolf Moriarty, Manager

FROM: Amanda Beaulieu, Asst. Manager

DATE: May 7, 19XX

SUBJECT: PHOTOS FOR FALL BROCHURE

Enclosed are the photos I selected for our exciting fall brochure. It should be a winner!

You will find two photos marked for page 7 of the brochure. Photo 7a is my preference; however, my concern is that the colors will appear too dark in the finished brochure. If this might be a problem, photo 7b would work well. It portrays a similar fashion but in lighter colors.

Please let me know what you think. With your input and approval, we will begin layout and copy work on Monday right on schedule.

layout

plan or design or arrangement of something that is to be reproduced by printing; a set of pages with the position of text and artwork indicated; a mock-up of a proposed publication

copy

text that will be set for printing

C A S E   S C E N A R I O

Institutionally Speaking

Ted Flanagan worked for a pharmaceutical company with a large advertising budget. Ted completed the *layout* and *copy* of an ad that was to appear in several medical periodicals, including the *New England Journal of Medicine*. He planned to send the ad to each of the branch managers so that they were familiar with its contents. Ted wrote the following transmittal memo:

MEMORANDUM

TO: All Branch Managers

FROM: Ted Flanagan

DATE: June 1, 19XX

SUBJECT: ADVERTISING LAYOUT AND COPY

Attached is a rough layout with copy of an advertisement which we are planning to publish.

As you will see, the ad is strictly "institutional"—no products are mentioned by name.

Please let me have your comments and suggestions, if any.

Does this memo follow the guidelines suggested for transmittal memorandums? Is there any information that you believe needs to be added? Why or why not?

---

3   USE YOUR JUDGMENT

List the information you would include in a transmittal letter to accompany an employee handbook, policy manual, and insurance forms for a new employee. Be as specific as possible.

WRITING INSTRUCTIONAL MEMOS

Many memos contain various instructions that are not linked by sequence. They often relate to a broad task or topic, such as "Preparations for Task Force Visit" or "Guidelines for Press Releases." The information contained within this type of **instructional memo** is important enough that readers must not only understand it, they must also be able to apply it.

Everyone appreciates having instructions in writing, but only if they are clear and easy to understand. The reader also needs to know why the information is important. This may be conveyed through the subject line or through one or two explanatory sentences at the beginning of the memo.

> **SUBJECT:** PAYROLL PROCEDURE FOR EXTRA VACATION DAYS
>
> The payroll procedure for extra vacation days differs slightly from the normal procedure. The Payroll Department will not issue payment for extra vacation days without the required paperwork:

As with all written documents, the planning stage of an instructional memo is important. Take time to think through exactly what you want your reader to do and what information the reader will need in order to comply before you write an instructional memorandum.

Guidelines for Writing Instructional Memos

- Be specific about what you want the reader to do.
- Number items so they can be readily identified.

Last Minute Memo

At the last minute, Kenya Drake was asked to attend an important marketing seminar in Chicago. Before leaving, Kenya arranged for an office floater—Harold Meyer—to take incoming calls and handle office details. In addition, there were some very specific items Kenya wanted Harold to handle in her absence. To ensure that Harold followed her wishes, Kenya wrote him an instructional memorandum:

MEMORANDUM

TO: Harold Meyer

FROM: Kenya Drake

DATE: October 3, 19XX

SUBJECT: DETAILS NEEDING ATTENTION IN MY ABSENCE

Please take care of the following items while I'm at the Marketing Seminar next week:

1. Make sure Stan Waller gets a complete presentation package for his booth at the Pharmacists Convention in Houston.

2. Contact all sales reps in Region B and find out what marketing materials they will need for next month.

3. Dr. Ada Quentin may call for me. Please tell her we have extended her deadline to October 15; if she has any questions, refer her to George Shapiro.

4. Reschedule my Friday lunch with Dan Redford for early next week.

Thank you for your attention to these matters. Have a great week.

How thorough is Kenya's memorandum? If you were Harold, would you be able to follow through? What information is missing?

Instructional Memos That Give Directions

When you must convey instructions that are directions, the *sequence* of the items is crucial. You must present the directions in the order in which they should be followed.

Clarity is important in any message, but particularly with directions. Focus on the action so the reader knows what to do.

Instead of: The amber posterior mechanism is activated by a sliding motion from left to right.

Write: Turn on the orange switch on the back panel by sliding it to the right.

Notice that the second direction starts with a verb. This construction is better because it identifies the action for the reader.

The memorandum below provides a fun example of clear directions written in a logical sequence:

MEMORANDUM

TO: Marion Hinkley

FROM: Arnette Wilson

DATE: May 29, 19XX

SUBJECT: SURPRISE PARTY PREPARATIONS—TOP SECRET!!

I appreciate your volunteering to help with Vicki's surprise party. Here's how I'd like you to pitch in:

1. Call Lindskoog Deli (555-9284) this week and place the attached order; tell them I want to pick it up at 10 a.m. on June 5.

2. Check with Dave Lundeen in Promotions (ext. 284) to see if we can use the helium tanks to blow up about 50 balloons. (Please let me know by Friday if he gives it the okay; otherwise, I'll need to make different arrangements).

3. Make sure Vicki is kept busy in the back office on the morning of June 5. We'll be preparing the conference room for the party at that time, so we don't want her nosing around there!

4. Bring Vicki to the conference room at 11:45 under the guise of a staff meeting. The door will be shut and the lights will be off, but we'll be ready for you!

Thanks so much for the help—and by all means, keep your lips sealed!!

Attachment: Deli order

Guidelines for Writing Memos That Give Directions

- Be specific about what you want the reader to do.

- Number items so they can be readily identified.

- Present items in their required sequence.

C A S E   S C E N A R I O

Copying Instructions

David Chan managed the office of a small financial planning company. On Monday the company received a new computerized copier-printer—something everyone in the office was looking forward to using. Because the equipment was new and quite expensive, David wanted to make sure everyone was aware of the correct procedure for making copies. After reading the copier manual and testing the machine for himself, David wrote the following instructions for a memo:

> The F87 copier-printer is finally here! To help you get acquainted with the new machine, I've assembled some easy-to-follow directions. Let's do our best to keep this machine in tiptop shape so it has a long, healthy life.
>
> 1. Turn on the copier at least 15 minutes before you wish to use it.
>
> 2. Check the control panel to see if toner needs to be added (see attached sheet for copier symbols); if the toner symbol lights up, add toner (stored in cabinet) per the instructions on the toner bottle.
>
> 3. Select the original paper size, copier paper cartridge, and number of copies on the control panel. You can also adjust for light/dark copies and reduced/enlarged copies. DO NOT ADJUST ANY OF THE PANEL FEATURES WHILE THE MACHINE IS MAKING COPIES.
>
> 4. Place the original face up on the incoming paper feed, aligned with the red markings. You can stack up to 50 incoming originals at a time using the multiple feed stack. DO NOT EXCEED 50 ORIGINALS AT A TIME—THIS WILL CAUSE THE MACHINE TO JAM.

5. Press start and the machine will begin to copy. Press "O" if you need to stop the machine for any reason. DO NOT TURN OFF THE COPIER TO STOP THE MACHINE IN MID-CYCLE. The machine will stop itself if it experiences a paper jam.

6. In the event of a paper jam, the machine will stop and the symbol for paper jam will light up in red. Open the front panel of the copier. Look for the symbol on the interior of the machine that is lit in red. This will indicate where the jam has occurred. Lift the lever by the red symbol to remove the excess paper. Then close the lid and press start to resume the copy cycle.

7. Remove all originals and copies when you are done using the machine.

8. Return the panel features to standard.

9. Turn off the machine only if it is after 4:30 p.m.

Thanks for your cooperation.

What is your impression of David's directions? Does the sequence seem logical? Find support for whether you believe the directions are or are not clear. Could the instructions be improved? How?

USE YOUR JUDGMENT 4

What would you include in a memorandum to give instructions to cashiers about handling credit card purchases? Do you think sequence will be important? Write the instructions.

IN BRIEF

❶ The primary organizational plan for messages that inform is to use a direct approach. The writer states the main idea and follows it with any necessary explanation.

❷ The indirect approach is preferred when the information may upset the reader. With this approach, writers begin with the explanation, which leads to the main idea.

❸ Whether relaying good or bad news, writers close messages that inform on a positive note, offering help or asking for action.

❹ Confirmation documents are used to verify important arrangements or agreements between business people. They must be both detailed and congenial.

❺ Transmittal documents accompany important materials. They relay relevant information pertaining to the materials and provide a written record of the transmittal.

❻ Memorandums that give instructions or directions must be specific. The reader will find it easier to comply when items are numbered and in sequence.

WORDS OF NOTE

Define each of these terms introduced in Chapter 12.

confirmation document
direct approach
indirect approach
instructional memo
transmittal document

CHECK YOUR RECALL

1 What organizational plan should you follow in writing messages that contain good or neutral news? How does the plan differ when writing bad news?

2 What is the purpose of a confirmation letter or memo? What are four guidelines to follow in writing a confirmation document?

3 What is the purpose of a transmittal letter or memo? What guidelines can you follow in writing a transmittal document?

4 What guidelines apply to writing an instructional memo? What additional guideline should you follow when giving directions?

SHARE YOUR PERSPECTIVE

1 Write a confirmation memo based on the situation described. State your specific purpose for writing and informally outline your memo before writing:

You are the administrative assistant to Leslie James, president of Maxwell Real Estate. One month ago, Ms. James scheduled a meeting of branch managers to discuss the slump in the real estate market and ways to boost sales. Ms. James wants you to send a memo to the five branch managers, reminding them of this meeting. She says this will be a brainstorming session and wants the staff to come prepared with ideas.

2 Write a transmittal memo based on the following situation. State your specific purpose and informally outline your document before writing:

You have completed a year-end report on the annual usage of your company's physical fitness center for Raymond Alvarez, budget director. The report is long, including data about hours used, number of classes, number of participants, and costs. You will be away from your desk all next week and want a record that the material was sent on time.

❸ Write a memorandum that relays the following information:

The purchasing director of Matlock Trucking Company, Tracy Rosetti, wants to inform all supervisors and managers who purchase office furniture and equipment that there is a sizable inventory of used but still usable office equipment and furniture at Matlock Trucking Company. These items include desks, chairs, electric typewriters, electronic calculators, tables, sofas, filing equipment, lamps, wall hangings, film projectors, and several other used items. Rosetti thinks a great deal of money can be saved if people see what the company has on hand at virtually no cost. The inventory is in Warehouse B, and those interested should call Rosetti at Extension 2174.

❹ Write the instructional memorandum that explains the following situation to sales representatives and advises them how to act:

You are a sales manager for Taylor, Aaron & Bache, a pharmaceutical company. Recently a report from the Food and Drug Administration sent out a scare about synthetic insulin products. Taylor, Aaron & Bache manufactures synthetic insulin, but not any of the products criticized in the report. However, the information that hit the newspapers was inaccurate and could mislead customers.

You want your sales representatives to provide all customers with accurate information on the FDA's findings as they pertain to your products—before the customers come to you. You have created a two-page analysis of the findings for this purpose. In addition, if customers have further questions, they can be referred to Taylor, Aaron & Bache's consulting physician, Dr. Orrin Linhouse.

Since this is a sensitive issue, advise the representatives to meet with customers in person to discuss the report. If a meeting is not possible, ask the sales representatives to mail the materials and follow up with a personal phone call.

❺ Write the instructional memorandum to give directions as stated in the following situation:

The national pharmaceutical convention is coming up next month. Three sales representatives from Taylor, Aaron & Bache will staff a booth at the convention. Before they go, they need to learn from you how to set up their convention booth. They will need directions regarding when to arrive at the convention center, who the contact person will be, how they should cover the tables in the booth, where to set up the video display, and what brochures to place on the tables. Write an instructional memorandum that provides this information in a logical sequence.

FOCUS ON THE FINE POINTS
Read the following background information. Then follow the
instructions to locate and correct grammar errors.

Background

Marc Mahli will soon graduate from Oklahoma State University with a degree
in Public Health Administration. After seeing an ad for a public health coordinator in the Sunday paper, Marc decided to write a letter of application.
Along with the letter, Marc sends his résumé and a list of his references.

Your Instructions

Each of the following documents contains up to 15 errors. Indicate and correct errors by circling the problem and noting the solution on a photocopy of
the page or on a separate sheet of paper. In each case, you may assume the
document is formatted correctly.

Note: If you have difficulty locating errors, turn to page 471 in the Appendix.
There you will find additional information about the errors in Document 1.

DOCUMENT 1: Letter

7575 West Oklahoma Street
Oklahoma City, OK 36503
May 15, 19xx

Ms. Paula Lewis
Riverton Medical Center
2000 Riverside Drive
Stillwater, OK 36421

Dear Ms. Lewis

This is in regards to you're add in Sundays' *Courier Express,* for a public health coordinator. I would welcome the chance to learn more about the position and about Riverton Medical Center.

In two week's time I will graduate from Oklahoma State University with a B.A. in Public Health Administration. In my four years as a student at OSU, I have worked in a hospital setting, as both an employee and a volunteer. I also spent a semester in East Africa, studying at the Royal Hospital school in Nairobi and traveling on three seperate occasions to the their hospitals in rural Kenya and Tanzania. A part from the semester abroad, I was the student assistant to the Dean of the School of Public Health Administration: professor Carol Kreutzer, during both my junior and senior years'.

I have enclosed a résumé and reference list. I hope you will find that my education and experience match the public health coordinator positions' qualifications.

I will call next week to see if you are interested in setting up an interveiw. Meanwhile, you can reach me at 617-555-7444.

Thank you very much.

Sincerely

Marc L. Mahli

Enclosures

DOCUMENT 2: Résumé

Marc L. Mahli
7575 West Oklahoma Street
Oklahoma City, OK 00000
000-555-7444

EDUCATION

1995 Oklahoma State University, Oklahoma City, OK

B.A. in Public Health Administeration. Spent one semester at the Royal Hospital School, Nairobi, Kenya.

WORK EXPERIENCE

September 1994 - Present
September 1993 - January 1994

Oklahoma State University, Oklahoma City, OK

Assistance to the Dean, School of Public Health Administration. Assisted with Research, and performed routine office tasks, including writing her routine correspondence and scheduling student appointments.

Summer 1993 and 1994

Tyrone County Public Hospital, Merle, OK

Intake Clerk. Interviewed (Non-emergency) patients before admittance to the hospital or it's out-patient medical office.

Summer 1992

Pauls' Steakhouse, Stillwater, OK

Night Host. Seated guests, assigned wait staff's tables; assisted wait staff as needed.

Summer 1991

Ben's Barbecue Barn, Stillwater, OK

Waiter. Worked full time at this World-Famous barbeque restaurant.

VOLUNTEER WORK

Summer 1993 and 1994

Tyrone County Public Hospital, Merle, OK

Patient Visitor. Visited patients and assisted them by reading to them, washing they're hair, writing letters, playing chess, etc.

REFERENCES AVAILABLE ON REQUEST:

DOCUMENT 3: List of References

REFERRALS

Each individual may be called at their office during regular office hours'. Where a home phone number is included, its alright to call their, as well.

Professor Carol Kreutzer, Ph.D.
Dean, School of Public Health Administration
Oklahoma State University
Public Health Building: Room 9
Oklahoma City, OK 00000
Office Phone: 000-555-7990

Howard Kisii, PH.D.
Instructor, Psychology
Oklahoma State University
Jesse Hall, Room 717
Oklahoma City, OK 00000
Office Phone: 000-555-7676

Kendra Saamata, M.D.
Hospital-School Liasson
Royal Hospital School
17 Mohuto Street
522313 Nairobi
KENYA

Paul McAllister, Owner
Pauls' Steakhouse
582 West Pioneer Trial
Stillwater, OK 00000
Office Phone: 000-555-2121
Home Phone: 000-555-0330

Samantha Jarvis, R.N.; L.P.N.
Tyrone County Public Hospital
100 Main Street East
Merle, OK 00000
Office Phone: 000-555-0004
Home Phone: 000-555-3230

Benjamin Smith
Ben's Barbecue Barn
1800 Crosstown Highway
Stillwater, OK 00000
Office Phone: 000-555-6667
Home Phone: 000-555-3963

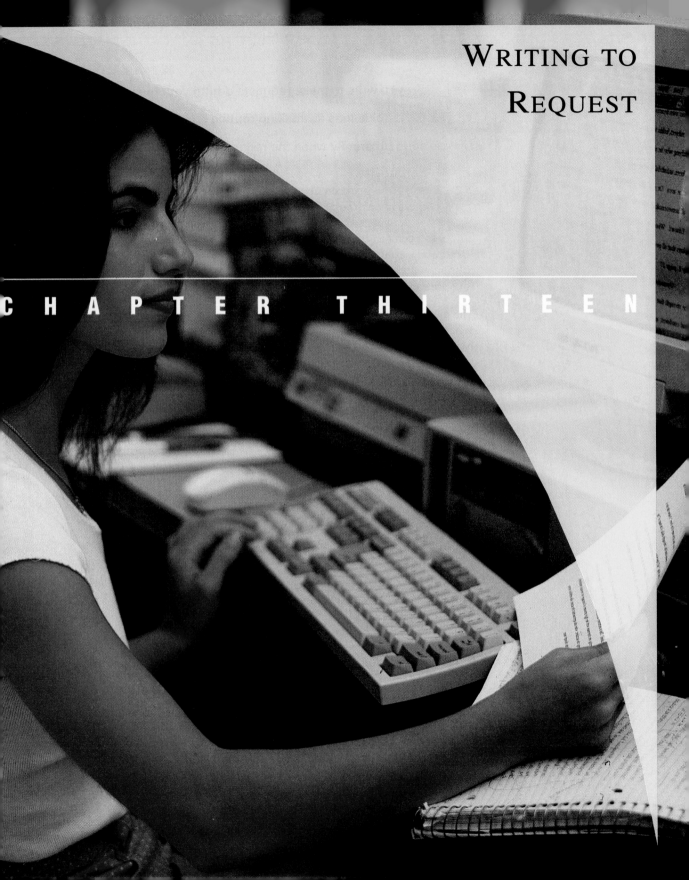

WRITING TO
REQUEST

CHAPTER THIRTEEN

Why might you write to make requests during your business career?

What are the guidelines for making routine requests?

Do you write differently when the request will be unexpected or unusual?

Y ou have a question about a particular product, and you write to ask for information. You read in a trade magazine about a new computer accounting service, and you write to get details. You are preparing a business proposal for a company, and you write to ask a company official for additional details. You are preparing an agenda for a meeting and you need background material for distribution with the agenda, so you send a memo to the proper department asking for it. In each of these business situations, you are writing to make a request.

The most efficient way to ask for important information is through a letter or memo. When you contact someone by telephone, the interaction is spontaneous and is easily sidetracked. On the other hand, seeing a request in written form lends it importance; it also gives the reader time to analyze the request, to think the problem through, or to locate and study the needed material before making a decision. A written request can also be used for permanent reference at a future date.

Most offices today are equipped with or have access to a facsimile or fax machine. A letter that once took days to reach its destination can be delivered by fax in a matter of moments. Now, even when time is a concern, you can make requests by letter and get fast results. In many cases you may also make requests by electronic mail.

WRITING AN EFFECTIVE REQUEST LETTER

Most of the requests you will make in business represent sales opportunities to those who receive them. For this reason, you can assume that you will generally receive favorable responses without delay. You do not need to do a selling job—it's to the recipients' benefit to help you in any way they can. Yet if the request is important to you and you want it to be businesslike, your **request letters** should contain the ingredients discussed in the following pages.

Clear, Specific, and Accurate Information

Your reader should not have to struggle to determine what you are asking for in a request letter. State what you want plainly. Make it easy for the reader to respond to your letter or memo—if you have more than one item or question that the reader must respond to, use bullets or asterisks. If there is a logical sequence to the items, use *enumeration.*

enumeration

the listing of one item after another; the numbering of items

Use language that is as specific as possible when making your request. For example, if you want to book a flight to New York, mention which airline you want to travel with as well as the date and time you wish to leave. Do not assume the reader will know what you want. For example:

> *Please arrange for my travel on Tuesday, November 15, to New York City. I would like to leave Boston in the morning and arrive at LaGuardia Airport by 1 p.m. If possible, I would like a non-stop flight on Regency Airlines.*

Before making a request, double-check to make sure you have the correct information included with your request. With a little care, you can easily avoid mistakes such as requesting a speaker to present on April 19 when your annual meeting is scheduled April 21. While it may take you more time to prepare your message when you have to verify information, ultimately you will save time (yours and your reader's) by being accurate.

The Nelsons cut a fine figure as they head across the lobby for an evening with the Glen Miller Big Band.

◀ **FIGURE 13.1**

Giving the wrong information can be embarrassing and inconvenient for all concerned.

Adequate Information for a Response

Your reader needs to know if you are expecting a face-to-face meeting, phone call, letter, or fax in response to your message. Your reader also needs to know about deadlines. Be sure to include this information in your communication. To enable the reader to get you the response you want when you want it, include your name, address, phone number, and fax number on any correspondence.

Background Information about Your Request

Let your reader know why you are requesting the information. That way, the reader will know the context of the request, which may make him or her feel more comfortable responding. For example, a request to obtain employee data may not be granted until you let your manager know that it will be used internally by Human Resources and will be kept strictly confidential.

When you supply relevant **background information**, you give your reader an opportunity to be more helpful. Then your reader, who is likely to know more about the information or service you need, will be better equipped to anticipate other needs that you may not realize you have in the situation. For example, perhaps the programmer whom you asked to make a demonstration diskette knows that the program you requested will not run on the equipment in your office. Because he was informed about how you would use the diskette, he can apply his own knowledge to avoid sending you a diskette you will not be able to use. He is then able to suggest another program that is compatible with your equipment.

Figure 13.2 shows a request letter that provides ample background information to enable the reader to respond quickly and completely.

Your readers will appreciate it when you provide sufficient background information to a request as this letter writer does.

Common Courtesy

Always be courteous when making a request. However, your courtesy should be sincere, not sugary. Say thank you, but don't overdo it. Better to say "The entire department is grateful for your contribution to this project" than to say "Words cannot express how grateful the entire department is for your contribution to this project."

The words *please* and *thank you* are always in style. Even when you are a customer and your reader has solicited your request, it is more effective to ask rather than demand. People tend to be more helpful when they are treated with respect.

You can be courteous by providing your reader with an easy means of responding to your request. If you need data, create a simple form that the reader can fill in and return (see Figure 13.3). Let your reader know the form can be sent by fax, or include a stamped, self-addressed envelope to encourage a quick turnaround.

LANGER PRINTING

17202 West River Way
Memphis, TN 38111
(901) 555-0200
Fax (901) 555-0245
Toll Free (800) 555-3333

January 9, 19XX

Order Department
PrintCo
186 Central Avenue
Nashville, TN 38404

Dear Order Department:

Last March I ordered several cases of 100 percent cotton rag stock from your paper division. We were very pleased with the quality of this paper and would like more. Unfortunately, we have disposed of the boxes and cannot locate the exact order numbers that correspond to the paper. Your catalog describes over 10 varieties of cotton rag stock.

Can you help me by checking your records to find the exact product ordered by PrintCo in March, 1994? We ordered the stock in white and cream. I would appreciate a confirmation of the product numbers, paper weight, and price by return fax immediately. Thanks for your help.

Sincerely,

Marcus Muggli
Inventory and Control Manager

◀ **FIGURE 13.2**

Request Letter

Common courtesy also means offering to *reciprocate,* if appropriate. If you are conducting a survey, offer to share the results. If you are assembling a proposal, let people know their contributions will be acknowledged.

reciprocate

to return in kind; to return a courtesy

A Reasonable Request

Make sure that what you are asking for is reasonable. Particularly if you are in a position of authority, it is not fair to ask someone to do something that is unethical or will require extreme sacrifices on the person's part. Be willing to do your share, and let the reader know that. You are more likely to get cooperation when your reader does not feel taken advantage of.

FIGURE 13.3 ▶

You are more likely to get a response to a request if you provide a form that the reader can fill in. This form is to be distributed among employees interested in computer training.

EMPLOYEE COMPUTER TRAINING

Course	Dates Available
Beginning Word Processing	09/19/XX 09/21/XX 09/27/XX
Intermediate Word Processing	09/19/XX 09/22/XX 09/27/XX
Advanced Word Processing	09/15/XX 09/22/XX
Spreadsheet I	09/20/XX 09/22/XX 10/06/XX
Spreadsheet II	09/21/XX 09/23/XX 10/07/XX

••

DEPARTMENT: _____ NO. OF EMPLOYEES_____

Employee Name	Course	Date
1. _____		
2. _____		
3. _____		
4. _____		
5. _____		
6. _____		
7. _____		
8. _____		
9. _____		
10. _____		
11. _____		
12. _____		

Please return to Human Resources by August 5, 19XX. Thank you.

There will be times when your request is unusual or asks a lot of the reader. Perhaps you need a speaker on short notice, or you would like the respondent to complete a lengthy questionnaire and return it within several days. In these situations, you can use an indirect approach, balanced with plenty of courtesy and background information, to get the response you need.

C A S E   S C E N A R I O

The Play's the Thing

Reginald Cornish was in charge of the student activity program at a small college in Brattleboro, Vermont. In the summer he would be hosting a group of international students who were registered for a six-week course in English as a foreign language.

Reginald wanted to provide them with several cultural activities during their stay at the college. He saw in the newspaper a listing of the New London Barn Theater's summer productions and decided to write to request more information regarding group attendance (20 students, one in a wheelchair) on either of two Saturdays in August. He wanted to make this as much of a learning experience as he could, so he decided to inquire about a backstage tour as well.

Reginald drafted the following letter to be sent by fax:

> Dear Theater Manager:
>
> I would like to arrange for a group of international students to attend a matinee performance of Meet Me in St. Louis on either Saturday, August 4 or 11. Do you have a large block of seats available for either of those afternoons? Also, do you offer a student discount on the price of tickets for matinee performances? If we can, we would like to stay after the performance and get a short informational tour of the backstage area of your theater.
>
> I need this information from you by June 15. Thank you very much.
>
> Sincerely,

What do you think of Reginald's letter? Did he include all the information the theater manager will need to respond? How might Reginald improve his message in content and format?

USE YOUR JUDGMENT

You work for a test publishing company. You plan to conduct several focus groups on a Saturday next month. You need to hire a caterer to deliver box lunches for 30 people. Before you can hire the caterer, you need a menu, with prices, and assurance that the caterer is available on the Saturday in question. Write the necessary document.

WRITING A ROUTINE REQUEST

Routine requests are the bulk of request letters sent by businesses. They are letters in which the writer asks for materials, information, and services. Often the items requested are advertised or promoted and the recipients are prepared for your requests.

The most frequent mistake made by those writing routine requests is to include too much or too little information. You can avoid either scenario by thinking ahead to what information the recipient will need to fulfill the request.

Look at the examples below. Notice how the request letter progresses from too little information (Letter A), to too much information (Letter B), to just the right amount (Letter C).

A ▶

Dear Office Supply House:

Send me all the free materials you have.

Sincerely,

Dear Office Supply House:

In consulting our files of catalogs of office equipment and supplies and checking them off against various manufacturers and distributors, I discovered that I do not have your latest catalogs and price lists and other information concerning your products. (I have some materials, of course, but they are out of date.)

I have just been promoted to the position of office services manager of Winston Associates, and I think one of the first things I must do is build a good reference source for me and my staff to use in selecting appropriate equipment, materials, and supplies. For this reason I would like to request that you send me your latest catalogs and price lists and other product information you may have in your possession at your earliest convenience. In addition, I would be most grateful if you would put my name on your mailing list so that I will receive all new materials.

Thank you.

Sincerely,

◀ B

Dear Office Supply House:

May I have your latest catalogs and price lists and other information about your office supplies and equipment. I would also like to be placed on your regular mailing list so that I will receive all new sales and promotional literature.

Thank you.

Sincerely,

◀ C

The letter below contains a request for an appointment. The writer provides sufficient information but no extraneous details, so that the recipient can accommodate the request.

Robertson Press

One Publishers' Place
Columbia, South Carolina 29201
803/555-1373
Toll Free 800/555-7788
Fax 803/555-1348

September 11, 19XX

Mr. Howard Cohen
Putnam Lowes Corporation
75 West Airdale Drive
Northbrook, IL 60637

Dear Mr. Cohen:

I will be attending the annual convention of the American Society of Office Administration at the Hyatt Hotel near O'Hare Airport October 9-12.

While I am in the area, I would like to visit Putnam Lowes in Northbrook and see the new electronic mailing system that you introduced a short time ago. Our present system for mail handling is somewhat antiquated, and I am greatly intrigued by the literature you have sent out on your equipment. Would you or someone else be available to see me on Tuesday, October 10? This is the only day I am free, but the hours are flexible. I suggest 2:30 p.m. If this is not a convenient time, please call to suggest another hour.

I will be stopping at the Hyatt, arriving early in the afternoon of October 9 and departing around noon on the 12th. You may leave a message for me with the concierge if at all necessary.

Sincerely yours,

Cynthia McBride
Shipping Manager

You are doing research for your employer, a recruiting company, and you need data from a local community college on the number of graduates and the degrees they were awarded over the last five years.

1. How might the contents of this letter differ from the letter in "Use Your Judgment" exercise 1 (page 354)? How will it be the same? Be as specific as possible, given the information provided.
2. Write the necessary document.

REQUESTING A SPECIAL FAVOR

Some of the request letters you write in the course of business will deal with requests that do not represent sales opportunities for the recipients. Your request may be more of a **special favor** that will be of benefit to you but of little, if any, benefit to those to whom you write. These are somewhat more challenging to write than routine requests, but they contain the same ingredients. The level of courtesy and *diplomacy* may be more important here, however, be sure to say please and thank you!

diplomacy

tact; skill in handling affairs without offending or arousing hostility

C A S E   S C E N A R I O

Special Appearance

Helen Barry was the new vice president of the St. Louis chapter of the Modern Management Society. One of her responsibilities was to plan the monthly dinner meetings and obtain interesting speakers for these occasions.

For the March 25 meeting she selected the topic of organization planning, a subject in which a number of members had expressed interest. It was

suggested that Professor William F. Kinsolving of Drury College in Springfield be invited to speak to the group on this topic. Several of the members were familiar with his writings and had heard him speak. The chapter had a small budget for guest speakers; it could pay an ***honorarium*** of $100 plus all expenses.

Helen prepared the following draft of a letter:

honorarium

a payment for a service (such as making a speech) on which custom or propriety forbids a price to be set

> Dear Professor Kinsolving:
>
> The St. Louis chapter of the Modern Management Association is planning to concentrate on the topic of organization planning at its March 25 dinner meeting.
>
> Would you be willing to serve as our speaker for the evening? We are in a position to pay you an honorarium of $100 plus all expenses. I look forward to having your acceptance.
>
> Sincerely yours,

If you were Dr. Kinsolving, what would you think of this request? Does it contain the necessary ingredients to make it effective? Why or why not? How would you change the letter?

3 USE YOUR JUDGMENT

You need to ask your landlord to release you from the last three months of your one-year apartment lease because you have accepted an out-of-state job.

1. How might the contents of this letter differ from those in "Use Your Judgment" exercises 1 and 2 earlier in this chapter? How will it be the same? Be as specific as possible, given the information provided.
2. Write the necessary document.
3. Find an advertisement that invites inquiries about the advertised item. Choose an ad for something in which you have some interest and about which you can generate some logical questions. Then do the following:
   a. Clip the advertisement.
   b. Write a letter requesting offered information and answers to your questions.
   c. Send the letter (by fax if possible) and then record how long it takes to get a reply. Keep a copy of the letter for yourself.
   d. Analyze the response you get to your letter. Was your request effective? Did you get a complete response?
   e. Write a memo to your teacher describing your relative success with the project. Attach the advertisement and a copy of your request letter.

Notice in the letter below how the writer is careful to explain the situation and expresses willingness to pay for the services provided, if necessary. The writer also offers to provide the results to Mr. Lipscomb as a courtesy.

BASSERETTE INDUSTRIES

3770 ST. CHARLES AVENUE
NEW DESERT, NV 89772
PHONE (702) 555-6612
FAX (702) 555-1757

July 17, 19XX

Mr. Elmer Lipscomb, President
Southern Library Association
2732 Trabajo Nuevo Road
Miami, FL 33003

Dear Mr. Lipscomb:

Our company is planning an expansion and modernization of its library, and I have been asked to assist in putting together a proposal for the project.

The library was organized many years ago when we were a very small company, and during the early years it satisfied our needs quite well. The recent rapid increase in the number of our personne— especially engineers, chemists, scientists, and executives—has added new demands that we simply cannot meet with our present space and equipment.

It occurred to me that perhaps the SLA has available various model layouts and recommendations for equipment and materials. If so, I would be grateful if you would share this information with me.

If you do have resource material and there is a charge for it, we will be happy to pay for it. If you do not have the information I need but know where it can be located, I would appreciate your recommending a reliable source.

Thank you very much, Mr. Lipscomb. If we are successful in our plans, I will make it a point to share the results with you, complete with diagrams and photographs.

Cordially,

Kenneth Rodriguez
Office Manager

IN BRIEF

❶ The best way to request information is by letter or memo. Business people are able to communicate in writing quickly and easily using a fax machine or electronic mail.

❷ Effective written requests are clear, specific, and accurate. The writer gets to the point, includes all relevant details, and makes sure the details are correct.

❸ A request is complete when it tells the reader when to respond and whether the response needs to be in person or by telephone, fax, or mail.

❹ Your reader will be better equipped to respond to your request if you provide sufficient, relevant background information.

❺ Business requests that get the job done are courteous and reasonable. The writer uses sincere words of appreciation, offers to return a favor when possible, and shares in the burden of the task as appropriate.

❻ Routine requests, where the writer asks for materials, information, or services, are usually anticipated by the recipient.

❼ Special favors require more diplomacy than the routine request; in these situations the writer must be particularly gracious and reasonable.

WORDS OF NOTE

Define each of these terms introduced in Chapter 13.

background information
request letter
routine request
special favor

CHECK YOUR RECALL

1 What can you assume in most cases about the recipient of your request letter?

2 What are the ingredients of an effective written request?

3 What mistakes are frequently made by people writing requests? What can you do to avoid these mistakes?

4 How might your approach to asking a special favor differ from writing a routine request?

SHARE YOUR PERSPECTIVE

1 Write a letter to a former teacher asking for a reference letter. Supply background information that relates what you have been doing since you were his or her student and describe what type of employment you are seeking.

2 Read the following situation and write the necessary request documents:

You work as an administrative assistant to Paul Norton, general merchandising manager of ProLine Products, a fishing lure manufacturer. Paul frequently asks you to write letters for him, and you prepare these letters and sign them over the title Administrative Assistant to Paul Norton.

Paul plans to visit the company's manufacturing headquarters in Minneapolis, Minnesota, on the second Wednesday in April this year. He asks you to write several documents to make the following arrangements:

　　a. Paul needs to confirm a meeting with Nadine Ashwell, Manufacturing Distributor, to review the manufacturing schedule of a new product, the Bi-Swivel Lure. He also wonders if she can give him a quick tour of the manufacturing assembly line. Paul wants to meet with Nadine some time before noon on April 10.

b. Paul hopes he can arrange an afternoon meeting on April 10 with Josh Siffert, Product Specialist, to discuss product and pricing specifications for the Bi-Swivel Lure. In the meantime, he wants Josh to complete and return a form that answers these questions: What are the recommended uses for the Bi-Swivel Lure? What materials are used to manufacture the Bi-Swivel Lure? Where would he place the Bi-Swivel Lure on the **continuum** of Pro-Line products in terms of price and quality?

continuum

a coherent whole characterized as a collection, sequence, or progression of parts varying by minute degrees

c. Paul will need accommodations at a hotel. Write a letter to send by fax to the Minneapolis Inn on Wayzata Drive. Make reservations for Tuesday and Wednesday evenings. Request a non-smoking room at the executive rate.

❸ You work in the dispatch office of The Hurried Courier. Write a request letter to all clients to accompany the following survey:

Name (optional): _____ Date of last service: _____

How often do you use our service? (Select the most accurate response):

_____Several times during the day

_____Several times during the week

_____Several times during the month

_____Several times during the year

Which service do you use most often?

_____One-hour delivery

_____Two-hour delivery

_____Four-hour delivery

_____Overnight delivery

Do you use other courier services as well as The Hurried Courier?

___Yes ___No

Rate your level of satisfaction with our services:

	Very Satisfied	Satisfied	Not Satisfied
Dispatcher courtesy	3	2	1
Courier courtesy	3	2	1
Timeliness	3	2	1
Rates	3	2	1

FOCUS ON THE FINE POINTS

Read the following background information. Then follow the instructions to locate and correct grammar errors.

Background

Sally Larson-Wilkes, vice president of fund-raising for the Windsor City Institute of Fine Arts (WCIFA), has decided to approach Lionel Lee, a board member who owns a successful video production company, to produce a "gratis" promotional videotape for a special exhibit the institute is making part of its permanent collection.

Sally drafts a letter to Lionel and encloses a chart with demographic projections and a draft of WCIFA's mission statement.

Your Instructions

Each of the following documents contains up to 15 errors. Indicate and correct errors by circling the problem and noting the solution on a photocopy of the page or on a separate sheet of paper. In each case, you may assume the document is formatted correctly.

Note: If you have difficulty locating errors, turn to page 473 in the Appendix. There you will find additional information about the errors in Document 1.

DOCUMENT 1: Letter to Video Company

WINDSOR CITY INSTITUTE OF FINE ARTS

1700
West
15th
Avenue
Windsor City
TN
38820

(615)555-9090
Fax
(615)555-9099

April 29, 19XX

Mr. Lionel Lee
Lee Teleproductions
222 Cannon View Road
Windsor City, TN 38823

Dear Lionel:

Having been so ill, I was delighted to see you back in the peak of health at the April board meeting. Both contracting such a rare illness as well as a quick recovery were quite remarkable—I can see why you feel like a "miracle in shoes"!

Lionel, I know you share my passion for finally seeing the textiles become part of WCIFA's permanent collection. This move will merit a healthy and much-needed boost in funding from the NEA. Further, sitting as you do on both this board and the Horton Foundation board, I know you understand the implications for future foundation grants. As we both also know, getting the word out to members, the community, and—most important of all—to participating institutes here and in England will be absolutely critical. We find ourself in the contradictory position of being poised to move into the "big time," but having to do this on a budget, which is decidedly small.

On behalf of the institute, the board, and I, may I ask you to consider giving an additional gift to WCIFA this year. What all of we have in mind is a gift in kind of a 15-minute promotional video on the institute and her incredible collection of textiles. Understanding how difficult it is for me to ask you this, I hope you will respond with a resounding "Yes."

If in need of additional persuading, I hope you will find the enclosed demographics summary of interest and will prompt an affirmative decision. (I've also enclosed the revised mission statement from the March board meeting.)

Thank you, Lionel. I'll look forward to hearing from you.

Best regards,

Sally Larson-Wilkes
Vice President of Fund-Raising

ttt

Enclosures

DOCUMENT 2: Mission Statement from Annual Report

Windsor City Institute of Fine Arts

Our Mission Statement

As the oldest institution of its kind in the city of Windsor, the mission of WCIFA is:

To bring to the community a diverse representation of art and artists around the world, spanning ancient times to modern, in a way that is respectful of each artist and his culture

To foster in the community an active physical relationship with art through education, scholarship, and juried member exhibits—be they children or adults

To maintain and build their soon-to-be-permanent collection of the textile crafts of the southeastern United States

To ensure that an ever-growing base of membership will grow along with interest and attendance of nonmembers by creating opportunities for experiential exhibits in both our main and satellite exhibit centers

To ensure their various permanent and traveling collections to remain intact for generations to come by maintaining a sound, well-managed budget

Revised 3/15/XX

DOCUMENT 3: Demographics Chart

As a sales tool, WCIFA can now boast one of the wealthiest, most consumer-oriented constituencies on the national arts scene. The graph shows

- Growth and the corresponding potential in corporate membership for growth in dollars for arts funding

- Growth and the corresponding potential in foundation support for sustaining dollars from various sources (NEA, Van Gogh Fund and their subsidiary foundation arms, Paris Group, etc.)

- Growth and the differences in per capita incomes in individual membership from members 1991- 1995 and projected for 1996-2000

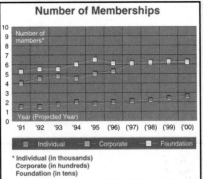

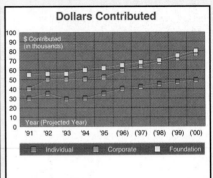

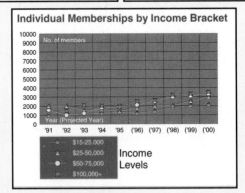

WRITING TO
RESPOND

CHAPTER FOURTEEN

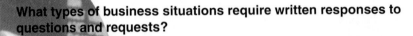

What types of business situations require written responses to questions and requests?

How are form letters composed and used?

What circumstances call for courtesy letters?

How do you respond to requests that are complex or require you to say no?

Many of the letters that businesses receive require some type of response. Whether that response is provided orally or in writing is determined by the situation. Those situations that require a written response can be separated into two groups: simple inquiries, orders, or comments and more complex inquiries, orders, or comments.

Orders come from customers, while inquiries and comments come from a number of sources—a student who is planning to write a report and who needs information about your company, a person who is planning to make a presentation for your firm, a potential client who has just become acquainted with your company through newspaper or catalog advertising.

Responding to any kind of a request takes employee time and costs money for paper, postage, and equipment. However, the investment is rather small when you consider the potential payback. Every request is a prospect for new or continued business if the response is handled quickly and efficiently. The conscientious business person will recognize that a written response is an opportunity to make a sale.

RESPONDING TO SIMPLE INQUIRIES, ORDERS, OR COMMENTS

If a business sells a product or service, it is likely to get the same types of **simple inquiries** and requests repeatedly. If it is a large company and very visible in the public eye, it probably receives a fair number of letters from citizens who comment on how the company conducts its business or on the effectiveness of a product or service. When the letter is routine, a well-written form letter will do in response. If a letter is unique, business favors the brief courtesy response.

The Form Letter Response

deluged

overwhelmed, swamped by an excess of something

Large companies are often *deluged* by requests for information. To handle such requests, they prepare special booklets and brochures that answer typical questions. To accompany these materials, they also prepare **form letters** that give details on how to get more information if necessary.

When preparing a form letter or **acknowledgment card** (printed on a postcard), follow these guidelines:

- Visualize a real person as you are composing your form letter.

- Use a personal salutation whenever possible ("Dear Ms. Hinten" rather than "Dear Customer").

- Write to communicate to your reader that the request is important and welcome.

- Invite further communication by providing a return address, phone number, and individual or department name.

The form letter below was prepared to respond to an advertising campaign for a new *font* package for personal computers (it will accompany a sample disk of the program). The writer used the ***mail-merge feature*** of a word processing program to personalize each response with the customer's name and address.

▲FIGURE 14.1

Computer word processing programs have made it efficient and easy to personalize and send mass mailings.

F O N T S

4757 Perimeter Road Cleveland, OH 45220
Phone [216] 555-FONT Fax [216] 555-3434 Toll Free [800] 555-FONT

January 12, 19XX

Arlene Quist
433 Vernon Hills Road
Cambridge, MA 02139

Dear Ms. Quist:

Thank you for your interest in Fab Fonts' new font package, Incredi-Fonts. For a short time only, we are offering a sample disk of Incredi-Fonts to interested customers. With the disk you can test our amazing array of fonts on your own system!

Incredi-Fonts features 24 text, headline, and script fonts for creating letters, faxes, reports, and other business documents. What's more, each font will print the way it appears on the screen. All this for just $35.95.

Complete the attached order form to get your Incredi-Fonts package without delay.

Sincerely,

Art Greene
Product Manager

Thank you for your recent request for information about our new line of lightweight, fully automatic video camcorders.

Your name has been added to our mailing list, and you should receive our new catalog of VCR equipment and supplies in time to order for holiday picture taking or gift giving.

For specific information about models and prices, please call our toll-free number (1-800-555-7823) between 8 a.m. and 5 p.m. any weekday.

Consumer Services Division

The printed postcard above was prepared to acknowledge general requests for information about a company product. Since it will be sent to hundreds of inquirers, it could not be personalized. It is worded to make the recipient feel that the request is important and welcome, and it extends an invitation to call for more information.

The Courtesy Response

goodwill

a kindly feeling of approval and support; the favor or prestige that a business has acquired beyond the mere value of what it sells

Frequently there is a need to write a letter simply to let a customer or a correspondent know that a message was received and acted upon. This type of response is called a **courtesy letter** because it is a gesture of *goodwill*. Courtesy letters provide businesses with opportunities to build trust and rapport with the general public as well as customers.

Businesses often send courtesy letters to acknowledge orders. This is particularly common when there will be a delay in filling an order. The following letter provides an example of this type of response.

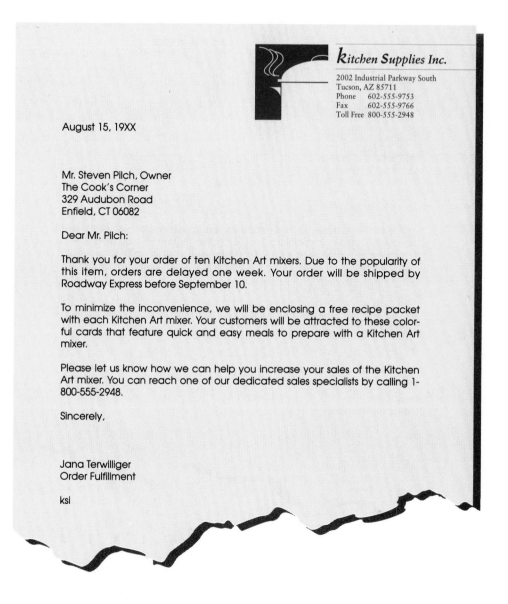

Kitchen Supplies Inc.

2002 Industrial Parkway South
Tucson, AZ 85711
Phone   602-555-9753
Fax   602-555-9766
Toll Free 800-555-2948

August 15, 19XX

Mr. Steven Pilch, Owner
The Cook's Corner
329 Audubon Road
Enfield, CT 06082

Dear Mr. Pilch:

Thank you for your order of ten Kitchen Art mixers. Due to the popularity of this item, orders are delayed one week. Your order will be shipped by Roadway Express before September 10.

To minimize the inconvenience, we will be enclosing a free recipe packet with each Kitchen Art mixer. Your customers will be attracted to these colorful cards that feature quick and easy meals to prepare with a Kitchen Art mixer.

Please let us know how we can help you increase your sales of the Kitchen Art mixer. You can reach one of our dedicated sales specialists by calling 1-800-555-2948.

Sincerely,

Jana Terwilliger
Order Fulfillment

ksi

Businesses often receive letters attesting to the quality of their products. You will want to acknowledge these letters to maintain your customers' goodwill. A short, personalized response (as demonstrated on page 372) tells the individual that you appreciate the feedback. Your company may also have special materials that you can mention and include in this type of response.

kitchen Supplies Inc.

2002 Industrial Parkway South
Tucson, AZ 85711
Phone   602-555-9753
Fax   602-555-9766
Toll Free 800-555-2948

August 15, 19XX

Mr. Stanley Dearstyne
88 Ashuelot Drive
Washington, NH 03240

Dear Mr. Dearstyne:

Your recent letter telling us how much you are enjoying your new Kitchen Art
mixer is the kind of feedback we enjoy getting from our customers. It was
thoughtful of you to write to us expressing your satisfaction with our equipment. We promise to be just as thoughtful if you ever need service or assistance with your Kitchen Art mixer.

We hope you will enjoy the enclosed tipsheet for making pasta with the
Kitchen Art mixer. We promise to keep you informed about any mixer attachments and recipe offers that may interest you.

Sincerely,

Nelly Pocai
Customer Relations

urs

C A S E S C E N A R I O

For Rent

Tory Hildebrandt worked at the Apartment Finders, an agency that helps
people find suitable apartments to rent. She received a letter from Evan
Masters inquiring about the services provided by Apartment Finders. Evan
planned to move to the area in six months and would need help finding a
place to live.

Tory took a minute to assemble the Apartment Finders brochure, preferences checklist, and a map of the area. Then she drafted the following letter
which she planned to use for other inquiries of the same nature:

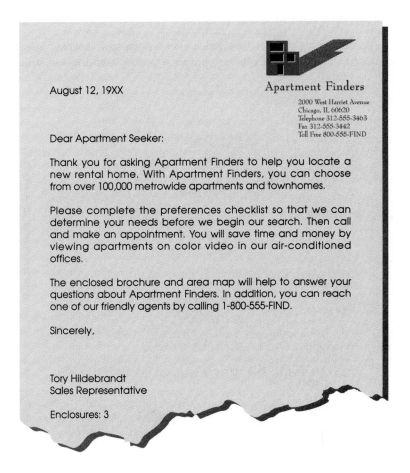

August 12, 19XX

Apartment Finders

2000 West Harriet Avenue
Chicago, IL 60620
Telephone 312-555-3463
Fax 312-555-3442
Toll Free 800-555-FIND

Dear Apartment Seeker:

Thank you for asking Apartment Finders to help you locate a new rental home. With Apartment Finders, you can choose from over 100,000 metrowide apartments and townhomes.

Please complete the preferences checklist so that we can determine your needs before we begin our search. Then call and make an appointment. You will save time and money by viewing apartments on color video in our air-conditioned offices.

The enclosed brochure and area map will help to answer your questions about Apartment Finders. In addition, you can reach one of our friendly agents by calling 1-800-555-FIND.

Sincerely,

Tory Hildebrandt
Sales Representative

Enclosures: 3

Is a form letter an appropriate response to this inquiry? Why or why not? Would you improve this response in any way? How?

USE YOUR JUDGMENT 1

What information would you include in a form letter in response to orders for a limited edition figurine that is on back-order? Outline the letter.

2   USE YOUR JUDGMENT

Analyze the following response to a request for a company's annual report from Julius Ambrosio, a student who is preparing a report for a business management class:

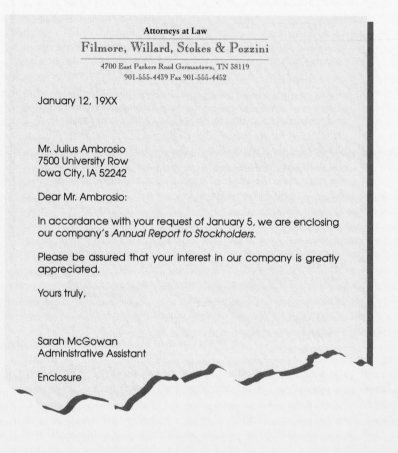

Attorneys at Law

Filmore, Willard, Stokes & Pozzini

4700 East Parkers Road Germantown, TN 38119
901-555-4439 Fax 901-555-4452

January 12, 19XX

Mr. Julius Ambrosio
7500 University Row
Iowa City, IA 52242

Dear Mr. Ambrosio:

In accordance with your request of January 5, we are enclosing our company's *Annual Report to Stockholders.*

Please be assured that your interest in our company is greatly appreciated.

Yours truly,

Sarah McGowan
Administrative Assistant

Enclosure

3   USE YOUR JUDGMENT

Write an improved letter to Julius Ambrosio to accompany the annual report.

RESPONDING TO THE COMPLEX INQUIRY

Complex inquiries require highly individualized responses. An inquiry is complex when you must provide detailed information or when the situation calls for extra tact.

The Detailed Response

Here are some guidelines for preparing a **detailed response** to an inquiry, order, or comment:

- **Express appreciation for the opportunity to be of service.** Inquiries about your product or service help sustain your business. Let your customers know that you are pleased that they have written. This can be done in a direct statement or reflected in the tone of your letter.

- **Be complete and specific when responding to questions.** It is easy to answer inquiries that are clear, concise, and specific. When responding to a letter listing several questions, answer each question completely and in the same order as presented in the original letter. For easy reading, you may even consider putting each answer into a separate paragraph.

- **Begin on a positive note.** If you can't say yes to every question, alter the format so that you don't have to begin with a negative answer. Strengthen your writing by starting with a positive response and working your way

◀ **FIGURE 14.2**

A positive beginning helps soften a negative answer.

down to the less favorable responses. A positive beginning sets the tone for your response and can soften bad news that follows.

- **Hold the customer's interest.** The inquiry itself shows that the customer already has an interest in your product or service. Your ultimate goal is to convert reader interest into action. Subtly try to persuade the recipient to take favorable action. Emphasize reader benefit by commenting favorably on your products.

- **Try to give something extra.** Doing something extra is a special gesture of friendliness. It is an offer to do something beyond what was requested and should be used when appropriate. We all react with a good feeling when we get a bonus or something more than we anticipated.

Read the product inquiry below and its accompanying detailed response. Notice how the response meets the guidelines presented in this section.

Product Inquiry

CONVAL CORPORATION

May 23, 19XX

3224 Pautuxet Avenue
Providence, RI 02933
401/555-8220
Fax 401/555-9222
Toll Free 800/555-7171

American Plastics
1257 Reedson Road
Worcester, MA 01601

Dear Product Manager:

My company is studying the potential use of shrink-wrap packaging in our operations.

We are a diversified manufacturer which produces electrical components, automobile parts, plumbing supplies, and canned foods as our major products.

Please send me technical specifications and price information on your shrink-wrap packaging machinery. Also, please send your recommendations for the application of this machinery to our operations.

Based on the information we receive from you and from two other companies, we will be scheduling formal presentations to our Budget Committee.

Thank you for your help.

Sincerely,

Constance Kennedy
Purchasing Assistant

Response to Product Inquiry

★ **AmericanPlastics**

1257 Reedson Road
Worcester, MA 01601
Phone (617) 555-4400
Fax (617) 555-8232

May 29, 19XX

Ms. Constance Kennedy
ConVal Corporation
3224 Pautuxet Avenue
Providence, RI 02933

Dear Ms. Kennedy:

Thank you for your letter of May 23 requesting information on our shrink-wrap multiple packaging equipment.

The enclosed fact sheets list the technical data and the price information you requested. In addition to packaging equipment, our company also manufactures other products that would be beneficial to your operations, particularly your canned foods division. Fact sheets for those products are also enclosed.

I would be pleased to make a formal presentation of our product line at your location at your convenience. Just let me know when you wish to schedule it.

Thank you for the opportunity to introduce our company line of products to you. You may call me collect at 617-555-4400 if you have further questions or if you wish additional information.

Sincerely yours,

Deanna Priazzi
Product Manager

Enclosures

C A S E S C E N A R I O

Calling Card

Trish LaVoy worked as a sales correspondent for Staffords, a company that sold promotional items to businesses. She read a letter from Robert L. Bromley, sales director for Olympus Products Corporation, asking for information about The Calling Card, one of Staffords' products. The price was $9.95 each and there was a 10 percent discount for quantities of 50 or more.

Bromley also wanted to know if the vinyl carrying case in the catalog could be obtained in blue with his company's logo imprinted on it in yellow. If so, he planned to order 120. He had enclosed a black-on-white photograph of the Olympus *logo*.

Trish checked the catalog and determined that the carrying case was available in blue (and other colors). She knew it was also possible to imprint the logo on the case in any color desired. The charge for the imprint was $1.00 each.

Trish quickly drafted the following letter in response to Bromley's inquiry:

November 25, 19XX

Mr. Robert L. Bromley
Olympus Products Corporation
17 West Markham
Columbia, SC 29233

Dear Mr. Bromley:

The Calling Card (Item G-7) about which you inquired can be obtained in blue at no extra cost—that is, $9.95 less a 10 percent discount on quantities of 50 or more.

Your company logo can be imprinted on the case. However, there is a charge of $1.00 for this extra service.

Sincerely,

Trish LaVoy
Sales Correspondent

How thorough was Trish's response to Bromley's inquiry? Did the letter have any personal touches? Do you think Bromley will be compelled to place an order? Why or why not? How would you have responded to Bromley's inquiry?

The Delicate Response

Sometimes you may not be able to provide the material, the answer, or the information that a writer has requested. While it is easy to say yes, it takes more time and creative talent to say no gently and tactfully. You may have to say no because the writer does not understand the nature of your company's business. Customers are often misled because they base their thinking on the name of the company. If you must say no, do so graciously. A negative response can still be courteous and effective. Use the occasion as an opportunity to build goodwill. Since you cannot be of service, suggest a reasonable alternative as that little "something extra."

When You Must Say No

- **Aim for a favorable start.** Begin with something that will cushion the negative reply. What would your reaction be to a letter beginning "I regret to inform you" or "Unfortunately, we cannot grant your request"? Compare this to a letter that begins "We appreciate your interest in our product, and always strive to do our best to meet our customers' needs."

- **Explain why you cannot say yes.** Perhaps the request is for information you are not allowed to give out. It is better to explain why you cannot honor such a request than to hide behind "company policy." Even if this is the reason, express the idea more sympathetically. Explaining your case prepares the reader to accept your refusal.

- **Offer an alternative solution.** This helps take the bite out of saying no. If you do not offer the product or service, direct the customer to someone who does.

- **End with a forward look.** The reader may be a future customer. Emphasize what you can do rather than what you cannot do. There are many things you can do—offer an alternative solution, express your desire to cooperate, or wish the reader success.

The letter below is a good example of **delicate response** to a complex inquiry.

Pet Suppliers Surplus

1700 South Pilgrim Street
Minneapolis, MN 55408
Phone (612) 555-2242
Fax (612) 555-2256
Toll Free (800) 555-PETS

February 1, 19XX

Mr. Michael Lindley
Pedigreed Pets Unlimited
520 Minnehaha Street
St. Paul, MN 55103

Dear Mr. Lindley:

Thank you for supplying me with the credit information I requested. I wish I could say, "Yes, we will be pleased to have you as a credit customer." However, on the basis of information I have received about the condition of your business and the comments of your creditors, I must give you a reluctant no at the moment. We truly believe that it would not be wise for you to take on other obligations at this time.

I say "at this time" because I am hopeful that things will change for the better for you. If so, please write me again when your financial picture has changed.

In the meantime, I hope you will find it possible to order from us on a cash basis. We appreciate your business and will do everything possible to see that you get what you want when you want it.

Cordially,

Catherine Brubaker
Credit Representative

C A S E   S C E N A R I O

Nursery Note

Xue Lee was the assistant manager at Addams Floral Nursery Inc. The nursery offered a wide range of cut flowers, plants and shrubs, and other nursery supplies to retailers and other commercial businesses. Xue handled all inquiries about products, prices, services, and quantity discounts.

Xue received a letter from Dennis Hogan who was interested in having the nursery prepare the floral arrangements for his daughter's wedding. It was not the first time the nursery had received inquiries from private individuals who mistakenly thought the nursery was a retail florist.

Xue wrote the following letter in response to Mr. Hogan:

47572 South Broadway
Des Moines, IA 52333
Phone
(515) 555-7745
Fax
(515) 555-7773
Toll Free
(800) 555-0003

December 10, 19XX

Addams Floral Nursery Inc.

Mr. Dennis Hogan
613 North Third Street
Des Moines, IA 52337

Dear Mr. Hogan:

Unfortunately, we cannot do the flowers for your daughter's wedding.

Our name is misleading. Everyone thinks we are florists, but we are not. We only sell to big businesses.

Try looking in the Yellow Pages. You might find a florist there.

Sincerely,

Xue Lee
Assistant Manager

How does Xue's letter fail to follow the guidelines of this type of response? How might she improve her message?

Write response letters to the following inquiries:

a. You are president of Jefferson Community College, and you have received a request from the students in Psychology 101 to conduct a campus survey on how students perceive television violence and how they think it affects children. The students have given you adequate information about how and when the survey will be conducted and which professor will supervise the program. You are happy to grant the class permission to conduct the survey on campus.

b. You work in the public relations department of Hanover's, a large retailing firm that sells merchandise by catalog and in stores nationwide. Throughout the years Hanover's has bought numerous small companies and stores. In corporate lingo these are referred to as "acquisitions." In Hanover's annual report to stockholders, the figures concerning acquisitions or subsidiaries are not broken down. The financial statements show only total income, expenses, and profits for the entire corporation. Of course, financial records are kept for each of the major divisions; however, these figures are not available to the general public.

Richard McIvey (not a stockholder) writes asking for information concerning Yamaguchi Appliances, a firm that McIvey held stock in before it was acquired by Hanover's. McIvey wants to compare the present figures for Yamaguchi with those before Yamaguchi was purchased. This information is not available to the general public, although major stockholders are provided with this information on an individual basis and with the approval of the board of directors. McIvey's request cannot be granted.

IN BRIEF

1 Businesses frequently use form letters to respond to simple inquiries, orders, and comments. In doing so, they save time and money.

2 For situations that are unique or that require a personal touch, businesses often send short, personalized responses.

3 Complex inquiries, orders, and comments demand immediate, personalized responses.

4 When a customer needs details, the best help you can offer is to provide them in full.

5 When a customer's request or order must be refused, you must craft a delicate response. Ways to do this include starting on a positive note, offering an explanation and/or alternative solution, and ending with a forward look.

WORDS OF NOTE

Define each of these terms introduced in Chapter 14.

acknowledgment card
complex inquiry
courtesy letter
delicate response
detailed response
form letter
simple inquiry

CHECK YOUR RECALL

1 In preparing a form letter for a response to a routine inquiry, what guidelines can you follow?

2 What should you consider in deciding whether to respond with a form letter?

3 What distinguishes a simple inquiry from one that is complex?

4 What guidelines can you follow in writing a detailed response?

5 When you must say no, what are some things you can do in your letter to build goodwill?

SHARE YOUR PERSPECTIVE

1 Write a form letter in response to the following situation:

Maureen Shaw, 3900 Cervantes Drive, Green Valley, NV 89014, writes requesting a review copy of the new magazine *Computer Novice,* which is published by your company, Computer Publishing Inc. You anticipate many requests for this item and need to prepare a response to accompany the magazine.

2 Write personalized letters in response to the following situations:

   a. Your company is Secure-It-T Systems. You receive an inquiry letter from Jon Rollins who is interested in having a safety-protection system installed in his home. Rollins has a wife and two young children. So far, no homes in his neighborhood have been burglarized or vandalized, but he doesn't want to take any chances with his young family. Write Mr. Rollins to arrange for an on-site demonstration of your system. Supply any information Rollins may need.

   b. Mrs. Diane Venezia has written to your company, Star Movers (a nationwide chain of long-distance movers) requesting information on moving her family's household goods three months from now from Cranbury, New Jersey, to Akron, Ohio. She is interested in overall cost, method of payment, packing, insurance coverage, etc. Write to Mrs. Venezia saying that you can provide this service. Emphasize safe, reliable service.

c. You work for a hardware supply house, Tweeden Supply. Stewart Walsh, owner of Walsh Hardware, placed an order for nails totalling $360.28, asking that the amount be charged to his account. Actually, Walsh has purchased nothing from Tweeden Supply for two years. Walsh Hardware and Tweeden Supply had a falling-out two years ago when Walsh Hardware did not pay its outstanding credit purchases. Tweeden had to threaten to place Walsh Hardware's account in the hands of an attorney. Walsh eventually paid and now wants to resume credit privileges, making no mention of past difficulties. You are willing to accept orders from Walsh on a cash basis for a one-year probationary period. At the end of this period, you'll be happy to extend credit privileges.

FOCUS ON THE FINE POINTS
Read the following background information. Then follow the instructions to locate and correct grammar errors.

Background

MaryBeth Prizziller is a customer service representative for Fishermen's Fleet. MaryBeth needs to respond to a customer inquiry about a blanket the Fleet no longer carries. She writes a letter to mail along with the Fleet's current catalog. In the catalog, she flags the page describing summer blankets and the page with the order form.

Your Instructions

Each of the following documents contains up to 15 errors. Indicate and correct errors by circling the problem and noting the solution on a photocopy of the page or on a separate sheet of paper. In each case, you may assume the document is formatted correctly.

Note: If you have difficulty locating errors, turn to page 475 in the Appendix. There you will find additional information about the errors in Document 1.

DOCUMENT 1: Letter of Response to Customer

Fishermen's Fleet

Outfitters

August 29, 19XX

Mrs. Martha Brisbois
753 Duck Lake Trail
Battle Creek, MI 49017

Dear Mrs. Brisbois:

RE: LIGHT-AS-AIR SUMMER QUILT

Thank you for your recent inquiry about a quilt, which you in the past have ordered from Fishermen's Fleet. We are happy to know you have found that the Fleet carried the more higher quality blankets than other bedding catalogers and were pleased to learn of your long history as a satisfactory Fleet customer.

Unfortunately, the quilt in question, once called Light-As-Air summer weight quilt, was discontinued several years ago. We do offer a very high-quality cotton summer blanket, but we are no longer carrying any nylon blankets nor do we at present sell silken blankets.

I am enclosing our more recent catalog and have flagged page 52, which features all currently available summer blankets. You are more than welcome to try out a blanket for 30 days and returning it in salable condition, for which we will cheerfully refund your money. If you do not find any of our blankets suitable, perhaps you will do more better with another bedding distributor.

Sincerely,

MaryBeth Prizziller
Customer Service Representative

Enclosure

150 Fishermen's Wharf Boston, MA 02111-0661
Phone 617/555-5115 Fax 617/555-5121

DOCUMENT 2: Catalog Page

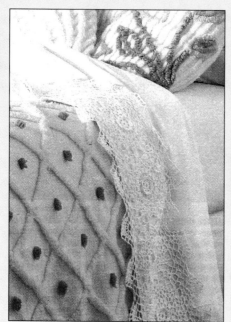

F. *Fluffy Chenille Coverlet*

This all-cotton bedspread recalls an earlier, less care-weary era with its motif of rose buds. It is by far the most softest bedcover available for the price. Inspired by 18th- century American folk art, roses and flowers are intertwined with geometric designs. Coverlet is all cotton, machine washable. For custom sizing, be specific about measurements and also specify white or off-white color.

FCC10HA Twin 80 X 110 $49.95
FCC10HB Full 96 x 110 $59.95
FCC10HC Queen-Size 102 x 120 $69.95
FCC10HD King-Sized 118 x 120 $79.95

FCC10CUS Custom sizing for antiquated beds:

81 X 110 to 87 x 110 $65.95
88 X 110 to 95 x 110 $75.95

G. *Feather-Light Cotton Afghan*

Available in solid colors or patterned after Old West designs, our cotton afghan is the perfect weight for cool summer nights. These will sell fast thus ordering early for best selection. Specifically state color (powder blue, cotton-candy pink, seafoam green, dusty rose, eggshell white, cream yellow) or style (Old West sunset or Old West design) one or the other. Sorry, we are not able to be filling customer orders for this item.

GAL10HA Twin 80 X 110 $29.95
GAL10HB Full 96 x 110 $35.95
GAL10HC Queen 102 X 120 $45.95
GAL10HD King 118 X 120 $55.95

DOCUMENT 3: Order Form

1 Your order is to be shipped to the above address unless you indicated otherwise or no address has been provided. In the former case, write your address completely on the lines below:

Name _____
Address _____
City_____ State _____ Zip_____
Daytime Phone ( )_____ Night Phone ( ) _____

2 May we ship to an alternative address?

☐ Yes, this is a gift. Please deliver my order to the address below.
☐ Yes, I'm not home during the day. It should be shipped to the address below.

Name _____
Address _____
Company (if applies) _____
Address _____
City_____ State _____ Zip_____

3 Message for gift: _____
_____
_____

4 I wish to pay by:

☐ Check or money order enclosed. (Enclose check made payable to Fishermen's Fleet.)
☐ VISA   Account number _____
☐ MasterCard   Account number _____
☐ Discover   Account number _____
☐ Amer. Express Account number _____

Expire date: __/__   Signature _____

5

Circle items to alternative address	Page	Item	Color	Qty	Price	Total Price
1	21	sheets	blue	2	$11.99	$23.98

Fishermen's Fleet

Merchandise total......$
Shipping total ....
(5% of total).............
TOTAL.....................$

WRITING TO
SELL

CHAPTER FIFTEEN

How can you increase your ability to sell through writing?

What are the ingredients of a sales letter?

What devices can you use in sales letters to gain reader attention and interest and stimulate reader desire and action?

Y ou have an idea that you are sure will increase productivity, and you want to convince your superior of its merit. You want to introduce potential customers to a new product line. You are about to launch a new service business, and you want to attract clients. In each of these situations, you want to introduce your idea, product, or service to a special audience. More importantly, you want to *persuade* them to do something—adopt your idea, buy your product, or sign up for your service.

When your primary goal is to persuade readers to take a certain course of action, essentially you are writing a sales letter. With the **sales letter,** you can apply the writing process just as you have for other types of documents. However, there are certain ingredients that you will want to include in your sales documents. There are also effective devices that will help you accomplish your purpose. You'll see these ingredients and devices in context as you learn about sales letters in this chapter.

USING THE SALES LETTER

Nearly every business letter sells something, even if it's only a point of view, an idea, or goodwill. But the true sales letter attempts to persuade people to spend money for a product or service immediately or to put them in the mood to do so later. If these letters are well written and sent to the right people, they can be your company's most economical and effective means of advertising.

When you write a sales letter, your purpose will be to convince readers of the value of your product, service, idea, or suggestion and to give them specific steps to follow. Your communication needs to answer what they are to do, by when, how often, how much, where, why it is important, and who needs to know.

Sales letters fall into the following categories:

- Those that provide information about a new product or service

- Those that support sales representatives by setting up a sales call

- Those that persuade the reader to buy a product or service

prospect

a potential buyer or customer

Sales letters are used to market and distribute goods and services to manufacturers, wholesalers, retailers, and directly to individual consumers. They are often used to find a market for new services and products or to reach out-of-the-way *prospects.* Sales letters often assist the sales personnel to make a sale.

Selling by mail has been a productive and legitimate tool for many years. This is true in spite of the fact that many of us have received poorly written sales letters which we categorize as "junk mail." Such experiences should not lead you to distrust the entire mail-order industry.

Mail-order shopping presents many advantages for the consumer. It is convenient; in fact, certain items are sold only by mail. Some items are even offered at a lower price than through retail establishments.

The disadvantage of buying by mail is that the customer cannot examine the merchandise before deciding to buy. The most vivid description and the most colorful photograph often will not adequately prepare the buyer for the real thing. Businesses that sell by mail must overcome this obstacle in their sales materials. Certainly, reliable businesses always offer the consumer the option to examine and return merchandise if it is not completely satisfactory, which is required by law.

Many businesses sell by mail because it is the most selective of advertising media. The selling public can be categorized by age group, occupation, family income, profession, geographical area, or leisure-time interests. If the list of prospective clients is carefully selected, the sales letter is an inexpensive form of advertising. A well-written sales letter can grab the reader's full attention; there are no distracting or competing ads. Also, the sales letter puts a larger concentration of material about the product or service before the reader.

The advantages of sales letters must be considered in light of the product you are selling. Sales letters are not economical for marketing all types of goods. You would not use a sales letter to sell toothpaste, groceries, film, or cameras since these are products that are used by everyone. These items are best advertised through mass media, such as radio, television, magazines, or newspapers. You would use a sales letter to sell specialized products such as decorative art pieces, coins, collectors' items, gourmet foods, specialized photographic equipment, professional periodicals, textbooks, investments, and so on.

▲**FIGURE 15.1**

Though a productive sales tool for many years, mail-order shopping is a constantly growing business. The challenge is to present a sales approach that distinguishes your product from the others and captures your potential customer's interest and imagination.

USE YOUR JUDGMENT **1**

Prepare a list of 15 *specific* products or services that could easily be sold by mail. Prepare another list of 15 items that do not lend themselves to being sold by mail.

PLANNING THE SUPER SALES LETTER

The super sales letter has a positive tone, reader orientation, realism, and dignity. Consider how each of these ingredients can strengthen your selling messages:

Positive Tone

If you want to be persuasive, learn to write with a positive tone—stressing the favorable and playing down the unfavorable.

Instead of: It takes up to a month to receive the product from the factory. We hope you can wait that long.

Try: Once you place your order, you will receive the product directly from the factory in 30 days or less.

Being positive doesn't mean bending the truth. For example, you wouldn't tell a prospect that your photocopier makes better copies than Brand X when you know it doesn't, but you might direct your prospect's attention to the fact that your machine costs $200 less than Brand X.

Reader Orientation

A reader-oriented letter has the needs of the reader in mind. By addressing and satisfying the readers' needs, you meet them on a personal level. You immediately gain reader interest. You also build trust and rapport.

Instead of: We are proud of our excellent automotive service record. We never let any car leave our service area until we're sure it is operating at peak efficiency. We wouldn't have it any other way.

Try: Because you care about your car, you will appreciate our excellent automotive service record. Your car will be operating at peak efficiency after each visit. We wouldn't have it any other way, because we know you wouldn't either.

Realism

A good sales letter promises only what it can deliver. It does not rely on exaggeration to make a sale. You are more likely to win the respect and allegiance of readers if you make reasonable, sound offers of your products or services. Instead of an exaggerated offer of service, try a more balanced approach.

Exaggerated: We never, ever will miss your call because our operators are standing by at all times.

Balanced: We do our best to keep our customer service operators available to you 24 hours a day.

Dignity

As the writer, you want to convey dignity—that you value your own dignity and your reader's. Talking down, lecturing, and making insinuations and accusations can "kill" any attempts at persuasion.

Instead of: Although it is very large and successful, Conover-Crane makes no distinction between small customers like you and giant corporations.

Try: Small, family-run businesses like yours are important to Conover-Crane.

Similarly, writing that is overly silly or filled with flattery will make you look silly too.

Instead of: It's time, oh precious customer, to stop "tocking" and "tick" off why you will want a McKenzie clock:

Try: Your time is valuable. That's why you'll appreciate how well the McKenzie clock keeps track of it:

USE YOUR JUDGMENT 2

Locate a sales letter or a full-page ad in a magazine. Study the letter or ad and find support for your answers to the following questions:

a. Is the message positive or negative?
b. Is the message reader oriented?
c. Is the message realistic?
d. Is the message dignified?

WRITING THE SUPER SALES LETTER

When you write a sales letter, you have specific purposes based on the circumstances. You may hope to sell a certain dollar amount or a certain quantity. You may just want your reader to take a step closer to purchasing by contacting a sales representative or accepting a trial offer. To achieve your purposes, you must:

1. Attract the reader's *attention*.

2. Build the reader's *interest*.

3. Create *desire* for the product or service.

4. Induce the reader to take *action*.

CASE SCENARIO

Top Forty

Regina Romano was the assistant manager of the Golden State Coastal Inn, a large hotel in Oceanside, California. Regina obtained a directory listing the names and addresses of over a thousand men and women who became company presidents before reaching the age of 40. She wanted to write a sales letter that would appeal to these decision-makers in promoting the facilities and services of the Golden State Coastal Inn.

After considering several different approaches and making several drafts, Regina produced the following sales letter:

GOLDEN STATE COASTAL INN

June 5, 19XX

Dear Company President:

"Thank you for helping us put on the best conference we have ever had. Your superb facilities, service, and know-how and helpful attitude all add up to one word: professionalism."

Pardon us for crowing just a bit, but the above message was received a few days ago from the vice president of one of the country's largest manufacturing companies. And it is typical of many we get from top executives who choose Golden State Coastal Inn as their host for meetings, conferences, seminars, and conventions.

At Golden State *your* meetings are *our* business. Making your meetings successful is our number one priority. Golden State Coastal Inn is not just another magnificent resort center that offers everything any meeting goer could ask for. Of course, we do offer all sports, including a championship golf course and tennis courts; outstanding cuisine; big-name entertainers; an almost ideal climate; elegant nearby shopping malls; and a stunning view of the Pacific Ocean. We are all those things, of course. But we are more.

By "more" we mean that we really are professionals when it comes to arranging space for your specific needs and providing every service you require to make outstanding meetings and conferences. At Golden State you will find a staff that is dedicated to personal and friendly hospitality.

Skeptical? Let me prove what I have said. Please look over the enclosed colorful folder, which shows our spectacular setting and elegant facilities. Then, to learn more about our professional side, mail the enclosed card for your free copy of *So You're Having a Meeting!*

Sincerely yours,

Regina Romano
Assistant Manager

Enclosure

52 SOUTH OCEAN DRIVE OCEANSIDE, CA 95050-4222
TELEPHONE (213) 555-7991 FAX (213) 555-7999

Does this letter contain the four ingredients of a sales letter? Does it strike you as an effective message? Do you think Regina should change anything in her message? How would you revise the letter?

Figure 15.2 illustrates how these four steps combine to make an effective sales letter. You can learn to use different techniques and devices as you follow these steps in your sales messages.

435 South Ironwood Drive
South Bend, Indiana 46675
219-555-5667   Fax 219-555-1234

Dear Subscriber:

Don Budge... Jack Kramer... Pancho Gonzales... Rod Laver... Fred Perry... Margaret Court... Bill Talbert... Billie Jean King... John Newcombe... Arthur Ashe... Lew Hoad...

Pardon Me for name dropping, but I have exciting news abouth these and other all-time tennis greats that I want to share with *Tennis Monthly* readers. You know, of course, that each of these players blazed the pro circuit in one era or another, leaving an indelible imprint on tennis history. But did you know that they were also prolific writers ont he subject?

Tennis Monthly has arranges to issue in book form the major writings of twenty of the greatest names in tennis. The first is *Don Budge on Tennis*, followed by similar books by those names above plus many of today's headliners whose names are instantly recognized by every tennis enthusiast.

I think you will find every volume in this series immensely exciting. Each will be profusely illustrated by America's leading tennis artist, Eklund Nillsen, and will be hansomely bound in a rich-looking leatherlike cover. The price of each book will be only $9.95, including postage.

Use the enclosed card to order your copy of *Don Budge on Tennis*. I will accept your personal check now, or I can bill you later. As each volume is released, I'll send you advance notice. I do not think you will want to miss a single one!

SPECIAL BONUS! If your order reaches me before May 15, I will include— absolutely free—a beautifully illustrated 24-page booklet, *Back to Fundamentals*. It could make a big difference in your game!

Sincerely,

Chris Hemby

Chris Hemby

◀ **FIGURE 15.2**

The four steps for writing an effective sales letter.

Attract attention. Those who receive Tennis Monthly will be familiar with these names, so their attention is captured at once.

Build interest. Once attention has been gained, the writer then explains the reason for "name dropping," gradually building sufficient interest on the reader's part to want to learn more.

Create desire. By the end of the third paragraph, it is expected that the reader has become interested enough to want to own them.

Induce. The assumption now is that a sufficient desire has been created to lead the reader to wonder. How do I get this series? This question is answered in paragraph five, and as an incentive to take action, a bonus is offered in the last paragraph.

Reader Attention

Most people are interested in their mail—even when it is apparent that a message is intended to persuade or sell. But there is always a risk that the reader will open your letter, read the first few lines, and then toss it before you've had a chance to make your pitch. You need to capitalize on your reader's slight interest in the opening paragraph. Make it stimulating so that the reader wants to finish the letter.

Openings

The following devices can be used to attract the reader's attention in the first paragraph:

A semipersonalized greeting:

> Dear Antique Collector:
> Dear Homeowner:

A pertinent question:

> Do you remember when SYNEC was selling for just $120 a share back in 1986?

A courteous command:

> Don't waste your time and energy housecleaning when you can hire Mary's Maids to keep your house in tip-top condition.

A provocative statement:

> Children must be seen and not hurt!

A special offer:

> WITHOUT ANY COST TO YOU, we'll mail you a handsome pocket diary.

A quotation:

> "You are judged by the company you keep." Sixty-five percent of our customers have kept company with us for ten years or more.

An anecdote:

> Choose an *anecdote* that is both entertaining and related to your sales message.

anecdote

a short narrative or account of an interesting, amusing, or biographical incident; a brief biographical story

Writing Style

You can modify your writing style to capture the interest of your reader. Apply different techniques as the situation allows. Limit yourself to one style within a document to ensure consistency.

Two popular styles for sales letters are:

Sentence fragments to give a casual, emphatic effect:

> Too much work. Not enough time.
> Great deals. Now.

An enthusiastic style supported by strong adjectives:

> You'll find *tremendous* savings at our four *convenient* locations.

Format Elements

These "eye-catchers" will liven up your document and attract reader interest:

- Color used for the letterhead, for certain words and phrases in the body of the letter, or for the signature

Western Distribution, Inc. ● 740 North Main St ● Santa Ana ● CA ● 92701 ● (310) 555 1600 ● Fax (310) 555 1699

- Boldface type, underlining, all-capitals, dashes, series of periods, exclamation points, or white space used to emphasize important information

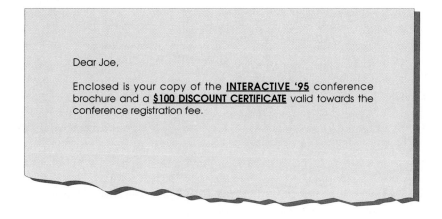

Dear Joe,

Enclosed is your copy of the **INTERACTIVE '95** conference brochure and a **$100 DISCOUNT CERTIFICATE** valid towards the conference registration fee.

- Bulleted lists that make it easy for the reader to locate key information

Featured presentations by leading authorities on:

- The multimedia and classroom convergence
- Strategies for experienced multimedia developers
- Interactive learning technologies

- "Handwriting" or a script or italic font to personalize the message

Dear Chris,

I think you will find this credit card offer hard to resist.

- Headings worded and formatted to look like newspaper headlines

TWO-COLOR PRINTING CAN BE YOUR BUDGET SALVATION IN THE '90s

Many print buyers are facing the '90s with smaller budgets and bigger demands. But fewer dollars don't necessarily mean fewer options. It simply means reevaluating your design and layout alternatives, and your printed pieces can still have the impact and appeal they've always had. The clutter of varishes, decorative match colors and fancy embossings are being replaced by a renewed and more creative emphasis on these basic design principles:

Reader Interest

It takes a skillful writer to capitalize on the interest your opening sentences arouse. Keep the message going by using language and style that is easy to read and understand. Lead the reader to think, "This sounds interesting. I want to know more about this product. I need this product." Your letter will hold the reader's interest if you can give evidence that your product will help the reader to enjoy life, to live more happily, or to do a better job:

> The world looks a little brighter when you start your day with a savory cup of Cravendale Select Blend Coffee.

> Your customers will love the smooth, resilient finish of our low-lustre Satinelle paints.

Reader Desire

You can use either of two basic appeals to make people desire things—appeal to emotions (through **descriptive technique**) or appeal to reason (through **argumentative methods**):

Appeal to emotions:

> You will sleep better, feel better, and look better after you spend a night on a Support Rest mattress.

Appeal to reason:

> Because of its superior construction, the Support Rest mattress cradles your body so that you sleep comfortably and safely.

Certain consumer appeals have universal acceptance: comfort, security, popularity, personal pride, desire for possession, economy, durability, ease of use, safety, healthfulness.

Consider your audience as you direct your appeal. For instance, you would probably use a rational appeal emphasizing the cost, construction, and efficiency of equipment in a letter selling air conditioners to a dealer. However, you would probably want to emphasize the joy of living in air-conditioned comfort when writing to the general public.

Avoid appeals that stir up negative reaction as this one does:

> A prowler may be entering your back door right now!

This scare tactic may make you think seriously about installing more secure locks, but it is not effective when it stands alone in an attempt to sell. Instead, use appeals that create friendly rapport between reader and writer:

> We're all shocked and saddened—and a little threatened—by the rising burglary rate. But there is something you can do to give yourself some peace of mind.

Reader Action

If you want your reader to make an immediate response to your sales letter, then think about all the objections your reader may have to your product. Anticipate reader reasons for delaying a decision to buy. Respond to these objections before your reader has a chance to think about them. You can do this in a number of ways:

- Give evidence to back up your statements.

- Capitalize on the satisfaction the reader will get from your product.

- Provide proof that your offer is sincere.

- Include a sample.

- Offer trial use of the product with a money-back guarantee.

- Refer your reader to an enclosure that is especially interesting.

FIGURE 15.3 ▶

Respond to possible objections before your reader has a chance to think about them.

The sale would guarantee Boswell a place in the folklore of The Crusher Garlic Press Company forever.

To encourage action, emphasize the positive points of your service, product, or company rather than make disparaging remarks about the competition. Wait for the best moment to talk about price and make sure that the reader understands that the product is worth the cost.

Lastly, do these three things in your sales letters to increase reader response:

1. Make a specific request for action.

    Please call our office today to receive your copy of *The Complete Gourmet Cookbook*.

2. Make it easy for the reader to respond.

    Just complete the attached order form and return it to us in the stamped, self-addressed envelope.

    We'd be pleased to have you attend any of our in-store demonstrations, conveniently scheduled every half-hour Monday through Friday.

3. Motivate your reader to respond promptly by giving some reason or incentive.

    Be the first one on your block to have a Simpure Water Purifying System.

    The first 500 callers will receive an original lithograph from the esteemed artist Jorgen Hansford.

    Supplies are limited, so respond today!

USE YOUR JUDGMENT 3

Locate a sales letter or a full-page ad in a magazine. Analyze the message to see how it accomplishes the four steps in selling (attract attention, build interest, create desire, and induce action).

Slim Interest

Cora Dienst worked for a public relations firm. She was asked by a client, Toras Nutrition, to produce a sales letter for a new weight-loss program called SLIM NOW. The client planned to send the letter to 1,000 people who subscribed to a nutrition and weight-loss newsletter it published. Cora drafted the following body of a letter:

Start now!

You'd like to put it off a little longer, we know, but you need to decide to just START NOW!

Because if you wait any longer to lose those extra pounds, you'll have to wait that much longer to enjoy how good you'll feel when you step on the scale . . . when you wear designer clothes. . . . when you see yourself reflected in a store window as you walk along the street.

START NOW with SLIM NOW, our proven weight-loss program. It's easy to follow and doctor recommended. Here are the ingredients:

- Over 300 simple yet elegant recipes to satisfy your appetite, meet your daily requirements, and keep you under 1,200 calories per day!

- A meal plan to help you turn off the food fantasies and stay focused on your goals!

- A daily dieter's meditation handbook to help you stay on track!

- Over 500 support groups nationwide!

We know it's hard to START NOW, so we work hard to make it easy. Just pick up the phone and dial 1-800-555-SLIM to talk to an operator about the SLIM NOW $99.95 starter package. You'll get incredible results within 60 days or your money back.

Don't delay! START NOW to get SLIM NOW!

We're waiting to hear from YOU!

What devices did Cora use to attract and build reader interest? How did she create reader desire for SLIM NOW? Did she induce the reader to take action? Identify how each sentence contributed to the overall purpose of the message.

USE YOUR JUDGMENT 4

For each of the items a-f, write a different phrase or sentence to accomplish the following:

1. Attract the reader's attention at the beginning of a sales letter.
2. Build reader interest.
3. Create reader desire.
4. Call for reader action.
   a. A phone-answering service
   b. A VCR with remote control
   c. A lawn-care service
   d. A seminar on communications skills for office workers
   e. A food-service wagon that will come to offices for morning coffee and lunch breaks
   f. A printing service that offers fast delivery

USE YOUR JUDGMENT 5

Evaluate the following draft of a sales letter:

Dear Mrs. _____:

Do you love your husband enough to help him stay alive? This Valentine's Day give your husband something that will really make his heart beat for you—our new blood pressure monitoring kit.

High blood pressure is the number one cause of heart attacks among men in this country, and our new kit will help you to prevent this affliction before it starts.

Our blood pressure monitoring kit is only $32.95 delivered, and it is approved by the American Heart Association. Don't delay, Valentine's Day is only a week away!

Sincerely yours,

IN BRIEF

1 Business sales letters either provide information about new products or services, set up sales calls, or try to convince readers to make a purchase.

2 Certain products can be sold effectively by mail; mail-order selling is very selective and is particularly effective for specialized products.

3 The super sales letter contains the following ingredients: positive tone, reader-orientation, realism, and dignity.

4 An effective sales letter attracts the reader's attention, builds the reader's interest, creates desire for the product or service, and induces the reader to take action.

5 Writers can attract the reader's attention through creative openings, varied writing style, and interesting format elements.

6 Reader interest can be maintained by writing clearly and connecting the product or experience to the reader's sense of well-being.

7 Writers can appeal to emotions or reason to stimulate reader desire.

8 Writers can encourage action by giving incentives, asking for the order, and providing all the information necessary to make a response.

WORDS OF NOTE

Define each of these terms introduced in Chapter 15.

argumentative method
descriptive technique
sales letter

CHECK YOUR RECALL

1. What are the three categories of sales letters?

2. What kinds of goods and services can be effectively promoted through sales letters? What kinds of products do not lend themselves to selling by mail?

3. What are the ingredients of a successful sales letter?

4. What four things must your letter do if you are to achieve your purpose?

5. What are some effective opening devices for a sales letter?

6. What are two popular writing styles for sales letters?

7. What are some formatting ideas to give your letter impact?

8. Suggest two different approaches for creating reader desire.

9. How can you help your letter by anticipating a reader's possible objections or reasons for delaying a purchase?

10. What else can you do to encourage your reader to act and buy your product or service?

SHARE YOUR PERSPECTIVE

1. Write the advertising copy to sell or rent your home.

2. Write a situation-wanted advertisement.

3. Secure at least three samples of form letters you or your family or friends have received. Determine the purpose of each letter and then evaluate each letter for:

    a. Length
    b. Appeal used
    c. Attention-getting quality of its opening
    d. The desire and conviction provided
    e. The effectiveness of the techniques used for inducing action
    f. The overall letter tone
    g. Special emphasis on descriptive, vivid, forceful words or phrases
    h. Evidence of the you (reader-oriented) approach
    i. Evidence of mechanical means of emphasis

④ Prepare a sales letter with a holiday theme for a suitable product.

⑤ Select a full-page magazine or newspaper advertisement. Study the ad and determine the following:

    a. What is the central selling point?

    b. Is reader benefit evident in the ad?

    c. Would you buy this product? (Do you need it? Do you want it? Can you afford it?)

    d. Is the ad an attention getter?

    Construct a sales letter developed around the advertisement you select. Choose your ad carefully—can the product easily be sold by mail?

⑥ Write a letter to a local business persuading that business to place an ad in your school newspaper (or magazine or yearbook). Persuade your reader that it will be worthwhile to do so.

⑦ As a representative of a personal shopping service, write a sales letter convincing your reader to register for such a service.

FOCUS ON THE FINE POINTS

Read the following background information. Then follow the instructions to locate and correct grammar errors.

Background

CitySpa is a full-service beauty and "wellness" salon that recently opened in a residential neighborhood. Delila Silver, its owner and manager, decided to mail a flyer and rate sheet featuring special gift packages for the holiday season. She wants to encourage people to purchase gift certificates for friends and family and to use the services of the spa for themselves as well.

Your Instructions

Each of the following documents contains up to 15 errors. Indicate and correct errors by circling the problem and noting the solution on a photocopy of the page or on a separate sheet of paper. In each case, you may assume the document is formatted correctly.

Note: If you have difficulty locating errors, turn to page 477 in the Appendix. There you will find additional information about the errors in Document 1.

DOCUMENT 1: Flyer

This holiday season, give the ultimate gift for these hectic times, a gift certificate to CitySpa for your spouse, friend, mother or daughter because, after all, who doesn't love to be pampered?

Imagine . . .

. . . relaxing in a thickly-soft velour robe while our specialist gives a heavenly facial?

. . . lying in a warm, dimly-lit room surrounded by gentle music for a massage that nurtures both body and spirit?

. . . a morning in a bath of sea salt, a nourishing lunch at a cozy table, and an afternoon's pedicure and hair conditioning?

CitySpa will give you all the pampering you can imagine from head to toe with hair conditioning and hot oil treatments, european mud facials, sea-salt baths, body wraps, leg waxing and therapeutic massage, and state-of-the-art manicures and pedicures.

Our gift certificates can be tailored for all people and budgets. While you're at it, why not put together a gift "package" for that other important person in your life—namely you! When you create your own pampering package with any combination of services, CitySpa will give you a discount of 15% on the complete Package.

DOCUMENT 2: Rates and Services Sheet

CitySpa gift certificates are currently-available in the following packages and you can additionally design a customized package for yourself. Or for a friend.

Hair Conditional Treatments

Hot oil conditioning	$25.00
Intense follicle rejuvenation	$35.00
Permanent or hair coloring	$55.00

Add a cut and styling to any of these three for $25.00

Cut and styling with CitySpa's patented-weekly conditioner	$37.00

Head-to-Toe Treatments

Facial		$50.00
Manicure		$12.00
Pedicure		$20.00
Waxing		$10.00-$75.00
Sea-salt bath	1/2 hour	$35.00
Body wrap	1 hour	$75.00
Full massage	1/2 hour	$30.00
	1 hour	$55.00
	1 1/2 hour	$75.00
Back, neck, head	3/4 hour	$60.00

Luncheon $15.00

(Luncheon is free-of-charge with any half-day package.)

Packages may be combined at reduced, overall, rates and gift certificates and packages do not include Gratuities. Because scheduling a variety of services for so many varying individuals is truly a complexity-laden process, we request that you provide 48-hour advanced notice for cancellations.

DOCUMENT 3: Gift Certificate

This gift certificate comes to you from

_____

who, wants you, to pamper yourself with

a Full Day at CitySpa?

Your day of pampering will include a facial, manicure, sea-salt bath, full-massage, shampoo, conditioning, and styling plus your choice of waxing or pedicure and a delighted, nutritious, luncheon, so please call us at 555-7210. To schedule your appointment for the more relaxing day you will ever experience.

WRITING TO REPORT

CHAPTER SIXTEEN

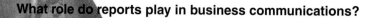

What role do reports play in business communications?

What are some different techniques for planning and organizing a well-researched report?

When is the memorandum report used?

What are the elements of a structured business report?

In many organizations, particularly large ones, information is exchanged among executives, managers, supervisors, and other employees through reports. Reports travel upward (to top-level executives), downward (as directives to subordinates), and laterally (to personnel of equal rank). Reports may also be sent to people outside of the organization such as government agencies, consultants, investors, or customers.

Reports play an important role in business because they are often used as the basis for decision making. Some reports are progress or **status reports** written on fill-in forms and submitted periodically (monthly, quarterly, annually) to those who need such information. Others are **narrative reports** that give detailed responses to requests for information, ideas, explanations, or recommendations. Some reports require extensive research and analysis related to a particular proposal. Business reports, depending on the need, will range from short, simple memos to complex, scholarly *dissertations*.

dissertation

an extended written treatment of a subject

Informal memorandum reports generally are short and list facts, figures, and opinions in the first person. A structured report is more lengthy, written in the third person, and supported by valid research techniques. Whatever the length or style of the report, your goal is to prepare a valid, useful, and informative message.

PLANNING A REPORT

There are no set rules for presenting material in reports. It is up to the writer to determine what is relevant and to arrange it in a logical sequence that is easy to understand. Listed in this section are some suggestions to use as you read, research, and think in preparation for writing a report:

1. **Take time to read over all of your notes.** Then ask yourself, is there a central theme that binds all of this information into a meaningful whole?

2. **Find the essential ideas.** Review the ideas that support your purpose and discard the nonessentials. Once you have all the facts you plan to use, arrange them in the order that will make your report effective.

3. **Plan your introduction.** You'll want to capture the reader's attention by showing the *mutual benefit* of the idea or recommendation you are presenting or by giving a brief overview of the report's contents.

4. **Think ahead to your close.** It will be effective if you summarize the key points and then emphasize one or two that require particular emphasis.

mutual benefit

shared advantage or good result; gain shared jointly

Selecting an Approach

As you prepare to write, select an approach that supports your material:

- **The chronological approach.** Start with the earliest events and proceed to the most recent. This approach is appropriate when you are reporting on the history of a situation.

- **The ordered approach.** List facts in order of importance. Use this approach when you are trying to inform readers of the relative importance of certain facts, ideas, or proposals.

- **The reasoned approach.** List facts or ideas followed by conclusions. This approach is useful when your report reflects a true investigation; you report your opinions only after careful research and fact-finding.

- **The direct approach.** Make a general statement of purpose and follow it with supporting details. As discussed previously, the direct approach works best when your readers are prepared for the message.

- **The indirect approach.** List supporting details as preparation for your general statement of purpose. Reserve the indirect approach for when you have a tough argument to make and your readers need convincing.

GATHERING AND ORGANIZING DATA

If you treat the research aspect of report preparation as an ongoing process, you can shorten what might otherwise turn into a long, complicated process. You can stay on target by evaluating your material as you go; this will enable you to identify needed changes in your initial plan and gather data accordingly.

Use note cards to organize your material. Use separate cards for each heading or idea and then arrange them in a natural, logical order. Note cards give you flexibility; you

almanac

a publication, usually annual, that contains statistical and general information; a publication containing astronomical and meteorological data for a given year and often including other general miscellaneous information

dedicated collection

a collection of books and other research materials given over to a particular subject

card catalog

a catalog in which the entries are arranged systematically on cards

▲FIGURE 16.1

You will find sources of secondary research at public, vocational, college, and professional school libraries.

can arrange and rearrange your ideas without having to rewrite. They also allow you to quickly identify weaknesses, redundancies, and omissions.

Secondary Research

Secondary research (data already assembled and recorded by someone else) will usually be the starting point for your research. Whatever problem situation you are trying to solve has probably occurred before in other organizations or with other individuals. You may find information related to these problems in business magazines, periodicals, newspapers, or other sources, perhaps even within your own company files. The problems reported may not be exactly like yours, but it will be helpful to investigate similar situations as you address your own problem.

The Library

Dictionaries, encyclopedias, yearbooks, *almanacs,* business manuals, guides to periodicals, and government publications are excellent sources of secondary research found at your local library. Your community probably has more than one library. In addition to public libraries, you'll find at least one library at an area vocational school, community college, or university near you. Law schools and medical schools have *dedicated collections;* many nonprofit organizations or societies also have material that is available to the public, sometimes for a fee or on a limited basis. Make a few phone calls to find out which library in your area will provide the best collection of materials related to your topic.

The *card catalog* is your key to the library. Use it to check on the availability of material. Many libraries have transferred their card catalogs to *microfiche* or use an *on-line catalog.* The catalog lists material alphabetically according to author, title, and subject matter. Each entry also provides descriptive information about the item that will help you to determine if the work contains information that might be helpful to you.

Computer-Accessed Information

Today a wealth of information is stored in *databases.* If you have a personal computer, you can subscribe to a database service by paying for the time you use the service. The types of information available by database include stock market news, weather, business reports, marketing studies, book reports, and catalog items for purchase.

In addition to their on-line catalog, many libraries also provide access to computerized databases. Research librarians use certain key terms to search through databases to obtain information about similar topics or research projects. You pay for this type of service according to the amount of time the database is used and according to whether the results are transmitted immediately over telephone lines, transmitted later at night rates, or mailed to the reporting location.

FIGURE 16.2

Today a wealth of information is stored in databases and available on-line through your home computer or by using a computer at a library.

on-line catalog

a catalog connected to, served by, or available through a computer or telecommunications system

microfiche

a sheet of microfilm bearing reduced photographs of rows of extremely small images of pages of printed matter

database

a collection of interrelated information that may be organized and sorted electronically

footnote

a note of reference, explanation, or comment usually placed below the text on a printed page

works-cited list

a list at the end of a report that provides full citations for all sources of borrowed information

It is essential—both legally and ethically—to cite sources of secondary research. When quoting, paraphrasing, or summarizing information from any source, you will want to use a consistent system for crediting these sources. Depending upon the number and types of sources, you may choose to use *footnotes*, a *works-cited list*, or text references to a works-cited list. One very efficient citation system is provided in the *MLA Handbook for Writers of Research Papers*. For facts of publication on this and a variety of other style guides, see page 285.

Robert is about to become an expert on the migratory patterns of the smew.

FIGURE 16.3

Most information librarians are extremely helpful in searching out sources and information.

Primary Research

Primary research is the collection of information by any method other than reading the words of others. It includes information gathered through interviews, surveys, direct observation, or from experimentation. Through primary research you can obtain new data for your report. You may also want to use primary research to *replicate* data obtained elsewhere; this is one way to strengthen your position.

replicate

to produce duplicate or identical results, as in a statistical experiment or research study

Interviews

Interviews are an effective method of gathering information and opinions from others, but they require special skill on the part of the interviewer. The interviewer should:

- Have a good knowledge of the subject as well as the person being interviewed.

- Carefully prepare questions beforehand.

- Be gracious, tactful, and understanding.

- Be prepared to get answers that were unanticipated.

- Be objective.

- Keep the interview short.

- Seek permission to record and use responses.

tabulate

to count, record, or list systematically

- Understand that the information acquired may be difficult to *tabulate* or interpret.

- Allow sufficient time for the interview.

Surveys

Surveys are useful tools when you want to collect a large amount of data from a group of individuals. A survey is highly structured and contains multiple items for response (see Figure 16.4).

Surveys can be conducted through personal interviews, over the telephone, or through questionnaires sent by mail. Your success will depend on how well you construct your **survey instrument.** Here are some things to consider before developing a survey or questionnaire:

1. **Ask yourself these questions:**

    a. Is a questionnaire the best method for getting the information?
    b. Who is the target audience?

    c.   How many people should receive it to get the response you need?

    d.   How will you go about selecting your sample?

2. **Make the questions easy to answer.** This may mean providing multiple choice answers or a scale on which respondents can rate their responses. These types of questions are also easier to tabulate than open-ended questions.

3. **Anticipate all likely answers.** Do this so you can gauge whether your questions are phrased to gather the right information.

4. **Check to make sure your questions do not "lead" respondents to a particular answer.** Biased questions produce biased data.

5. **Make room for comments.** Often the best information comes from unstructured responses.

6. **Put the questions in a logical sequence.** Group items and give them headings, when possible.

When a questionnaire is mailed, it should be accompanied by a cover letter. The **cover letter** is a type of sales letter; it identifies the purpose of the questionnaire and emphasizes reader benefit to solicit a response. Always enclose a stamped and addressed envelope to make it easy for respondents to return the completed questionnaires. As a courtesy, offer to share the results of your study with interested participants.

Direct Observation

Data can be gathered for a report by simply observing an activity or situation. The observer needs to maintain an objective *stance* during the observation. You can help by providing a checklist or series of questions to guide the observer and establish consistency from one observation to the next.

> **stance**
>
> intellectual or emotional position, outlook, or attitude

Retailers often use and undoubtedly request reports on direct observation of employees. For example, a retailer may hire a "shopper" to observe the manners and skills of its sales consultants. The shopper's observations are recorded and analyzed to determine if the retailer needs to provide its consultants with additional training.

Experiments

Depending on your topic and the circumstances, you may want to consider how the results of an experiment can support your position or idea. Testing a new process under *controlled conditions* or doing a trial run of a new marketing strategy and recording the results are two examples of experiments that can provide information for business reports.

> **controlled conditions**
>
> carefully regulated circumstances in which to conduct a study or experiment thereby eliminating outside influences that might affect or change an outcome

FIGURE 16.4 ▶

Surveys are useful tools when you want to collect a large amount of data from a group of individuals.

SEMINAR SPECIALISTS INC.

QUESTIONNAIRE FOR POTENTIAL CLIENTS

PURPOSE: To enable us to know you better as we work cooperatively with you to determine your training and/or seminar needs. Please answer all questions thoughtfully; each is designed to address one particular area of training.

QUESTIONS:

1.　Do you recognize an immediate training need within your organization?

　　☐　Yes
　　☐　No

　　If "Yes," describe it briefly on the lines below.

　　_____
　　_____
　　_____

2.　Are you aware of an immediate seminar need for your employees?

　　☐　Yes
　　☐　No

　　If "Yes," describe it briefly.

　　_____
　　_____
　　_____

3.　Would you be interested in attending a session "Assessing Training Needs in Today's Business Environment"?

　　☐　Yes
　　☐　No

4.　Would you be interested in meeting with your own individual training specialist from SSI?

　　☐　Yes
　　☐　No

　　If "yes," what is the best time of day to contact you? _____

5.　Have you ever contracted the services of a training/seminar specialist?

　　☐　Yes
　　☐　No

Construct a questionnaire that could be sent to graduates of your school, asking for information about what they studied in school and how they have done in the workplace (job placement, pay range, skills required, etc.).

Describe briefly how you would tabulate the data obtained from the questionnaire in "Use Your Judgment" exercise 1.

FOLLOWING GUIDELINES WHEN WRITING REPORTS

Report types, setup, content, and wording vary from one company to another, even by departments within the same organization. However, the following four basic guidelines pertain to all narrative business reports:

1. **Know who your readers are.** Your readers determine to a large extent the manner in which you write your report. You must take into account the readers' preferences as to language and style, biases regarding the subject (if any), knowledge of the subject, and familiarity with the terms the report contains.

2. **Make your purpose clear.** Have clearly in mind the purpose of the report and identify it for the readers. State it clearly at the beginning of your report. To make sure this important element is not overlooked, the structured report usually contains a paragraph titled "Purpose" or a statement of purpose within the introduction.

3. **Make sure that your report is believable.** It will be believable if you provide evidence in the form of supporting facts and figures from reliable sources. It will not be believable if you base your position solely on opinion or hearsay.

▲FIGURE 16.5

Computers allow you to use display that enhances both readability and eye appeal.

4. **Use display elements.** Display gives the report a readable appearance, particularly in longer reports. By **display** we mean headings, enumerations, indentions, tables, and special illustrations. These displays may include computer graphics, which are charts, graphs, and pictures that a computer produces automatically from verbal or numerical information.

WRITING THE MEMORANDUM REPORT

The **memorandum report** is used frequently in the business world. It is generally longer and usually pertains to more weighty subjects than those treated in everyday memos. For example, a memorandum report may contain the results of the following types of business inquiries:

- A study of how to obtain a larger share of a certain market

- Projections for growth in sales and profits in five and ten years

- An analysis of whether it is more cost-effective to lease automobiles for sales representatives or purchase them outright

Memorandums are the chosen format for periodic reports and reports on informal studies. Writers can make it easy on themselves and their readers by following certain guidelines when preparing these documents.

The Periodic Report

Periodic reports are reports that are written according to a specified schedule—daily, weekly, monthly, quarterly, and so on. More often than not, such reports consist mainly of figures—monthly financial statements, weekly reports on overtime worked by employees in various departments, daily reports of articles produced in a factory, annual reports of employee turnover, and so on.

In writing periodic reports, follow these guidelines:

- When possible, set up the memorandum as a fill-in form that can be duplicated and used over and over again. Many companies use or create *computer templates* for this purpose.

- If narrative comments may be required in the periodic reports, leave space somewhere on the memorandum form for writing these comments.

computer template

a standard form or a standard part of a document stored on disk to be used repeatedly, perhaps with slight modification each time; also called a boilerplate

A periodic memorandum report is shown on the following page. Its shell can be used over and over again to report sales data; only the date and quarter, sales figures, and comments need to be entered.

The Informal Study

Often you will write reports that are based on **informal studies,** investigations, and research. These reports may be self-initiated or prepared at the request of someone higher up in the organization. For many such reports, you may use a memorandum, depending on the preferences of those who are to read them.

MEMORANDUM

TO: Richard Lundell

FROM: Bernice Eversham

DATE: July 15, 19XX

SUBJECT: QUARTERLY SALES REPORT

Quarter _2nd_   Year _19xx_

Item	This Year	Last Year	Increase	Decrease	Comments
TR-520	212	198	7%	--	
TX-948	320	275	16%	--	
TX-969	95	159	--	67%	discontinued mid-quarter
WO-245	430	229	88%		

Additional Comments: The TR-520 2nd TX-948 continue to be consistent performers; the WO-245 is our new star due to zero competition.

In writing a memorandum report based on an informal study, follow these guidelines:

- State the purpose of the report. The statement may be merely a reference to a request memorandum, a telephone call, or a personal visit.

- Use suitable side headings to guide the reader. Among the most important are "Method" (describing the method you used to obtain the data for your report), "Findings," and "Recommendations" (including "Procedure").

- Unless otherwise instructed, use informal language, including personal pronouns.

The following memorandum report illustrates how to present the findings of an informal study in an organized, coherent, and concise fashion.

M E M O R A N D U M

TO: Drew Harkness

FROM: Hilary Novotne

DATE: July 7, 19XX

SUBJECT: REVIEW OF CUSTOMER CORRESPONDENCE

I have completed the review of customer correspondence (your memorandum of May 16) for the period May 21 through June 21. As you suggested, I read copies of all outgoing letters written by the four correspondents in the Customer Services Unit. (These were sent to me daily at your request.) During this period, 1,079 letters were written and mailed to customers.

METHOD

As I read each letter, I assigned a grade to it: A (excellent), B (good), C (passable), and D (poor). The elements considered in assigning these grades were tone (friend-liness), helpfulness, accuracy of information, organization, and grammatical cor-rectness.

Findings

The findings follow:

Number of Letters	Grade Assigned
146	A
212	B
527	C
194	D
1,079	

Although my evaluations were necessarily subjective, the grade distributions indi-cated above would appear to give credence to the sales representatives' criti-cism. As they mentioned to you at the conference, there are many examples of indifference, carelessness with facts, repetition and circumlocution, and negativism. It seems apparent, based on the 1,079 letters examined, that the standard of cus-tomer letters in Bigelow is much lower than it should be.

As might be expected, most of the letters in the C and D categories were written by the same people, and the same is true of the A and B categories. However, at times, individuals in the C and D categories produced good to excellent letters. By the same token, a few individuals whose letters fell mostly in the A and B categories occasionally wrote some letters that were barely passable.

RECOMMENDATIONS

Based on this quick study, I recommend that we set up a special written communications course for all sales correspondents. I believe the logical person in the company to teach the course is Dorothy Fasnacht in Human Resources Training. She is a communications specialist (last year she organized and taught a course for credit correspondents, and according to the credit manager, Clark Pinson, it was a great success).

Procedure

I recommend that whoever handles the assignment might proceed as follows:

1. Prepare photocopies of perhaps 100 letters representing all categories and distribute them to the participants. All names would be concealed so that it would not be readily apparent who wrote the letters.

2. These letters would, in effect, serve as the textbook for the course. Each letter would be examined critically by the class, and everyone would be asked to contribute to a revision of those that contain flaws. In this way, we can get across all the basic elements of good letter writing in the most practical setting possible.

3. During the course the participants would continue to supply the instructor with copies of their outgoing letters to enable the instructor to measure the results being achieved in the course. Perhaps private sessions can be scheduled for those who continue to have difficulty.

I will be happy to assist in setting up the course and helping the instructor in any way that I can if you think these ideas are feasible.

C A S E   S C E N A R I O

Suggestions, Anyone?

Juanita Ortega was on the Operations Committee of Golneff Corporation. The committee was discussing the feasibility of establishing an employee suggestion plan for the company. The committee chairperson, Wayne Crier, asked Juanita to study the matter and present a brief report, including specific recommendations concerning how the system might be operated.

Juanita studied the suggestion plans at five different companies, compiled her results, and then wrote the following memorandum report:

MEMORANDUM

TO: Wayne Crier

FROM: Juanita Ortega

DATE: April 24, 19XX

SUBJECT: EMPLOYEE SUGGESTION PLAN

Suggestion plans of five different companies were studied, and the best features of all these were selected as most pertinent to Golneff.

The five companies referred to maintain that they have benefitted in three ways from having a suggestion system: Encourages workers to make improvements and eliminate waste. Provides an effective means whereby the worker can communicate with management. Improves morale—gives employees a sense of contributing.

Based on my study, I would recommend that the following procedures be established. A special form should be designed (sample attached hereto) and printed in quantity and distributed to employees, along with an announcement of the general plan. Suggestion boxes should be placed on each floor of the building and employees encouraged to drop their suggestions in the boxes. A committee of six people, each representing a different department, should be named to administer the awards. (This might be called the Suggestion System Committee.)

Two types of awards would be presented—Class A and Class B. As to Class A, where savings can be computed, an award equal to 25% of the first year's savings would be paid. If the award is $100 or more, half of the amount (based on <u>estimated</u> savings) would be paid as soon as possible after the suggestion is adopted. The remainder (based on <u>actual</u> savings) would be paid within a year after the suggestion is adopted. If the award is less than $100, the entire amount would be paid as soon as possible after the suggestion is adopted.

As to Class B awards, where savings cannot be precisely computed (for example, safety suggestions) awards from $25 to $50 would be made. When exceptional circumstances warrant, the committee referred to above should be authorized to offer an award up to $100 for such suggestions.

In terms of operating rules, all suggestions, on submission, would become the property of the employer. Suggestions would be collected daily and date-stamped. This date would become the official date of the suggestion. (A separate sheet is attached on which are listed 20 additional operating rules that might be adapted for our purposes.)

I trust the information given will be helpful to you.

How well did Juanita follow the guidelines for reporting an informal study? What, if anything, would you do differently?

USE YOUR JUDGMENT 3

Rewrite the memorandum report from Juanita Ortega in "Suggestions, Anyone?" above to make it easier to read and understand.

WRITING THE STRUCTURED REPORT

Longer reports that deal with particularly important issues and require substantial research are often highly structured. They are written on plain paper (or paper designed expressly for the purpose) and are not memorandums. Following are some of the subjects that **structured reports** deal with:

- Reorganization of one or more larger departments in the company

- Plans for acquiring one or two smaller companies and fitting them within the present organization

- Establishment of new concepts and strategies that affect the entire company

- Reexamination of the company's objectives that may represent a sweeping change in personnel, managerial responsibilities, and methods of operations

- An intensive study of current products being marketed or of taking on new products

- Studies of customer preferences as to product and method of distribution

- An overhaul of the company's policy on retirement—age, retirement pay, life insurance, and medical benefits

Structured reports are usually a bit more formal in tone than memorandum reports, and their format gives them a scholarly appearance that sets them apart from routine communications. Often such reports are distributed widely, and for this reason they are frequently bound in special folders.

The parts of a formally structured report vary according to the needs of the writer, but in general, there are at least five:

1. **The title page.** This shows the title of the report, the person or group for whom the report was written, the name of the author, the date, and sometimes other information such as the position of the author and the name and location of the company.

2. **A summary.** In this part the main points covered in the body of the report are capsuled for the readers, the assumption being that this is all that some people will want to read. It is sometimes called the **executive summary** or abstract.

3. **An introduction.** This often covers the following, although not necessarily in the order given:

   - The history or background—a description of the events leading up to the preparation of the report
   - The purpose—the reason why the report was written
   - The need, or *justification*, for the report (this is often included with the purpose)
   - The method—an explanation of how the data for the report was gathered
   - The **scope**—a statement of what the report covers and, if necessary, of what it does not cover
   - The definition of terms that may present problems for certain readers

justification

the proof or evidence that something is right or reasonable; the just reason why something exists

4. **The body.** This is the main part of the report.

5. **Conclusions and recommendations.** The conclusions should be based on the information presented in the body of the report. They should flow logically from the facts and lead to your recommendations. If you make a "leap" at either point, you risk losing credibility with your readers, and the entire report may become suspect.

Figures 16.6 to 16.10 demonstrate the five parts of a formally structured report.

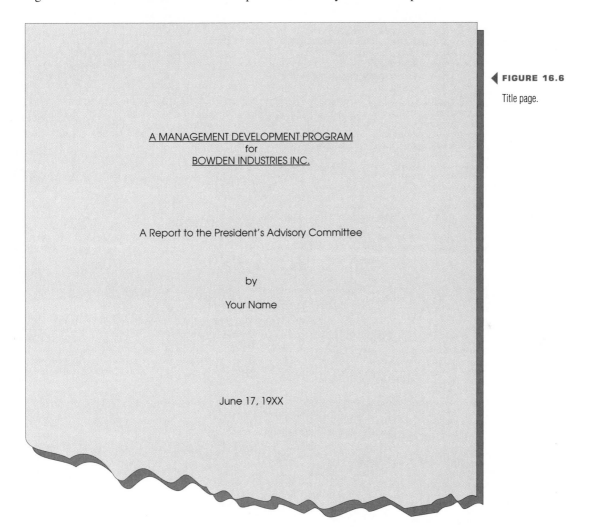

A MANAGEMENT DEVELOPMENT PROGRAM
for
BOWDEN INDUSTRIES INC.

A Report to the President's Advisory Committee

by

Your Name

June 17, 19XX

◀ FIGURE 16.6

Title page.

FIGURE 16.7 ▶

Report Summary.

EXECUTIVE SUMMARY

The President's Advisory Committee of Bowden Industries Inc. commissioned this study to investigate why the company has difficulty filling management positions and to determine an appropriate solution to the problem. A thorough examination of hiring, training and development, management, and promotion practices was conducted. The data suggests that management positions at Bowden require a high level of training, experience, and education and that there is no established route to provide this combination of preparedness for those entering management. The attached report recommends that the company create a formal, well-rounded training program under the guidance of an appointed director and a Management Education Committee for the purpose of training candidates for managerial positions.

A MANAGEMENT DEVELOPMENT PROGRAM
for
BOWDEN INDUSTRIES INC.

◀ **FIGURE 16.8**

Introduction.

INTRODUCTION

Bowden Industries Inc. is often referred to as "a family that keeps outgrowing its home." This implies that in the company's twelve years of existence there was little planning, innovation, and management leadership. This is simply not so. How else can one account for an over 500 percent increase in sales and staff increase from about 300 to nearly 2,500? Product diversification, innovative marketing and manufacturing, and sound financial management all attest to the effective leadership with which the company has been blessed.

But what of the future? The continual need to adapt management strategies to new technologies, an increasingly complex business environment, and the proliferation of aggressive competition—indeed, the simple fact of company size—all will call for especially skilled and aggressive managerial talent in the years ahead.

At the May 9 meeting of the President's Advisory Committee, the question "Where will the managerial expertise needed for future growth and expansion come from?" was asked. The purpose of this report is to provide possible answers to that vital question.

HISTORY

In the past, Bowden has depended largely on universities and executive placement agencies for sources of managerial talent—and, of course, on its own promotion-from-within policy. By and large these have been good sources and no doubt will continue to be used. However, training and developing those people the company puts into management positions has been through hit-or-miss, largely unstructured on-the-job supervision. The results are mixed. Some people were well trained and quickly moved up when bigger jobs became available. Others languished and, seeing no opportunity for growth, left the company.

SCOPE

The term "management" in this report refers to all positions from first-line supervisors (classified as Levels 13 and 14 by the Human Resources Department) right on up to the top executive positions. No attention has been given to lower-level jobs in this report, although this is obviously a subject that deserves full exploration later.

FIGURE 16.8 ▶
CONTINUED

NEED

During the past year, 44 vacancies occurred in management positions. Of that number, 22 were the result of retirement because of age or health; 13 resigned to
accept better positions in other companies; and the remaining 9 were the result of
newly created positions within the company.

It is interesting to find that 27 of the 44 openings had to be filled from the outside. In
other words, only 17 employees were considered ready to accept the greater
responsibilities of management. Actually, few of the people recruited from the outside were actually ready either (the unknown often looks better than the known);
many required a long break-in period. Besides having a negative effect on employees who were denied promotion, outside recruiting and on-the-job adjustment are
very expensive.

The time seems right, then, for a thorough examination of the company's education
posture, for it seems apparent that no matter how successful we are in attracting
bright management talent, we will not obtain the leadership required for the future
without an effective management development program.

JOB REQUIREMENTS

LEVELS 13 AND 14 (FIRST-LINE SUPERVISORS)
LEVEL 15 (ASSISTANT DEPARTMENT MANAGERS)
LEVELS 16 AND 17 (DEPARTMENT MANAGERS)
LEVEL 18 (DIVISION MANAGERS)

ON-THE-JOB TRAINING

ESTABLISHING OBJECTIVES
ORGANIZATION PLANNING
DELEGATION OF AUTHORITY
JOB COUNSELING

JOB ROTATION

PRINCIPLES OF JOB ROTATION
ADVANTAGES
PROBLEMS

IN-COMPANY COURSES

BASIC MANAGEMENT TECHNIQUES

Supervision
Psychology of Motivation
Internal Communications
External Communications
Interpersonal Relationships
Management Decision-Making
Organization Planning and Control

JOB-RELATED TRAINING

Company Structure and Objectives
Long-Range Planning
Refresher Technical Training

OUTSIDE SOURCES

UNIVERSITIES AND COLLEGES

Typical Programs Available
Cost

MANAGEMENT EDUCATION GROUPS (THE SEMINAR CONCEPT)

Types of Seminars Offered
Cost

SABBATICAL LEAVES

PURPOSES
SOURCES
ADVANTAGES AND LIMITATIONS

◀ **FIGURE 16.9**

Headings for the
body of the report.

FIGURE 16.10 ▶

Recommendations.

RECOMMENDATIONS

On the basis of this study, there would appear to be a definite need for a well-rounded education program at Bowden Industries Inc. There are numerous possible methods of operating and conducting it. The following recommendations are offered:

1.   Appoint a Director of Management Development, preferably a person with sound academic credentials (possibly a Ph.D.), teaching experience in management at the undergraduate and graduate levels, and broad business experience in supervision and management. The person appointed would report directly to the executive vice president or to the president.

2.   Appoint a Management Education Committee, consisting of the top executive of each of the six divisions in the company and the executive vice president (ex officio). This committee would advise the director of management development in planning and operating the program, utilizing as many of the sources described in this report as seem feasible.

4 **USE YOUR JUDGMENT**

Go to the library and locate a report of some kind. Describe the report and its contents. Note how data is presented. Then analyze its organization and effectiveness. Note any changes that you believe would make it better.

IN BRIEF

❶ Reports are prepared in the workplace to communicate important information to individuals within and/or outside of the organization. The material contained within a report often is used to make business decisions.

❷ Reports generally contain the results of careful research; this research requires extra time to plan and gather.

❸ The report writer can select from a number of different approaches (chronological, ordered, reasoned, direct, and indirect) to deliver the message in a way that suits the material and purpose.

❹ Secondary research is data that is already assembled by someone else; the report writer simply must locate it and relate it to the topic. Sources of secondary research include the library and computer databases.

❺ Primary research is data collected by the writer or an associate through interviews, surveys, direct observation, or experimentation.

❻ The periodic report is a memorandum written on a schedule (every three or six months, for example). It typically contains many figures and is often formatted for reuse.

❼ The informal study is often reported by memorandum. It may contain side headings to guide the reader.

❽ The structured report usually takes a formal tone and has five parts: title page, executive summary, introduction, body, and conclusions and recommendations.

WORDS OF NOTE

Define each of these terms introduced in Chapter 16.

body
chronological approach
cover letter
direct approach
display
executive summary
indirect approach
informal study
introduction
memorandum report
narrative reports
ordered approach
periodic report
primary research
reasoned approach
scope
secondary research
status reports
structured report
survey instrument
title page

CHECK YOUR RECALL

1 What are some ways that status reports and narrative reports differ?

2 What are four general guidelines to follow in preparing to write a report?

3 Identify and describe five different report-writing approaches. Explain why you would use each approach.

4 What is secondary research? What are some sources of secondary research?

5 What is primary research? What are four ways to gather primary research?

6 What are some considerations that go into choosing and planning to use a questionnaire?

⑦ What might be some practical applications for direct observation as a research approach?

⑧ What guidelines should you follow in writing your report?

⑨ What are two types of memorandum reports? How is each used?

⑩ What might be some applications for a structured report?

⑪ What are the five parts of the structured report?

SHARE YOUR PERSPECTIVE

❶ Design a report form based on the requirements of the situation that follows. Give the report a title, and allow for other appropriate identification data:

> You have decided to ask the seven regional managers to keep a record of the expenses of each of their sales representatives and send you a report once a month. The information you want includes the name of the representative; car mileage, per-mile rate, and total cost; other transportation expenses (plane, bus, taxi); hotel and motel expenses; the cost of meals; expenditures for the entertainment of customers; and miscellaneous expenses (telephone calls, postage, and tips).

❷ Write a report based on the following situation. Use all the elements of a structured report to present the data and your conclusions and recommendations:

> You are the general manager for Wiggins Stereo Outlet, a chain of six retail stores in and around Des Moines, Iowa. In the past six months there have been three burglaries and one fire. The president of the company, Amanda Wiggins, has asked you to evaluate three different alarm systems. Wiggins is concerned about cost, but primarily she wants a system with features that will make it an effective and efficient choice to protect the stores against both burglaries and fires.
>
> Here's the data you have gathered:
>
> Each store is 5,000 square feet, has two door entries and two windows. None has a burglar alarm currently installed; all have battery-operated fire alarms.

	System Features	Cost
Allsafe	Window and door wired system, heat sensors, and fire sprinklers linked to an around-the-clock security service that automatically contacts police or fire	$24,000 for all 6 stores plus monthly per store service fee of $29.00
Prevention One	Window and door wired system and heat sensors that set off several loud alarms	$16,000 for all 6 stores
Strong Arm	Window and door wired system, heat sensors, and fire sprinklers linked to an around-the-clock security service that automatically contacts police or fire	$23,000 for all 6 stores plus monthly per store service fee of $39.00

FOCUS ON THE FINE POINTS

Read the following background information. Then follow the instructions to locate and correct grammar errors.

Background

PC-2000 is a computer manufacturer going head-to-head with two other leading computer companies. The executive committee asked Bretta Dauhlgoron, one of PC-2000's market researchers, to conduct a study of mid-sized companies and their computer buying patterns. In her report, Bretta paid special attention to the executive summary, key findings, and recommendations because she knew these would be carefully scrutinized by PC-2000's executives.

Your Instructions

Each of the following documents contains up to 15 errors. Indicate and correct errors by circling the problem and noting the solution on a photocopy of the page or on a separate sheet of paper. In each case, you may assume the document is formatted correctly.

Note: If you have difficulty locating errors, turn to page 479 in the Appendix. There you will find additional information about the errors in Document 1.

DOCUMENT 1: Executive Summary

EXECUTIVE SUMMARY

In March, 19xx, PC-2000 implemented a market research study of corporate purchasers of personal computers. Having made the decision to move aggressively into the mid-size market, the purpose of the study are to provide the strategic planning committee with sensitive and projectable information about the specific computer purchasing processes of mid-sized companies.

Study Objectives

1. Profile the demographic characteristics of mid-sized companies by:

    a. Type, age, and annual sales volume

    b. Current number of personal computers

    c. Current age of personal computers

    d. Projected computer-related needs for the next ten years

2. Pinpoint present attitudes and perceptions on purchase price, operating cost, durability, and service availability

3. Project date and type of purchase by:

    a. Number of computers purchased each year

    b. Anticipated calendar quarter of next purchase

    c. Primary factor(s) in purchase decisions

Key Findings

The interviewed sample of equipment purchasers show they to have steady product loyalty divided equally between the two major computer companies *over eight of the last ten years.* This changed abruptly, however, with the advent two years ago of PC-2000's next-generation computer line. Already having had meaningful market impact, the study clearly shows that PC-2000, their hardware, software, and multimedia lines, are in a position to experience unheralded growth.

Findings also indicates that specific leading-edge companies offers greater opportunity for early sales growth, while more conservative operations provides the sustained sales growth needed to carry PC-2000 into the next century.

DOCUMENT 2: Detailed Key Findings

DETAILED KEY FINDINGS

Timing of Purchases

Taken as a group, the fiscal quarter timing of computer purchases, both hardware and software, follow no particular patterns, yet there are notable differences between leading-edge and conservative companies.

Only the leading-edge companies lean toward one specific fiscal quarter for their purchases. Half of these companies indicates that they make major computer purchases in the first quarter. This has a major impact on how us at PC-2000 plan production scheduling and staffing. Conservative companies make up nearly 80% of total purchasing power in both dollars and units. There's strong implications that PC-2000 should staff three full shifts during the third and fourth quarters in preparation for their rush of orders early in the first quarter. While they tend to purchase more erratically, another finding is that PC-2000 had to scramble to meet the very large orders they are not prepared to fill. Leading-edge companies seem to buy almost on impulse and in volumes that requires intensive production and shipping efforts in a very concentrated period of time.

The chart on page 7 shows patterns of purchase timing for both conservative and leading-edge companies by fiscal quarters.

Confusion about Product Loyalty

Product loyalty showed a sudden upset early in 1992. Focus groups were asked to cite where it was presently turning when computers, computer equipment, software, and training materials need to be purchased.

Computer Hardware and Software Purchases

In the focus groups, most purchasers who has not yet bought any PC-2000 models express confusion about how them and their companies will make decisions over the next several years.

Additional focus groups were arranged to determine marketing strategies to persuade purchasers to make the switch to the PC-2000 line. Having been loyal for years to a particular product, PC-2000 is well positioned to move into the niche this confusion has created and to build a new loyalty base for computers and computer servicing.

Based on focus group participants' comments, several strategies seem viable although none were singled out as potentially more effective than any of the others.

The chart on page 8 shows the changes in companies' product loyalties and its effect on PC-2000 and both major competitors.

Service Contracting

Of note, too, is the unexplained tendency by many purchasers to make sudden switches to different service providers. Since these companies have spending power, PC-2000 needs to find a way to set the industry service standard and communicate this to purchasers.

DOCUMENT 3: Recommendations

RECOMMENDATIONS

Short-Term Recommendations

1. Take advantage of the current climate of shifting product loyalties to move quickly into the position of market leader through immediate, intensive marketing efforts.

2. Plan now to staff three full production shifts in the third and fourth quarters of this fiscal year in order to meet the orders marketing generate for the first quarter of next fiscal year.

3. In the first quarter of next fiscal year, plan now to staff three full shipping shifts so orders will be shipped without them being delayed.

4. Owing to its erratic purchasing patterns, determine a plan for filling unexpected large orders from leading-edge companies.

Long-Term Recommendations

1. Develop a focus on service with a goal of making PC-2000's service the industry standard.

    a. Implement ongoing training of customer support staff.

    b. Implement an ongoing marketing campaign to get the word out about the PC-2000 service standard.

2. Strategize marketing, product improvement, and new product plans that maintains and builds purchaser loyalty.

3. Review salary and benefits at all levels of the company, with a goal of recruiting and keeping the most talented and dedicated work force in the industry. Of particular importance is:

    a. Research and Development. Money well spent, pay top-dollar in this area and budget for mistakes, which are shown by the study to be an essential element of creativity.

    b. Production. Implement team building and benefits packages to ensure their loyalty to the company.

    c. Sales and Marketing. Implement a bi-level bonus plan that reward both sales and ongoing customer loyalty.

UNIT V

COMMUNICATE FOR RESULTS
For each of the following situations, write the appropriate document:

1 The Program Committee of the Montana Internal Auditors Association, of which you are a member, is planning an afternoon meeting and dinner on June 12 at the Executive Motor Inn in Missoula. The committee chairperson has asked you to make reservations. You talked to the assistant manager of the inn by telephone and made tentative reservations for (a) a private meeting room for ten people; (b) single sleeping rooms for six (yourself, Judy Patterson, Leo Frailey, Peter Musette, Jane Logan, and Morris Haritan) for one night; and (c) dinner (to be selected from the menu) for ten in a private dining room. The hotel is to supply the meeting room without charge and is to bill MIAA for the dinner. Each person staying overnight is to pay for his or her own room (the rate is $50). Confirm your reservation request by letter.

2 Your company, BioEssence, a manufacturer of skin and hair care products, is considering distributing some of its products in Russia, China, and Mexico. Your supervisor has asked you and two coworkers to do some research into the potential of each of these markets. Specifically, she wants you to prepare a report she can present to the Executive Committee. The report should outline how each market differs from the U.S. and Canadian markets, including what pitfalls and opportunities exist in each country and what kinds of cultural differences might affect working with the foreign distributors and clients. Work with two other classmates as your "coworkers." Each of you is to select one country to research. Then work together to prepare a report to present to your supervisor.

3 Last week you attended the monthly dinner meeting of the Modern Management Society of which you are a long-time member. The speaker, Dr. Dianne Lewisohn, spoke on the topic "Management Communication in the Computer Age," and you thoroughly enjoyed her talk. In her talk Lewisohn mentioned that there are companies with outstanding corporate communications programs. She indicated that many of these companies would be willing to share their ideas and materials with others. She did not, however, mention any names.

You are interested in seeing the materials referred to, and so you decide to write Lewisohn at Boston University to ask for the names of some companies whose corporate communications programs she considers outstanding.

④ You work in the office of a NAPA parts dealership. You are to place an order for 16 bowling shirts from Torrington Mills with whom you have not established credit. Of the 16 shirts, 4 are to be small, 6 medium, and 6 large. Each shirt is priced at $18. You have chosen white as the base color of the shirts, and the lettering "NAPA PARTS" is to appear in bright yellow across the back. For the lettering design, you refer to the circular arrangement shown on page 16 of the supplier's catalog.

This is to be a COD order, which requires you to pay when the merchandise is received. Shipping charges are to be paid by the supplier.

⑤ You work in the public relations department of a hotel chain, Delaney Suites. Lloyd Demaret, a partner in an investment counseling firm, wrote to say he had seen a copy of the publication *Inside Delaney Suites* and asked to be put on the mailing list for six copies of the publication. This monthly bulletin contains confidential financial information, and its distribution is restricted to the officers of the company. You don't know how Demaret got his hands on a copy. Write an appropriate response to the request.

⑥ You are the membership director of The Art Collector's Guild, a group formed for the purpose of selling lithographs and etchings by outstanding modern artists. You have obtained the mailing list of the Philanthropic President's Club, a group you know includes many individuals interested in art and collecting. You want to write to the members of the club, encouraging them to become members of the guild. Here are some details (not necessarily given in the order in which they might be featured in your letter) supplied by your advertising manager:

   a. The guild is offering original art for the people who appreciate aesthetic value as well as its investment value.
   b. Enclosed with the letter will be a folder (announcement) that shows samples of the art that will be available to members.
   c. Each work is signed by the artist, numbered, authenticated, and framed.
   d. The cost of each work will be less than half its appraised value—from $600 to $1,000.
   e. The artists who are represented are only those whose works have been displayed in galleries and museums and recognized by critics for their beauty and financial potential.
   f. Those who join risk nothing—they are not required to purchase a single work of art.

g. The membership fee is $20, and subscribers will be billed for this amount only after they have received a free, framed original etching or lithograph, which they must request.

h. A postage-paid card is to be enclosed, and all the reader has to do to enroll as a member and receive a free original etching or lithograph is to complete the card and mail it.

7. You work as an administrative assistant to the head of the Chamber of Commerce in your hometown. The Chamber has established a campaign to promote tourism in your area. Write a structured report to your supervisor highlighting the attractions in and around your area that a tourist might be interested in visiting.

THE RRTWRP PROCESS

(Read, Research, Think, Write, Revise, Proofread)

STEP ONE: READ, RESEARCH, THINK

Goal: To think through what you want your document to say and do

- Identify your purpose.
- Identify your audience.
- Identify the ideas you want to communicate.
- Identify your sources of information.
- Identify your deadline.
- Identify your approach and medium.

STEP TWO: WRITE

Goal: To create a first draft that gets your meaning across

- Write with your purpose and audience in mind.
- Write to include important information.
- Write in the sequence you find fastest and easiest.

STEP THREE: REVISE

Goal: To improve the structure and meaning of your document and to eliminate errors in spelling, grammar, and usage

- Evaluate your document using the editing checklist.
- Evaluate the overall structure of your document; correct so that the order of information is clear and logical.
- Evaluate the paragraphs; correct so that each is strong and organized in a coherent manner.
- Evaluate the sentences; correct so that there is parallel structure and subject-verb agreement.
- Evaluate the words; correct spelling, define terms, eliminate jargon and clichés.
- Evaluate the content; correct so that important details are included and extraneous information is deleted.
- Evaluate the emphasis of your message; correct so that your meaning is clear.

STEP FOUR: PROOFREAD

Goal: To eliminate errors in data, spelling, and punctuation

- Check a hard copy of the document; use proofreaders' marks to note corrections.
- Check, crosscheck, and correct dates, numbers, and other data.
- Check and correct spelling.
- Check and correct punctuation.

ABBREVIATED
GRAMMAR
REFERENCE

A P P E N D I X

A s you have learned throughout this text, the purpose of communication is to share ideas. The "message" is truly the most important part of communication; however, how the message is presented, i.e., correct language, format, grammar, and usage, is also vital.

This appendix, an abbreviated reference tool, focuses on the grammar and usage problems that you, as business students and employees, are most likely to experience. It was created for use with the Focus on the Fine Points exercises, which appear at the end of each chapter to assess your knowledge of grammar, punctuation, and usage rules. If used simultaneously with these exercises, this appendix should help you to identify and correct the most common language and usage errors as they appear in a variety of business documents.

Each document contains errors from three or four of the categories listed below:

1. Words in the message are spelled incorrectly and may be confused with similar words that have different meanings.

2. The message is punctuated incorrectly and words within the message are not capitalized when necessary.

3. The message contains sentence fragments or run-on sentences.

4. The subjects and verbs within sentences do not agree in number (singular or plural).

5. The verb forms in the message are not all in the same tense.

6. Possessives are used and punctuated incorrectly.

7. Pronouns are not used accurately and when necessary.

8. The message contains incorrect usage of both dependant and independent clauses.

9. The message contains dangling modifiers.

10. Adverbs and adjectives are used incorrectly throughout the message.

Use this appendix as a reference manual whenever you are working on the Focus on the Fine Points exercises. First, this tool will help you correctly identify the category or categories of errors in the document. Second, by studying the rules and examples given, this reference tool will help you correct each grammar and usage error in the document. The solution to the first document is provided for your reference. Check the solution after you have tried to solve the problem on your own. Your instructor has solutions to documents 2 and 3.

CHAPTER 1

The three documents in this chapter's "Focus on the Fine Points" include errors in the following areas:

1. Words in the message are spelled incorrectly and may be confused with similar words that have different meanings.

   - Use a dictionary to determine the correct spelling of a word that can be spelled more than one way, such as *complementary/complimentary.*

   - Always use a dictionary or spell checker to make sure your document has no misspelled words.

2. The message is punctuated incorrectly and words within the message are not capitalized when necessary.

   - Use a comma to separate the items in a series. It is common business practice to use the comma before the conjunction in a series.

   - Use a comma to set off days and dates in a sentence.

   - Use a comma to set off nonessential modifiers, such as *however.*

   - An apostrophe indicating a possessive of two or more units of time usually follows the final *s.*

   - Generally, do not capitalize occupational titles such as *officer,* unless those titles appear in direct address.

3. The message contains sentence fragments or run-on sentences.

   - Use grammatically complete sentences in your writing. Incomplete sentences are called *sentence fragments.* The simplest general rule is that a sentence must contain both a subject and a verb.

   - A second type of faulty sentence structure is a *run-on sentence*—two or more sentences punctuated as a single sentence. Run-on sentences can be separated with a period into two sentences or with a semicolon into two separate parts.

CHAPTER 1, DOCUMENT 1 Solution
Your instructor has solutions to Documents 2 and 3.

M E M O R A N D U M

TO: Regional Managers

FROM: Tulisa Wirthe, Vice President of Marketing

DATE: September 28, 19XX

SUBJECT: UPCOMING QUARTERLY MEETING

The fall quarterly meeting will be held Tuesday thru Thursday, October 17, 18 and 19 at the home office conference center. Lyn Pucetta has booked a block of rooms at the Bluefin Breeze Hotel. Please call Lyn (Extension 233) by Monday, October 2, to indicate your preference for a smoking or nonsmoking room assignment. Lyn will do her best to accomodate everyone's preferences. There will be no smoking during meetings however ice water and complementary hard candies will be provided.

Your input has been a great help in organizing the meeting. You'll be pleased to see that the enclosed agenda allows a full morning for discussion of the new sales formulas and at the suggestion of Leo Schwalm, we've also arranged for each of you to have lunch with your home office and territory team members.

The highlight of the weeks events will be the presence of Charles Pettinger, a principle officer of Old World Coffee Ltd. Charles will join us for a social hour and dinner Tuesday. On Wednesday morning he will present our joint plans for introducing GFD in Great Britain. Charles is a highly respected broker As well as an entertaining speaker. His visit is a great opportunity for you to meet him and learn more about our exciting new partnership!

If you have questions about the meetings or wish to add an item to the agenda, please call Lyn or Leo.

We're all looking forward to what promises to be a productive meeting with an emphasis on team building.

TW/lp

Enclosure

Distribution: K. Ardour
                J. Doennes
                A. Filipovic
                T. Mendez
                L. Schwalm
                M. Zeibert

CHAPTER 2

The three documents in this chapter's "Focus on the Fine Points" include errors in the following areas:

1. The subjects and verbs of some sentences do not agree in number (singular or plural).

   - A singular subject must have a singular verb. A plural subject must have a plural verb.

   - Do not shift from the singular to the plural when referring to the same subject in the same sentence. For example, *members* (plural) becomes *they* (plural), not *he or she* (singular).

   - When a subject is preceded by *each*, the verb is always singular.

2. The verb forms in the message are not all in the same tense.

3. Possessives are used and punctuated incorrectly.

   - A singular subject must take a singular possessive (*his, her, one member's*); a plural subject must take a plural possessive (*their, our, two members'*).

   - Some possessives can be confused with contractions that are spelled differently, such as *its* (possessive) and *it's* (a contraction for *it is*). Use a dictionary to determine the correct spelling.

   - An apostrophe indicating a possessive of one unit of time usually precedes the final *s*. An apostrophe indicating a possessive of two or more units of time usually follows the final *s*.

   - The possessive of singular nouns is usually formed by adding an *apostrophe* followed by *s* ('*s*) to the noun (*family* becomes *family's*). The possessive of plural nouns is usually formed by adding an *apostrophe* (') to the noun (*families* becomes *families'*).

CHAPTER 2, DOCUMENT 1 Solution

Your instructor has solutions to Documents 2 and 3.

FAMILY FITNESS CENTER

602 West Coast Road Highway
Solon Springs, NH 03452
(603) 555-6767
Fax (603) 555-6890

February 12, 19XX

Dear Family Fitness Center Member:

To better serve member's needs, Family Fitness is conducting a survey to learn what activities and services members find most useful, how he or she would change activities and services, and what additional activities and services members wanted to have available. We have enclosed a brief questionnaire and asked that you complete and return it in the enclosed postpaid envelope at you're earliest convenience.

As a thank-you for taking time to complete the questionnaire, we will send you a coupon good for one guest visit to the Solon Springs Family Fitness Center or to one of it's satellite centers in Freeport or Rocky Crest. A member need not accompany their guest on the visit. Additionally, if your guest become a member of Family Fitness, you will be credited with two month's dues absolutely free.

Thank you for your help. Each of us at Family Fitness are eager to serve your families fitness needs and in responding to any questions.

Sincerely,

Monty Schwarz
Scheduling Coordinator

Enclosures: survey and envelope

CHAPTER 3

The three documents in this chapter's "Focus on the Fine Points" include errors in the following areas:

1. Pronouns are not used accurately and when necessary.

   - Use *nominative case* pronouns (*I, we, he, she, they, who, it, you*) when the pronoun is the subject and/or when the pronoun follows a linking verb (*is, are, am, was, were, be, been*).

   - Use *objective case* pronouns (*me, us, him, her, it, them, whom, it, you*) when the pronoun is the object of a verb or of a preposition. (Remember that the object answers the question "who" or "what" after the verb.)

   - Maintain consistency of person. For example, when addressing your reader, do not switch from second person (*you*) to third person (*he, she, they*).

   - A singular pronoun (*that, this*) must replace a singular noun or single antecedent. A plural pronoun (*those, these*) must replace a plural noun or plural antecedent.

2. The message contains incorrect usage of both dependent and independent clauses.

   - Parallel dependent clauses should have a parallel construction: *Facing problems <u>from employee borrowing</u> of company supplies to <u>insider trading</u> on the stock market, . . .*

   - A dependent clause that modifies a sentence should be set off from the main clause with a comma.

3. The message contains dangling modifiers.

   - A *dangling modifier* is a clause or phrase that seems to modify a word it does not modify. Often the word or subject the modifier refers to has been omitted. For example, *As a manager who cares about corporate integrity* does not refer to *there* or *a company*; it refers to the reader, *you*. A dangling modifier is found most often at the beginning of a sentence.

4. Adverbs and adjectives are used incorrectly throughout the message.

   - Avoid redundant adverbs and adverbial phrases. For example, in the phrase *no longer seem evident of late*, the words *of late* are not necessary.

CHAPTER 3, DOCUMENT 1 Solution
Your instructor has solutions to Documents 2 and 3.

Public Service Announcement (PSA), 45 seconds

Dates: _____

Are you a manager ~~that~~ *who* is concerned about ethics in the workplace? Are you discouraged by the many business people today for who*m* the very idea of reconciling the bottom line with the common good has become merely "quaint" or "old fashioned"? Do you want to find a way to build a real commitment to "doing the right thing" at all levels of your organization?

Just between you and ~~I~~ *me*, if your answer to any of these questions is yes, you are not alone. More and more managers are concerned about ethics in the workplac*es* *facing problems*. Companies everywhere are recognizing and addressing these concerns. ~~From the~~ *e* ~~problem of an~~ *of* employee "borrowing" company supplies to insider trading on the stock market *;* companies around the world are looking for ways to refocus their organizations on "doing the right thing."

We all know that ethical standards, once universally held, no longer seem evident *you will be glad to know* ~~of late~~. As a manager who cares about corporate integrity, ~~t~~here is a company dedicated to guiding t~~hem~~ *you* and ~~their~~ *your* organization toward the highest ethical standards and practices. Oscar Pratt, author of the international best-seller *Business: Doing It Right*, has formed Oscar Pratt Associates to do just ~~those~~ *that.* OPA offers businesses custom seminars in workplace ethics. OPA is in its fifth year of helping companies large and small develop solid, realistic plans to establish and maintain a company-wide commitment to integrity. For a no-obligation consultation with a professional OPA representative, take down this number now: 1-800-557-4448. That's 1-800-55-RIGHT. Join the thousands of managers ~~whom~~ are facing the vital issue of ethics head on and are working to make their workplace the very best it can be!

▶ CHAPTER 4

The three documents in this chapter's "Focus on the Fine Points" include errors in the following areas:

1. The subjects and verbs of some sentences do not agree in number (singular or plural).

    - A singular subject must have a singular verb. A plural subject must have a plural verb.
    - When a subject is preceded by *which*, the verb is always singular.

2. The verb forms in the message are not all in the same tense.

3. Adverbs and adjectives are used incorrectly throughout the message.

    - Do not misuse adjectives or adverbs after forms of the verb *to be*. For example, the meaning of the sentence "We will *hopefully* be able to approve the notes" is "We hope to be able to approve the notes."
    - When using adjectives or adverbs to compare two things, use the *comparative form* of the modifier. Use the *superlative form* when comparing three or more things. For example, the comparative form of *good* is *better*. The superlative form is *best*.
    - Avoid redundant adverbs and adverbial phrases. For example, *unanticipated* and *unexpected* have the same meaning.
    - Place an adverb or adjective as close as possible to the word or phrase it modifies.
    - *Farther* and *further* are generally not interchangeable. *Farther* is an adverb meaning *more distant*. When used as an adverb, *further* means *in addition* or *to a greater degree*; when used as an adjective, *further* means *additional*.
    - When deciding whether an adjective should end in *al,* consider meaning carefully. For example, a workshop that is about music is a *music workshop*. A sound that is melodic is a *musical sound*.

CHAPTER 4, DOCUMENT 1 Solution

Your instructor has solutions to Documents 2 and 3.

MEETING OF THE CEDARREST WORKSHOP PLANNING COMMITTEE

July 10, 19XX

AGENDA

1. Call to order: 1:00 p.m.

2. Approval of minutes from June 12 meeting:

   a. Note that since Joel ~~had been~~ *was* ill on the meeting day, the June minutes were a group effort.

   b. Before we meet, please read the rough notes from that meeting (which ~~is~~ *are* presently circulating). We ~~will~~ hopefully ~~,~~ *to* be able to approve the notes without extensive discussion.

3. Old business:

   a. Report on search for new workshop possibilities:
      • Yvonne will be recommending which of the two native dance people look ~~best.~~ *better.*
      • Gregor will report on his interviews with four journal workshoppers.
      • Paul will present a wide array of potentially ~~good~~ music workshops.

   b. Report on progress with kitchen coordination. The issues are:
      • Doing the daily cooking for guests.
      • Accommodating the herbal remedies group.
      • How to ~~work~~ *-ing* side by side with the canning/preserving group.

4. New business:

   a. Unanticipated, ~~unexpected~~ registration overload for outdoor meditation and primitive camping:
      • What ~~to~~ *can we* do about it this year?
      • How can we handle it in future years?

   b. Decisions on music, fine art, and dance workshops. Come prepared to:
      • Evaluate both this fiscal year and next—the farther we can look ahead (particularly for musical workshops), the better off we will be.
      • Consider simultaneous presenters and topics.
      • ~~We will~~ consider the best site for each workshop.
      • Vote on our ~~final~~ choices in all three categories.

   c. Other.

5. The meeting will adjourn at 4:00 p.m.

CHAPTER 5

The three documents in this chapter's "Focus on the Fine Points" include errors in the following areas:

1. Words in the message are spelled incorrectly and may be confused with similar words that have different meanings.

    - Use a dictionary to determine the correct spelling of a word that can be spelled more than one way, such as *there/their*.
    - Always use a dictionary or spell checker to make sure your document has no misspelled words.

2. Pronouns are not used accurately and when necessary.

    - Use *nominative case* pronouns (*I, we, he, she, they, who, it, you*) when the pronoun is the subject and/or when the pronoun follows a linking verb (*is, are, am, was, were, be, been*).
    - Use *objective case* pronouns (*me, us, him, her, it, them, whom, it, you*) when the pronoun is the object of a verb or of a preposition. (Remember that the object answer the question "who" or "what" after the verb.)

3. Possessives are used and punctuated incorrectly.

    - A singular subject must take a singular possessive (*its*); a plural subject must take a plural possessive (*their, our*).
    - Do not attribute gender to organizations or other nonliving entities. For example, *New Generation Preschool* takes the possessive pronoun *its*.
    - Some possessives can be confused with contractions that are spelled differently, such as *its* (possessive) and *it's* (a contraction for *it is*). Use a dictionary to determine the correct spelling.
    - The possessive of singular nouns is usually formed by adding an *apostrophe* followed by *s* ('*s*) to the noun (*parent* becomes *parent's*). The possessive of plural nouns is usually formed by adding an *apostrophe* ('); however, when the plural form of the noun does not end in *s*, add *apostrophe s* (*children* becomes *children's*).

CHAPTER 5, DOCUMENT 1 Solution

Your instructor has solutions to Documents 2 and 3.

Y O U N G
CHILDREN'S
EDUCATION
COALITION

Febuary 12, 19XX

Dear _____:

You are invited to attend a special presentation hosted by YCEC at this year's Preschool Education Association meeting. At the meeting I will be addressing executives from the education industry about an exciting demonstration project the Story County YCEC has initiated to improve the odds for at-risk children.

No doubt you are aware of the acclaimed New Generation Preschool in California's La Linda County. In its six years of operation, New Generation has had *their* measurable success in improving children's skills acquisition and in raising ~~there~~ parents' level of involvement. Eight seperate studies have documented the results of New Generation's program.
a

One of the most important factors in La Linda Counties' *y's* success has been the assistance of private secter businesses in building and maintaining ~~their~~ program. *its* Contributions from the education industry, in money and in kind, continue to sustain New Generation in ~~her~~ ongoing service to the children and families of La Linda. The ultimite benefit, of course, is to us all.
its

With that background, I invite you to join other education professionals and ~~I~~ for a *me* social hour and presentation:

Thursday, April 5
Geneva Hotel, New Amsterdam Room
Social Hour 4:00-5:00 P.M.
Presentation 5:00-6:00 P.M.

I hope you will come to hear about the progress many of ~~we~~ in Story County are *us* making in ~~its~~ effort to help New York's children and families.
our

Best regards,

Gerri Toensing
Director

sem

CHAPTER 6

The three documents in this chapter's "Focus on the Fine Points" include errors in the following areas:

1. Adverbs and adjectives are used incorrectly throughout the message.

- Avoid overly wordy adverbs and adverbial phrases. For example, in the phrase *next of all*, the words *of all* are not necessary.

- *Adjectives* modify nouns and pronouns. *Adverbs* modify verbs, adjectives, and other adverbs. Because they both modify, adjectives and adverbs are sometimes confused. For example, *efficient* is an adjective; *efficiently* is an adverb. In the phrase *to work as efficiently as possible*, *efficiently* modifies the verb *to work*. Your dictionary will help you with difficult adjective and adverb forms.

2. The message is punctuated incorrectly and words within the message are not capitalized when necessary.

- There is no need to hyphenate adverb-adjective combinations because the grammatical construction makes the meaning clear.

- Use a comma to separate the items in a series. It is common business practice to use the comma before the conjunction in a series. However, when one part of a compound sentence contains a comma because of a transitional phrase, use a semicolon to separate the parts.

- Use a comma to set off nonessential modifiers, such as *however*.

- Use a colon to introduce long quotations.

3. The message contains dangling modifiers.

- A *dangling modifier* is a clause or phrase that seems to modify a word it does not modify. Often the word or subject the modifier refers to has been omitted. A dangling modifier is found most often at the beginning of a sentence.

4. The message contains incorrect usage of both dependent and independent clauses.

- Place a dependent clause and the clause it modifies in a sequence that is easy to read and understand.

- A dependent clause that modifies a sentence should be set off from the main clause with a comma.

CHAPTER 6, DOCUMENT 1 Solution

Your instructor has solutions to Documents 2 and 3.

Page: 4.1

Date: 03/03/XX

Voice Mail Procedures

The use of voice mail has become widely accepted. The technology of voice mail helps us all manage our jobs efficiently. However, Alternatives Inc. does not want to sacrifice courtesy in its efforts to work as efficient as possible. It is Company Policy to return calls promptly, to provide callers the option of speaking to a "live body", and to ensure ready access to an operator, a customer service representative, or a secretary. To ensure that this will happen, the following guidelines are to be strictly observed:

1. Each Department will designate one full-time clerical employee as "telephone clerk." Employees are to program their telephones to go to the telephone clerk's extension *immediately* if the line is busy or *after the second unanswered ring.*

2. The telephone clerk will screen all calls and will route them into department members' voice mailboxes at callers' requests.

3. All employees *not* designated "telephone clerks" are to begin their voice-mail messages with this statement: Hello. My name is _____. I (am/am not) in the office today."

4. Next of all:

   a. If you are out of the office, state the date you will return. If you are not on vacation, state that you will check your messages each day. *Follow through by checking your messages, returning your calls, and referring any inquiries to the appropriate person.*

   b. If you are in the office, state the following: "I'm not able to take your call right now, but I will call you back as soon as possible. Please leave a message at the tone, or press 0 for an operator."

5. ~~Being closed~~ between 5:00 p.m. and 8:00 a.m. all telephones must be programmed to switch to the message for before-and-after-hours calls. For programmable instructions, see page 5.2.

6. Always keep in mind that as an Employee of this company, the telephone customer's first impression is up to you.

CHAPTER 7

The three documents in this chapter's "Focus on the Fine Points" include errors in the following areas:

1. The subjects and verbs of some sentences do not agree in number (singular or plural).

    *   A singular subject must have a singular verb. A plural subject must have a plural verb.

2. The message contains sentence fragments or run-on sentences.

    *   Use grammatically complete sentences in your writing. Incomplete sentences are called *sentence fragments.* The simplest general rule is that a sentence must contain both a subject and a verb.

    *   A second type of faulty sentence structure is a *run-on sentence*—two or more sentences punctuated as a single sentence. Run-on sentences can be separated with a period into two sentences or with a semicolon into two separate parts.

3. The message contains incorrect usage of both dependent and independent clauses.

    *   Place a dependent clause and the clause it modifies in a sequence that is easy to read and understand.

    *   A dependent clause that modifies a sentence should be set off from the main clause with a comma.

CHAPTER 7, DOCUMENT 1 Solution
Your instructor has solutions to Documents 2 and 3.

DataSmart Style Guide

PAGES IN A TUTORIAL

This section begins by listing and defining the different pages in a tutorial. And explaining the use of each (Parts 1, 2, and 3). Parts 4 through 9, respectively, moving beyond these fundamentals. Covers the following pages: title, name, introduction, practice, question, and glossary.

You should not neglect to read this section. If you have written PRMs for other computer programs, they will not necessarily have followed the same page style.

GRAPHICS ON A PAGE

This section defines the different types of graphics that are available: line art, full-color art, and logos and icons.

- Line art (including horizontal and vertical bar graphs, pie charts, flow charts, and loop charts) which is typically used in higher-level tutorials, and for line art, the writer should include a rough sketch using the writing software's "draw" function.

- Full-color art includes any kind of art that can be generated by a computer artist.

- Logos and icons includes those that can be generated by the computer. And if any, those that can be created by a programmer.

CHAPTER 8

The three documents in this chapter's "Focus on the Fine Points" include errors in the following areas:

1. Words in the message are spelled incorrectly and may be confused with similar words that have different meanings.

   - Use a dictionary to determine the correct spelling of a word that can be spelled more than one way, such as *shear/sheer*.

   - Always use a dictionary or spell checker to make sure your document has no misspelled words.

2. The verb forms in the message are not all in the same tense.

3. Adverbs and adjectives are used incorrectly throughout the message.

   - When using adjectives or adverbs to compare two things, use the *comparative form* of the modifier. Use the *superlative form* when comparing three or more things. For example, the comparative form is *more*. The superlative form is *most*.

   - The use of *former* and *latter* is limited to a relationship of two ideas. *Former* refers to the first idea mentioned; *latter* refers to the second, later idea. When comparing three ideas, use *first* and *second* rather than *former*; use *last* rather than *latter*.

CHAPTER 8, DOCUMENT 1 Solution

Your instructor has solutions to Documents 2 and 3.

Mix It Up Grill gets mixed review

If you've got a group of people with widely differing tastes, you may want to try the Mix It Up Grill. Billed as a restaurant "where no two meals are ever alike," the Mix It Up Grill lived up to its promise on two out of three recent visits.

The first visit was for Sunday brunch. One member of our group of four opted for the design-your-own omelet (choosing olives, pimientos, basil, and goat cheese with a side of fried potatos) for $6.95. A second chose a seafood pizza--a typical mix of seafoods (shrimp, scallops, and clams) in a nontypical presentation-- for $7.95. Both declared their meals excellent. My other dining companion and I tried our luck at the buffet ($8.50). Her selection of vegetarian lasagne turned out to be a case of false representation, unless sausage has recently been categorized as a vegetable. My peppered walleye brushed with lemon-thyme butter in a white wine sauce was dry, and my palette could discriminate no hint of lemon or thyme. On the plus side, the coffee is rich, the unusual selection of fresh juices (papaya, grapefruit, kiwi, carrot, mango) delightful, and the service more competent.

Our second visit, for a weekday lunch, proved disastrous. Having told our server that we had exactly one hour, we found ourselves waiting thirty-five minutes for our entrées, one of which almost didn't arrive at all. When three of us were finally served, the eggplant parmigiano ($8.95) and poached halibut in wine sauce ($10.95)--both billed as "light" and "very low in salt"--were so salty that one of our party could not even eat hers; my Waldorf salad ($8.95) included cashews rather than walnuts and a blend of pears and apples. Our other dining companion had to take his entire Monte Cristo sandwich in a doggie bag and found it unedible by the time he got it back to the office.

Surprisingly, visit number three proved more enjoyable of all. The skewered lamb appetizer (six kabobs for $7.95) included a pungent, spicey mint sauce. Miniature Cape Cod crab cakes (four for $6.95) are crispy on the outside, light and flavorful on the inside. The black bean soup with sour cream ($3.75 a cup) was shear heaven. Of our four entrées--peppered rib eye in a hearty burgundy sauce ($21.95), lamb a la Provençal ($22.95), nutty wild rice with artichoke-stuffed mushrooms ($15. 95), and swordfish baked with apples and mustard ($18.95)--only the latter was mildly disappointing, due in larger part to the fact that the burgundy sauce is less hearty than it was skimpy. The specialty desert of the house, an orange poppy seed cake, was exquisite.

The verdict on the Mix It Up Grill: Give it a try, but be willing to experiment and come prepared for a few disappointments along with the happy surprises!

CHAPTER 9

The three documents in this chapter's "Focus on the Fine Points" include errors in the following areas:

1. The subjects and verbs of some sentences do not agree in number (singular or plural).

   • A singular subject must have a singular verb. A plural subject must have a plural verb.

2. The verb forms in the message are not in the same tense.

3. Pronouns are not used accurately and when necessary.

   • A singular subject must take a singular possessive pronoun (*its*); a plural subject must take a plural possessive pronoun (*their, our*).

   • When referring to a single person, use pronouns that represent both genders, such as *his or her*, *she or he*, and so on.

4. The message is punctuated incorrectly and words within the message are not capitalized when necessary.

   • Omit the comma before or after essential modifiers.

   • Use a comma to separate the items in a series. It is common business practice to use the comma before the conjunction in a series.

   • Use a comma before *etc.*

CHAPTER 9, DOCUMENT 1 Solution

Your instructor has solutions to Documents 2 and 3.

PLAN FOR RECRUITING VOLLEYBALL LEAGUE PARTICIPANTS

I. Use direct mail to inform and motivate the community.
    a. Send a letter to all singles (using the list developed through
       cooperative market research with CompuTec) inviting ~~him or her~~ *them*
       to participate.
    b. Send a letter to every CompuTec manager inviting his *or her*
       participation and requesting financial support.
    c. Send a letter to Directors of adult singles groups, in local churches
       and synagogues asking for their support and requesting an
       opportunity to speak to ~~its~~ group in the near future.
       their

II. Use print media to get the word out and further motivate the
    community.
    a. Invite a local sports columnist to write an article for ~~their~~
       newspaper about the league in Sweetwater and explains why
       such a league would be a great idea for Fairfield County.
    b. ~~Running~~ classified ads in the local newspaper to support the
       article and recruit participants and coaches.
    c. Run an article and ad in CompuTec's company newsletter inviting
       interested people to call.
    d. Carry out a poster campaign using donated services and
       materials. Display the posters in churches, in synagogues, at
       CompuTec, and at other places of business such as stores,
       restaurants, etc.

III. Using television and radio to further motivate the community and
     neighboring towns.
     a. Seek free radio and television time for public service
        announcements.
     b. Consider running an ad or announcement on electronic mail. (To
        do this, explore whether public service announcements can be
        made in this way, and if so, finds a person who knows how to take
        advantage of this mode of communication.)

CHAPTER 10

The three documents in this chapter's "Focus on the Fine Points" include errors in the following areas:

1. The message contains sentence fragments or run-on sentences.

   - Use grammatically complete sentences in your writing. Incomplete sentences are called *sentence fragments*. The simplest general rule is that a sentence must contain both a subject and a verb.

   - A second type of faulty sentence structure is a *run-on sentence*—two or more sentences punctuated as a single sentence. Run-on sentences can be separated with a period into two sentences or with a semicolon into two separate parts.

2. The message contains incorrect usage of both dependent and independent clauses.

   - Parallel dependent clauses should have a parallel construction.

3. The message contains dangling modifiers.

   - A *dangling modifier* is a clause or phrase that seems to modify a word it does not modify. Often the word or subject the modifier refers to has been omitted. A dangling modifier is found most often at the beginning of a sentence.

CHAPTER 10, DOCUMENT 1 Solution
Your instructor has solutions to Documents 2 and 3.

M E M O R A N D U M

CONFIDENTIAL

TO: All Employees

FROM: LeAnn Metzger

DATE: June 12, 19XX

SUBJECT: RETIREMENT DINNER FOR PAUL ARCHER
                FRIDAY, JULY 3, 6:00 P.M.

The retirement dinner for Paul Archer will take place Friday evening, July 3, at 6:00 p.m. in the Fern Room of the Garden Court Hotel.

As you know, while Mr. Archer is aware of the dinner, he is not aware of some of the activities we are planning in his honor. ~~Having said this,~~ please take care not to accidentally give away any of the surprises!

~~Besides the~~ [or a] multimedia tribute [In addition] ~~that~~ long-time client Barbara Mulligan of Stratford Films is planning, all employees are invited to create a page for a memory book that we will present to Mr. Archer. What you do with your page is entirely up to you. Some suggestions might include writing about a past event (using the format of a paragraph, short personal note, or poem), providing a photograph with a caption, or incorporating a small souvenir along with a brief description of the occasion remembered.

As the founder of Archer, Feldman, Archer, & Moroni, ~~we all owe it to~~ Mr. Archer [deserves] ~~to give him~~ a memorable send-off, ~~As well~~ as one that is respectful and in keeping with his stature and dignity. I mention this because, in planning how you will present your memory, the end result should be something Mr. Archer will treasure. [You will want to]

Should you wish to contribute to the book, please turn in your page to me or to Sandra Blake on or before Friday, June 19, and Sandra and I will assemble the book and arrange for printing and binding.

If you are able to come to the dinner, plan to arrive no later than six o'clock; if not, you are still welcome to crate a page for the book. [If you plan to come]

Please let either Sandra or me know. We need an exact head count by June 26. If you have questions, call me at extension 333 ~~or by calling~~ Sandra at extension 338.

Remember: Mum's the word!

CHAPTER 11

The three documents in this chapter's "Focus on the Fine Points" include errors in the following areas:

1. Words in the message are spelled incorrectly and may be confused with similar words that have different meanings.

    - Use a dictionary to determine the correct spelling of a word that can be spelled more than one way, such as *cite/site*.
    - Always use a dictionary or spell checker to make sure your document has no misspelled words.

2. The verb forms in the message are not in the same tense.

3. Possessives are used and punctuated incorrectly.

    - Some possessives can be confused with contractions that are spelled differently, such as *its* (possessive) and *it's* (a contraction for *it is*). Use a dictionary to determine the correct spelling.

CHAPTER 11, DOCUMENT 1 Solution

Your instructor has solutions to Documents 2 and 3.

REGISTRATION INFORMATION

Deadlines for Spring Classes

February 14:	Registration begins
February 28:	Registration ends
March 1:	Late registration begins
March 12:	Late registration ends

We will ~~except~~ *accept* registrations beyond the late registration date only for classes that are not filled. This year we are not accepting registrations for audited classes.

How to Register

To register by mail   Use the registration form on page 7. Complete the form and mail (or ~~have it faxed~~) it to the main registration office.

~~For~~ *To* registering in person   If you are interested in particularly popular courses (denoted by an asterisk * in the course descriptions), we advise you to use this method. Many of our most popular courses fill to capacity on or before the second day of registration. *Registrations ~~that we have~~ received by mail or fax will be applied at the close of business on the day received. Those received after 3:00 p.m. ~~will apply~~ be led at the opening of the next business day.*

How to Pay

To pay by check   Make your *or* check payable to "International Business School." Include your invoice number, course number, and telephone number on your check.

~~If~~ *To* paying by credit card   We can accept tuition charged on VISA, MasterCard, or Discover. Sorry we ~~are not~~ *cannot* accepting American Express.

Additional Services

Devices for hearing impaired individuals are available for all classes. Call at least three business days ahead of your first scheduled class to arrange for this assistance.

Child care is available at the East Shelby site only.

The International School of Business is an equal opportunity school. For a copy of its bylaws, call the information office at 555-0101.

CHAPTER 12

The three documents in this chapter's "Focus on the Fine Points" include errors in the following areas:

1. Words in the message are spelled incorrectly and may be confused with similar words that have different meanings.

- Use a dictionary to determine the correct spelling of a word that can be spelled more than one way, such as *add/ad*.
- Always use a dictionary or spell checker to make sure your document has no misspelled words.

2. The message is punctuated incorrectly and words within the message are not capitalized when necessary.

- Omit the comma before or after essential modifiers.
- Use commas to set off a person's professional position or educational degree.

3. Possessives are used and punctuated incorrectly.

- A singular subject must take a singular possessive (*its*); a plural subject must take a plural possessive (*their*).
- Some possessives can be confused with contractions that are spelled differently, such as *its* (possessive) and *it's* (a contraction for *it is*). Use a dictionary to determine the correct spelling.
- An apostrophe indicating a possessive of two or more units of time usually follows the final *s*: *two weeks' time*.
- The possessive of singular nouns is usually formed by adding an *apostrophe* followed by *s* (*'s*) to the noun (*position* becomes *position's*). The possessive of plural nouns is usually formed by adding an *apostrophe* (*'*) to the noun.

CHAPTER 12, DOCUMENT 1 Solution
Your instructor has solutions to Documents 2 and 3.

7575 West Oklahoma Street
Oklahoma City, OK 36503
May 15, 19xx

Ms. Paula Lewis
Riverton Medical Center
2000 Riverside Drive
Stillwater, OK 36421

Dear Ms. Lewis

This is in regards to you're add in Sundays *Courier Express* for a public health coordinator. I would welcome the chance to learn more about the position and about Riverton Medical Center.

In two weeks time I will graduate from Oklahoma State University with a B.A. in Public Health Administration. In my four years as a student at OSU, I have worked in a hospital setting as both an employee and a volunteer. I also spent a semester in East Africa, studying at the Royal Hospital school in Nairobi and traveling on three seperate occasions to their hospitals in rural Kenya and Tanzania. A part from the semester abroad, I was the student assistant to the Dean of the School of Public Health Administration professor Carol Kreutzer, during both my junior and senior years.

I have enclosed a résumé and reference list. I hope you will find that my education and experience match the public health coordinator positions qualifications.

I will call next week to see if you are interested in setting up an interveiw. Meanwhile, you can reach me at 617-555-7444.

Thank you very much.

Sincerely

Marc L. Mahli

Enclosures

CHAPTER 13

The three documents in this chapter's "Focus on the Fine Points" include errors in the following areas:

1. Pronouns are not used accurately and when necessary.

    *   Since *our* is plural and *self* is singular, *ourself* is incorrect; *ourselves* is the correct form.
    *   In choosing between *which* and *that* for beginning a modifying expression, always use *which* when the phrase or clause is nonessential and *that* when it is essential.
    *   Use *nominative case* pronouns (*I, we, he, she, they, who*) when the pronoun is the subject and/or when the pronoun follows a linking verb (*is, are, am, was, were, be, been*).
    *   Use *objective case* pronouns (*me, us, him, her, it, them, whom*) when the pronoun is the object of a verb or of a preposition. (Remember that the object answers the question "who" or "what" after the verb.)
    *   Do not use pronouns that attribute gender to organizations or other nonliving entities.

2. The message contains incorrect usage of both dependent and independent clauses.

    *   Parallel dependent clauses should have a parallel construction.
    *   A dependent clause that modifies a sentence should be set off from the main clause with a comma.

3. The message contains dangling modifiers.

    *   A *dangling modifier* is a clause or phrase that seems to modify a word it does not modify. Often the word or subject the modifier refers to has been omitted. For example, *Having been so ill* does not refer to the writer of the letter (*I*); it refers to the reader. A dangling modifier is found most often at the beginning of a sentence.

CHAPTER 13, DOCUMENT 1 Solution

Your instructor has solutions to Documents 2 and 3.

WINDSOR CITY INSTITUTE OF FINE ARTS

1700
West
15th
Avenue
Windsor City
TN
38820

(615)555-9090
Fax
(615)555-9099

April 29, 19XX

Mr. Lionel Lee
Lee Teleproductions
222 Cannon View Road
Windsor City, TN 38823

Dear Lionel:

~~Having been so ill,~~ I was delighted to see you back in the peak of health at the April board meeting. Both contracting such a rare illness ~~as well as~~ *and making such* a quick recovery were quite remarkable—I can see why you feel like a "miracle in shoes"!

Lionel, I know you share my passion for finally seeing the textiles become part of WCIFA's permanent collection. This move will merit a healthy and much-needed boost in funding from the NEA. Further, sitting as you do on both this board and the Horton Foundation board, ~~I know~~ you understand the implications for future foundation grants. As we both also know, getting the word out to members, the community, and—most important of all—to participating institutes here and in England will be absolutely critical. We find ~~ourself~~ *ourselves* in the contradictory position of being poised to move into the "big time," but having to do this on a budget, ~~which~~ *that* is decidedly small.

On behalf of the institute, the board, and I, may I ask ~~you~~ *me* to consider giving an additional gift to WCIFA this year. What all of ~~we~~ have in mind is a gift in kind of a 15-minute promotional video on the institute and ~~her~~ *its* incredible collection of textiles. ~~Understanding how difficult it is for me to~~ ~~ask you this,~~ *ask you this and will* I hope you will respond with a resounding "Yes."

If in need of additional persuading, ~~I hope~~ *I hope it* you will find the enclosed demographics summary of interest ~~and~~ will prompt an affirmative decision. (I've also enclosed the revised mission statement from the March board meeting.)

Thank you, Lionel. I'll look forward to hearing from you.

Best regards,

Sally Larson-Wilkes
Vice President of Fund-Raising

ttt

Enclosures

CHAPTER 14

The three documents in this chapter's "Focus on the Fine Points" include errors in the following areas:

1. The verb forms in the message are not in the same tense.

2. Adverbs and adjectives are used incorrectly throughout the message.

    *   Avoid redundant adverbs and adverbial phrases. For example, *more higher* and *more better* are incorrect; instead, simply use *higher* and *better*.
    *   Place an adverb or adjective as close as possible to the word or phrase it modifies.
    *   When using adjectives or adverbs to compare two things, use the *comparative form* of the modifier. Use the *superlative form* when comparing three or more things. For example, the comparative form is *more*. The superlative form is *most*.
    *   Different adjectives formed from the same root word have different meanings. For example, a *satisfactory customer* is a customer who satisfies the vendor; a *satisfied customer* is a customer who finds the vendor satisfactory. Your dictionary will help you select the correct adjective and adverb forms.

3. The message contains incorrect usage of both dependent and independent clauses.

    *   Place a dependent clause and the clause it modifies in a sequence that is easy to read and understand.
    *   A dependent clause that modifies a sentence should be set off from the main clause with a comma.
    *   Parallel dependent clauses should have a parallel construction.

CHAPTER 14, DOCUMENT 1 Solution

Your instructor has solutions to Documents 2 and 3.

Fishermen's Fleet
Outfitters

August 29, 19XX

Mrs. Martha Brisbois
753 Duck Lake Trail
Battle Creek, MI 49017

Dear Mrs. Brisbois:

RE: LIGHT-AS-AIR SUMMER QUILT

Thank you for your recent inquiry about a quilt, which you in the past have ordered from Fishermen's Fleet. We are happy to know you have found that the Fleet carried the more higher quality blankets than other bedding catalogers and were *~~are~~* pleased to learn of your long history as a satisfactory Fleet customer.

Unfortunately, the quilt in question, once called Light-As-Air summer weight quilt, was discontinued several years ago. We do offer a very high-quality cotton summer blanket, but we are no longer carrying any nylon blankets nor do we at present sell or silken blankets.

I am enclosing our more recent catalog and have flagged page 52, which features all currently available summer blankets. You are more than welcome to try out a blanket for 30 days and returning it in salable condition, for which we will cheerfully refund your money. If you do not find any of our blankets suitable, perhaps you will do more better with another bedding distributor.

Sincerely,

MaryBeth Prizziller
Customer Service Representative

Enclosure

CHAPTER 15

The three documents in this chapter's "Focus on the Fine Points" include errors in the following areas:

1. The message is punctuated incorrectly and words within the message are not capitalized when necessary.

   - Use a comma to separate the items in a series. It is common business practice to use the comma before the conjunction in a series.
   - There is no need to hyphenate adverb-adjective combinations because the grammatical construction makes the meaning clear: *a dimly lit room.*
   - Capitalize proper nouns and geographical place names and regions.

2. Adverbs and adjectives are used incorrectly throughout the message.

   - *Adjectives* modify nouns and pronouns. *Adverbs* modify verbs, adjectives, and other adverbs. Because they both modify, adjectives and adverbs are sometimes confused. For example, *a thickly-soft velour robe* is incorrect. *A thick, soft velour robe* is correct: *thick* modifies the noun *robe,* not the adjective *soft.*
   - Avoid redundant adverbs and adverbial phrases. For example, in the phrase *namely you*, the word *namely* is not necessary.

3. The message contains sentence fragments or run-on sentences.

   - One type of faulty sentence structure is a *run-on sentence*—two or more sentences punctuated as a single sentence. Run-on sentences can be separated with a period into two sentences or with a semicolon into two separate parts.

4. The message contains incorrect usage of both dependent and independent clauses.

   - Place a dependent clause and the clause it modifies in a sequence that is easy to read and understand.
   - Parallel dependent clauses should have a parallel construction.

CHAPTER 15, DOCUMENT 1 Solution

Your instructor has solutions to Documents 2 and 3.

This holiday season, give the ultimate gift for these hectic times, a gift certificate to CitySpa for your spouse, friend, mother, or daughter, because, after all, who doesn't love to be pampered?

Imagine . . .

. . . relaxing in a thickly-soft velour robe while our specialist gives a heavenly facial?

. . . lying in a warm, dimly-lit room surrounded by gentle music for a massage that nurtures both body and spirit?

enjoying
. . . a morning in a bath of sea salt, a nourishing lunch at a cozy table, and an afternoon's pedicure and hair conditioning? *in the afternoon*

offer CitySpa will give you all the pampering you can imagine from head to toe with we hair conditioning and hot oil treatments, european mud facials, sea-salt baths, body wraps, leg waxing and therapeutic massage, and state-of-the-art manicures and pedicures.

Our gift certificates can be tailored for all people and budgets. While you're at it, why not put together a gift "package" for that other important person in your life—namely you! When you create your own pampering package with any combination of services, CitySpa will give you a discount of 15% on the complete Package.

CHAPTER 16

The three documents in this chapter's "Focus on the Fine Points" include errors in the following areas:

1. The subjects and verbs of sentences do not agree in number (singular or plural).

   • A singular subject must have a singular verb. A plural subject must have a plural verb.

2. Pronouns are not used accurately and when necessary.

   • Use *nominative case* pronouns (*I, we, he, she, they, who*) when the pronoun is the subject and/or when the pronoun follows a linking verb (*is, are, am, was, were, be, been*).

   • Use *objective case* pronouns (*me, us, him, her, it, them, whom*) when the pronoun is the object of a verb or of a preposition. (Remember that the object answers the question "who" or "what" after the verb.)

   • Do not shift from the singular to the plural when referring to the same subject in the same sentence. For example, *PC-2000* (*the company*—singular) takes the possessive pronoun *its* (singular), not *their* (plural).

3. The message contains dangling modifiers.

   • A *dangling modifier* is a clause or phrase that seems to modify a word it does not modify. Often the word or subject the modifier refers to has been omitted.

4. The message contains incorrect usage of both dependent and independent clauses.

   • Place a dependent clause and the clause it modifies in a sequence that is easy to read and understand.

CHAPTER 16, DOCUMENT 1 Solution

Your instructor has solutions to Documents 2 and 3.

EXECUTIVE SUMMARY

In March, 19xx, PC-2000 implemented a market research study of corporate pur-chasers of personal computers. Having made the decision to move aggressively into the mid-size market, the purpose of the study are to provide the strategic plan-ning committee with sensitive and projectable information about the specific com-puter purchasing processes of mid-sized companies.

[handwritten annotations: was; company's; in conducting]

Study Objectives

1. Profile the demographic characteristics of mid-sized companies by:

    a. Type, age, and annual sales volume

    b. Current number of personal computers

    c. Current age of personal computers

    d. Projected computer-related needs for the next ten years

2. Pinpoint present attitudes and perceptions on purchase price, operating cost, durability, and service availability

3. Project date and type of purchase by:

    a. Number of computers purchased each year

    b. Anticipated calendar quarter of next purchase

    c. Primary factor(s) in purchase decisions

Key Findings

The interviewed sample of equipment purchasers show they to have steady prod-uct loyalty divided equally between the two major computer companies *over eight of the last ten years.* This changed abruptly, however, with the advent two years ago of PC-2000's next-generation computer line. Already having had meaningful market impact, the study clearly shows that PC-2000 their hardware, software, and multimedia lines are in a position to experience unheralded growth in its.

[handwritten annotations: s; them; can]

Findings also indicates that specific leading-edge companies offers greater oppor-tunity for early sales growth, while more conservative operations provides the sus-tained sales growth needed to carry PC-2000 into the next century.

[handwritten annotation: can]

GLOSSARY

A

acknowledge
to take notice of; or make known the receipt of

acknowledgment card
special type of form letter that is printed on a postcard

acquainted
made familiar or known

acquisition
something acquired or gained

active listening
to participate fully in any listening situation by (1) considering the speaker's purpose, (2) evaluating what the speaker is saying, (3) showing attention by taking notes, asking questions, and making comments when appropriate

active reading
to participate fully in reading situations by (1) considering the writer's purpose, (2) anticipating what the material will say, and (3) relating what you read to your past experience

active voice
verb quality within a sentence in which the subject is the doer of the action

advantage
benefit resulting from some course of action

affect
feeling or emotion as shown by one's facial expression

allegiance
devotion or loyalty to a person, group, or cause

almanac
a publication, usually annual, that contains statistical and general information; a publication containing astronomical and meteorological data for a given year and often including other general miscellaneous information

alternative
a proposition or situation offering a choice between two or more things only one of which may be chosen

ample
generous or more than adequate in size, scope, or capacity

analogy
a resemblance in some particulars between things otherwise unlike; a comparison or parallel made about two unlike things based upon a particular aspect they have in common

anecdote
> a short narrative or account of an interesting, amusing, or biographical incident; a brief biographical story

antiquated
> obsolete; outmoded or discredited by reason of age

argumentative method
> a technique that appeals to the reader's reason to create desire for something

assertive
> aggressive; disposed to or characterized by bold or confident assertion

asterisk
> a star-shaped character * used in writing as a reference mark or in formatting to highlight or set off important information

astute
> having or showing shrewdness; clever, shrewd, wily; intelligent

attest
> to affirm to be true or genuine

authority
> power to influence or command thought, opinion, or behavior

B

background information
> information essential to understanding of a situation

banquet
> an elaborate and often ceremonious meal for numerous people often in honor of a person

bar graph
> graph that uses vertical or horizontal bars to measure and/or represent data

belonging needs
> needs satisfied by involvement with and recognition from management and coworkers

beneficial
> conducive to personal or social well-being

bias
> prejudice; a personal and/or unreasoned distortion of judgment

biological needs
> needs that must be satisfied for survival

block style
> letter style characterized by a streamlined appearance; each letter part and paragraph begin at the left margin

body
> the main part (message) of a letter, memorandum, or report

bottom line
> the line at the bottom of a financial report that shows the net profit or loss; financial considerations such as cost, profit, or loss; or the crux, the essential point; the most important consideration

brainstorm
> a problem-solving technique that involves the spontaneous contribution of ideas

C

capitalize
> to write or print with an initial capital letter or in all capital letters

caption
> the heading of an article or document; title

card catalog
a catalog in which the entries are arranged systematically on cards

chronological approach
an approach to writing that starts with the earliest events and proceeds to the most recent. This approach is appropriate when reporting on the history of a situation

circumlocution
the use of an unnecessarily large number of words to express an idea; evasion in speech

classification
a systematic arrangement in groups or categories according to established criteria

clause
a group of words that contains a subject and a related verb and that is part of a sentence

cliche
a trite phrase or expression

closing sentence
the sentence that serves as the closing of a message

coherent
logically or aesthetically ordered or integrated

commensurate
proportionate; corresponding in size, extent, amount, or degree

communication
the sharing of ideas or information

communication process
a process by which information is exchanged between individuals through a common system of symbols, signs, or behavior

compatible
capable of existing or operating together in harmony

compensation
something that constitutes an equivalent

compile
to compose out of materials from other documents

complex
complicated, intricate; hard to separate or analyze

complex inquiry
a request for information that requires a detailed response or extra tact

compliance
the act or process of conforming to a desire, demand, or proposal

complimentary close
word or words (e.g., Sincerely) that mark the end of the body of a letter

computer template
a standard form or a standard part of a document stored on disk to be used repeatedly, perhaps with slight modification each time; also called a *boilerplate*

concept level
singular concepts in reading from which the reader can recall prior knowledge of a word or phrase, attach new knowledge of the word or phrase, and act accordingly

concise
brief; free from all elaboration and superfluous detail

condolence
an expression of sympathy

confidential
> private or secret; containing information not to be disclosed

confirmation document
> document that is written and distributed for the sole purpose to confirm that something has been done or received

connotation
> something suggested by a word or term that is not part of its direct, specific meaning—connotation depends on the culture and past experience of the persons using or hearing a word or term

conscientious
> careful

consecutive
> following one after the other in order

consider all factors
> a method for evaluating reading where the reader systematically focuses on all factors relating to what is being read

consistent
> constant; free from variation or contradiction

context
> the words and ideas that surround a word, term, or idea and can throw light on its meaning; the environment or setting in which something occurs or is communicated

continuum
> a coherent whole characterized as a collection, sequence, or progression of parts varying by minute degrees

controlled conditions
> carefully regulated circumstances in which to conduct a study or experiment thereby eliminating outside influences that might affect or change an outcome

convention
> an assembly of persons met for a common purpose

copy
> text that will be set for printing

copy notation
> part of a letter that indicates other personnel who received a copy of the letter

cordial
> gracious; warm and genuinely affable

corporate
> of or relating to a corporation

correspond
> to communicate with a person by exchange of letters

courtesy letter
> letter that lets a customer or a correspondent know that a message was received and acted upon

cover letter
> a type of sales letter that accompanies a questionaire. It identifies the purpose of the questionnaire and emphasizes reader benefit to solicit a response

credence
> mental acceptance as true or real

credential
> something that gives credit or confidence

cuisine
> style of cooking

D

database
a collection of interrelated information that may be organized and sorted electronically

dedicated collection
a collection of books and other research materials given over to a particular subject

deficiency needs
biological needs and safety needs, both of which are essential to survival

delicate response
response to a complex inquiry that says "no" gently and tactfully

deluged
overwhelmed, swamped by an excess of something

demographics
the statistical characteristics of human populations (such as age and income) used to identify markets

demonstration
a showing of the merits of a product or service to a prospective consumer

denotation
the direct, specific meaning of a word or term as found in the dictionary

descriptive technique
a method that appeals to the reader's emotions to create desire for something

detailed response
a response to a complex inquiry that includes complete and specific information

developmental sentence
one of several sentences that expand and develop the topic sentence of a paragraph

dignified
showing or expressing honor or esteem

dignitary
one who possesses extreme rank or holds a position of dignity or honor

diplomacy
tact; skill in handling affairs without offending or arousing hostility

direct
to guide others in what they must do to accomplish something

direct approach
an approach in writing where information is presented in the clearest, most logical way possible, beginning with a statement of the main idea and moving on to support that main idea

direct order
an approach to writing where the topic sentence is followed by descriptive details

discard
to cast off or reject

disdain
a feeling of scorn or contempt

display
exhibition; a presentation of something

dissertation
an extended written treatment of a subject

diversification
to produce variety

downtime
time during which work is stopped, often due to unanticipated waiting periods, scheduling problems, or mechanical breakdowns

downward communication
interaction that takes place between someone in a position of authority and a subordinate

durability
the ability to exist for a long time without significant deterioration

E

economical
thrifty; marked by careful, efficient, and prudent use of resources

ego needs
our needs for personal worth and our need to feel valuable, to have a high opinion of ourselves

elicit
to draw forth or bring out

e-mail
electronic mail: messages keyed and sent from one computer terminal to others on the same computer network

embedded
enclosed closely; made an integral part of

enclosure notation
part of a letter that alerts the reader to materials that are included along with the letter

enumeration
the listing of one item after another; the numbering of items

enunciate
to pronounce words very clearly

esteem needs
our drives for personal worth and our needs to feel valuable, to have a high opinion of ourselves

ethics
the discipline dealing with good and bad and with moral duty and obligation

euphemism
an expression that is a substitute for a term or phrase

evaluation
appraisal; to determine the worth or value of something by careful appraisal or study

executive summary
a summary of the main points of a report

exhibit
show; display

ex officio
by virtue or because of an office

external communication
communication that takes place with anyone outside of the organization

extraneous
existing or coming from the outside; not an integral part of

eye appeal
the quality of something that makes an impression on the viewer

F

facsimile (fax)
material transmitted through telephone connections

feature
a prominent part or characteristic

feedback
a response to a message that indicates that the receiver has received and understood the message

first draft
the preliminary attempt at writing complete sentences and paragraphs from notes and outlines

font
a specific type size and style of a character; an assortment or set of type all of one size and style

footnote
a note of reference, explanation, or comment usually placed below the text on a printed page

format
the size, shape, and general makeup of something printed

former
of, relating to, or being the first of two things mentioned, referred to, or understood

form letter
special letter that often is prepared in advance to answer typical questions and concerns of customers

foster
to encourage; to promote the growth or development

G

goodwill
a kindly feeling of approval and support; the favor or prestige that a business has acquired beyond the mere value of what it sells

gross profit
overall profit before the deduction of charges and outlay such as wages, taxes, and insurance

growth needs
the second level of Maslow's hierachy of needs that includes our drive to achieve and to be free and independent

guarantee
an assurance for the fulfillment of a condition

guidance
advice

H

hamper
restrain; to interfere with

handouts
material that a speaker distributes to an audience

hard copy
printed form of a letter, memo, report, or other written document

hard data
definite, factual information used as a basis for reasoning or discussion; firm measurements or statistics used as a basis for calculation

hierarchy
a graded or ranked series or set of levels

honorarium
a payment for a service (such as making a speech) on which custom or propriety forbids a price to be set

I

idiom
dialect; the language peculiar to a people or to a district, community, or class; an expression having a meaning that cannot be derived from the combined meaning of its individual words (for example: *Monday week* for *the week after next Monday*)

immediacy
the quality or state of being immediate

impede
to hinder; to interfere with or slow the progress

imperative
necessary; not to be avoided; of utmost importance

implication
something implied; the implied or suggested meaning; a statement exhibiting a relationship of implication

incentive
a motive; something that encourages a particular action

inclusive
covering all items, costs, or services

indirect approach
approach in writing where material is presented in a way that gradually leads the reader to the point; the message then prepares the reader to respond in a desired way.

indirect order
approach in writing where details precede the topic sentence

informal study
study that is self-initiated or prepared at the request of someone higher up in the organization

information in / information out
a method for evaluating reading where the reader focuses on what information is missing. The information provided in the reading is information in. The information not included is the information out

innovation
the introduction of something new

inquiry
a request for information

inside address
part of a letter that includes the addressee's name and title, the company name, street address, city, state, and ZIP code

instructional memo
memo that contains various instructions that are not linked by sequence

intentional
purposeful; to do by design, by planning

internal communication
communication that takes place within an organization

intimidate
to make timid or fearful

intonation
the rise and fall in pitch of the voice in speech

introduction
a preliminary passage that introduces a topic and includes history, purpose, justification, method, and scope of the topic

J

jargon
the technical terminology or characteristic idiom of a special activity or group; obscure and often pretentious language marked by unnecessarily long words and descriptions

justification
the proof or evidence that something is right or reasonable; the just reason why something exists

K

keynote speaker
speaker who presents the most important speech at a business or social event, often evoking the main theme for the specific gathering

lateral communication
communication that takes place among peers

latter
of, relating to, or being the second or the last of two things mentioned, referred to, or understood

layout
plan or design or arrangement of something that is to be reproduced by printing; a set of pages with the position of text and artwork indicated; a *mock-up* of a proposed publication

legitimate
justified; lawful; accordant with established requirements

line graph
a type of graph that uses lines to represent data

logo
a company's motto or identifying statement, usually having a specific design

M

mailable letter
a letter in its final form, when it is ready to be mailed

mail-merge feature
a feature of word processing programs that lets the user create a form letter in one file and combine the letter with names and addresses from a second file

marginal
close to the lower limit of qualification, acceptability, or function

Maslow's Hierarchy
A study of human needs conducted by psychologist Abraham Maslow where human needs were grouped into several levels that formed a pyramid

medium
the form one uses to deliver communication, information, or entertainment

memorandum
brief communication written for interoffice circulation

memorandum report
a brief report written as a memorandum for interoffice circulation

merger
the combining of two or more organizations or business concerns

merit
reward

message
a communication in writing, in speech, or by signals; the basic content of communication

microfiche
a sheet of microfilm bearing reduced photographs of rows of extremely small images of pages of printed matter

modified block style
letter style characterized by balance; the date, complimentary close, and signature block begin at the horizontal center of the letter

modifier
a grammatical qualifier; a word, phrase, or clause that affects (changes, restricts, enlarges) the meaning of another word or group of words

monotone
a succession of syllables, words, or sentences in one unvaried key or pitch

mutual benefit
shared advantage or good result; gain shared jointly

N

narrative report
report that gives detailed reponses to requests for information, ideas, explanations, or recommendations

net profit
profit remaining after the deduction of all necessary charges and outlay such as wages, taxes, and insurance

nonverbal communication
communication through gestures and other body movements

O

objectively
fairly; undistorted by personal feelings, prejudices, or interpretations

obstacle
something that impedes progress or achievement

on-line catalog
a catalog connected to, served by, or available through a computer or telecommunications system

oral communciation
communication through speaking

ordered approach
an approach to writing where facts are listed in order of importance. This approach is used when you are trying to inform readers of the relative importance of certain facts, ideas, or proposals

original
being the first source from which a copy, reproduction, or translation is or can be made

outline
a breakdown of a particular topic into main and sub topics

overage
surplus, excess

P

parallel structure
consistency within the structure of communication; for example, if one heading begins with a verb, start all your headings with a verb

paraphrase
to restate a spoken or written idea, giving it meaning in another form or other words

passable
tolerable; good enough

passive
acted upon by an external agency; receptive to outside influences; not active

passive voice
verb position within a sentence in which the subject is the receiver of the action

peer
an equal; a person of equal standing with another based on age, grade, status, education, or work position

periodic report
report that is written according to a specified schedule; e.g, daily, weekly, monthly, quarterly

personal business letter
a letter written by a private person (perhaps a consumer) to a business organization about a business matter

personal pronoun
a word used to refer to a person, a group of people, or an object, such as I, you, he, she, it, we, they, me, my, your

persuade
to move by argument, entreaty, or postulation to a belief, position, or course of action

persuasive talk
spoken words used in an attempt to change someone's attitude or behavior

persuasive writing
written words used in an attempt to change someone's attitude or behavior

pertinent
relevant; having a clear decisive relevance to the matter in hand

pie chart
a graph that is shaped like a circle, which is then divided into sections to represent data

pitch
the difference in the frequency of the voice that contributes to the total meaning of speech

politically correct
a strict compliance to current societal trends, dress, and standards of speech and action

positive-negative-questionable strategy
listening technique whereby the listener categorizes incoming information based on whether it is positive, negative, or questionable

postscript
a note attached to a completed letter, article, or book

posture
the position of the body

potential
something that can develop or become actual

predominant
prevailing; being most frequent or common

preference
a desired choice

presumption
something that is assumed or believed without question; a belief based on probable or assumed reliability

primary readers
those to whom you direct your writing

primary research
the collection of information by any method other than reading the words of others

prioritize
to list or rate in order of priority; to rank beginning with what is most important

privilege
a right granted as a benefit or favor

proliferation
rapid production and growth

prospect
a potential buyer or customer

protocol
a code prescribing strict adherence to correct etiquette and precedence; custom or etiquette which is strictly followed

provocative
something that excites or stimulates

proximity
closeness, nearness—the quality or state of being nearby or very close

Q

quotient
quota, share

R

rapport
accord; relationship marked by harmony

rate
speed at which one speaks or reads

reader processing
the complex interaction between the words on the page and the way those words are manipulated and processed by the reader

reasoned approach
approach to writing where facts are followed by conclusions. This approach is useful when your report reflects a true investigation

receiver
person to whom communication is directed

reciprocate
to return in kind; to return a courtesy

reconciliation
the action of restoring friendship or harmony

redundancy
an instance of needless repetition

reference initials
the initials of the person who keys the document if different from the writer of the document

relevant
significant; related to the topic of interest, having significant bearing on the matter at hand

replicate
to produce duplicate or identical results, as in a statistical experiment or research study

request letter
correspondence written for the purpose of asking for services, supplies, or assistance

resilient
capable of withstanding and adjusting easily to change

revision
a step of the writing process where the writer improves the quality of the message by creating a corrected version

rigorous
very strict

routine request
the most common type of request letter in which the writer asks for materials, information, and/or services

RRTWRP
a process for writing that involves **R**eading, **R**esearching, **T**hinking, **W**riting, **R**evising, **P**roofreading

S

sacrifice
to give up

safety needs
our needs for security, shelter, and freedom from danger

sales letter
letter that sells a product or service

salutation
part of a letter that names the person or people addressed

scanning
process of reading where the reader glances from point to point in search of a particular item

scope
range

secondary readers
those readers who need to know that a communication has taken place or who need to know specific information contained in a communication; these readers are not those to whom the writing was primarily intended

secondary research
data already assembled and recorded by someone else

self-actualization needs
our drives for competence and mastery

self-talk
strategy for listening where the listener sifts incoming information by silently asking questions to him/herself

sender
the person who transmits a message

sequence
a continuous or connected series

shades of meaning
the property of words or phrases to be interpreted in more than one way

simple inquiry
a request for information that does not require a detailed, tactful response

situation level
broad concepts in reading from which the reader can recall prior knowledge of a situation, attach new knowledge of the situation, and act accordingly

skeptical
doubtful, mistrusting

skepticism
an attitude of doubt; a degree of mistrust

skimming
a process of reading where the reader glances through content to find the chief ideas

social-business correspondence
executive correspondence addressed to high-level company officials and/or dignitaries

social needs
our drives to give and receive affection and love

soft copy
    material that has been created and appears on electronic media. Once the material is printed, it becomes hard copy

solarium
    a glass enclosed porch or room

sophisticated
    finely experienced and aware

spacious
    vast or ample in extent; roomy

special favor
    request letters that do not represent sales opportunities for the recipients, but do benefit the writer

spontaneous
    arising from a momentary impulse

stance
    intellectual or emotional position, outlook, or attitude

statistics
    a collection of data relating to a topic

status report
    a fill-in form that reports on progress of something and is submitted periodically to those who need such information

structured report
    a report that contains distinct elements, such as a title page, a summary, an introduction, a body, and conclusions

style
    a distinctive manner of expression, as in writing or speaking

subjective
    of or relating to personal perceptions

subtlety
    indirectness; the quality of being obscure, difficult to understand or distinguish

succinctly
    precisely, exactly; without wasted words

summarize
    to tell in a reduced, abbreviated way

survey
    a structured tool used to collect a large amount of data from a group of individuals

survey instrument
    method through which a survey is conducted; e.g., personal interview, telephone, or questionnarie sent by mail

sympathetic
    compassion, friendliness, and sensitivity to other's feelings

T

table
    a systematic arrangement of data in rows and columns for ready reference

tabulate
    to count, record, or list systematically

tactic
    a method for accomplishing an end

tentative
    not fully worked out or developed

territory
    an assigned area

thesaurus
    a book or computer program of words and their synonyms

title page
part of a formally structured report that shows the title of the report, the person or group for whom the report was written, the name of the author, and the date

tone
style or manner of expression in speaking or writing

topic sentence
the sentence that makes the main point of any communication

transition
a passage from one subject to another

transitional words
words that lead from one subject or paragraph to another

transmit
send

transmittal document
a memo or letter that accompanies an important document or other material

transparency
a picture or design on film designed to be viewed by light shining through it or by projection

transposition
the act of shifting from one place to another

trend
a current style or preference

trendy word
a term marked by superficial or faddish appeal

typographical
of or relating to letters or characters that have been typed, keyed, or typeset

U

unscrupulous
unprincipled; not acting in strict regard for what is considered right or proper

upward communication
communication with someone who is a superior

usage
the way in which words and phrases are actually used in a language

V

validity
logical correctness, justifiability; soundness

value
an idea held in importance

verbal communication
communication through words

visual aids
visuals that enhance communication, such as graphs, charts, photographs, and cartoons

vivid
bright

vocational aptitude
talent, ability, or suitability for a skill or trade being pursued as a career

volume
loudness

W

word level
singular concepts in reading from which the reader can recall prior

knowledge of a word or phrase, attach
new knowledge of the word or phrase,
and act accordingly

works-cited list
a list at the end of a report that
provides full citations for all sources
of borrowed information

writer's block
a psychological inhibition preventing
a writer from proceeding with a piece

INDEX

Y

PHOTO CREDITS